ARGUMENT EVALUATION

Wayne Grennan

UNIVERSITY
PRESS OF
AMERICA

LANHAM • NEW YORK • LONDON

Copyright © 1984 by

University Press of America,™ Inc.

4720 Boston Way
Lanham. MD 20706

3 Henrietta Street
London WC2E 8LU England

Printed in the United States of America

ISBN (Perfect): 0-8191-4267-0
ISBN   (Cloth): 0-8191-4266-2

All University Press of America books are produced on acid-free
paper which exceeds the minimum standards set by the National
Historical Publications and Records Commission.

TO THE MEMORY OF MY PARENTS

TABLE OF CONTENTS

This book has been written for the typical first-year college student. It is intended for use as a text in courses designed to develop the student's ability to accurately evaluate the logical adequacy of arguments that might be encountered in everyday life. The evaluation approach is a critical one: arguments are rated favorably to the extent that they survive a critique of their assumptions and inferences.

The text differs from others in the non-formal logic vein in at least one conspicuous way. The evaluation procedure is applied to 20 inductive argument patterns that I regard as frequently occurring in a variety of guises in everyday life. Each pattern can be embodied in arguments that prove their conclusions to a considerable extent, unlike the fallacies that are often given pride of place in texts of this genre. (I do present a compendium of 33 fallacies in Chapter Nine, however, but these are not a major preoccupation in the text.) It seems to me that studying fallacies before studying the more acceptable argument patterns is like studying pathology before studying anatomy!

The material herein was developed for a 25-week course in "baby" logic, so that it is possible to include some elements of symbolic logic without stinting on the non-formal topics. In a 15-week "pure" non-formal logic course I would recommend covering Chapters One through Five plus Chapter Eight and possibly Chapter Nine. Chapter Six presents the use of the short truth table method for testing deductive inferences, both those cast in propositional logic and (in conjunction with Venn diagrams) syllogisms. I cover this chapter in four weeks. It is worth doing because it provides the simplest general strategy for dealing with deductive inferences. Some treatment of these inferences must be provided in a text of this type and I think this approach is superior to covering a number of common valid and invalid deductive patterns in an ad hoc way as some books do. The material is no substitute for a course in symbolic logic, but it does seem to whet the appetites of some students for such a course.

Chapter Seven presents strategies for the evaluation of arguments by the identification of needed but unstated assumptions. This chapter is, in effect, an extension of Chapter Five. The approaches presented can be used to produce more effective responses to arguments but they are more difficult to apply than those presented in Chapters Five and Six.

It should be unnecessary to remind people that this is a text on practical argument evaluation techniques, not a treatise on the theory of the topic. As such, I have provided no more theory than necessary to ensure that the reader understands why the various techniques work. My use of other peoples' texts leads me to believe that too many writers succumb to temptations to be philosophically and logically rigorous to an extent that they fail to present enough useful evaluation strategies.

A comment on the examples and exercises is in order. In general the ones presented are somewhat artifically expressed versions of patterns that are encountered in everyday life. Except in Chapter Eight, which is devoted to the analysis of arguments as they appear in their logically untidy "natural habitat", I have presented them in linguistically clear form. Linguistic complexity and logical untidyness interfere with the application of evaluation techniques. Most texts seem to overestimate the ability of college freshmen to analyze the logical structure of passages containing arguments. Anyone who uses this text and feels a need for more examples is advised to do what I do, that is, borrow from other texts. The ones in Chapter Seven can be used to supplement the corresponding sets in Chapter Five, or vice versa.

The model for this text in the beginning was Michael Scriven's REASONING. It has evolved in a number of ways, but I have adopted his diagram format for displaying argument structures as a key device in my evaluation procedure. I have also drawn on other writers, although I am not now able to say it what way. Some may recognize their influence and I want to thank them for their help.

I am happy to acknowledge the influence and help of Anne Bastedo and Sheila Kindred, both of whom have used this material in their courses. The latter, in particular, continues to provide useful constructive criticism.

Very special thanks are due to Florence Elliott, my secretary, who was prepared to undertake the typing of the final version of the book on my word processor with a very tight deadline. Her success in meeting the deadline is all the more remarkable as this was her first exposure to word processor technology.

Finally, I want to thank my wife Eleanor for helping to support the family so that I can teach philosophy and write books.

Wayne Grennan

Saint Mary's University

Halifax, Canada   B3H 4A9

CHAPTER ONE: INTRODUCTION

(1.1) INTRODUCTION: The ultimate aim of this book is to improve the reasoning skills that you rely on in arguing--making a case for a belief or course of action. This aim is pursued indirectly by showing you how to evaluate the logical adequacy of other peoples' arguments. This is easier to learn and if you become a good critic of other peoples' arguments, you will also be well-equipped to argue effectively yourself, simply because you can apply your acquired critical skills to your own arguments.

Very likely you are using this book as a text in a course. It is intended to teach you logical skills, it is not intended to force on you any theories or doctrines about human beings and the world they live in. The information that is provided is there to teach you some of the logical skills that humanity has acquired during its history. These skills have been found to be reliable in helping us to arrive at true beliefs rather than false ones, and this has enabled us to gain control of nature for our benefit.

If you are using this book in a course you should think of your instructor as you would think of an athletics coach. She or he is someone who can play the logic "game" successfully and you should try to do the assigned exercises in the way the instructor does them. Do not think that there are a variety of ways to be logical so that you can say "The instructor is logical in his/her way, I'll be logical in mine!" Logic does not work like this because it is reality, not peoples' preferences, that determines the most logical way of dealing with any particular argument. Whether the reasons the arguer gives are good ones is determined by the facts, not whether or not you accept them.

Learning to be more logical by taking a course in logic is a lot like learning a golf swing from a golf pro. Everyone who can do it well does it pretty much the same. By listening to the pro describe the procedure, watching her/him do it and trying to imitate the motion, you will soon learn it, and learn quicker than those who try to learn on their own.

This analogy will also help stress an important point. DO NOT THINK THAT YOU KNOW HOW TO DO THE EXERCISES JUST BECAUSE YOU READ AND UNDERSTOOD THE MATERIAL AND CAN FOLLOW THE INSTRUCTOR WHEN HE/SHE DOES THE EXERCISES IN CLASS. The instructor is trying to impart skills. The test of whether you have a skill or not is whether or not you can satisfactorily do the exercises yourself. You would not be so naive as to think you can swing a golf club like a pro just because you have read a book about it and seen it done. Don't be naive about the skills presented in the course either. Guided practice is the key to success and this is why there are exercises to be found in most of the chapters. Do them, then see how the instructor does them. When your results start to be about the same you will be well on your way to mastering these skills.

(1.2) PERSUASION: One of the activities humans engage in is persuasion. This is a characteristically social activity because if someone is engaged in persuading then there must be someone whom they are trying to persuade. Persuasion is directed to one of two ends: to get someone to believe something, or to get them to do something. To persuade someone to do something we must create in them the belief that that is what they ought to do, so it turns out that all persuasion is concerned with creating or changing beliefs.

There are two main kinds of persuasion: persuasion by giving reasons and persuasion by force. I might try to persuade a child to go to bed by giving him reasons like: "You promised to go to bed early"; or "You'll be tired in school tomorrow if you stay up later". Here the persuasion takes place against a background of freedom. The child can choose what to do, and I am attempting to influence his conduct by rational appeal. On the other hand, I might try to persuade him by threat of force. In this case the child's freedom of choice is not respected and regardless of how carefully he weighs up the other reasons for and against going to bed, the prospect of punishment will be an overriding reason against staying up.

These two methods of persuasion differ in important ways. In logical persuasion the persuader is attempting to influence only by words. No physical intervention is intended. In using threats, however, the person being addressed is expected to respond to the prospect of physical intervention. It is not so much what I say to the child, as what I may do that influences him.

Logical persuasion is superior to other kinds in a profoundly important way. When you attempt to convince people that they should believe something on the basis of reasons, you are showing that you regard them as autonomous persons who are free to make up their own mind. Indeed, persuasion by any other means is widely regarded as treating human persons as less than human or less than persons.

(1.3) WHY BE LOGICAL? Although studying this book can teach you some logical skills, whether or not you ever use them is up to you. But if you choose to be illogical in life you should realize that there is frustration ahead for you if you ever want to influence the beliefs of others. And most of us do want to influence the beliefs of others because there are things we want them to do. If you do want to be persuasive, yet do not want to be logical, you have to realize that most other people do want to hear good reasons when asked to believe something, so your attempts at persuasion will often be unsuccessful. Very few people are likely to believe what you say simply because it is you who say it, and you will not be taken very seriously if it is known that you seldom have reasons to support your assertions on controversial matters. And there is nothing more frustrating than having a deep conviction and not be able to get others to accept it.

In effect, it has been suggested that if you wish to interact successfully with other people you should cultivate a logical approach to life because most people do. But if one were philosophical about this one might want to hear why anyone at all should be logical. After all, it is possible to act and believe according to one's feelings. Traditionally, people who have taken this approach to life have been individuals who have thought that humans, by stressing logicality, have ignored the emotional side of our nature. People who have taken this position in their writings are often labelled 'Romantics'. In this century a conspicuous example is the novelist D. H. Lawrence who thought that we, as a society, were losing our ability to respond emotionally because of our stress on logic in thinking. For him, our feelings were the best guide to what is true.

As it happened, Lawrence became an acquaintance and correspondent of Bertrand Russell, the British philosopher who was one of the most effective users of the principles of logic who has ever lived. He was, in fact, one of the most important figures in the development of symbolic logic. Lawrence saw that Russell was a paradigm of the logical man and wrote to him on one occassion: "Do stop working and writing altogether and become a creature instead of a mechanical instrument . . . become a mere nothing, a mole, a creature that feels its way and doesn't think" (quoted by Russell in THE AUTOBIOGRAPHY OF BERTRAND RUSSELL, Volume One, page 22). At the time of their discussion (1915) Russell was writing a book about how Europe ought to be reorganized politically after World War I. Lawrence, the apostle of feeling, also had strong views on the subject but in debate with Russell he was hopelessly ineffective, as this somewhat comical exerpt from one of Russell's letters shows:

"He is undisciplined in thought, and mistakes his wishes for facts. He is also muddleheaded. He says 'facts' are quite unimportant, only 'truths' matter. London is a 'fact' not a 'truth'. But he wants London pulled down. I tried to make him see that that would be absurd if London were unimportant, but he kept reiterating that London doesn't really exist, and that he could easily make people see it doesn't, and then they would pull it down. He was so confident of his powers of persuasion that I challenged him to come to Trafalgar Square at once and begin preaching. That brought him to earth and he began to shuffle . . he regards all my attempts to make him acknowledge facts as mere timidity, lack of courage to think boldly . . . When one gets a glimmer of the facts into his head, as I did at last, he gets discouraged, and says he will go to the South Sea Islands, and bask in the sun with six native wives." (AUTOBIOGRAPHY, Vol. 1, p.53)

If Lawrence had followed through on his last promise (or threat), the literary world would have been the worse for it. Some of his novels are considered modern classics. Unlike many illogical people, Lawrence was a gifted writer who was able to influence people through his novels by constructing characters who lived out various aspects of his philosophy of life. But it is certain that he was nowhere near as successful at persuading others to his views as he would like to have been. Had he been prepared to take a logical approach, of course, he might have discovered that some of his positions were untenable. He was a man of passion who thought others should be able to see the truth in his views without being given good reasons.

Russell was also passionate about the social causes he supported but his certitude came from having made a diligent attempt to locate all of the evidence for and against a particular position. Furthermore, his respect for the facts made him aware that many people could not be persuaded by reasoning. He would also be aware of the difficulty in persuading anyone to be logical.

Human beings have the freedom to choose to be logical, (as Russell did) or to be illogical (as Lawrence did). What, then, does being logical have to offer other than the advantage of being taken seriously by most other people? The main advantage, and a great one it is, is that BEING LOGICAL IS THE MOST RELIABLE WAY OF GETTING TRUE BELIEFS. False beliefs can lead one into doing things one shouldn't do. In general, truth has survival value for us, although as we all know sometimes the truth hurts.

A further advantage, related to the preceding one, is that being logical helps us to maintain our individual autonomy. If we cannot think for ourselves then we cannot be our real selves. A great many of our beliefs are acquired from others, who tell us things in person, in textbooks, amd in the media. If you do not have, or do not use, logic skills you will have to depend on others to tell you what you should believe and you will be manipulated by them for their own ends without realizing it.

(1.4) WHAT BEING LOGICAL INVOLVES: There are two basic requirements that being logical about beliefs involves. These are (1) one's certainty about the truth of a proposition is to be proportional to the logical adequacy of one's reasons for it (another way of putting this is to say that the degree of conviction is to be proportional to the evidence one has); (2) the avoidance of inconsistency--in the above passage Russell is relating how he tried to show Lawrence that he was being inconsistent in thinking both that London doesn't exist and that it ought to be pulled down.

The first requirement, of course, implies that the logical person must have good reasons before he/she will regard any controversial proposition as true. Of course, with the world being the way it is we frequently find that a proposition has evidence counting both for and against it. In this situation the rational person will "weigh up" the evidence and decide whether the evidence for the proposition outweighs the evidence against it.

The requirement to avoid inconsistency is easier to adhere to because we can usually tell when two propositions are inconsistent, whereas in trying to adjust conviction to evidence we often have the problem of deciding how much evidence is enough. Inconsistency is perhaps the greatest logical fault and can be avoided to some extent by insisting on having good reasons before believing something, that is, by taking the first requirement seriously. Another way of uncovering inconsistency is to think out what follows from particular propositions. In general, when we have incompatible propositions on our hands one will entail a certain proposition and the other will entail the opposite.

In using this book you will receive practice in judging whether the evidence for a proposition is good enough to warrant accepting it. Since reasons (and what they are reasons for) constitute arguments, you will, putting it another way, receive practice in sizing up arguments.

(1.5) ARGUMENT: Arguments are constructed in languages. They consist of assertions, at least one of which the arguer is trying to persuade the "arguee" to believe, on the basis of reasons which the arguer thinks the arguee already believes. Thus, we say that arguments consist of conclusions and reasons for them, called "premises."

There are other uses of the term 'argument'. Sometimes we say people have been arguing when we mean they have been quarreling or disagreeing. But disagreeing does not necessarily involve arguing, as we will use the term here, because disagreeing can be simply a matter of one person asserting something and the other denying that the assertion is true, without any reasons being given on either side. An argument, in the sense in which we are using the term here, involves giving reasons for what one says is true or false. There must be at least one conclusion, but it can exist only in an argument. By itself it is an assertion. The notions of premise and conclusion are interdependent in that if

5

one assertion is a conclusion there is another that is a premise. This does not guarantee that just any two (or more) assertions taken together represent an argument. For example, suppose someone says: "The sun is shining. The sky is blue." This will not be construed by hearers as an attempt to persuade them about anything: the speaker is simply reporting some things about the world. Each assertion is neither premise nor conclusion beccause the speaker had not asserted that either one is a reason for the other. Suppose instead the speaker said "The sun is shining. SO the sky is blue." Here an argument has been uttered. The word 'so' indicates that what follows it is being concluded from the assertion preceding. The assertion that the sun is shining is being given as a reason for the hearer to believe that the sky is blue. The utterance is an argument because it contains an inference. It is this that determines whether or not a set of assertions constitute an argument. In a simple argument such as this, one assertion is being made on the basis of another which is said to be a reason for it. We can define 'conclusion', then, as that which is inferred from (or derived from or implied by) a premise or premises.

We could have defined 'premise' in terms of 'conclusion' and 'inference' had we chosen to do so. But it would not do to define 'inference' in terms of the other two. One assertion is a premise and another a conclusion because someone has attempted to infer the conclusion from the premise. We can't have a premise or conclusion unless an inference is made.

An argument, then, consists of at least one premise and a conclusion that the aruger is trying to infer from it. Sometimes it will be logically legitimate to infer the conclusion from the premises in an argument and sometimes it won't. When it isn't, the argument cannot prove its conclusion but it still counts as an argument. Any collection of assertions becomes an argument when the assertor tries to infer one of the assertions from the others. Even when the conclusion has no logical relation to the premises we still count what is said or written as an argument. It is just that in such cases we have a bad argument. But even a bad argument counts as a genuine argument.

(1.6) WHAT IS LOGIC? This is a good point to describe what the subject of logic is. Very likely you have not studied the subject before and it is not unreasonable to expect to be told what it is about.

In this book logic will be regarded as the science that tries to state the principles of good reasoning of a certain kind, that is, the principles we can use to distinguish good inferences from bad.

Argument evaluation, the skill that this book is concerned to

6

develop, has two aspects to it:inference evaluation and premise evaluation. A good argument proves its conclusion to be true by starting out with true premises and legitimately inferring the conclusion from them. Inference evaluation is a matter of applying the principles of logic. Premise evaluation is a matter of establishing facts by observation, research, and testing.

It is important that you realize at the beginning that logic cannot by itself show you what is true. By helping you to see when an inference is valid it can help you to acquire new knowledge, but inferences must be made from premises that are known to be true if you are to come to know the conclusion. So usually you can make a complete evaluation of an argument only if you have independent knowledge about the premises. However, you should realize that inferences can be evaluated without knowing whether or not the premises are true. For example, you can see that in the following argument the inference is valid even though you may not know whether the premise is true: "The man who is captain of the Boston Red Sox has a child. Therefore, he is a father."

You can know that the inference in the argument is a good one because you know the meaning of each sentence in the argument. You do not have to find out anything about the person referred to in the premise. You do not even have to know the man's name. Of course, you would not want to accept the conclusion as proved until you are satisfied that the premise is true, but you can make an informed and correct judgment about the inference. Furthermore, since a good argument (one that proves its conclusion) must have true premises and a good inference, you can say that an argument with a poor inference has not proved its conclusion without even taking steps to check its premises. In summary: some bad arguments can be identified as such without knowledge of their premises, but we must also establish that the premises are true to be sure that arguments with good inferences actually prove their conclusions.

(1.7) SUMMARY: In this chapter the following points were made:

1. The material to be studied is intended to teach logic skills.

2. These logic skills are best learned in the way other skills are: by reading the theory and putting it into practice under supervision.

3. The best test of your skill is how well you can apply it, not how well you understand the text.

4. Logical persuasion relies on convincing people by giving reasons for what you want them to believe.

5. Logical persuasion is ethically superior to the use and threat of force because it involves treating others as autonomous persons with a right to make up their own minds.

6. It is worthwhile being logical because most people are, and you will not be persuasive if you aren't too.

7. It is possible to be illogical like D.H. Lawrence, but you will not be taken seriously by most people.

8. The best reason for being logical is that it is the most reliable way to acquire true beliefs.

9. Not being logical opens us to being manipulated by others since most of our beliefs are obtained from others.

10. Being logical involves adjusting the strength of one's convictions to the adequacy of the evidence, and also being consistent.

11. Arguments consist of premises (reasons) and conclusions, what the reasons are reasons for.

12. In accepting a conclusion on the basis of premises we are making an inference, so arguments contain inferences.

13. Logic is the science that tries to discover the principles of good inference making.

14. Argument evaluation involves premise evaluation and inference evaluation, and the study of logic helps you do the latter more effectively.

CHAPTER TWO: ASSUMPTION EVALUATION

(2.1) INTRODUCTION: One of the necessary steps in deciding whether an argument proves its conclusion is to decide whether its assumptions are true, dubious, or false. The assumptions are the premises that are the starting points of the argument. They are starting points because they are not argued for. This truth-value decision is to be based on an attempt to gather all the important facts relevant to the assumptions, then weighing individually the facts that support them against the facts that undermine them.

Obviously, being able to reach a reliable decision about a particular assumption requires information. If we do not have knowledge of most of the facts for and against an assumption we are not likely to reach the right judgment. Lack of knowledge is a severe handicap in argument evaluation when the question of assumption truth is to be settled. In general, there are three main sources for knowledge: (1) one's own experience, (2) personal observation, and (3) testimony of an authority. Each of these is useful in different ways and each can fail us in different ways.

(2.2) EXPERIENCE: Since we are normally only required to evaluate arguments relevant to our personal concerns we will often be able to reach a decision on the basis of our own experience. For example, suppose someone says to you: "Some high school courses are beneficial so high school is not a complete waste of time." You may very well be able to accept the premise as true because you yourself have taken a beneficial high school course, or you know at second hand of some courses that are beneficial.

(2.3) PERSONAL OBSERVATION: Sometimes we do not know whether an assertion is true, dubious, or false, but we are in a position to personally investigate the matter. Suppose someone says "Professor Dull is a very boring lecturer, so you shouldn't take any of his courses." The premise of this argument might be investigated by asking students who have taken courses from Professor Dull whether or not they found his lectures boring. However, given the rather subjective criteria for deciding what is boring, you would do better to sit in on a few of the Professor's classes and decide for yourself.

Most of us overestimate the reliability of direct observation. Magicians are not the only ones who exploit this tendency. Many a politician on a fact-finding tour abroad has been duped by stage-managed activities.

(2.4) AUTHORITY: More often than not we must rely on the testinmony or others in deciding on the truth value of an assertion. Most of the knowledge we have is acquired from books and various media, but of course we also acquire most of our mis-information from these sources also. The problem is to be able to distinguish people and sources who are in a position to know from those who are not. The following points are important:

(a) An authority here is an expert, not someone in a position of power. Authorities are identified by establishing what others acquainted with the subject think of them. If you are not well acquainted with the subject you are not in a position to identify the authorities reliably. Of course, most questions do not require the testimony of the most authoritative person in the field. Usually anyone with, say, a Ph.D. in an academic subject is a reliable authority for settling most questions in the subject.

(b) Every subject area has its controversial topics at any given time, so that not even the greatest experts can be counted on to tell us the truth. They will, however, if they are reputable, make it clear that their opinions are tentative and give reasons for them. In the early sixties U.S. President John Kennedy wondered if lowering personal income taxes would stimulate the sluggish U.S. economy, so he asked the opinions of eight top economists. It was said that four said it would help and four said it would not! Such matters are obviously highly complicated, to such a degree that even experts disagree. Therefore, when you find the experts disagreeing the best you can do is take note of their reasons for differing views, "weigh" them up, and either reach your own conclusions based on these reasons or withhold judgment. If you decide to withhold judgment about the truth of a premise you ought to rate it as dubious.

(c) Keep in mind that an authority in one area is not ncessarily a legitimate authority in any other. Accepting as true the opinion of someone who is not an authority on the matter is a fallacy. Baseball players who want men to use a particular brand of after-shave lotion because they say it is the best, are not to be taken very seriously. Skills at baseball and knowledge about it do not equip anyone for identifying the best shaving lotion. On a more serious level, physicians are not necessarily authorities on when a developing human fetus is a human being. Physicians cam reliably tell us about the attributes and abilities of the fetus at the various stages of its development because this is something medicine is an authority about. This information is necessary for deciding when a fetus is a human being but does not by itself provide an answer. The answer depends on what factors are relevant for being a human being, and establishing what these are is a question of conceptual analysis. Conceptual analysis is a characteristically philosophical acitivty, one in which physicians are not normally trained, so that we ought to be wary of believing (for example) that a newly fertiliZed human egg is a human being just because some prestigious medical researcher or practitioner says so.

(d)   We   also   count   the   testimony   of   people   as   authoritative
when   they   are   eyewitnesses   to   events.   They   have   acquired   their
knowledge   by   perception   rather   than   from   someone   else's
description.   Evaluation   of   claims   made   by   such   people   is   a   matter
of   deciding   whether   the   person   was   in   a   position   to   perceive   what
she/he   has   claimed   to   have   perceived,   and   whether   the   person
reliably   tells   the   truth.   Normally   it   is   desirable   to   try   to
discover   others   who   were   witnesses   so   that   we   can   check   the   story.
Obviously,   the   farther   back   in   the   past   the   event   occurred   (or   was
supposed   to   have   occurred)   the   more   difficulty   we   might   have   in
checking   the   claim.   Historians   are   faced   with   difficulties   here
of   a   kind   that   a   detective   investigating   a   recent   crime   is   not.

(2.5)   CAUTIONARY   COMMENTS.   Before   getting   into   specifics
about   particular   kinds   of   assertions   some   further   comments   need   to
be   made.   First,   sometimes   it   is   inappropriate   to   require   an   arguer
to   defend   an   assumption   that   strikes   you   as   dubious   or   false.   The
arguer   may   know   more   about   the   subject   being   discussed   than   you
do.   It   is,   in   certain   circumstances,   satisfactory   for   the   arguer
to   refer   to   a   defence   of   the   assumption   he/she   has   provided
elsewhere.   This   situation   can   occur   in   the   academic   journals,
where   someone   uses   a   conclusion   from   one   article   as   an   assumption
in   a   further   one.   It   is   appropriate   for   the   arguer   to   provide   a
reference   to   the   earlier   paper   instead   of   giving   a   justification
of   the   premise   in   the   present   paper.

Secondly,   it   is   not   unreasonable   to   tentatively   accept   an
assumption   even   though   you   find   it   doubtful   and   the   arguer   has   not
provided   a   defence   elsewhere,   providing   the   arguer   promises   to
provide   a   justification   for   it   on   another   occasion.   On   some
occasions   there   is   just   not   enough   time   to   deal   thoroughly   with   an
argument.

Thirdly,   it   is   sometimes   useful   to   posit   a   dubious   premise   or
one   whose   truth   value   is   unknown   just   to   see   what   logically
follows   from   it.   In   this   situation   the   truth   value   of   the   premise
is   irrelevant   since   the   validity   of   any   inference   made   is
independent   of   the   truth   of   the   premise.   Scientists   do   this   when
they   want   to   test   a   theory.   They   reason   that   IF   the   theory   is
true   THEN   certain   phenomena   would   be   observed   under   certain
experimental   conditions.   Having   made   such   an   inference   they
proceed   to   make   the   experiment.   People   who   are   arguing
hypothetically,   as   we   call   it,   will   very   often   preface   their
argument   with   words   such   as   "suppose   for   the   sake   of   argument"   or
"let's   assume   that",   etc.

(2.6)   A   CLASSIFICATION   OF   ASSERTIONS.   To   effectively
criticize   or   evaluate   an   assumption,   you   must   present   the
appropriate   evidence   and   not   all   assumptions   are   of   the   same
logical   kind.   Thus,   it   will   be   necessary   to   distinguish   the

various kinds and discuss how each can be approached. The classification best suited to our purposes is the one given below:

    (a) Relational: X is bigger than Y, X is whiter than Y

    (b) Singular: X is Y

    (c) Universal Generalizations: All X's are Y, No X's are Y

    (d) "Soft" universals: X's are Y's, X's are not Y's

    (e) Weak Generalizations: Most X's are Y's, Some X's are Y's, etc.

    (f) Semantical Assertions: (definitional claims)

    (g) Evaluative Assertions

    (h) Logically Complex Assertions :

    (i) Negations: Not A

    (ii) Conjunction: A and B

    (iii) Alternations: Either A or B

    (iv) Conditionals: If A then B

    (v) Propositional Attitude Assertions: X believes that A, X feels that A, etc.

Each of the above kinds is logically different from the others so that effective criticism of each must be done differently. The remainder of this chapter is given over to describing the logical features of the kinds of assertions and how to criticize them.

    (2.7) RELATIONAL ASSERTIONS. These are not especially tricky to evaluate in most cases. There are relational assertions that are a matter of degree, usually expressing comparisons, for example: "Sludge soap washes clothes whiter than the most popular brand," "Sweden has a higher standard of living than Canada". Others are non-quantitative, such as "New York is south of Boston."

In evaluating quantitative comparisons you should remember that they can be misleading. Even a very small difference between brands will entitle the Sludge soap people to say that their product washes clothes whiter than the most popular brand. Even 1%

whiter is whiter, but hardly an overwhelming reason for buying
Sludge! Whenever you are asked to believe that one thing is
bigger or better than another in some respect, ask 'how much?'
The current stress on high fuel efficiency for cars has led the
manufacturers to make claims such as "the highest mileage for cars
in this class", but checking the government figures often reveals
that the competitors are within 5% of their mileage figure. For a
fairly efficient car using about 400 gallons of fuel a year we are
talking about a difference of only 20 gallons or so--about $40.00
per year. Hardly a large enough difference to play a part in
determining a choice of car, especially when there are also many
other factors that are relevant, such as durability and comfort.

(2.8) SINGULAR ASSERTIONS. These attribute a property to a
particular thing: "Friedrich Nietsche is the greatest enemy
Christianity ever had," "Margaret Thatcher is the first female
Prime Minister of Britain", "The Grand Canyon is over a mile
deep". Establishing the truth or falsity of singular assertions
is normally easier than deciding about general claims (to be
discussed next) since the properties of only one thing need be
investigated.

(2.9) UNIVERSAL ASSERTIONS. These are of two forms: 'All
(or each or every) X's are Y' and 'No X's are Y'. Both of these
are used to assert something about an entire class of things,
which is why they are said to be universal assertions.

In evaluating a premise of the form 'All X's are Y's' our
attempts at refutation involve counter exampling, trying to think
of an X (or more than one) that is not a Y. These universal
assertions are very susceptible to refutation. People who
regularly make such strong claims are guilty of being incautious.
Often people who use universal claims as premises do so because
they feel very strongly about something and allow their feelings
to overcome their logical prudence. Here is an example:

"All homosexuals are sexually aggressive, so we must keep
them away from our young people."

More than one sexually "straight" individual has used this
argument. The inference is to some extent satisfactory, perhaps,
but we could refute the argument regardless of the quality of the
inference by identifying for the arguer ome ordinary homosexual
who is not sexually aggressive. One example serves to show the
premise is false but to be convincing we should get an example
that is normal or typical, a clear-cut case. Marginal or unusual
cases are less convincing just because there is something
exceptional or dubious about them. For the present example, it is
less satisfactory to cite an older homosexual than one "in the
prime of life" sexually, since it is generally believed that human
sex drives become less intense with advancing age. Identifying a

well-controlled younger individual as a counter-example will prevent the arguer from evading the objection by claiming that the individual is a special case.

Theoretically, a single genuine counter-example proves a universal claim to be false and arguers should concede that their premise has been refuted when they have conceded the existence of one counter-example. However, most people are psychologically unable to accept that one case could overthrow their claim, so that more than one counter-example must be identified for them. It often does little good to explain that universal assertions allow of no exceptions, and in this case we simply identify counter-examples until they concede.

Negative universal assertions of the form 'No X is Y' are criticizable by identifying examples of X's that are Y. Anyone who claims that no homosexuals are sexually aggressive could be refuted by identifying some who are. The same considerations in choosing examples apply here as for claims of the form 'All X's are Y'.

It is appropriate here to discuss what we might call "soft" generalizations, since they are best understood by contrasting them with strict universal generalizations.

Suppose, in the anti-homosexual argument just discussed, the premise had been 'Homosexuals are sexually aggressive' instead of 'All homosexuals are sexually aggressive'. Is the former version as susceptible to refutation as the latter? Perhaps you might say it is because the arguer no doubt meant to refer to all homosexuals. Perhaps in some cases, evem in most, we are entitled to "read in" the word 'all' in generalizations when it is missing. However, very often it is unfair to do so because it exposes the speaker unnecessarily to refutation. People often do not intend 'all' to be read into their generalizations. Instead of meaning that ALL homosexuals are sexually aggressive, in saying "Homosexuals are sexually aggressive", someone might mean only that they normally or usually are, or that the typical homosexual is, or that most are. If this is the sort of thing that was meant it would be inadequate to try to refute the arguer by identifying a few counter-examples. Refutation is only possible by establishing that the majority of homosexuals are not sexually aggressive. This, of course, might be difficult to do. A statistical approach is one way of settling the matter. If, on some qualitative scale homosexuals were found, on average, to be no more sexually aggressive than heterosexuals then the claim would be disproved.

(2.10) WEAK GENERALIZATIONS. These, in effect, make "soft" generalizations about a certain proportion of things of a particular kind, but they use an explicit qualifying term to

14

indicate that the claim being made is not universal. In English we have a variety of terms that can be used to make particular generalizations as weak or as strong as we like.

There seem to be two kinds of qualifying terms used in weak generalizations. One sort allows us to make claims about a proportion of the members of a class, only some of which are arithmetical expressions, e.g. 'half', 'one-third', etc. The others are vaguer, e.g. 'nearly all', 'most', 'the majority', etc.

To refute claims made using these proportionate terms we need to show, at the minimum, that besides the proportion exempted by the claim itself, there is another significant proportion that lacks the attribute. With the arithmetical terms this is relatively clear-cut. For example, if it is said that "Half the people in the world are males", we could refute this by showing that only one-third are. The original claim allows for 50% not being male, and if it could be shown that an additional significant proportion are not male the original claim would be refuted. Intuitively, it would seem that about 20% counts here as significant, but this figure is not necessarily reliable in all contexts.

Stating what might be a "significant proportion" in dealing with the non-arithmetical terms is even more difficult because of their vagueness, but we can state in appropriately vague language the minimal claims that could refute some of them:

'Nearly all X's are Y's' is refuted by: 'At least one-quarter of X's are not Y's'

'Most X's are Y's' is refuted by: 'At least half of X's are not Y's'

'The majority of X's are Y's' is refuted by: 'At least half of all X's are not Y's'

The second sort of term used in making weak generalizations is exemplified by 'many', 'some', 'a few', etc. These seem to refer directly to quantities rather than proportions, and they are quite vague. The three terms mentioned can be used to generate weak generalizations that can be minimally refuted as follows:

'A few X's are Y's' is refuted by: 'No X's are Y's'.

'Many X's are Y's' is refuted by: 'Only a few X's are Y's'.

'Some X's are Y's' is refuted by: 'No X's are Y'S'.

You should be aware that the use of expressions such as

'many', which refer to quantity rather than proportion is a dubious practice. If the class of individuals is a very large one 'many' could legitimately refer to a large number but the large number may at the same time represent only a few per cent of the total. For example, if someone arguing for better air safety regulations in the U.S. claims that "many Americans are killed in commercial air crashes every year" this could be regarded as true, perhaps, since most years more than one hundred are killed this way (163 killed in 1978) and over a hundred is quite a few isn't it? But the claim is misleading since, after all, this represents less than one American in a million! The airlines' record looks even more impressive when we discover that in 1978 there were, on average, about 150 Americans killed on the highway EVERY DAY. So when someone uses words like 'many' or 'a lot' or 'a large number' ask then for actual numbers amd then establish how big a proportion is being talked about. As the example shows, 'many' or similar terms can be used correctly, although misleadingly, when one in a million is being talked about.

EXERCISE 2 - 1

This exercise is intended to test your ability to criticize generalizations. Each question consists of an assertion and several potential criticisms of it. You are to choose the best criticism for each and say why the others are less satisfactory. For purposes of the exercise regard each criticism as true. Answers to 1 and 3 are given in the back.

1. "Left-handed people have more dexterity with their right hand than right-handed people have with their left."

   (a) Virgil Crump is left-handed and he's no better with his right than I am with my left.

   (b) Zeke Peevish is a lefty and he is no better at throwing with his right than the average right-hander is in throwing left.

   (c) In a study involving 20 right-handers and 20 left-handers the subjects were asked to trace a star-shaped figure with their non-favored hand. The average percentage of errors for the two groups was about the same.

2. "All short people feel inferior."

   (a) Zeke Peevish is only 5 foot 4 inches and he doesn't feel inferior.

   (b) Zeke's son, Abner, who is three, has plenty of confidence.

16

(c) Virgil Crump is 5 foot 8 inches and doesn't seem to feel inferior.

(d) A test to measure inferiority feelings was given to 20 jockeys. Their average score was within 5% of the score for people of average height.

3. "College students are less serious about their studies these days."

(a) The typical student is just as serious about studies as he/she has ever been.

(b) Most students in this class are about as serious as those in last year's version.

(c) The good students are just as serious as in the past.

4. "Some roses are blue."

(a) Nearly all roses are red.

(b) More roses are white than blue.

(c) Blue roses are rare.

(d) There are no blue roses.

5. "English people are arrogant."

(a) English women are not arrogant.

(b) I've met hundreds of English people and only a few seemed arrogant.

(c) The English are no more arrogant than high-born Bostonians.

(d) Only the upper-class English people are arrogant.

(e) Nigel Seldom-Slypshod is English and he is not at all arrogant.

(2.11) SEMANTICAL ASSERTIONS: Some assertions used in
arguments are not true or false because of any correspondence with
reality, as ordinary factual claims are, but because of the
meaning of the words used to make them. The most common kind of
semantical assertions are assertions of definitions. Definitions
are not established as correct or incorrect by means of observing
reality or conducting scientific investigations. They are correct
in virtue of whether they account for the usage of the term that
is being defined. Usage, of course, is a conventional matter much
as matters of etiquette are. We can describe a culture's etiquette
by observing their social behavior and formulating rules that
account for it. We say, for example, that in situations in which
one person has done something beneficial for another, there is a
rule applying to the effect that the person for whom the "good
turn" was done must express gratitude by saying "thank you" or
something equivalent.   We can say there is a rule to this effect
in our society because people who do not express gratitude are
criticized for not doing so. Censure for omission is a very
reliable sign that a rule has been violated. Traffic offences are
a good example.

Similarly, language use can be conceived of as rule-governed
behavior with the rules arising from linguistic conventions.
Deviation from these rules (calling a cat "a dog", for example)
prompts other users of the language to regard the speaker as
having made a mistake. The rules and ultimately the conventions
are the basis on which we decide whether or not an assertion of a
definition is correct.

Sometimes the task of judging the correctness of a definition
is relatively easy because the word in question has been formally
defined, a definition has been laid down. To verify that in
Euclidean Geometry a triangle is a three-sided plane figure we
need only consult a geometry book. This can even be done when
there are already some rules governing the term that have arisen
in the ordinary use of the term. The CONCISE OXFORD DICTIONARY
has to deal with this problem in defining 'fish'. They end up
providing two definitions, one reflecting popular use of the term
("animal living in the water") and a strict definition, one that
has been laid down by zoologists ("vertebrate cold-blooded animal
having gills throughout life and limbs (if any) modified into
fins"). Zoologists are interested in classifying animals, so they
want a formula by which any newly-discovered species can be
classified.   Therefore, they stipulate a precise definition. The
popular definition, intended to do justice to the ordinary
person's use of the word, can be thought of as an hypothesis
intended to account for that use. The ordinary person's purposes
and interests are very often different from those of specialists
and we must expect differences in definitions as a result. For
example, under the popular definition whales count as fish, but
under the technical definition they do not, because whales are not

18

cold-blooded. There are many words that can be said to have both popular and technical definitions, so do not dismiss a definition as incorrect because it does not conform to a technical one. There might be a popular use of the term that is accounted for by a definition in the dictionary, and the definition given in the argument might be close enough to it to warrant its acceptance. The context determines whether a popular or technical definition is to be preferred. In an argument in the field of zoology, the popular definition of 'fish' would be unacceptable.

The basic test for a definition (when it is supposed to account for the use of a noun expression) is this: does the definition pick out ALL AND ONLY those things that are legitimately referred to by the expression? For a predicate expression the test is: does the definition pick out ALL AND ONLY those things that the predicate can legitimately be said to apply to?

A definition can be inadequate for several reasons but no definition can be adequate if it applies to things the term itself does not apply to, or does not apply to some things the term does apply to. To criticize a definition we do two things: (1) we try to think of something correctly described by the definition but which is not an instance, (2) we try to think of an instance of the kind of thing that is not correctly described by the definition. Some definitions can be attacked in both ways.

Suppose someone claims that "murder is the intentional killing of human beings." Are there cases of the intentional killing of human beings that do not count as murder? Yes, there are several in fact: killing in self defence and killing the enemy in wartime. So the definition is inadequate because it does not take in ONLY those cases that count as murder.

Suppose someone defined 'valid argument' as 'any argument whose premises prove their conclusion'. Are there any arguments that fit the definition but are not valid arguments? No, because an argument cannot prove its conclusion unless it has a valid inference. So the definition applies to ONLY arguments that are valid, which means that it meets one requirement for a good definition. But does the definition apply to ALL valid arguments? Clearly not, because an argument can be valid and fail to prove its conclusion by having false assumptions.

Some definitions are doubly defective. The ancient Greek philosophers were fond of defining the species word 'man' by saying that the word means 'rational animal'. First we ask: are all men (and women) rational animals? Rationality is to some extent a matter of degree but it would seem that there are adult humans who are sufficiently retarded or disorganized in their thinking to not count as rational. So not all men and women are rational, although we all count as animals.

To complete the task of evaluating the definition we should ask if only humans count as rational animals. As it happens, the great apes have considerable intelligence, so they may count as rational animals. Thus, the definition is somewhat defective because:

(a) Not all men and women are rational, and

(b) Perhaps not only humans have rationality.

One of the most common defects in arguments containing definitions arises because arguers take the liberty of putting forward definitions that do not reflect established usage but which help them to prove their point. Here is an example: "Abortion is murder of the unborn. Murder is morally wrong. Therefore, abortion is morally wrong."

In this argument the inference is valid and the second premise is true. However, the argument fails because the first premise is not a correct definition in all circumstances. The word 'murder' is a legal term, defined as 'unlawful killing of a human being with malice aforethought'. Thus, if this definition of 'abortion' is to be correct legally it is necessary that 'the unborn' have the legal status of a human being. However, in some jurisdictions this is not so. For instance, the Canadian Criminal Code (Section 206 (1)) says this:

"A child becomes a human being . . . when it has completely proceeded, in a living state, from the body of its mother . . "

Thus, in Canada at this time unborn children do not legally count as human beimgs, which is to say they do not have the protection of the law. (This does not prevent the passing of laws regulating the performing of abortions, it only means that there is no possibility of laying murder charges.) With reference to Canada and some other jurisdictions, then, the argument cannot prove its conclusion. We simply point out to the arguer that the definition is faulty. It is at best a legal proposal, not a legal fact. But it is one thing to claim that something is a legal fact and another to say it ought to be.

EXERCISE 2 - 2

This exercise is intended to develop your ability to evaluate definitions. Remember, a definition is adequate to the extent that it refers to ALL things that the defined term applies to, and ONLY to those things. Give examples to support your criticism. Some may be defective in both ways at once. Answers are given in

20

the back for 1,4, and 8.

Example:"A shoe is a covering for the bottom of the foot."

Socks qualify as shoes under this definition, so it fails to apply to only those things that count as shoes.

1. A university is a group of persons gathered in a particular place and offering instruction in various subjects at the post-High School level.

2. A person is a human being.

3. Instruction is the presentation of information resulting in learning.

4. Plagiarization is the word-for-word use of other people's writings without acknowledgement.

5. A game is an athletic activity governed by rules.

6. Logic is the science that studies the principles of reasoning.

7. Murder is the non-accidential killing of a human being.

8. Rape is sexual intercourse with a human being involving the use of force.

9. War is armed conflict between nations.

10. A car is a four-wheeled self-propelled vehicle designed to transport people.

(2.12)   EVALUATIVE   ASSERTIONS.   As the label suggests, the
assertions   embody   judgments about the value of an action, event,
state of affairs, or thing.   Ultimately such judgments reflect our
opinions   about   the   desirability   of   the   "thing" being judged.
Almost   anything   can   be   judged   on a good-bad scale in terms of
whether   it promotes benefit or harm. A human action can be judged
morally good because it benefits people. The weather can be judged
as good because it helps farmers grow crops.   The criteria used in
making evaluative judgments are those that are inferrable from the
function   the   judger   takes the "thing" to have.   This means that
judgment   takes   place   in a context so that judgments are relative
to the kind of thing being judged.   The more broad the category in
which   we   place   a   thing   when   we judge it the more general the
criteria   we   base our judgment on.   Thus, we may say the music of
the Beatles is great music or we may be more cautious and say that
their   music   is   great POPULAR music.   The   criteria used   to
determine   the   truth of the two judgments are somewhat different.
Perhaps   as   a   result   the music of the Beatles can be said to be
great   popular   music   but   not   great as music in general.   It is
usually   futile   to   try   to   determine   the   truth of evaluative
judgments   when things are placed in very broad categories because
there is not likely to be an agreed-upon set of standards that can
be   used in judging. This is the basis for futile disputes such as
whether the Beatles created better music than Beethoven.   The fact
is   that   not all music is created for the same purpose or for the
same   audience,   so   the   tests   for   success   can be varied.   The
Beatles'   music   is great popular music while Beethoven's music is
great classical music.

Since   evaluative judgments are based on appeals to standards
it is essential, if a judgment is to be appraised accurately, that
the   claimant's   standard   be   identified.   In   effect   this is a
semantic   problem.   When someone says they've just seen a "great"
movie   we   should   ask   (if   we want to establish whether they are
correct   or   not):   "What   do   you   mean   by   'great movie'?"
Disagreements   about evaluations often occur because of the use of
different criteria for 'best', 'goodness', 'greatness', etc.   Here
is a commonplace example.

Virgil   and   Zeke are baseball fans and they have gotten into
one   of their many disputes about the game.   Virgil argues that in
1979   Fred   Lynn   of the Boston Red Sox was the best hitter in the
American   League   because   he finished the season with the highest
batting   average.   Zeke disagrees, he argues that Jim Rice of the
Red Sox was the best hitter because he hit for the greatest number
of   total   bases.   (In   baseball   parlance   Rice   was   the leading
"slugger".   Slugging   percentage   is   calculated   by   adding   the
hitter's   singles   plus two times the number of doubles plus three
times   the   number   of   triples plus four times the number of home
runs, then dividing by times at bat.)

The   two   arguments   seem to have incompatible conclusions so

22

that we are disposed to say that at least one of the arguments is defective. But that isn't necessarily so. The source of the dispute is semantic or conceptual. Virgil and Zeke are using different criteria for the expression 'best hitter'. Is the best hitter the person with the greatest number of hits for times at bat (Lynn) or Rice, the top slugger? With Virgil and Zeke defining 'best hitter' differently they will not be able to decide who is right. THERE MUST BE AGREEMENT ON WHAT STANDARDS ARE BEING USED BEFORE ANY CLAIM CAN BE ESTABLISHED AS TRUE OR FALSE TO THE JOINT SATISFACTION OF THOSE ARGUING.

In criticizing evaluative claims, then, the first step is to identify the standard the claimant is basing the claim on. If that standard is appropriate then the criticism must be one that shows the thing doesn't come close enough to the standard to make the evaluative judgment true. In English we have many words available so that we can "tailor" evaluative judgments to be accurate.

(2.13) LOGICALLY COMPLEX ASSERTIONS. These assertions are ones that, as we shall see in Chapter Six, contrast with simple ones that we shall symbolize using single letters. There are four such forms that will be discussed here: 'not A', 'A and B', 'A or B', and 'If A then B'.

(2.14) NEGATION: 'NOT A'. This is the simplest of the logically complex forms. Asserting "Not A" is the same as saying "A is false" so in evaluation we merely try to identify the relevant facts supporting and undermining A. If those supporting A outweigh those indicating it is false then the premise must be considered either dubious or false.

(2.15) CONJUNCTIONS: 'A and B'. A conjunction is true only when both conjuncts are true, so to refute a conjunction we need only show that one of the conjuncts is false. Obviously, the whole assertion is dubious to the extent that either one of the conjuncts is dubious, and the best strategy is to pick on the one that appears the most difficult to defend.

(2.16) ALTERNATIONS: 'A or B'. These are false only when both alternates are false so that the task of refutation is more difficult than with conjunctions, since you have to show that neither alternate is true. Alternations are, in general, more cautious assertions since the assertor is not committed to the truth of any partiular proposition mentioned in the assertion.

EXERCISE 2 - 3

This exercise is intended to develop your appreciation of what is needed to effectively criticize an alternation. Each

23

alternation has several assertions given below it, which are to be regarded as true. For each main assertion decide which of the others disproves it. Remember, to refute an alternation an assertion must be incompatible with ALL alternates. Nos. 1 and 4 are answered in the back.

1.   Either God created the Universe or it has always existed

    (a)   There is no God

    (b)   The universe came into existence on its own as a result of a great explosion that converted pure energy into matter.

    (c)   Nothing can come into existence without being created.

2.   General Motors makes the best cars or Ford does.

    (a)   Sone foreign cars are better than either GM or Ford products.

    (b)   Chrysler and AMC products are as good as any.

    (c)   We should buy North American built cars.

3.   Homosexuality is either an illness or an acquired taste.

    (a)   Homosexuals are born, not made.

    (b)   Homosexuality is not a physical illness.

    (c)   Sexual preferences are not a matter of taste.

    (d)   Homosexuality is a social vice.

4.   Students are either lazy or lacking study skills.

    (a)   Most students are fairly well-prepared and industrious.

    (b)   These students simply have deficient study skills.

    (c)   Having poor study skills is not the student's fault.

5.   To reduce fuel consumption home owners should either install wood stoves or install better insulation.

    (a)   There is a limited supply of wood.

    (b)   Very little fuel can be saved by these tactics.

    (c)   People should move to a warmer climate instead.

(2.17) CONDITIONALS: These are logically trickier than any of the other forms. The important point is that conditionals state truth guarantees, so that to refute them you must show that the truth guarantee fails. There are two ways to do this.

(1) THE FACTUAL APPROACH. When the antecedent is in fact true you might try to show that the consequent is not in fact true; for example if it is asserted that "If the moon appears circular then it is shaped like a Frisbee" you can show that the truth guarantee fails by asserting that the moon does in fact appear circular, yet evidence provided by the space program shows that the moon is a sphere so it is not shaped like a Frisbee. Thus, the antecedent is in fact true and the consequent is in fact false, which shows that the conditional is false. The truth guarantee made by the conditional is defective, as shown by the facts.

(2) THE CONCEPTUAL APPROACH. The factual approach is somewhat limited because you cannot use it to disprove all defective (false) conditionals. For example, you cannot show "If New York is more than 10 miles from Boston then New York is more than 12 miles from Boston" is false by the factual method because both the propositions embedded in this conditional are true. The factual approach can be successful only when the antecedent is true and the consequent false. For the other combinations of truth values (true-true, false-true, false-true) you must rely on a hypothetical or conceptual approach. This involves asking yourself "Regardless of whether the antecedent is true, would it make the consequent true if it was true?" When you ask such a question you are separating questions of antecedent and consequent truth from the question of whether the conditional provides a truth guarantee. This approach has the advantage of often permitting us to evaluate a conditional without having to know what truth values the antecedent and consequent actually have. In these cases it is sufficient to understand what these mean. For example, we can deal with "If the moon appears circular then it is shaped like a Frisbee" without knowing what the back side of the moon looks like, because the truth of the antecedent does not guarantee the truth of the consequent. We can claim this because we know that not all things that appear round are shaped like Frisbees. Some are spheres, others are oblong or irregular in shape, and some are even cylinders being looked at endwise! So our everyday experience enables us to show this conditional is false without any help from the space program. Similarly, the example about Boston and New York can be shown to be false without our actually knowing how far apart these cities are. The conceptual approach to evaluating conditionals is much more useful than the factual one since you don't have to show that the consequent of the conditional is in fact false, which sometimes could be difficult to do. However, there is one species of conditional assertion that cannot be evaluated without factual information.

25

These assertions represent statements of causal links, either of particular events or states of affairs, or of kinds of events or states. Here is an example of the first sort: suppose Zeke and Chloe are going away for a two-week vacation and Chloe just bought a large container of milk yesterday having forgotten they were going away: Zeke argues "If we leave it here then it will be sour when we get back, so we'd better give it to someone." How should Chloe deal with Zeke's premise? It clearly isn't one that can be known to be true or false without factual investigation. Zeke's conditional premise is really Just a particular version of a more general one: if fresh milk is kept in a refrigerator for two weeks then it will go sour. To verify or falsify Zeke's original premise they need only conduct the "experiment of leaving the milk in the refrigerator and seeing what it is like when they get back, but this isn't very useful because the milk will be wasted if indeed it does go sour. Zeke and Chloe want to know what to do now, so what they need to do is to find a source of information about the storage properties of milk. Perhaps a cook book gives them the answer, or perhaps the last useable date is stamped on the container. At any rate, conditionals that assert that a certain effect will occur, given a certain event or state, can only be verified or falsified by knowledge of how the world works.

The kind of causal link assertion just examined asserts that a particular phenomenon or kind of phenomenon will cause another. That is, the antecedent represents a cause and the consequent represents its supposed effect. When we are given a phenomenon and want to link it with another that we think brought it about, our antecedent represents the effect and the consequent represents the supposed cause. Let us suppose that Zeke and Chloe have finally sorted eveything out in the house and have gotten in the car to leave on vacation. The car makes the familiar starting noises but won't start. Zeke says, "If it won't start then the ignition system has quit." If Chloe wants to challenge this claim she could suggest some alternative cause of the problem, which would amount to saying that ignition failure isn't guaranteed by the fact that the car won't start. Failure to start might be caused by fuel delivery system failure (fuel pump, carburetor, etc.) or simply by lack of fuel. What happens here is that the original assertion represents one explanation of the phenomenon observed and it is being challenged by the presentation of other plausible explanations. Conditionals of this kind that represent good truth guarantees are ones that exclude any other plausible causes of the phenomenon mentioned in the antecedent. That is to say, the effect can guarantee that a particular phenomenon is its cause only if there is 'just the one probable cause. Experience indicates that most phenomena can be caused in several ways so that conditionals of this kind often fail to come close to providing a guarantee. Actually, they are put forward as hypotheses by most people--speculations to be investigated and confirmed or disconfirmed.

26

One particular mistake in criticizing conditionals is to try to refute them by claiming or showing that the antecedent is false. For instance, many people would respond to the assertion that "If the moon is made of cheese then it has a high protein content" by saying that the moon isn't made of cheese. This is true of course, but it does not refute the conditional, since the conditional is logically equivalent to "If it was true that the moon is made of cheese then it would be true that the moon has a high protein content." Written in this form it should be clear that the speaker is not saying the moon is made of cheese. The speaker has taken no position whatever on what the moon is made of, so denying that the moon is made of cheese cannot possibly refute the assertion. The only way to attack the assertion would be to give reasons why, if the moon was cheese, this fact would not guarantee that it had a high protein content. We would need, in particular, to identify kinds of cheese that are not high in protein or at least to show that there COULD be genuine cheese that was not high in protein. The lesson to be learned from this example is that showing that the antecedent of a conditional is false is irrelevant to showing that the conditional itself is false.

EXERCISE 2 - 4

This exercise is intended to develop your appreciation of what is needed to effectively criticize a conditional. Each conditional has several assertions given below it. Assume each is true and determine which disprove the main assertion. Nos. 1 and 3 are answered in the back.

1. If the Yankees win the American League pennant then they can win the World Series.

    (a) Kansas City Royals will win the pennant.

    (b) The Yankees can win the pennant but the National League pennant winner will win the World Series.

    (c) The World Series will be won by Montreal this year.

2. If the moon looks circular then it must be a sphere.

    (a) The moon looks circular but it is actually shaped like a cylinder--we see it end-on.

    (b) The moon is a saucer, not a sphere.

    (c) The moon doesn't look completely circular.

3. If a cow jumped over the moon then a cow was the first animal

in space.

(a) No cow ever jumped over the moon.

(b) A monkey was the first animal in space.

(c) A cow did jump over the moon but a kangaroo did it first!

4. If we have the government restrict wage settlements then prices won't increase so fast.

(a) Restricting wage settlements won't prevent companies from increasing prices as they have been doing.

(b) The government can't effectively keep track of wage settlements.

(c) It's not possible to control prices in a free market system.

(2.18) PROPOSITIONAL ATTITUDE ASSERTIONS. This class of assertions is characterized by the total absence of any link between the truth value of embedded propositions and the assertion itself. For example, assertions of the form 'X believes that A', where 'X' stands for a person and 'A' for a proposition do not depend at all for their truth or falsity on the truth of 'A'. "X believes the earth is flat" is false if asserted about you, but true if asserted about many individuals who lived during the middle ages. So we cannot disprove assertions of the form 'X believes that A' by directly attacking 'A'. Instead, we have to show, whatever the proposition, that the individual does not believe it. Propositional attitude assertions use a variety of terms to ascribe degrees of certainty that a person has about the truth of a proposition. Besides 'believe', there are 'feels', 'thinks', 'doubts', 'suspects', 'is certain', and others.

In establishing whether or not a person has a particular attitude to a particular proposition it is obviously most effective to ask that individual because normally no one knows better what an individual believes, feels, or thinks about something than that individual. Often on important matters this is not possible because the individual is dead or otherwise inaccessible. In these circumstances we have to rely on the reports or records of others who are (or were) in a position to know. Newspapers and books, especially biographies, are the usual sources for establishing the views of well-known people.

When someone presents you with a premise of the form "X believes/feels/thinks that A" you should be prepared to ask them how they know that it is so if it seems doubtful to you that X would believe/feel/think that A.

There is a fallacy (a fallacious argument form) that depends on attributing a belief or attitude to someone that they do not have. It has the Latin name IGNORATIO ELENCHI, which shows how old it is! The fallacy arises from an over-enthusiastic desire to refute an opponent's view. To do this you attribute to the opponent a view that appears to be his/hers, except that it is distorted to a degree that allows you to prove it false. This gives the arguee the impression you have refuted the opponent. Here is an example.

Person X is a politician running for office in an area where people are notably conservative on abortion. In a panel discussion he has conceded that he believes that when a woman's life is threatened by pregnancy she should be permitted to have an abortion. X's opponent, anxious to gain some political mileage at X's expense, argues thusly at a rally: "X approves of abortion, which shows he has no respect for innocent human life. We cannot allow such a man to hold a responsible office."

29

Here, the audience is against abortion and if it fails to note that X's view is different, the arguer is likely to gain some ground. The premise "X approves of abortion" does not do justice to X's view on the subject. It is far too general. If you were part of the audience and aware of X's views you could attack the premise by objecting that X only approves of abortion in special circumstances, when a woman requesting it does so in self-defence. Of course, to refute premises attributing views to someone you have to know what the person's position actually is.

Be suspicious of arguments intended to refute someone's views when that person is not around to defend him/herself.

(2.19) SUMMARY. We have discussed the approaches to be followed in evaluating the various kinds of premises to be encountered in arguments. A brief summary will be useful.

RELATIONAL ASSERTIONS: Examples: (1) Sweden has a higher standard of living than Canada, (2) New York is south of Boston.

Dealing with comparative cases such as (1), remember to establish the degree to which the one thing is superior to the other. The difference might be insignificant.

SINGULAR ASSERTIONS: These ascribe properties to particular individuals. Example: The Grand Canyon is over one mile deep.

Refute by showing that the "thing" referred to does not in fact have the property.

UNIVERSAL GENERALIZATIONS: Example: All red-haired people are hot tempered.

Refute by identifying as a counter-example someone who is red-haired and not hot-tempered.

In selecting counter-examples do not use odd cases, use otherwise typical individuals.

Don't take claims like 'red-haired people are hot tempered' to mean all red-haired people are hot tempered. These are soft generalizations that can only be refuted by showing that the claim is true of less than half of the individuals in that category.

WEAK GENERALIZATIONS: These are of two kinds: (1) proportionality claims ('most X's are Y's', etc.) which are refuted by showing that a significantly greater proportion are exceptions than the original claim allows; (2) non-proportionality claims ('many X's are Y's', 'some X's are Y's', etc.) which are

30

refuted by establishing the truth of a non-proportionality claim that is incompatible with the original one (e.g., 'many X's are Y's' is refuted by 'a few X's are Y's').

SEMANTICAL ASSERTIONS: Example : Man is a rational animal.

Definitions can be criticized by showing that either (a) the expression given as the definition does not apply to all the things that the term being defined refers to, or (b) it applies to more things than the term being defined does.

Semantical assertions can be verified also by using a dictionary.

Beware of people who give personal definitions that help them prove their point.

EVALUATIVE ASSERTIONS: These can be dubious either because the standard against which the thing is being judged is unsatisfactory or because the thing does not measure up to the standard.

When criticizing make sure you are clear about which of the two criticisms you are making.

Any propositions belonging to any of the other categories can be evaluative.

NEGATIONS: These are simply denials of assertions of one of the other kinds. Refute by showing the affirmative version is true.

CONJUNCTIONS: Example: She's a model and she's an actress. Refute by showing that one or both of the conjuncts is false.

CONDITIONALS: These have the form 'If A then B'. Example: If it rains then the umpire will cancel the game.

To refute show that either (1) A is true and B is false (factual approach), or (2) B could be false when A is true (conceptual approach).

Conditionals that express causal inferences can be refuted only by appeal to causal links, not by the conceptual approach.

Conditionals cannot be refuted by showing that A, the antecedent, is false.

ALTERNATIONS: These have the form 'Either A or B'. Example: Either there is life on Mars or there are no genuine canals there.

31

To refute you must show that both alternatives are false.

PROPOSITIONAL ATTITUDE ASSERTIONS: These have the form 'X believes that A', 'X feels that A', etc. Example: Leo believes the earth is flat.

Can't be refuted by showing A is false.

To refute you must show that X does not believe/think/feel that A.

CHAPTER THREE: VALIDITY

(3.1) INTRODUCTION: In Chapter One you were told that arguments consist of premises and conclusions that are inferred from them. A good argument is one that proves its conclusion or, to put it another way, it has true premises that guarantee the truth of the conclusion inferred. In future we will call a good argument, one that proves its conclusion, a "proof". We will also say that the inference in such an argument is "valid". Conversely a bad inference will be called "invalid" and a bad argument will be said to be "unsound". To avoid confusion you should always follow these linguistic conventions. Do not interchange the words 'true' and 'valid' by calling premises 'valid' or inferences 'true'.

An argument, then, is evaluated by answering two questions: (1) are the premises true?, and (2) is the inference valid? Affirmative answers to these questions require us to say that the argument proves its conclusion. We can express the requirement in an equation.

Proof = True Premises + Valid Inferences.

Obviously, false premises cannot prove anything, regardless of how logically adequate the inference is. The notion of premise truth is probably a familiar one. The idea of inference validity, however, is likely to be somewhat unfamiliar. In essence, inferences are the logical steps taken to get the conclusion from the premises in an argument.

(3.2) VALIDITY: An argument has a valid inference when the premises, if they were true, would guarantee that the conclusion was true. The condition for validity must be stated in the form of a conditional for several reasons.

First, VALIDITY IS INDEPENDENT OF THE TRUTH VALUE OF THE PREMISES.

Here are four arguments that illustrate how validity is independent of the truth value of premises:

Example 1:

Boston is more than 10 miles from New York. Therefore, Boston is more than five miles from New York.

Example 2:

Boston is more than 10,000 miles from New York. Therefore, Boston is more than five miles from New York.

Example 3:

Boston is more than 5 miles from New York. Therefore, Boston is more than 10 miles from New York.

Example 4:

Boston is more than 10,000 miles from New York. Therefore, Boston is more than 11,000 miles from New York.

Examples 1 and 2 have valid inferences but Example 1 has a true premise whereas Example 2 has a false one. On the other hand, Examples 3 and 4 both have invalid inferences but Example 3 has a true premise and Example 4 has a false premise. These examples prove that knowing the truth value of premises will not help us establish whether or not an argument has a valid inference. There just is no correlation between premise truth (by itself) and inference validity.

A second aspect of validity that follows from defining it with the conditional 'if the premises were true then the conclusion would be true' is that VALIDITY IS INDEPENDENT OF CONCLUSION TRUTH VALUE TAKEN BY ITSELF. Referring back to Examples 1 and 3 you will note that each argument has a true conclusion, yet Example 1 has a valid inference and Example 3 does not.

Compare also Example 4 with the following one, Example 5: "Boston is more than 10,000 miles from New York. Therefore, Boston is more than 5,000 miles from New York."

Both Examples 4 and 5 have false conclusions yet Example 4 has an invalid inference and Example 5 has a valid one. Thus, we cannot judge an argument to have a valid inference on the sole ground that it has a true conclusion.

The discussion of the five examples has shown that if we know that the premises of an argument are true, we cannot from this alone know that the argument contains a valid inference. If you think about it, this makes good sense because if true premises guaranteed a valid inference then every argument with true premises would be a proof (would prove its conclusion) and we know that some arguments with true premises do not prove their conclusions. Some have true premises that fail to make the conclusion true, either because they do not provide enough good evidence or because they are not evidence for the conclusion at all--they are irrelevant. Furthermore, if we know that the conclusion of an argument is true we cannot know from this alone that the inference is valid, and if it need not be valid then it need not be a proof either. It is a common error to think an

34

argument must prove its conclusion (be sound) when it has a true conclusion. But it only does so when it has a valid inference from true premises. Examples 2 and 3 are instances of arguments that have true conclusions but which do not prove those conclusions true. Example 2 has a false premise and Example 3 has an invalid inference. Perhaps you find it difficult to understand how a conclusion can be true yet belong to an argument that does not prove it. This is understandable once we distinguish between conclusions that are true for reasons not stated and conclusions that must be true because of the premises given in the argument. Examples 1 and 2 can illustrate this distinction. They have the same true conclusion (Boston is more than five miles from New York) and the truth of the premise in Example 1 makes the conclusion true, yet Example 2 has a false premise (Boston is more than 10,000 miles from New York) so that the argument cannot prove the conclusion. In this case the conclusion is true for reasons relating to geographical factors, not because of the premise. Thus, Example 2 has a true conclusion but does not prove its conclusion true.

We have just come upon a reason why it won't always be satisfactory to deal with other people's arguments by attacking their conclusions, which is the favorite approach used by most people who haven't studied logic. Sometimes an arguer's reasoning will be defective even though the conclusion being argued for is true. It will be a waste of time in such cases to try to show the conclusion is false because it is true, and nothing true can be proved false by any argument. (No set of true premises can guarantee the truth of a proposition that is not true). You can, however, point out the logical defect in the argument that prevents it from proving its conclusion. You might not necessarily want to do this simply to show the arguer he or she made an error. You might be engaged in a cooperative effort to find good reasons for believing something you both want to believe. You might, perhaps, be trying to prove a theorem in geometry together.

Having seen that validity is independent of premise truth value and conclusion truth value taken separately, it should be noted that validity can occur with any combination of these, EXCEPT when the premises are true and the conclusion false. In this case the inference can only be invalid, since when an inference is valid, true premises guarantee a true conclusion. The existence of true premises and a false conclusion shows the guarantee is defective.

Since it is not possible to have an argument with a valid inference, true premises, and false conclusion, there will (according to the theory of combinations) be seven possible arrangements for premise, conclusion, and inference values. Here are examples of the two others to "round out the set".

Example 6 has an invalid inference, a false premise, and a true conclusion:

Boston is 5 miles from New York. Therefore, Boston is more than 10 miles from New York.

Example 7 has a true premise, an invalid inference and a false conclusion:

Boston is more than 10 miles from New York. Therefore, Boston is more than 10,000 miles from New York.

It will be helpful for further discussion to list the combinations in a table:

EXAMPLE	PREMISE	INFERENCE	CONCLUSION	PROOF
1	True	Valid	True	Yes
2	False	Valid	True	No
5	False	Valid	False	No
3	True	Invalid	True	No
7	True	Invalid	False	No
6	False	Invalid	True	No
4	False	Invalid	False	No

The first combination in the table, of which Example 1 is an instance, is the only one that a proof can have, since proof equals true premises and a valid inference. It follows from this, of course, that only arguments with true conclusions can be proofs. However, it does not follow that ALL such arguments will be proofs, as several of the other examples show.

Examples 2 and 5 show that, given a false premise and a valid inference, the conclusion could be either true or false. This is what we would expect because the conclusion is guaranteed true in a valid argument only on condition that the premise is true. The absence of premise truth when the inference is valid does not, however, guarantee that the conclusion is false, as Example 2 shows. The guarantee provided by validity is a truth guarantee only, and conditional on the premise being true.

Examples 3 and 7 show that, even with true premises, the absence of the truth guarantee provided by validity keeps us from knowing the truth value of the conclusion. Just as Examples 2 and 5 show that validity is not enough to prove a conclusion, Examples 3 and 7 show that true premises are not enough by themselves either.

Examples 6 and 4 represent the most defective kinds of arguments, those in which we have neither true premises nor a

36

valid inference. Arguments like these can be successfully attacked on two fronts.

(3.3) SUMMARY: The simple arguments given in this chapter are intended to familiarize you with the concept of inference validity. The main difficulty people have in gasping this concept is with the relationship between the truth value of the assertions in an argument and validity. The examples were used to make the following points:

(1) An argument with true premises and a false conclusion is always invalid, with any other combination of truth values it can be either valid or invalid (see Example 7).

(2) An argument with a true conclusion can be invalid because it is possible for the premises given not to guarantee the truth of the conclusion: in such cases the conclusion is not proved true by the argument, it is true for other reasons (see Examples 3 and 6).

(3) Conversely, an argument with a false conclusion can be valid although it cannot be a proof since it is impossible to prove a false assertion to be true. Such arguments cannot have all their premises true because arguments with a valid inference and true premises are proofs and no proof can have a false conclusion.

(4) Proof = True Premises + Valid Inference.

CHAPTER FOUR: AN ARGUMENT EVALUATION PROCEDURE

(4.1) INTRODUCTION: In this chapter a procedure will be presented that will enable you to arrive at a judgement about the extent to which an argument proves its conclusion. This judgement represents the "bottom line" of an argument evaluation.

A key element in the procedure is the construction of an accurate logical "picture" of an argument. This picture will take the form of a diagram and the inference and assumption judgements will be recorded on the diagrams in the form of ratings. When we arrive at a rating for the degree of proof of the final conclusion we have completed a logical "audit" of an argument.

Actually, arriving at the argument rating will not be the last step in the evaluation procedure. The final step will be the formulation of a response. Often we must respond to the arguer and not simply form a private judgement of the quality of her/his argument. This response cannot, obviously, take the form of showing them a diagram with ratings on it, unless they know what the diagram means. Since only those who have read this material will know that, it is essential to express one's evaluation judgement and the reasons for it in a logically non-technical way.

(4.2) STRUCTURAL DIAGRAMS: It is essential to understand the logical structure of an argument if one is going to evaluate it accurately. One must be clear about what the conclusion is and how the premises relate to it and to each other. One way of ensuring that we have a clear understanding of the logical relations in an argument is to produce some sort of illustration of it. The method of depiction to be presented here will be the basis for a methodical step-by-step approach to the overall evaluation of arguments.

The method of depiction to be used is very simple yet it can portray arguments of any degree of complexity in a way that a written description could not. The diagrammatic approach lets us look at the whole argument at once whereas a written version does not. A single capital letter will be assigned to each distinct simple proposition in an argument, starting with the letter 'A' and proceeding alphabetically. Whole assertions will be contained in circles on the diagram and assertions that are reasons for others are linked to them by arrows whose arrow-heads touch the circle representing the conclusion. The conclusion is to be placed below the premises. For example, suppose someone says "Pedestrians are using umbrellas, therefore it is raining." We can let 'A' stand for 'pedestrians are using umbellas' and 'B' for 'it is raining', and draw the argument "picture" as shown on the next page:

The argument diagram shown above is the one corresponding to the simplest argument, one with only two assertions. The next-most complex argument naturally has three assertions in it, a conclusion and two premises. There are two different structures these arguments have:

The diagram on the left says that the assertions A and B are not considered to be logically related by the arguer. They are independent reasons for C and, when taken together are thought to be sufficient to make C true. Here is an example: "Boston is north of New York. New York is north of Washington. Therefore, Boston is North of Washington." Here we can call the first assertion "A", the second "B", and the conclusion "C". In this argument B is not inferred from A. That Boston is north of New York does not give us any reason for thinking that New York is north of Washington. And neither can A be inferred from B. This is why the arguer gives no indication that he or she thinks A and B are logically linked. They are simply two independent premises that, taken together, seem to prove C.

The diagram on the right differs from the other in that the arguer is saying that A and B are logically linked. A is being given as sufficient reason for believing B, and B in turn is thought to be a sufficient reason for C. Here is an example of this argument pattern: "Since San Francisco is about 250 miles north of Los Angeles, San Francisco is colder than Los Angeles. Therefore, Los Angeles has a more comfortable climate than San

39

Francisco." If we label the assertions "A", "B", and "C" in sequence, the diagram will be a picture of the argument. In contrast to the previous argument this one has two inferences (A to B and B to C). We will adopt the principle that THERE ARE AS MANY INFERENCES AS THERE ARE CONCLUSIONS DRAWN, so that the first argument has only one inference but the second has two because it contains two conclusions. B is a conclusion drawn from A and C is a conclusion drawn from B. In this example, assertion B serves as both premise and conclusion, so to avoid confusion B and other assertions that have this dual status will be called "intermediate conclusions". Intermediate conclusions, it must be remembered, also function as premises. Premises that are not argued for will be called "assumptions". They are the starting points of the argument. This does not mean that they cannot be argued about, it only means they are not being argued for in the argument at hand. Obviously, one way of criticizing an argument is to show that the assumptions are dubious or false.

To summarize the terminology: in the left-hand diagram there are two assumptions and one inference, in the right-hand diagram there is one assumption and two inferences. These are the only patterns that three-assertion arguments can have. Of course, theoretically, arguments can contain any number of assertions. But in practice we try to avoid using complex arguments because they are difficult to follow. This might not seem like a good reason but it is. You cannot persuade people to accept your conclusion if they cannot follow your argument. Normally when we need to get people to accept a conclusion requiring a number of inference steps we simply break the argument down into a series of simpler arguments. However, you will frequently encounter arguments containing more than three assertions. The possible arrangements for four-assertion arguments are shown below:

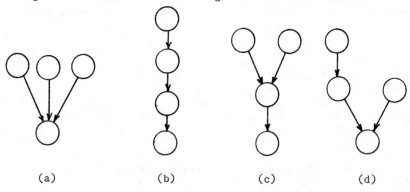

(a)   (b)   (c)   (d)

Using the terminology we have adopted, (a) has one inference and three assumptions, (b) has three inferences and one assumption, (c) has two inferences and two assumptions, and (d) has two inferences and two assumptions. As extra assertions are added the number of different structures increases, but this complexity will not present problems when we use the diagrams in criticizing arguments. What we will do is deal with complex arguments by evaluating each inference separately--a piece-meal approach. By recording our decisions about the goodness of each inference and the plausibility of each assumption on the diagram we will have a "bird's eye view" of the logical adequacy of each part of an argument, and so we will be able to make overall judgements of even very complex arguments without getting confused. Complexity can be dealt with by being analytical and methodical.

In the next four chapters you will not be required to construct argument diagrams that are very complex. Most will contain no more than three assertions, consisting of two independent premises and one inference. The arguments you will be diagramming will also be clearly stated so that there will be no difficulty in identifying the conclusion and the premises. In Chapter Eight problems of analyzing arguments in ordinary English will be discussed.

(4.3)   THE RATING SYMBOLS: $\sqrt{}$, ?, X

Three symbols only will be used in conducting logical audits on the diagrammatic versions of arguments. The rough-and-ready nature of the judgement process makes it difficult to defend the use of a more precise set of rating terms. On the other hand, using only '$\sqrt{}$' and 'X' would involve an unnecessary sacrifice in accuracy since we often will want to say that an argument provides some good grounds for its conclusion while falling short of being a proof. Thus, there is a need for the '?' symbol.

The three symbols chosen will serve triple duty in that assumptions, conclusions and inferences will all be rated using them. It is important to keep in mind, though, that one of these symbols beside a conclusion expresses the degree of proof for that assetion, while the same symbol beside an assumption (an assertion not argued for, a starting-point for the argument) expresses a probability that the assumption is true. When the symbol is used as an inference rating, on the other hand, it will express the probability that premise truth guarantees conclusion truth.

To keep things simple it is possible to define the symbols quantitatively in the same way for each of their three distinct uses. The symbol '$\sqrt{}$' will be understood to represent the "quality range" from 75% to 100%. The symbol '?' covers the range 50% to 75% and 'X' covers the range 0% to 50%. To further clarify the meanings of the rating symbols in their various uses here are the nine situations that can arise in a two-assertion argument.

41

The truth of A makes the probability of B at
    least 3/4.

Appraisal: "The inference from A to B is valid".

The truth of A makes the probability of B between
    1/2 and 3/4.

Appraisal: "The inference from A to B has
    appreciable validity".

The truth of A makes the probability of B less
    than 1/2.
Appraisal: "The inference is invalid".

The probability of A being true is at least 3/4.

Appraisal: "A is true".

The probability of A being true is between
    1/2 and 3/4.

Appraisal: "A is dubious".

The probability of A being true is less than 1/2.

Appraisal: "A is false".

The probability that B is proved is at least 3/4.

Appraisal: "B has been proved by A".

The probability that B is proved is between 1/2 and 3/4.

Appraisal: "B has been proved to an appreciable extent".

The probability that B is proved is less than 1/2.

Appraisal: "B has not bee proved by A".

The foregoing should provide you with a "feel" for the meanings of the three rating symbols in their different uses. The major confusion that can occur has to do with the last three ratings. These ratings do not directly express judgements of the truth value of the conclusions. When the conclusion is "√" rated, of course, we are committed to claiming it is true, but this is because the "√" rating shows we regard it as PROVED true. When the conclusion is rated "?" this does not show that we regard it as dubious. We may well regard it as true. The rating indicates the extent to which it has been proved true. The same applies when the conclusion is rated "X". Consider this example from Chapter Three: "Boston is more than 5 miles from New York. Therefore, Boston is more than 10 miles from New York."

We can construct a diagrammatic version of this argument and rate it as follows:

A = Boston is more than 5 miles from New York.

B = Boston is more than 10 miles from New York.

43

The verdict on the argument is indicated by "X" beside B, i.e. the conclusion is not proved. However, we do know B is true. The evaluation procedure would not be followed correctly if we had put a "√" rating by B, since the task is to decide whether B has been proved by A. It has not, because the inference is invalid. The point is this: EVALUATE ASSUMPTIONS ONLY AS TRUE, FALSE, OR DUBIOUS--NEVER INTERMEDIATE OR FINAL CONCLUSIONS.

(4.4) RATING ARGUMENTS. Arriving at the correct overall rating for an argument can be tricky when inferences involve several premises. In the simplest case, with only one premise, rating is easy. Since the probability of the conclusion bring proved true is the product of the inference validity probability and the premise probability, the conclusion rating will be the lowest rating of the two, except when both are rated "?", in which case the conclusion is rated "X". This diagram portrays the situation for each of the nine combinations.

Inference ＼ Premise	√	?	X
√	√	?	X
?	?	X	X
X	X	X	X

This simple situation does not apply for more complex inferences, even when there are only two premises. For example, one assumption may represent very good evidence while the other represents very slight evidence. When this is so the falsity of the latter will not be as crucial for the argument as would the falsity of the former. An example will clarify this.

Suppose we have these three assertions:

A = Students at Podunk University study very little.

B = Most students at Podunk have part-time jobs.

C = Podunk students don't learn a lot in college.

Further suppose that the argument has this form:

In evaluating this argument we can judge the inference to be quite good. A certain amount can be learned in classes but a fair amount of study is needed to master the material assigned. Let us rate the inference with a '√':

Now suppose we investigate the situation at Podunk to see how we should rate the premises, and we find that A is true but that B is false because Podunk is situated in a small town where few part-time jobs are available. We enter ratings based on our investigations:

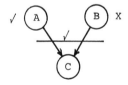

Now we must make a judgement about the overall adequacy of the argument. Should we say that since one premise is true and one false that this amounts to an overall premise rating of "dubious"? That would be unrealistic because A is much better evidence for C than B would be if it were true. In fact A is very good evidence for C. That being so we would not be far wrong to judge the argument as sound.

This example is intended to show that you cannot just "average out" the premise ratings when there are two or more premises. Some premises represent much better evidence than others. This does not present a problem when all the premises are true but you should be aware of it when some are true and some are false or dubious.

(4.5) THE BASIC ARGUMENT EVALUATION PROCEDURE. In its essentials the procedure presented below will be followed, with appropriate revisions, throughout the book.

STEP ONE: CONSTRUCT AN ACCURATE DIAGRAMMATIC VERSION OF THE ARGUMENT.

In the early chapters this will not be difficult but later you will be expected to rely on the argument analysis information presented in Chapter Eight to construct diagrams of more complex arguments that may contain ambiguous sentences and vague terms. Remember to draw the diagram as the arguer would. Sometimes you may want to draw it so that it makes the best sense, but make sure you do not deviate from the arguer's intentions when you do this.

STEP TWO: EVALUATE EACH INFERENCE AND ASSIGN A RATING TO IT.

Draw a line horizontally, cutting across each arrow going to the conclusion and place your rating above it. Remember, no matter how many arrows there are going to a conclusion, there is only one inference. The question to be answered for each inference is: would the premises taken together, if true, make the conclusion true? The technique for arriving at the correct answer are different for different kinds of arguments. The first kind, evidential arguments, will be dealt with in the next chapter. The second kind, structural arguments, are dealt with in the chapter after that.

STEP THREE: EVALUATE EACH ASSUMPTION AND ASSIGN A RATING TO IT.

The strategy to follow is to try to refute each one using relevant facts and the information contained in Chapter Two.

STEP FOUR: DETERMINE THE EXTENT TO WHICH EACH INTERMEDIATE CONCLUSION IS PROVED AND ASSIGN THE APPROPRIATE RATING.

This is simply a matter of relying on the ratings of the inference and each premise. Do not bring any new evidence to bear because we only wish to know whether the conclusions are proved by their premises and inferences. If you feel that a rating resulting from premise and inference ratings is too high or too low this means that you have rated one of these inappropriately.

46

STEP FIVE: DETERMINE THE EXTENT TO WHICH THE FINAL CONCLUSION HAS BEEN PROVED AND ASSIGN THE APPROPRIATE RATING TO IT.

This rating represents your overall judgements of the quality of the argument. It is based on the inference to the final conclusion and the premises from which it is inferred. These premises may be intermediate conclusions, in which case we rely on their proof ratings: or they may be assumptions, in which case we rely on their truth ratings.

STEP SIX: FORMULATE A RESPONSE TO THE ARGUMENT.

The response should be in plain English, or as plain as the subject matter permits. It should express your overall judgment, as arrived at in Step Five: the conclusion has been proved, has been proved to some extent but not satisfactorily, or has not been proved. You must also say why any weaknesses in assumptions or inferences are genuine weaknesses by giving good reasons.

You have now been acquainted with the fundamental concepts and procedures for argument evaluation. In the next two chapters you will find many examples of evaluations and there will be examples provided for you to work on. One last reminder: the issue is not whether the final conclusion is true, but whether it is PROVED true by the assumptions the arguer has started from.

EXERCISE 4 - 1

Identify the ratings that should appear in the blocks associated with each diagram. Nos. 2 and 4 Are answered in the back.

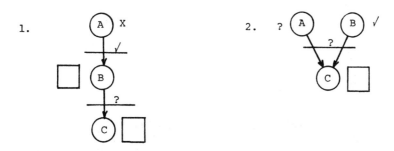

1.

2.

47

3.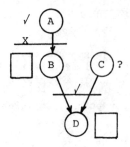

4.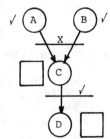

5.

EXERCISE 4 - 2

Assign the appropriate assumption, inference, and conclusion ratings to each argument. (Boston is about 200 miles from New York). Nos. 2 and 4 are answered in the back.

1.   A = Boston is more than 10 miles from New York.

B = Boston is more than 5 miles from New York.

2.   A = Boston is more than 10,000 miles from New York.

B = Boston is more than 5 miles from New York.

3.   A = Boston is more than 5 miles from New York.

B = Boston is more than 10 miles from New York.

4.

A = Boston is more than 10,000 miles from New York.

B = Boston is more than 11,000 miles from New York.

5.

A = Boston is more than 10,000 miles from New York.

B = Boston is more than 5,000 miles from New York.

6.

A = Boston is 5 miles from New York.

B = Boston is more than 10 miles from New York.

7.

A = Boston is more than 10 miles from New York.

B = Boston is more than 10,000 miles from New York.

49

CHAPTER FIVE: EVIDENTIAL VALIDITY

(5.1)   INTRODUCTION: The outcome of the process of inference evaluation is an answer to the question "IF the premises of the argument were true would they make the conclusion true?" If you can answer "no" and have good justification for saying so then you have shown that the argument does not prove its conclusion, even if the premises happen to be true. Of course, if the inference seems valid to you then you must also examine the premises to establish whether or not they are true.

We can distinguish between two kinds of inference validity: (1) evidential validity, and (2) structural validity. When we have an argument with one or more conditional assertions (if . . . then . . ., etc.) or alternations ("or" assertions) it is possible for such an argument to have structural validity, a property that arises entirely from the way the propositions in the argument are related. This is an all-or-nothing affair that can be checked by "mechanical" procedures. In Chapter Six one such procedure will be presented. Structural validity can also arise when the assertions in an argument are categorical ones. For example, arguments of this form are structurally valid: All X's are Y's. All Y's are Z's. Therfore, all X's are Z's. A method of testing such arguments will be presented in Chapter Six.

In this chapter we will be concerned with principles of evidential validity. To the extent that the assertions given as evidence could prove the conclusion (if they are true) we will say the argument is evidentially valid. Each premise is given as evidence for the conclusion.

Evidential validity, unlike structural validity, cannot be established using mechanical procedures. The principles and procedures of evaluation are varied and can only be mastered by practice. Also, again unlike structural validity, evidential validity is a matter of degree. Some arguments contain better evidence for their conclusions than do others, so that we will have to talk about inferences being "somewhat valid", "very nearly valid", etc. In such cases the degree of proof will be less than 100% even if all premises are true. Total evidential validity is normally only an ideal since the premises cannot usually guarantee the truth of a conclusion. Even this argument has a slightly defective inference: "The sun has risen for billions of years, therefore, it will rise tomorrow." Why? Well, the truth of the premise does not guarantee that between now and the next scheduled sunrise the sun won't blow up or otherwise cease to exist!

An exception here are arguments that rely on definitional or conceptual truths. Example One in Chapter Three is an instance: "Boston is more than 10 miles from New York. Therefore, Boston is more than 5 miles from New York." Because of what the terms '10',

50

'5', and 'mile' mean it would be contradictory to assert the assumption and deny the conclusion. Thus, it is impossible for the former to be true and the latter false, which makes the inference 100% valid.

(5.2) EVIDENCE AND RELEVANCE: These two important concepts are related.   An assertion that is irrelevant to the truth or falsity of another is one that is neither evidence for nor evidence against it.   Thus, if a proposition is evidence for or against another, then it is relevant to it. In an odd way, evidence is a "truth-neutral" concept. Our ability to judge that a proposition is evidence for or against another being true does not depend on our actually knowing that the propositions are true. Thus, we can see that 'The moon is made of cheese' would be evidence for 'The moon has a high protein content' even if we happened to know nothing at all about the moon. We do know that cheese has lots of protein and this is our basis for saying that the one proposition is relevant to the other.

Sometimes we can tell that one proposition is not evidence for another simply because we understand what they mean. We need no background information about how the world works. Here is an example. Someone called upon to support the claim that corn flakes are nutritious, said "as for the nutritional value of corn flakes, the milk you have with your corn flakes has great nutritional value."

This argument has the premise 'the milk one has with corn flakes is nutritious', which is supposed to prove the conclusion that corn flakes are nutritious. But it is clear that the nutritional value of milk is neither evidence for or evidence against the nutritional value of corn flake BY THEMSELVES. Thus, the premise is irrelevant to the conclusion so the inference is invalid. And because the inference is invalid the argument is not a proof. Notice that this argument can be found inadequate without our even verifying the premise. Most people know that milk has nutritional value, of course, but it was not necessary to know this. All we needed to know was that 'corn flakes' does not refer to milk or a milk product, which is simply a matter of knowing the meaning of the sentences used in the argument.

Relevance is not merely a matter of meaning, of course, because at bottom the assertions relevant to a particular one are relevant because of causal connections among phenomena. Thus, our ability to judge relevance is a function of what we know about how the world works. We now know, for example, that the position of the moon is relevant to tidal behavior on earth, but there was a time when no one would have taken the moon's position as being relevant to the state of the tide.

One unusual thing about the concept of evidence is that a

proposition that is false can have true propositions that count as evidence for its truth. For example, the proposition 'The moon looks round' is evidence for the truth of 'The moon is a giant Frisbee'. This sort of thing really seems to bother some people. In everyday life we frequently discuss propositions for which we have evidence counting for and against. The proposition 'Creatures from outer space have visited Earth' is an example. There is some evidence in favor and some against, but of course the proposition is either true or false. If it is false then what we take to be evidence for it is misleading us, but it is still evidence all the same. There is no impossibility about having evidence for the truth of it or vice versa. What is not possible is that such evidence could prove the proposition true. At one time people mistakenly thought that we had enough evidence to prove the earth was flat. They were not wrong about the truth of the propositions representing evidence (that the sea looks flat, etc.) for the earth being flat. What they were wrong about was thinking that they had enough evidence.

The existence of evidence both for and against controversial propositions leads some people to the conclusion that it does not matter which side one takes. This is a fallacy. There is only one situation in which this conclusion is appropriate--when the evidence for and against is equal. Usually this is not so, the evidence on one side usually has greater "weight." If you wish to adopt a position on the issue you must ascertain which is the weightier side and favor that. That is, if you wish to be logical about it.

EXERCISE 5-1

The purpose of this exercise is to improve your ability to recognize assertions that are relevant to others and recognize when there is relevance. For each of the five main assertions several others are given. You are to decide whether these others count for, against, or are neutral (irrelevant), with respect to proving the main assertion. In the parentheses enter "+" (for), "-" (against),or "0" (irrelevant). Answers for 1 and 3 are given in the back.

1. "Last month was a dry month."

    ( ) My well went dry.

    ( ) There was no rain after the middle of the month.

    ( ) There was a big rain storm on the fifth of the month.

    ( ) There was as much rain as in the month before that.

    ( ) Normally it is dry this time of year.

52

( ) We're getting plenty of rain this month.

2. "University students are interested in a degree rather than an education."

( ) Most students would not complain if the number of credits needed for a degree were halved.

( ) Most students do the work required of them.

( ) Lots of students come to university to learn.

( ) An education doesn't help you get and hold a job.

3. "England was a happier place in Victorian times."

( ) No major war was fought during this period.

( ) The mortality rate for children was many times higher than it is now.

( ) In those days people knew their place

( ) The British Enpire was at its peak.

( ) Queen Victoria had no sense of humor.

4. "Men are stronger than women."

( ) In Olympic competition the men's record in the shot put has always been longer than the women's.

( ) Men are taller than women, on average.

( ) For a given body weight men can lift more than women.

( ) On average, women live longer than men.

( ) Physical strength isn't as important as it used to be.

(5.3)   EVIDENTIAL   VALIDITY: An   argument   has   evidential
validity when its premises would be sufficient to prove the
conclusion if they were true. The first point to be made about
this is that we are interested in whether the premises TAKEN
TOGETHER prove the conclusion. It is not necessary that any one
premise prove the conclusion, as a separate inference to be
evaluated. Suppose someone argued as follows: "The starter of my
car won't turn the engine fast enough to start. The lights are dim
when turned on. Therefore, the battery is discharged."

The first two assertions are individually some evidence for
the conclusion, but neither one by itself comes close to proving
it.   The starter might be able to turn the engine fast enough
because its connection to the battery is poor. The lights may be
dim sometimes because of a poor electrical connection. But it
would be an error to say that the argument is not valid because
neither premise individually can prove the conclusion. Taken
together, the two premises come very close to proving it because
it is unlikely that two separate faults will occur at once to
cause them to be true. It is much more likely, given that both
functions rely on battery power, that a single fault (a discharged
battery) is responsible for both.

A second point to be noted is that assumptions may be
redundant.   If in the last example, the proposition 'The battery
fluid has a specific gravity close to 1.10' was an assumption the
other two assumptions would be redundant since this one by itself
comes as close as one can get to being sufficient to prove the
conclusion.   The other two do not really improve the inference
when this one is present. Thus, not all relevant premises have to
be true in all arguments for the argument to be a proof or
near-proof.

(5.4)   EVALUATING   EVIDENTIAL   ARGUMENTS: The   argument
patterns selected for this chapter have been chosen because they
are frequently used by most of us, so that they are frequently
encountered.   Since the assertions found in these arguments are
logically different the detailed application of evaluation
strategies will be different, but the underlying forms of the
strategies are pretty much the same.

The policy presented is that of evaluation through criticism.
If we fail completely in an attempt to show an assumption is
untrue or an inference invalid we should judge it to merit a " "
rating.   If our criticism casts doubt on the assumption or
inference but is nowhere near conclusive we should rate it "?".
If our criticism is strong, leaving no major doubts, we should
assign an "X" rating. The general crititicism considerations are
different for assumptions and inferences, of course.

(5.41)   ASSUMPTION   EVALUATION: In evaluating assumptions the first and most important thing is to ensure that you have correctly identified the logical type of the assertion. Failure to do so will result in your criticisms missing the mark. For example, the assertion 'The earth is flat' is logically different from the assertion 'Leo believes the earth is flat'. Evidence that can refute the first cannot refute the second. Most of the common logical types of assertions and the criticisms appropriate for each were discussed in Chapter Two. Some general considerations to keep in mind when the logical type of the assertion has been correctly identified are these: Is the arguer relying on an authority? If so, is that person in a position to know? Is the arguer giving her/his own opinion? If you have reason to doubt the arguer's reliability, check the facts. If you have doubts about the claim check the facts too, even if the arguer is reliable. How do you "check the facts"? Consult an encyclopedia or other reference work if the assumption is a general knowledge claim. Or ask an expert personally. Or, if the claim is an observation, consult other witnesses to the event.

There are three sorts of situations that warrant rating assumptions lower than "√": (1) when the facts you have make the likelihood of the assumption being true less than 50% you rate it "X", (2) when the facts you collect make the likelihood of it being true less than 75% but geater than 50% rate it "?", (3) when claims you think are true but cannot verify would, if true, make the likelihood less than 50%, rate the assumption "?". An example: suppose someone asserts "Leo believes the earth is flat" and says this proves Leo is a fruitcake. If we could consult Leo in person and he says he would swear in court that the earth is not flat, we have a type (1) situation and can rate the assumption "X" (providing Leo is not known to lie). If instead all we have available is some knowledge of Leo's behavior that seems to show he acts like the rest of us, we have type (2) evidence and can rate the assumption "?" because a person who believes the earth is flat can be expected to behave differently from those who think it is a sphere. If we have only reports from reliable acquaintances of Leo that Leo has told one or two of his closest confidantes that it is all a put-on, then we have type (3) evidence. This warrants rating the assumption "?". If we know Leo had said this we would have type (1) evidence, but we have only indirect reports.

The preceding may give you a "feel" for what is needed to justify the ratings of assumptions. Rating inferences is a relatively more complex matter.

(5.42) INFERENCE EVALUATION. The correct strategy in criticising inferences in evidential arguments will depend on the context in which the argument is produced, as well as on the content of the assertions constituting the argument. In a sense, then, every inference must be approached differently.

Fortunately, however, there are two basic general strategies that can be applied to all evidential arguments. Some knowledge of the theory behind these strategies, as well as of the nature of the strategies themsleves, will make the argument patterns to be discussed in this chapter much more intelligible.

Evidential arguments are normally expressed in the form 'P, therefore C'. However, as was noted already, C cannot normally be inferred with 100% certainty from P. No matter how good P is as evidence, there is usually some chance that some factor will be at work to make C false even though P is true. Thus, the proper form for expressing most such arguments is really 'P, therefore C unless U'. The symbol 'U' here represents whatever factors prevent C from being true when P is true. Obviously a satisfactory inference exists when no very probable "U-factor" exists, and the inference is less than satisfactory when there are such factors.

It turns out that there are two types of U-factors because evidential arguments can be divided into two classes. When the truth of P can be thought of as producing (in a causal sense) the truth of C, U-factors are ones that interfere to break the causal link. Consider this argument: "Thunderclouds are coming our way, so we will have a thunderstorm." Under certain circumstances the premise (assumption) can be true and the conclusion false. For instance, perhaps the wind changes and the clouds go in another direction, or perhaps the clouds will not be "mature" enough to produce lightning when they arrive. These are U-factors that could interfere with the conclusion coming true. We can call them "I-factors".

The second kind of U-factor is associated most frequently with arguments that move from effect to cause. That is, the truth of C would produce the truth of P. Just as an effect can be produced by more than one cause, in these arguments P is often good evidence for other assertions besides C. For example, suppose I am waiting for John outside a store and notice that, having paid the cashier and received his change, he hands some back. I reason: "John gave the cashier back some change, so John thinks he was given too much change." Here the truth of the conclusion could produce the truth of the assumption, but the inference I've made goes in the other direction. In the circumstances, the assumption is good evidence for at least one other assertion. John may have decided to buy something he sees at the cashier's counter. This U-factor is an alternative to C and a plausible one, so that my argument needs to be modified if I want to be entitled to infer C from P. That is, I need another assumption, one that rules the alternative out. We call alternatives to C "A-factors." They are incompatible with C, so that both could be false but both cannot be true.

The ideal form for evidential arguments, then, is this: 'P, therefore C unless I or A.' The expression 'C unless I or A' can be written as 'either C or I or A' since I-factors and A-factors are incompatible with C.

The argument now has the form 'P, therefore either C or I or A'. To simplify, let us replace 'I or A' with 'U', so we now have 'P, therefore either C or U'. Now using the techniques of symbolic logic to be introduced in the next chapter it can be shown that this argument can be transformed into this one:

P and not-U, therefore C.

This latest form should seem correct since if C is to be true when P is true, all of the plausible U-factors must be false. Let's complicate the argument again by introducing two plausible U-factors:

P and not-U1 and not-U2, therefore C.

Now some elementary probability theory is needed. Since the inference is valid, the probability that C is true ("p(C)") is the probability that the premises are jointly true. Now if we assume the premise is true then we say:

$p(C) = p(\text{not-U1 and not-U2})$.

We now have a situation in which, if P is true, C is true to the degree of probability p(not-U1 and not-U2). This formula represents a measure of the quality of the inference.

A probability theorem allows us to write this:

$p(\text{not-U1 and not-U2}) = p(\text{not-U1}) \times p(\text{not-U2})$

Another theorem allows us to write this:

$p(\text{not-U1}) \times p(\text{not-U2}) = (1 - p(U1)) \times (1 - p(U2))$.

At this point we introduce a new symbol "R" representing the probability of U relative to the probability of C:

$R = p(U) / p(C)$

Using this new symbol we can write:

$p(C) = (1 - R1 \times p(C)) \times (1 - R2 \times p(C))$

We can rewrite the last equation as this:

$p(C) = 1 / (1 + (R1 + R2) - R1R2p(C))$

57

This complex equation can be simplified. For values of R1 = 0.5 and R2 = 0.5 the actual value of p(C) is 0.536, but if we ignore the 'R1R2p(C)' term the value of p(C) is 0.500. For R1 = 1.0 and R2 = 1.0 the actual value of p(C) is 0.382 and the approximate value is 0.333. As an approximation the latter figure is realistic because it is a bit lower and usually there are other U-factors present which, although less plausible than the best two, still tend to make the actual value of p(C) lower. Thus, we get a fairly good value for p(C) using this equation:

$$p(C) = 1 \ / \ (1 + R1 + R2)$$

The above equation gives us a probability figure for C being true when P is true and there are two U-factors present. Now, as was specified in the previous chapter, we have adopted the policy of rating inferences "√" when their numerical rating is above 0.75. When they are under 0.5 we rate them "X". Ones between 0.5 and 0.75 are rated "?". Given these limits our equation yields inference ratings for specific values of R1 and R2, the relative probabilities of U1 and U2 with respect to C.

Not all U-factors have a relative probability that is significant for inference quality. We will be interested, in evaluating inferences, only in PLAUSIBLE U-factors, those that are at least half as likely to be true as C is. By calculating p(C) values using one, two, and three U-factors with relative probabilities of 1/2, 2/3, 1, 1-1/3, and 1-1/2, some interesting and useful results are obtained. It turns out that if there are two or more plausible U-factors with relative probabilities of 1/2 or greater, the inference rating will be "X". If there is one U-factor and it has a relative probability of less than 1, the inference rating will be "?". And if there is one and its relative probability is 1 or greater, the inference rating will be 'X'. With no plausible U-factor the rating will be '√'.

These results can be better seen in a table:

SITUATION	RATING
(1) No U-factors	√
(2) One U-factor, less probable than C	?
(3) One U-factor, at least as probable as C	X
(4) Two or more U-factors	X

The above table is the basis for the inference criticism procedure followed in this chapter. The procedure is described below. To evaluate arguments you do not need to remember the above probability discussion but you do need to know this.

(a)   TRY TO IDENTIFY TWO U-FACTORS THAT ARE PLAUSIBLE (i.e., are at least half as probable as C, given the premises).   If the argument follows an effect-to-cause direction you will find that these are A-factors, alternatives to the conclusion for which the premises are evidence.   Ask yourself: "What else besides this conclusion are these premises evidence for?"

If the argument has a cause-to-effect direction, look for I-factors.   Ask yourself: "What might prevent the conclusion from coming true when the premises are true?"

It is useful to try to decide which direction the argument follows but sometimes this is difficult to do.   When it is not clear simply proceed to ask both of the questions given above.

Remember that arguments are presented in a context and this can often be relied on to yield U-factors.   Other than that, you will have to rely on your own knowledge of how the world and people work.   Remember also that only two plausible U-factors are needed to condemn an inference as "X", so if you think up more than two, use the two most plausible ones when you formulate your inference criticism.

(b)   IF YOU IDENTIFY TWO PLAUSIBLE U-FACTORS, RATE THE INFERENCE "X".

(c)   IF YOU CAN ONLY IDENTIFY ONE AND IT IS AT LEAST AS PROBABLE AS THE CONCLUSION, GIVEN THE PREMISES, RATE THE INFERENCE "X".

(d)   IF YOU CAN ONLY IDENTIFY ONE AND IT IS LESS PROBABLE THAN THE CONCLUSION, GIVEN THE PREMISES, RATE THE INFERENCE "?".

(e)   IF YOU CANNOT IDENTIFY ANY PLAUSIBLE U-FACTORS, GIVEN THE PREMISES, RATE THE INFERENCE "√".

The remainder of this chapter will be taken up with the evaluation of some common evidential argument patterns, which will involve (among other things) the application of these inference quality criteria.

Each argument pattern to be included will be presented in the same format and one or more examples will be evaluated according to the six-step procedure set out in the previous chapter. Examples for you to evaluate are also provided.   Keep in mind that although the examples evaluated are all deficient in some way, each of the patterns can have instances that are actually good arguments.   Thus, you can, by being aware of the pitfalls of each pattern, avoid then in creating arguments of your own.

(5.5)   ARGUMENTS INVOLVING CAUSAL LINKS: The six patterns

59

to be discussed are of two broad types. The first pair depends on prior knowledge of causal 'laws' to prove that a certain phenomenon has occurred or will occur, based on the occurrence of another. The last four patterns are ones commonly used to try to prove the existence of a causal link between kinds of phenomena. These patterns were articulated by the philosoher John Stuart Mill and have come to be called "Mill's Methods." These four patterns are more fundamental than the other two because they are used in proving the existence of causal laws that we rely on in using the other two patterns.

(5.51) ARGUMENTS FROM EFFECT TO CAUSE

(1) INTRODUCTION: This is a very common reasoning pattern in everyday life. We often try to prove that some unobserved phenomenon has occurred because something it often causes is known to have occurred. The pattern is found in several professional fields also, notably history, accident investigation, detective work and pathology.

(2) TYPICAL EXAMPLE. The irate houseowner has noticed a small round hole in his picture window, the sort of hole made by a pellet fired by a pellet gun. He resons: "My window has a small round hole in it, so someone has fired a pellet gun at it."

(3) BASIC LOGICAL FORM:

E has occurred.

Therefore, C has occurred.

(4) INFERENCE CRITICISM STRATEGY. Try to identify plausible alternatives to C that could have caused E. In the example we could try to show that there is a good chance the hole in the window was caused by a BB gun or flying pebble. If we wanted to be thorough this would involve getting data on the relative frequencies of window holes caused by these three sources. Window installers might have such information.

(5) ASSUMPTION EVALUATION. To decide whether or not E has occurred we try to observe it or its results personally. Otherwise we accept the arguer's testimony if he/she is reliable, or we get corroborating testimony from others.

(6) VARIANT VERSIONS. None.

(7) EVALUATION OF EXAMPLES. Example (a): "Elmer had a bad day today so he must have walked under a ladder this morning."

Step One: construct an accurate diagrammatic version of the

argument.

A = Elmer had a bad day today.

B = He must have walked under
    a ladder this morning.

Step Two: evaluate the inference. Are there any rival alternatives to walking under a ladder as the cause of Elmer's bad day? Certainly, quite a few that are more likely to have been the cause. Perhaps Elmer's performance was impaired by a hangover, perhaps he had been putting off doing some unpleasant things that he finally had to do today. Perhaps there was no single factor but just coincidence. Given that any of these factors are likely to have caused Elmer's bad day, we should rate the inference "X".

Step Three: evaluate the assumptions. Whether Elmer had a bad day today is to be judged in comparison with what is a normal day for him. Even his best day might qualify as a bad day for you. Let us suppose that what the arguer tells us about his normal day and his day today leads us to agree with the assumption, so we rate it '√'.

Step Four: determine the extent to which intermediate conclusions are proved. There are none in this argument.

Step Five: determine the extent to which the final conclusion is proved. With the assumption rated "√" and the inference rated "X" the conclusion has not been proved to any appreciable extent, so we rate the argument "X". The rated version of the argument looks like this:

Step Six: state a response to the arguer. A good response is this: "Even though your assumption is true it cannot prove that Elmer walked under a ladder this morning. Perhaps things went badly because he had a hangover, or maybe he had to do a lot of things he'd been putting off, or maybe it was just coincidence. Any of these is more likely to be the cause than that he walked under a ladder."

EXAMPLE (b): "Gasoline prices are increasing so there is an oil shortage."

Step One: construct an accurate diagrammatic version of the argument.

A = Gasoline prices are increasing.

B = There is an oil shortage.

Step Two: evaluate the inference. What rival alternatives to an oil shortage would account for increasing oil prices? Here are some: taxes on gasoline have increased, companies have raised prices to improve their profit margins, increased labor costs have led them to raise prices. Each of these is as plausible as an oil shortage and any one might be responsible for gasoline price increases. Thus, we rate the inference as "X".

Step Three: evaluate the assumption. Let us concede that our experience indicates gasoline prices are rising. We rate the assumption "√".

Step Four: determine the extent to which intermediate conclusions are proved. There are no intermediate conclusions in the argument.

Step Five: determine the extent to which the final conclusion is proved. With A rated "√" and the inference rated "X" we should rate the conclusion as not proved to any significant extent. The rated argument looks like this:

Step Six: state a response to the arguer. A good response is this: "Although gasoline prices are rising this does not go very far to prove there is an oil shortage. Prices might be

62

increasing because taxes have been increased, or the companies
have incereased their profit margin, or are trying to offset
increasing labor costs."

EXERCISE 5 - 2

Each of the following arguments makes an inference from an
effect to a cause. Complete steps one and two for each argument.
Numbers 2 and 4 are answered in the back.

1. "There is a lower conviction rate for possession of "soft"
   drugs nowadays. Therefore, there is less use of "soft" drugs
   now."

2. "The postal clerks strike frequently. Therefore, they must be
   underpaid."

3. "The fact that the glass has lipstick on it proves that a
   woman was here."

4. "In the last ten years food prices have risen more quickly
   than other prices, so supermarket chains have increased their
   profits more than most other businesses."

5. "More professional basketball players are black than white,
   therefore blacks have more natural ability for basketball than
   whites."

(5.52)   ARGUMENTS FROM CAUSE TO EFFECT:

(1)   INTRODUCTION.   This   pattern   is   less common than the
previous one, but is still frequently found.   Often an arguer will
try to prove that something is going to happen because something
else has happened.   This depends on the background claim that the
two kinds of phenomena are causally linked.

(2)   TYPICAL EXAMPLE.   "Thunder-clouds are coming, so we will
have a thunderstorm."

(3) BASIC LOGICAL FORM:
C has occurred.
Therefore, E will occur.

(4)   INFERENCE VALIDITY ANALYSIS.   Inference quality depends
on (a) the existence of a causal law that links phenomena of kind
C with phenomena of kind E, and (b) the absence of any factor that
might intervene to prevent the particular phenomenon E from
occurring after C has occurred.

With respect to the first condition, note that it does not
state that the particular phenomena C and E must be linked
causally,   only   that   phenomena   of   these   KINDS are linked.
Competent arguers can often arrange for their arguments to meet
this condition since they know a great deal about causal relations
in the subject area.

The   second   condition   is   difficult   to   meet.   Causal
interaction takes place in a context and the context involves many
conditions that must obtain if E is to follow C. I might push a
car on a level road and expect it to move, but it won't if the
handbrake is on or it is in gear.

(5)   INFERENCE CRITICISM STRATEGY.   Two strategies can be
tried.   Sometimes it is possible to show that E will not follow C
because there is no causal link between the two kinds of
phenomena.   When it is not possible to do this, try to identify
factors in the context that might intervene to prevent E from
happening.

In the example, there is a causal link between the arrival of
thunderclouds and the onset of a thunderstorm, so we would have to
try to point out factors that might prevent the storm. Perhaps
conditions in the clouds are not yet right.

One difficulty in effectively criticizing cause-to-effect
arguments is identifying them as such.   It is easy to mistake them
for effect-to-cause arguments.   The trick is to identify the
phenomenon the arguer regards as the cause.

A fundamental principle of causality is that effects never
64

precede their causes. Often, enough information is given to enable us to rely on this principle to identify the cause. For instance, when it appears a prediction is being made we can tell that the cause is the factor used to make the prediction.

When this principle is not adequate to show which pattern we have, we must fall back on our knowledge of what causes what. Common sense is the touchstone here. For instance, if someone about to go sailing says "The sky will be clear so the water will be blue," we can tell that this is a cause-to-effect pattern because we know that the reflection of the sky in the water makes it look blue, whereas water color does not affect sky color. Be careful in using this approach, however. Remember, it is the arguer's version of the argument that we wish to identify.

(6) ASSUMPTION EVALUATION. To decide whether C has occurred you can accept the arguer's word if he/she is trustworthy, or you can investigate yourself or rely on reliable witnesses.

(7) VARIANT VERSION. A variant version involves claiming that the absence of some condition, rather than the presence of one, is a ground for believing that something else will or will not occur. To criticize try to show that some factor intervenes that will result in the opposite of E occurring.

(8) EVALUATION OF EXAMPLES.

Example (a): "Women's hem-lines are going up this year, so the stock market will rise too:

Step One: construct an accurate diagrammatic version of the argument.

A = Women's hem lines are going up this year.

B = The stock market will rise this year.

Step Two: evaluate the inference. Is there any known causal link between the height of women's hem-lines and stock-market performance? Someone once discovered that there was a good correlation over a number of years between hem-line height and the Dow-Jones stock index that is used to report market performance, but no one succeeded in showing that there was any causal connection between the two. Thus, the inference fails to meet the first condition validity requires. This failure is enough to warrant rating it "X".

65

Step Three: evaluate the assumption. Assuming that the arguer is speaking about the current year we might want to check his/her sources. After all, A itself is actually a prediction. Let us suppose that the arguer has good backing for A, so we will rate it "√".

Step Four: determine the extent to which intermediate conclusions are proved. There are none.

Step Five: determine the extent to which the final conclusion has been proved. Given that A is rated "√" and the inference is rated "X" we will rate the argument quality as "X". The assumption does not provide any basis for the conclusion being claimed true. We have here a case in which the argument can be rated "X" even without checking the assumption.

The rated version of the argument looks like this:

Step Six: formulate a response to the arguer. A good response would be: "Maybe hemlines are going up but that does nothing to prove the stock market will too. There just isn't any causal connection between the two so that if the market rises it is mere coincidence."

EXAMPLE (b): Someone reading the local paper says: "They've just passed a tougher law against drinking and driving. Therefore, there will be a lot fewer drinking-related accidents."

Step One: construct an accurate diagrammatic version of the argument.

A = They've just passed a tougher law against drinking and driving.

B = There will be a lot fewer drinking-related accidents.

Step Two: evaluate the inference. There is some causal connection between laws and the conduct they are intended to

66

influence. Are there any factors that might intervene to prevent a reduction in drinking-related accidents even though laws do influence the behavior they are intended to influence? Several come to mind: failure to conscientiously enforce the law will result in no long-term effect on drinking-related accidents, or it may be that most of the drinking drivers now are habitual offenders who cannot be deterred by tougher penalties. The second factor here is probably not a plausible one, but the first one is, although it is less probable than B at this stage in the campaign against drinking and driving. We can rate the inference "?".

Step Three: evaluate the assumption. Let us suppose the reader has reported the situation correctly in A. Rate it true.

Step Four: determine the extent to which the intermediate conclusions have been proved. There are none in this argument.

Step Five: determine the extent to which the final conclusion is proved. Given the "√" rating of A and the "?" rating of the inference the argument gets a "?" rating. The rated argument is shown below.

Step Six: formulate a response to the arguer. A good response would be: "The passing of a new, tougher, law against drinking and driving is a good but not conclusive reason for claiming there will be a lot fewer drinking-related accidents. The law might not be effectively enforced because of pressure from the community".

EXERCISE 5 - 3

Each of the following arguments makes an inference from a cause to an effect. Complete steps one and two for each. Numbers 1 and 3 are answered in the back.

1. "The trends indicate that more beer and liquor will be sold this Christmas than was purchased last Christmas. Therefore, holiday drunkenness will increase again this year".

2. "Loud music is played at student parties, so there is not much discussion there".

3. "The unemployment rate has increased from September to November so we must expect an economic depression soon".

(5.53) ARGUMENTS FOR CAUSAL CONNECTIONS: The two preceding argument patterns are used to prove that some phenomenon has occurred or will occur by citing the occurrence of another. Such arguments depend on the existence of causal links between phenomena of these kinds. Furthermore, effective criticism of weak instances of these patterns must be based on knowledge of causal connections also. How do we learn about such connections? By making inferences from observations made in our surroundings and as the result of conducting experiments. The logical structure of inference patterns most commonly relied on were described and named by the logician John Stuart Mill (1806-1873) in his book A SYSTEM OF LOGIC. Mill's analysis has stood up remarkably well and in what follows we will examine four of the inference patterns that he identified as commonly used in deducing causal connections.

(5.54) THE METHOD OF AGREEMENT.

(1) INTRODUCTION: Very frequently we try to find the cause of a kind of phenomenon by looking for a common factor that was present on occasions when it occurred. This strategy can be followed when there are at least two different cases of the same effect. Apparently as human beings we have a natural preference for following this strategy, rather than some of the others that will be described.

(2) TYPICAL EXAMPLE. In the autumn of 1980 aproximately 10 people from various places in Britain become ill with pneumonia of the type known as legionnaire's disease. In tracking down the source of the outbreak the investigators found that one thing the victims had in common was that they had recently visited Benidorm, Spain, and stayed at the Rio Park Hotel. The investigators reasoned like this:

"Persons 1, 2, 3, 4, etc., who developed legionnaire's disease had stayed at the Rio Park Hotel. Therefore, something at the hotel was the cause of their illness."

(3) BASIC LOGICAL FORM:

Cases 1, 2, 3, etc., are cases of E and have C in common.

Phenomenon C preceded phenomenon E.

Therefore, C is the cause of E.

(4) INFERENCE VALIDITY ANALYSIS. Validity depends on there being only the one relevant phenomenon (C) common to all cases in which the phenomenon E has occurred. Obviously, the word 'relevant' is important here because just about any group of

68

things has several attributes in common. (Question: What do you and the sun have in common? Answers: Both occupy space, both are located in our solar system, both are greater than one cubic centimeter in volume, etc.). In general, most investigators have some conception of what common phenomena might be potential causes. In the example, investigators were looking for some link between the people that might point to the cause.

(5) INFERENCE CRITICISM STRATEGY. To criticize, try to identify other factors besides C that might be common to E and which might be causally linked to it. These factors might be related to E in such a way that they do not follow E in time.

The best criticism is to try to show that even though the assumptions are true, some other factor might have caused E. This could be done by experimenting or by studying what has been written about E.

(6) ASSUMPTION EVALUATION. Whether or not cases observed are cases of E and have phenomenon C in common is simply a matter of observation or accepting testimony. When testimony is relied on make sure those who provide it are in a position to observe accurately and that they are objective.

Determining whether C preceded E or occurred at the same time is a matter of making sure C did not begin after E. Causes cannot begin later than their effects.

(7) VARIANT VERSIONS. None.

(8) EVALUATION OF EXAMPLES. Example (a): Lush has taken to drinking in the evenings but notices he feels poorly in the morning. Thinking back, he recalls the following:

Monday night I drank scotch and soda.

Tuesday night I drank rye and soda.

Wednesday night I rank rum and soda.

Thursday night I drank tequila and soda.

From this he reaons as follows: "On Tuesday, Wednesday, Thursday, and Friday mornings I had a headache and in each case my drink the night before contained soda. Therefore, soda was the cause of my headaches." (Adapted from Copi, INTRODUCTION TO LOGIC)

Step One: construct an accurate diagrammatic version of the argument.

A = On Tuesday, Wednesday, Thursday, and Friday mornings I had a headache.

B = In each case my drink the night before contained soda.

C = Soda was the cause of my headache.

Step Two: evaluate the inference. Is there any ingredient (other than soda) that might have been common to all the drinks Lush drank? Mixed drinks contain many chemical compounds but the most obvious one besides soda (in this case) is alcohol. Thus, even though there is a correlation between headache and soda, it is more likely that alcohol caused Lush's headache, given what we know about the effects of alcohol. The inference should be rated "X".

Step Three: evaluate the assumptions. Assuming Lush's memory is not faulty, we can accept the assumptions as true.

Step Four: determine the extent to which intermediate conclusions are proved. This does not apply here.

Step Five: determine the extent to which the final conclusion is proved. Given the assumption ratings and the inference rating the conclusion has not been proved to any significant extent. The rated version looks like this:

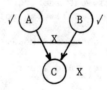

Step Six: formulate a response to the arguer. We could respond to Lush by saying: "That you had soda the night before each headache doesn't prove soda caused the headaches. They were caused by the alcohol that was in each kind of drink."

EXAMPLE (b): In many places uneducated farmers believe that a full moon causes frost in the autumn. Apparently this belief was arrived at by this reasoning process:

"Every autumn when the moon is full there is a frost. Therefore, the full moon can cause frost."

70

Step One: construct an accurate diagrammatic version of the argument.

A = Every autumn when the moon is full there is a frost.

B = The full moon can cause frost.

Step Two: evaluate the inference. Are there other common factors that might produce the frost when the moon is full? There are several possibilities. The frost results from a lower-temperature air mass that has moved into the area. Or, the earth is not being heated as much by the sun in autumn so the overnight temperature drops lower. A third possibility takes account of the observed correlation between full moon and frost: people especially notice the moon is full when the sky is clear at night. When the sky is clear the earth cools more at night than when it is cloudy. Clouds act as insulation to hold in some of the heat the earth receives during the day from the sun. Thus it is the clear sky, rather than the full moon, that is responsible for the frost on nights when the sky is clear and the moon is full. This is a common flaw in arguments of this kind. Phenomena X and Y are correlated and we conclude that one causes the other. However, it turns out that some other phenomenon, Z, causes both of them. Here, the clear sky causes the full moon to be noticeable and also causes the frost. Given the alternatives mentioned as common factors, and especially the last one, we should rate the inference as "X".

Step Three: Evaluate the assumption. The assumption can be challenged because the observations are restricted to occasions when the moon can be seen to be full. What about when the moon is full and the sky is cloudy? We can, to cast further doubt on the assumption, note that uneducated people are not very scientific about making observations. They tend to remember only examples that supported their case. Let us rate the assumption as "?".

Step Four: determine the extent to which intermediate conclusions are proved. Not applicable here.

Step Five: determine the extent to which the final conclusion is proved. Given the ratings of A and the inference from A to B, we should regard the conclusion as not proved to any great extent. The rated version is shown on the next page.

Step Six: formulate a response to the arguer. Our response to the farmers can be this: "You probably only notice that the moon is full when the sky is clear. What about when the sky is cloudy? But even if there is always a frost in the autumn when the moon is full, that doesn't prove the full moon causes the frost. A cold air mass could do it."

(9) ASSOCIATED FALLACIES. See "Post Hoc Ergo Propter Hoc" in Chapter Nine. It is the fallacy of thinking that correlation alone proves causation.

EXERCISE 5 - 4

Evaluate each of the following arguments. Each follows the method of agreement pattern. No. 1 is answered in the back.

1. The college student says: "Sometimes I get really worried before an exam. When I do I always do poorly. So worry is the cause of my poor performance."

2. A professor has found out that the players on the college football team are poor academic performers: "Research indicates that a relatively high proportion of our football players receive low grades, so football must be a distracting influence on the players."

3. The witchdoctor tells the tourists: "Whenever I dance a rain dance we have rain within a few days. So rain dances cause rain."

4. Statistics show that in 1979 the median age of first marriage for American men and women was 23.4 years and 21.6 years respectively. This prompts someone to argue: "Women typically marry men several years older than themselves. At 23.4 years a man will normally have begun a career, so an interest in financial security is behind the tendency to choose men older than themselves."

5. "Not a lot of old people are fat so getting old causes weight loss."

(5.55) THE METHOD OF DIFFERENCE:

(1) INTRODUCTION. What Mill called the "method of
difference" is the next most common method for determining causes.
It requires at least two cases with different outcomes, and
usually the cases to be investigated are compared with some cases
of the same type whose outcome is considered normal or usual.
Thus, the outcome in the case or cases of interest often represent
an unexpected outcome that we wish to have explained. This is the
situation in accident investigations: circumstances at some point
were the same as those in a normal case but then something happens
that leads to the unexpected outcome. Thus, we have a difference
in the phenomena leading up to a different outcome. The different
phenomenon preceding the effect is said to be its cause.

This method is often used in conjunction with the method of
agreement to ensure that the common factor identified as the cause
by the method of agreement is the only one that could be the
cause. Thus, in the example of the outbreak of legionnaire's
disease given in the previous section, researchers would compare
those afflicted with other people who had visited Benidorm but had
not stayed at the Rio Park Hotel. Noticing that this is the
difference between the two groups would reinforce the claim that
something in the Rio Park Hotel caused the disease. Thus the two
methods reinforce each other.

(2) TYPICAL EXAMPLE. A few years ago a Turkish airliner
crashed in Paris shortly after takeoff. By examining the wreckage
and studying flight recorder data, investigators were able to
argue as follows: "All pre-flight preparation was normal except
that a luggage compartment hatch cover was improperly secured.
Therefore, the improperly secured hatch cover caused the crash by
opening after takeoff."

(3) BASIC LOGICAL FORM:

Cases 1,2,3, etc., differed from cases a,b,c, etc., in respect C.

Cases 1,2,3, etc., differed from cases a,b,c, etc., in having
outcome E.

Phenomenon C preceded (or occurred at the same time as) E.

Therefore, C is the cause of E.

(4) INFERENCE VALIDITY ANALYSIS. Validity depends on there
being only one difference (C) between the two groups of cases,
other than the outcome E. However, no things are exactly alike in
all respects except one, so as in the last section C must be a
potential cause of E. In the example, the Turkish airliner had a
different paint scheme than other DC-10's but this difference

would be ignored as having no potential for explaining the crash. On the other hand, an improperly secured hatch cover is a potential cause because if it opens the aircraft is subjected to a sudden depressurization in the luggage compartment, creating a pressure differential in the aircraft (the cabin is still pressurized) that could bend it.

(5) INFERENCE CRITICISM STRATEGY. To criticize, try to identify factors other than C that might be the difference between the kinds of otherwise similar cases, and which are potential causes of E.

(6) ASSUMPTION EVALUATION. Checking on the assumptions is a matter of being sure the observed phenomena were observed accurately and that the observer and reporter were unbiased.

(7) Variant Versions. None.

(8) EVALUATION OF EXAMPLE. People claim that vitamin C tablets have the power to prevent colds based on this reasoning: "Each time I have noticed the onset of cold symptoms and have done nothing, I have gotten a cold. The last time I noticed symptoms I took a large daily dose of vitamin C tablets and did not get a cold. Therefore, vitamin C tablets prevented my cold."

Step One: construct an accurate diagrammatic version of the argument.

A = Each time I have noticed the onset of cold symptoms and done nothing, I have gotten a cold.

B = The last time I noticed the onset of cold symptoms I took a large daily dose of vitamin C tablets and did not get a cold.

C = Vitamin C tablets prevented my cold.

Step Two: evaluate the inference. Are there any other differences between the cases that might be potential causes for no cold resulting in the last case? One possibility is that the individual did other things, besides taking vitamin C. Perhaps the day the cold symptoms were noticed the victim stayed at home and rested because it was Saturday. This in itself could make the difference between catching cold and not catching cold. Another possibility is that on this last occasion the person was in exceptionally good health, whereas in the other cases recalled she/he was run down. Either of these factors might have prevented the cold from developing and since we do not know if either was operative or whether some other ones were, we will rate the inference "?".

Step Three: evaluate the assumption. Assumption B we will treat as true since we have no basis for doubt. Assumption A might be challenged. Most people do not keep permanent records of these matters. When trying to prove a conclusion like the one in this argument, their memories tend to be selective. They forget, or do not notice, occasions on which the symptoms appeared but did not develop into a cold. This provides an element of suspicion that warrants us rating A as "?".

Step Four. Determine the extent to which intermediate conclusions are proved. Not applicable here.

Step Five: determine the extent to which the final conclusion is proved. Given the ratings arrived at for the assumptions and the inference, we should admit that the argument provides some degree of proof but nowhere near enough. We can show the rated version as follows:

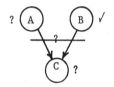

Step Six: formulate a response to the argument. We can respond to the arguer by saying: "Are you sure that EACH time you have noticed the onset of cold symptoms and done nothing, you have gotten a cold? You may have forgotten occasions when you didn't get one. Anyway, even if your assumptions are correct, they don't quite prove that the vitamin C prevented your last cold. Perhaps you were especally healthy and your system was able to fight it off on its own. Maybe you took it easy the day you were getting it. Rest is supposed to help as much as anything."

(9) ASSOCIATED FALLACIES: "Post Hoc Ergo Propter Hoc", in Chapter Nine.

EXERCISE 5 - 5

Evaluate each of the following arguments. Each relies on the method of difference. Number 1 is answered in the back.

1. Several years ago, despite significant opposition, the Canadian weather office stopped reporting temperatures in Fahrenheit and

adopted the Celcius (Centigrade) scale. About this time the weather patterns started to become unusually unstable. One militant opponent of the Celcius scale wrote a letter to a paper containing this argument: "The weather people started reporting temperatures in Celcius two years ago. Since then the weather has been very unsettled. Therefore, the change to Celcius caused the weather to become unsettled."

2. Some time ago when they realized that oil reserves were not unlimited many of the third-world petroleum exporting countries got together and increased the price of their crude oil dramatically. This forced the U.S. oil companies to raise their gasoline prices proportionately. There was a demand made on the government to try to reduce dependency on foreign oil by whatever methods could be devised. One obvious way was to reduce automobile fuel consumption. One tactic the U.S. government used was to get the individual states to lower their highway speed limits to 55 m.p.h., since this would theoretically decrease fuel consumption on the highway by 10 to 20% for most cars. After a year or so the government produced data on fuel consumption and argued that lower observed consumption was due to lower speed limits: "After the speed limit was lowered fuel consumption dropped. Therefore, lowering the speed limit caused the observed decrease in fuel consumption."

3. As a freshman in introductory psychology Elroy read the text but seldom went to class. He failed. On the second try he re-read the text, went to class, and passed. He reaoned: "Going to class was what I did differently. Therefore, what I learned in class made the difference between failing and passing".

(5.56) METHOD OF CONCOMITANT VARIATIONS:

(1)   INTRODUCTION: Using this method we infer from the fact
that one phenomenon varies at the same time another does, that
that one is the cause of the other. In scientific work
experiments can be designed so that one factor (called the
"independent variable") can be varied. Then observations are made
of the changes in other factors (the dependent variables). This
enables us to not only establish that two phenomena are causally
linked, but also what the quantitative relationship is: does E
increase or decrease?, does it increase twice the amount C
increases?, and so on.

(2) TYPICAL EXAMPLE. The French scientist-philosopher Pascal
developed the hypothesis that our atmosphere is a "sea of air."
We are on the bottom and should find that the higher we go the
less the weight of the air that presses on us. He tested the
behavior of a mercury barometer (it measures air pressure) as it
was moved to higher elevations. He found the barometer reading
decreased. He reasoned: "As the person holding the barometer
climbs higher, the barometer reading decreases. Therefore, the
change in altitude causes the barometer reading to decrease."

(3) BASIC LOGICAL FORM:

E varies when C varies.

Therefore, C is the cause of E.

(4) INFERENCE VALIDITY ANALYSIS. The inference quality
depends on the direction of causality and the absence of
coincidental variations. Both phenomena are varying at the same
time and when neither is under the cocntrol of the observer it is
possible to mistake the direction of causality. Although the
tides and the moon's position vary together, the moon causes the
tides, not the other way around. Furthermore, there must be no
possibility of variations just happening to have a similar
pattern. Someone once noticed that the Dow-Jones Index, a measure
of stock market performance, had, for a fairly long period, the
same pattern of variation as the height of women's dress hemlines!
But of course they weren't causally linked.

One source of coincidental variation was mentioned in the
discussion of the Method of Agreement. A third phenomenon may be
the cause of the variations of both the observed ones. This is
only a problem when no variable is controlled.

Even when a variable is being controlled, as in the Pascal
example, there is still the possibility that some unidentified
third factor is the cause of the observed variation. Had the
world worked differently, the change in the barometer reading

might have been due to the decrease in air temperature at higher altitudes (it drops about two degrees Celcius for each thousand feet). It could have been the case that the temperature drop caused the mercury to shrink in volume, thus accounting for the change in the length of the mercury column. Pascal knew in advance that this was not true.

(5) INFERENCE CRITICISM STRATEGY. The strategies used depend on whether or not the value of C, the supposed cause of E, is controlled. If it is, then we try to identify factors other than C which are also varying and which are potential causes of E.

If no variable is being controlled then there are two approaches to criticism. The least promising is to try to show that E might be the cause of C rather than the other way around. More often than not there is only one direction causation can take and the arguer knows this as well as you do. The other approach is to try to show that the concomitant variation is coincidental, that either two causes are at work or some third factor is causing the variations in C and E.

(6) ASSUMPTION EVALUATION. The same considerations apply as for the preceding methods.

(7) VARIANT VERSIONS. None.

(8) EVALUATION OF EXAMPLE. The harassed home owner gives us this argument as he cuts his grass for the third time this spring: "The more often I cut the grass the faster it grows. So frequent cutting must cause the grass to grow faster."

Step One: construct an accurate diagrammatic version of the argument.

A = The more often I cut the grass the faster it grows.

B = Frequent cutting of grass causes it to grow faster.

Step Two: evaluate the inference. In the argument one variable, the grass cutting, is controlled so it is clear that if there is a causal link the grass-cutting is the cause of growth and not the other way around. A critic must try to show that there is some other phenomenon varying and functioning as the cause of accelerating grass growth. There is one possible phenomenon. Since it is spring, the air is getting warmer and

78

this stimulates the grass to grow. As the temperature levels off with the coming of summer the rate of growth will level off. This actually is what happens. Since this alternative cause is more plausible than the grass cutting, one can rate the inference "X".

Step Three: evaluate the assumption. A expresses an observed concomitant variation between frequency of cutting and growth rate. Since the observer has not kept any written records on the variation pattern there is some room for doubt, but not enough to warrant a "?" rating. Let us rate A as true.

Step Four: determine the extent to which intermediate conclusions are proved. Not applicable here.

Step Five: determine the extent to which the final conclusion is proved. With A true and the inference rated "X" the conclusion is not proved to any appreciable extent. The overall argument rating is "X". The rated version of the argument looks like this:

Step Six: formulate a response to the arguer. We can respond to the arguer by saying: "It may be true that the grass growth rate and frequency of cutting are correlated, but that doesn't prove at all that the cutting causes the growing. Since it's spring, the rising temperature is probably causing the growth. Plants just generally grow faster this time of year."

(9) ASSOCIATED FALLACIES. The fallacy of "Post Hoc Ergo Hoc" is discussed in Chapter Nine.

EXERCISE 5 - 6

Evaluate each of the following arguments. Each follows the concomitant variation pattern. Number 1 is answered in the back.

1. Cigarette smokers who cannot quit are happy to find advantages in smoking. Many of them find their weight goes up when they quit and drops back when they have a "relapse" and take it up again. Some like this argument: "When I quit smoking my weight goes up. When I take it up again my weight drops. Therefore, smoking consumes calories."

2. The beginning tennis player is frustrated by inconsistency: "When I try hard the shots are not so good, but when I don't try so hard they are better. So trying gets in the way of successful shot-making."

3. Scholastic Aptitude Tests (S.A.T.'s) are widely used to determine suitability for university. There has been a decline of about 40% in the mean score over the last 15 years for those writing the Mathematics test. There is also a much larger percentage of average and below-average students writing the test. This last fact has been seized upon by defenders of the school system: "The Math S.A.T. scores have declined as a greater and greater proportion of high school students have elected to write the test. Therefore, the poorer performances of an increased proportion of average and below-average students has been responsible for the lowering of the mean score."

4. You have probably noticed that when a full moon rises from below the horizon it looks unusually big, but as it rises it appears to become smaller. Consider this argument: "Since the moon appears to become smaller as its elevation (angle above the horizon) increases, its elevation causes it to appear to become smaller."

5. Smiley Grassman, the marijuana farmer, decided to go scientific to see if he could increase his crop yield. He decided to test the effects of fertilizer, so he spread a slight amount over his acreage and noticed the crop yield was up 5%. The next spring he used twice as much fertilizer on the same acreage and the crop was up 10% above the base year (the year before he started fertilizing). He reasons: "After fertilizer was added, yield increased in proportion to the amount. So fertilizer causes cannabis to grow more."

(5.57)   THE METHOD OF RESIDUES.

(1)   INTRODUCTION.   Sometimes we find that known causes cannot account for all of an observed phenomenon. We then seek to identify the cause of the remaining portion. There are several ways of doing this, depending upon whether a controlled experiment can be set up.

(2)   TYPICAL EXAMPLE. The most famous example of the use of the method of residues for discovering and proving a causal link occurred in astronomy in the nineteenth century. In 1821 Bouvard published tables of the motions of some of the planets, including Uranus. Within a few years the position of Uranus calculated from the tables differed from its observed position. In 1845 Leverrier became interested in the discrepancy. He knew that Bouvard had based his tables on the assumption that there were seven planets in our solar system. Leverrier hypothesized that there was another planet, as yet undiscovered, beyond Uranus, and which was responsible for the deviation in the motion of Uranus. He was able to calculate where such a planet would be and asked Galle in Berlin to look in the area. Galle found an object that had not been charted before in about an hour and on the next night it had moved appreciably, thus indicating it was a planet. It was later named Neptune. Leverrier's reasoning can be crudely expressed as follows:

"The presence of the sun and the other planets cause the motion of Uranus to be such as it is. The sun and the other six known planets cause all but a small portion of Uranus' motion. Therefore, some unidentifed planet causes that small portion of Uranus' motion."

(3) BASIC LOGICAL FORM:

C is the cause of E.

C1 (one part of C) is the cause of E1, one part of E.

Therefore, C2 is the cause of E2, the rest of E.

(4)   INFERENCE VALIDITY ANALYSIS. Inference quality depends on the extent to which there can be only one phenomenon causing E2. In the example, Leverrier's inference was somewhat dubious because more than one additional planet might have caused the discrepancy in Uranus' motion. Often when we use this argument pattern we have identified all of the potential causes of E so that the pattern represents a process of elimination. If all potential causes are cited then inference quality will be good.

(5)   INFERENCE CRITICISM STRATEGY.   Try to show that some unnoticed potential cause of part of E might be the cause of E2.

(6)   ASSUMPTION EVALUATION.   The same general considerations apply as for the other methods.

(7)   VARIANT VERSIONS.   None.

(8)   EVALUATION OF EXAMPLE.   The house-plant lover has the habit of talking to her plants much like some of us talk to our pets.   The extraordinary health of the plants prompts her to reason as follows: "Environmental factors cause plant health. Natural environmental factors (soil, nutrients, sun, water, temperature) cause normal health in plants.   Therefore, the exceptional health of my plants is caused by my talking to them."

Step One: construct an accurate diagrammatic version of the argument.

A = Environmental factors cause plant
    health.

B = Natural environmental factors
    cause normal health in plants.

C = The extra health of my plants is
    caused by my talking to them.

Step Two: evaluate the inference.   Is there some unnoticed potential cause of the extra healthiness of the arguer's plants? One that comes to mind is that the woman's plants live under optimum natural environmental conditions.   Anyone who tends to treat plants as pets is very likely to be especially conscientious in looking after them.   This high level of care is more likely to be the cause of the extraordinary health of the plants than the talking.   A second potential cause could be one of the natural environmental factors.   For instance, some kinds of plants do not do well at the temperatures many people keep their houses. Perhaps this woman keeps her house cooler than most of us and the plants find this congenial.

A third potential cause of the extraordinary health of her plants may be genetics.   She may have specimens that are "the cream of the crop", so to speak, because they have inherited certain qualities.   This is not likely to be as plausible as a factor if the woman has many plants, unless of course she bought them partly-grown.   She may have a very good eye for choosing healthy ones.

Given these alternative potential causes, and the fact that they all are much more plausible than the cause argued for, it seems appropriate to rate the inference "X".

Step Three: evaluate the assumptions.   Both A and B seem

correct so they can each be rated "√".

Step Four: determine the extent to which intermediate conclusions have been proved. Not applicable in this case.

Step Five: determine the extent to which the final conclusion has been proved. With A and B rated "√", and the inference rated "X", the conclusion C has not beem proved to any appreciable extent. The diagrammatic version of the argument, with its ratings, is shown below.

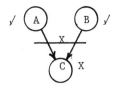

Step six: formulate a response to the arguer. A response to the arguer could be this: "Your assumptions, although true, do not go very far at all toward proving your conclusion. Several factors are more plausible causes of the extraordinary health of your plants: you simply take care of them better, or some environmental factor (other than talking) is especially favorable, or else maybe you are very good at choosing healthy plants when you go buying them."

EXERCISE 5 - 7

Evaluate each of the following arguments. Each follows the Method of Residues pattern. Number 1 is answered in the back.

1. A closely-fought election yielded a somewhat surprising victory for party X over party Y. The polls had shown that, of those intending to vote, 45% favored Y, 40% favored X and 15% were undecided. When the returns were in X had 52% of the vote and Y had 48%. The losers reasoned: "They always get the support of their faithful 40% so the support from the uncommitted segment put them ahead of us."

2. The scotch fancier notices that a bottle of his best scotch seems to be less full than he remembers it. He recalls having a drink with his wife and one with a friend, but this does not seem to account for the quantity that is missing. He reasons: "I've had two drinks, my wife had one, and my pal Lester had one. So the missing quantity was consumed by the baby sitter who was here last night."

3. A tourist finds he is able to buy a liter-sized bottle of the

83

Mexican coffee-flavoured liqueur Kaluhua for $7.00 in Mexico and finds it selling for $12.00 in his local liquor store. A little research reveals that import duties are about $2.00 on each bottle. He then reasons: "$2.00 of the $5.00 difference is due to import duty, so the remaining $3.00 must be the result of extra markup by the retailer here."

4. A European car manufacturer stored a large number of cars at an Atlantic coast storage facility and it was noted that their bright-metal parts (bumpers, trim, etc.) quickly started to tarnish with rust. A number of explanations for the unusual rapidity of the tarnishing were put forward, including this one: "Part of the accelerated rusting is due to the fact that the cars were never washed while stored. It can also be accounted for in part by the high concentration of salt in the air at the storage area, but these do not account for the high rate of tarnishing. Therefore, exposure to salt air prior to their arrival from Europe is the cause of the extra-fast corroding."

5. A college president has noted with delight an unexpected increase of 20% in admissions at the college. He surveys the freshman class and uses the survey results to argue as follows: "Half of the increase is caused by an increased desire for better job qualifications in econonmic hard times, and one-quarter is due to an increased interest in education for its own sake."

(5.6) ARGUMENTS INVOLVING RATIONALES. The following three argument patterns all involve the identification of rationales, reasons people have for their actions, motives, beliefs, attitudes, and policies. The first pattern to be examined is used to make inferences from behavior to the rationale for it. The second one is used to do the reverse, to infer future behavior from some rationale the individual might possess for doing what we predict. The third pattern is used to infer explanations of actions, motives, beliefs, aattitudes, and policies.

In contrast to Section 5.5, in which the phenomena of interest were, in principle, publicly observable, here we are dealing also with private ones. A person's reason for doing something is private and need not be revealed. Motives, beliefs, attitudes, and policies must be seen as internal phenomena that can only be identified indirctly from behavior or the person's testimony. The possibility of deception tends to make inferences of the kinds to be discussed much more chancy. At all events, the appraisal of evidence in such cases is a somewhat different matter than it was in Section 5.5.

(5.61) ARGUMENTS FROM ACTIONS TO PSYCHOLOGICAL STATES

(1) INTRODUCTION: Very frequently we try to prove that people have certain beliefs, attitudes, motives, or policies by citing their behavior as evidence. Behind this practice is the assumption that there are general psychological laws that associate particular kinds of behavior with particular kinds of psychological states. Indeed, these informal "laws" represent our understanding of human nature. Each of us acquires such an understanding based on our dealings with others, and of course from what we know of ourselves.

(2) TYPICAL EXAMPLE: Following the cessation of hostilities after the Israeli invasion of Lebanon in 1982, the Israeli Army allowed Lebanese militiamen to enter Palestinian refugee camps. The militiamen killed many civilians and there was great indignation world-wide, which ultimately was focused on the Israli Defence Minister, Mr. Sharon. Supporters of Mr. Sharon argued: "Sharon allowed the militiamen to enter the camps. Therefore, he wanted them to hunt down the Palestine Liberation Army (P.L.O.) members who were hiding there."

(3) BASIC LOGICAL FORM:

N did X.

Therefore, N believes / wants / has attitude / follows policy Y.

X = The action or set of actions done by N, including speech acts as well as more purely physical acts.

85

(4) INFERENCE VALIDITY ANALYSIS: The inference structure of this type of argument is similar to an effect-to-cause pattern. This means that a good argument will have an assumption that excludes the possibility that any factor other than the one mentioned in the conclusion is linked with the action. As we all know, just about any action can be based on a number of different psychological factors, so that it might seem that arguments of this type are never going to have very good inference quality. However, every action occurs in a setting, circumstances external to the person, as well as an internal context consisting of the person's history and current state of mind and feeling. The setting tends to restrict the factors that could be the basis for the particular action by this particular person.

The factors mentioned in the conclusions of these arguments require different sorts of evidence. Proving existence of a belief can be done by citing a pattern of behavior or a single instance of behavior, depending on the content of the belief. The existence of a want can often be proved by a single action. Attitudes, such as value positions and attitudes to persons are difficult to prove by citing a single action. The young man who wants to be sure that a young woman loves him had best observe many different things she does in his company. A single smile when they meet just isn't enough evidence. The existence of policies definitely require the existence of a pattern. We cannot prove that someone makes a practice of drinking too much at parties on the ground that we have seen them do this once.

In the example, validity requires that the desire to have the militia hunt down the P.L.O. members was the only plausible factor in Sharon's decision to allow the militia into the camps.

(5) INFERENCE CRITICISM STRATEGY: To criticize the inference in arguments of this kind we follow the strategy applied to effect-to-cause arguments. That is, we try to identify other factors that might plausibly be linked with the observed behavior, taking into account the overall setting.

In the example, only one plausible alternative comes to mind: that Sharon wanted Palestinians of any status killed, not just P.L.O. members. Some people did argue for this.

(6) ASSUMPTION EVALUATION. Whether or not N did X is checked by personal observation or by relying on testimony.

(7) VARIANT VERSIONS. No common ones.

(8) EVALUATION OF EXAMPLES. Example (a): "Lavinia is trying to get into medical school. Therefore, she wants to make a lot of money after college."

Step One: construct an accurate diagrammatic version of the argument.

A = Lavinia is trying to get into medical school.

B = She wants to make a lot of money after college.

Step Two: Evaluate the inference. What are plausible factors that might be Lavinia's reason for trying to get into medical school? Two come to mind: (1) she wants to help fight disease, (2) she wants job security. Both of these are good reasons for trying to become a physician or surgeon, which is enough to cast doubt on the inference. Without knowing more about Lavinia we are not in a position to claim that one of these alternatives is her reason for trying to get into medical school, but since these are reasons for trying to do so, we can rate the inference from A to B as "?".

Step Three: Evaluate the assumption. Let us suppose the arguer is correct, since we have no information on the matter. Rate A as "√".

Step Four: determine the extent to which intermediate conclusions are proved. There are none in this argument.

Step Five: evaluate the extent to which the final conclusion is proved. Given the inference and assumption ratings, we should place a "?" by B, indicating that B has been proved to some extent but not conclusively. The evaluated diagrammatic version looks like this:

Step Six: formulate a response to the arguer. A response to the arguer might be this: "That Lavinia is trying to get into medical school is some evidence for thinking she wants to make a lot of money after college. But she may be doing it because she wants to fight disease or to qualify for a job that gives job security."

87

EXAMPLE (b): Simon and Virgil are strangers participating in a meeting. The matter being discussed is imporant to both of them. After Virgil makes a presentation supporting the decision he thinks should be made, Simon attempts to refute each of his arguments. Virgil thinks: "Simon attacked every argument I made, so he dislikes me."

Step One: construct an accurate structural diagram of the argument.

A = Simon attacked all Virgil's arguments.
B = Simon dislikes Virgil.

Step Two: evaluate the inference. Virgil is trying to infer that Simon has a certain attitude from Simon's behavior at the meeting. Might there be some other reasons for Simon's attack? One possibility is that Simon was merely in a bad mood and would have attacked anybody's presentation. Whether this is a plausible alternative depends on what Simon is like. Does he sometimes have bad moods that make him irascible? A second possibility is that Simon simply wishes to get to the correct decision and sees that this involves assessing all the evidence supporting the various alternatives regardless of who advocates them. It is difficult for some people, and Virgil seems to be one, to separate criticism of what one says from criticism of the person who says it. This is part of what is involved in being objective when discussing issues. Given that Virgil is a stranger to Simon it would seem that either one of the alternatives is a better explanation of Simon's behavior than B, so we should rate the inference "X".

Step Three: evaluate the assuumptions. Given the background information as correct, we can rate A as true.

Step Four: determine the extent to which intermediate conclusions are proved. There are none.

Step Five: determine the extent to which the final conclusion is proved. Since A is rated "√" and the inference from A to B is rated "X" we should judge the argument to have failed to have gone very far toward proving B. Place an "X" by B.

The evaluated argument is shown below.

Step Six: formulate a response to the arguer. Virgil needs

to be told this: "That he attacked all your arguments doesn't at all prove he dislikes you. He may have just been in a bad mood or he may have been trying to make sure the right decision is made by challenging your case."

EXAMPLE (c): Mr. X is running for the legislature and has the impression that his constituents are jealous of their right to own firearms. His opponent has suggested X is "soft" on gun control so X has said frequently in his speeches that he cannot support gun-control legislation. A voter reasons as follows: "X has said a number of times that he cannot support gun-control legislation, so X opposes gun control."

Step one: construct an accurate diagrammatic version of the argument.

A = X has said a number of times that he cannot support gun-control legislation.

B = X opposes gun control.

Step Two: evaluate the inferences. In the argument the voter is trying to infer that X has a policy based on some past behavior of X. Given the behavior, could X have a different policy? Perhaps X is not against gun control but may be prepared to go against his conscience to please his constituents. (This is not necessarily hypocrisy. In a representative democracy the representative must represent the interests of the constituents, although sometimes their own real interests are different from their expressed interests.) There is also the possibility that X is lying when he says he cannot support gun-control.

Whether either of the above possibilities are as plausible as the conclusion can't be decided without knowledge of X's integrity, and information on what he had said about gun control before he decided to run for office. But they might be plausible enough (especially the first) to warrant rating the inference as "?".

Step Three: evaluate assumptions. Given the correctness of

the background let us rate A as true.

Step Four: evaluate the extent to which the intermediate conclusions are proved. Not applicable here.

Step Five: evaluate the extent to which the final conclusion is proved. With the ratings given the assumption and the inference, a rating 'of "?" is appropriate. A proves B to some extent but not conclusively.

The diagram will now look like this:

Step Six: Formulate a response to the arguer. We could respond to the arguer by saying: "That he has said a number of times that he cannot support gun-control legislation does not prove conclusively that he has a policy of opposing it. He may personally favor it, but is prepared to oppose it because we do. Then again, maybe he is lying and only saying these things to win votes."

EXERCISE 5 - 8

Evaluate each of the following arguments. They are all examples of the action-to-psychological state pattern. Number 1 is answered in the back.

1. A young woman whose car had a flat tire is helped by a man who stops. Afterwards she thinks: "He changed my tire even though he was a stranger, so he is one of those people who help people in need."

2. The professor finds that the rare joke he tells in class gets a good response: "The students laugh at my jokes so they think they're amusing."

3. Former acquaintances Ivan and Ernest meet on the street. After the usual hellos and inquiries they part. Ivan reasons: "Ernest said to stop by for a visit sometime so he wants to talk over old times."

4. Marvin gets a letter from his estranged wife's lawyer

90

announcing she wishes a divorce: "She has filed for divorce so she doesn't love me any more."

5. A man opens a door for a woman. She thinks to herself: "He opened the door for me. He must believe I like being waited on."

(5.62)   BEHAVIOR PREDICTION ARGUMENTS

(1)   INTRODUCTION.   Frequently   people   try   to   infer predictions   about   other   people's   future   behavior   based on what they   know   about the person, their background, amd circumstances. Logically   speaking   this   practice   is   inherently   risky,   since normally   each   of   us   is   free   to   act   in   different   ways   in   a given situation.   This means that we are free to falsify any prediction about   our behavior if we choose to, but in most serious matters a person   will   not   act   with   the   goal   of   falsifying   someone   else's prediction.

(2)   TYPICAL EXAMPLE.   In early March of 1983 the members of O.P.E.C,   the   oil   producer's   cartel,   found   themselves   unable   to agree   on   a   per-barrel   price   for   their   oil.   Several   commentators put   forward   this   argument: "The O.P.E.C. members can no longer agree on a minimum price for their oil.   Therefore there will be a price war among them."

(3)   BASIC LOGICAL FORM:

A

Therefore, N will do X.

(4)   INFERENCE   VALIDITY   ANALYSIS.   Claims   used   to   infer predictions   are   of two kinds, those about external phenomena and those about internal phenomena.   External phenomena are those that might   be   publicly   observed   without   the   person's   testimony   being needed.   They might be situations in which the person is involved, as   in   our   example,   or   they might be past behavior of the person. Although   premises reporting external phenomena are more likely to be   confirmed   as   true   than reports of internal phenomena, from the point   of   view   of inference quality they are more remote from the person's   conduct   than   the   latter.   This   is   because   the best possible   basis   for   prediction   of   behavior is knowledge of the reasons   the   person   has   for   ultimately   doing what we predict. These   are   private   and   our   only   access   to   them   is   through testimony.   External   phenomena   can   only   provide   clues   to   the presence   of   reasons   and   are   thus   at   one   remove   from   what   might determine behavior.

Internal   phenomena,   then,   provide   the   best   grounds   for prediction.   They   include the person's beliefs, wants, attitudes, and   policies.   A   distinction   can   be   made   between situation-specific   and   more   general   factors.   The   more situation-specific   the   factor,   the better basis it provides for prediction.   To   illustrate the distinction and its relevance let us consider an example.

Elroy   is   at   the   racetrack   and   we   know   he   is   going   to   bet   on

92

the fifth race. In the fifth there is a horse of dubious quality, named Sluggard, who is the only longshot in the race. Now consider two situations. In the first one we know Elroy is sympathetic to underdogs. In the second we know that, even though he is not generally sympathetic to underdogs, he is sympathetic to old Sluggard toward whom the bettors have shown their contempt. In the first situation Elroy has a relatively general attitude. In the second, he has a situation-specific attitude. That is, his attitude is toward a single individual and its present circumstances. Now if we wanted to argue that Elroy will bet on Sluggard we would have better grounds if we knew Elroy was sympathetic to Sluggard. Given that he was sympathetic to underdogs our inference would be a lot shakier, because without more information we cannot be sure that Elroy's general attitude of being sympathetic to underdogs extends to racehorses. Perhaps he is very hard-nosed about his betting, as many people are.

Of the four types of internal factors (beliefs, wants, attitudes, and policies), only policies are intrinsically general, although the degree of generality is variable. Policies are like rules and as such apply to kinds of situations, which means they can be applied to an indefinite number of particular situations of that kind.

In the example about O.P.E.C., the premise is a report of collective behavior that points clearly to a desire of some member countries to sell more oil. The inference quality depends on those countries choosing to lower prices as a means to sell more oil, and since other means have obviously not worked, this seems the best tactic. Thus, it seems likely that some countries will lower their oil prices, which in turn is likely to lead others to do so if they wish to maintain sales.

(5) INFERENCE CRITICISM STRATEGY. This argument pattern is comparable in structure to that of reasoning from cause to effect. We cite in the premise a factor that will, in the circumstances, lead to behavior of a certain kind. In criticizing an inference from cause to effect the strategy is to identify factors that might interfere with the effect coming into existence. The same strategy works here.

In criticizing the inference, try to identify factors that, given the one cited in the premise, might lead the person to act differently than the conclusion predicts, or not act at all.

In the example about the O.P.E.C. group we need to think of considerations that might result in there not being an oil price war, given failure to agree on a minimum price. Here are several candidates: (a) most countries may not need to sell their oil in quantity so they can hold their price, (b) economic and other pressure may be exerted on the countries ready to cut prices so that they make only small cuts. Although these may be the most important factors that might prevent a price war from occurring, experts would probably consider them both less than half as likely to occur as a price war, so the inference must be considered of good quality.

(6) ASSUMPTION EVALUATION. Special care is needed when the assumption refers to character traits. A character trait is confirmed by behavior in a variety of contexts over a period of time. One instance cannot prove a trait exists.

(7) VARIANT VERSION. Besides using this pattern to support predictions of future conduct, we also follow it when we try to prove that a person or group has done soemething in the past. Typically, this is what detectives do when they gather facts relevant to a crime. They try to identify motives of suspects, and then conclude that the perpetrator was a certain individual.

The same considerations for inference quality apply as for the predictive version but in general better quality is obtainable because the action has already occurred and purely external phenomena can often be relied on to show that the person has done it.

(8) EVALUATION OF EXAMPLES. Example (a): Supporters of generous foreign aid policies sometimes use this argument to incite support for a larger effort:

"The third world countries are envious of the prosperity we have. Therefore they may take what we don't give them."

Step One: Construct an accurate diagrammatic version of the argument.

A = Third world countries are envious of the prosperity we have.

B = They may take what we don't give them.

STEP TWO: Evaluate each inference. What factors might, given A, prevent B from coming true? Some possibilities: (a) they may lack the power to take what they need, (b) they may manage to become prosperous with the help we now provide. Of these two, (a) seems more probable than (b), and (b) plausible but less probable than B. Power of the kind needed here springs from wealth, which third world countries lack. The less prosperous a country is, the less troublesome it will be to other countries. This is a poor inference, meriting a "X" rating.

STEP THREE: Evaluate the assumption. Are third world countries envious of the prosperity we have? Given the way human nature is, those who are acquainted with our standard of living undoubtedly are envious. Strictly speaking, countries can't be envious, only individuals can. But if we interpret "countries" to mean "leading citizens in these countries," as we probably should, we can accept the assumption as true.

STEP FOUR: determine the extent to which intermediate conclusions have been proved. There are none in this argument.

STEP FIVE: Decide the extent to which the final conclusion has been proved. With the assumption A rated "√" and the inference A to B rated "X" we can say the conclusion has not been proved to any appreciable extent. The rated version of the argument looks like this:

STEP SIX: formulate a response to the arguer. Responding to the arguer we can say: "Although your assumption that third world countries are envious of the prosperity we have is no doubt correct for those who know about us, it cannot prove your conclusion. Power to take at the international level depends on wealth, and the third-world countries lack wealth."

EXAMPLE (b): An example from the fantastic world of U.S. college football. A running back with the University of Georgia, Herschel Walker, was considered the top pofessional prospect in 1982. The creation of the United States Football League led to speculation that Walker might drop out of college without completing his senior year to play in the U.S.F.L. SPORT magazine predicted in its January 1983 edition that Walker would remain in college for his senior year. They gave this argument:

"Hershel Walker wants to compete as a sprinter in the 1984 Olympics. To be eligible he must not be under contract to play any sport professionally. So he will not play pro football until after the summer of 1984."

Step One: Construct an accurate structural diagram of the

argument.

A = Walker wants to compete as a sprinter in the 1984 Olympics.

B = To be eligible for Olympic competition he must not be under contract to play any sport professionally.

C = He will not play pro football until after the summer of 1984.

STEP TWO: Evaluate the inferences. In this case there is only the one inference, from A and B to C. Is there anything that might intervene to lead Walker to sign with a pro football team in the spring of 1983, even given that he does want to compete in the Olympics? Whenever an assumption asserts the existence of a want there is always the prospect that a stronger want, or more immediate want, will override the one cited. In this case, an opportunity to sign a very large contract might tempt Walker. His desire for wealth might lead him to put aside any Olympic aspirations he might have, especially when we realise that he comes from a poor family. Given that he might get a bigger contract for the U.S.F.L.'s first season of operation than he might later, there is a distinct possibility that the SPORT prediction might fail.

Another factor in deciding inference quality is the likelihood that the want can be satisfied. If, in the mind of the person, the goal is not very likely to be attained, then a rational individual is not likely to act to pursue it. In this case, a check of the records indicates that although Walker has run a 10.23 second 100-meter sprint, he was not ranked in the U.S. top ten in January 1983. Thus, it should appear to Walker that a berth on the Olympic team is not a realistic prospect for 1984.

There are, then, two I-factors that are plausible relative to C so we should rate the inference "X".

Step Three: Evaluate the assumptions. Assumption B is true, so it gets rated "√". To judge assumption A we need to do some research into what Walker has said about his track aspirations. One place to look is in the press, of course. The most efficient way to proceed is to consult the READERS GUIDE TO PERIODICAL LITERATURE. This work indexes the articles published in about 200 North American popular magazines, including SPORT and SPORTS ILLUSTRATED. The indexing is by subject and by name, so that in this case we look to see what recent entries there are listed under "Herschel Walker".

The October 4, 1982, issue of SPORTS ILLUSTRATED contains a

story on Walker that indicates he was a track star in high school, but says nothing about his future track aspirations. The September 1982 issue of SPORT has a brief physical analysis of Walker intended to explain how he can run with a football so well, but there is no mention of track.

Another source of information is the various newspaper indexes. The best known American one is THE NEW YORK TIMES INDEX. These indexes also classify by subject and name. The New York Times Index reveals that there was an article in the January 20, 1981, edition that discussed Walker's track interest. On consulting it we find him saying that at that time he liked track better than football, but there was no mention of a desire to compete in the Olympics.

Given the above research, and especially the last item, we can regard assumption A as dubious at best, so it should be rated "?".

Step Four: determine the extent to which intermediate conclusions have been proved. There is no intermediate conclusion in the argument.

Step Five: determine the extent to which the final conclusion has been proved. Given the ratings of A, B, and the inference, it seems that the argument does not go very far to prove the conclusion. We can rate it as "X". (Of course, other evidence might come closer to proving the prediction, but this is irrelevant for this argument.)

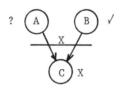

Step Six: formulate a response to the arguer. In responding to the SPORT prediction one could say this: "Your argument provides poor support for its conclusion. It is dubious that Walker really wants to compete in the 1984 Olympics, since he has not said so publicly. And even if he did want to, he may be more interested in the money to be had from signing a pro football contract. Furthermore, it is unlikely that he wants to try to qualify for the Olympics given the slim chance he has of making it. He is not even ranked in the top ten in the 100-meters, his best event." Note: in March, 1983, Walker signed a contract with a team in the U.S.F.L., thus making the SPORT prediction incorrect.

Evaluate each of the following arguments. Each has a behavior prediction pattern. No. 1 is answered in the back.

1. Alvin has talked to his philosophy prof. several times and has the impression the prof. likes him. He thinks to himself: "The prof likes me, so he will give me a few breaks on the tests."

2. "Both the U.S.S.R. and the western powers are engaged in arms build-ups. Therefore, a nuclear war is inevitable."

3. The technology is now available to enable TV watchers to express their opinions on issues presented on TV by having a modest computer terminal in each home attached to a central computer that records the responses. It can be argued that: "Governments find unofficial opinion surveys useful as guidance in policy formulation. Therefore, the developed countries will implement electronic survey systems very soon."

4. "Professor P often says he wants everyone in the class to pass the course, so he will not demand much on his exams."

5. The varsity football star finds an attractive girl in one of his classes expresses an interest in the team's performance. He thinks: "She talks to me about the team so she will go out with me."

(5.63) ARGUMENTS FOR BEHAVIORAL EXPLANATIONS.

(1) INTRODUCTION. In trying to understand our fellow human
beings we are primarily concerned with their actions, beliefs,
attitudes, wants, and policies. What we seek is explanations of
such things in terms of each other: "Why did she do that?
Because she loves him", "Why does he believe white people are
racially prejudiced? Because he has been discriminated against
unjustifiably", "Why does she love him? Because she believes he
loves her", "Why does he want to go to Hawaii? Because he wants
to see a live volcano".

Explanations are intended to help us make sense of some fact
about someone. We normally seek them when we find something
puzzling or we want to fill in a certain kind of gap in our
knowledge. The gap is a factual one, but the fact we seek is one
that allows us to see a connection between human phenomena. To
identify a person's reason for an action we link the action to the
person. Persons are seen as initiators of behavior analogous to
the way natural phenomena initiate other natural phenomena.

The term 'reason' has a broad meaning. It can refer to those
considerations that we might give weight to in deliberating on a
course of action (reasons in the strict sense). But the term is
also used to refer to what are more properly called causes. Thus,
we might say that the reason someone went off the road in their
car is that he fell asleep while driving, but falling asleep
cannot be a reason in the strict sense. Rather, it is a cause,
since the driver was not functioning as an agent of action when
the accident occurred. Beliefs, attitudes, and wants can be
explained sometimes by citing causes. We might explain why
someone believes he is worthless as a person by finding out that
he is taking a drug that has been known to cause depression. Here
the person's belief that he is worthless comes not from a rational
appraisal of himself and his accomplishments and relationships,
but is an effect of the drug. The person cannot help holding the
belief regardless of what the factors are. The situation is one
in which coming to hold the belief is something that has happened
to him, not something he has inferred from the evidence.

The argument pattern to be discussed here tries to prove that
something about someone (they did something, believe something, or
want something, or have some attitude) is explainable by arguing
that one of perhaps several good reasons is actually their reason
as shown by facts about them and their situation. Do not confuse
the strategy for finding correct explanations with a justification
for an explanation being the correct one. An arguer presumably
uses some strategy to discover an explanation, then when called
upon to defend it she/he uses the information relied on to prove
that this explanation is the correct one, or the best one. The

99

discussion to follow will present factors that make for good justifications of explanations.

Note that a distinction was made in the last paragraph between good reasons and the individual's reason. Almost any kind of action can be done for several possible reasons, but to explain a particular instance of this kind of action we must identify not a good reason, but that person's reason. None of the common or good reasons may be the actor's reason. Since only the actor can know for sure what her/his reason was, we can only hope that the best explanation (as we see it) is indeed the correct one when we do not have the actor's testimony to go on.

(2) TYPICAL EXAMPLE. When Adolf Hitler, the German Chancellor, unexpectedly signed a non-aggression treaty with Russia in 1939 many students of European politics were puzzled because they knew he was opposed to Communism. This argument tries to prove one explanation to be correct:

"Hitler wanted the Russians to not interfere in his planned invasion of Poland. Therefore, this explains why he signed a non-aggression treaty with Russia."

(3) BASIC LOGICAL FORM:

A

Therefore, A explains why B.

> A = The action, belief, attitude, policy,
> or desire that the person has that
> is supposed to be her/his reason
> for B.

> B = The action, belief, attitude, policy,
> or desire to be explained.

(4) INFERENCE VALIDITY ANALYSIS: There are two conditions that must be met to have a valid inference. First, things of kind A must be a good reason for things of kind B. The above example meets this requirement because a desire to keep others from interfering with one's plans is always a good reason to get them to promise not interfere.

The second condition is that no other possible good reason for B is the person's actual reason for it. The inference in the example is valid only if Hitler had no other good reason for signing the treaty with the Russians. This second requirement is often difficult to meet since individuals can usually have any one of several good resons for their actions, beliefs, attitudes,

100

wants, and policies. Indeed, we often have more than one reason.

(5) INFERENCE CRITICISM STRATEGY: First, we try to show
that A cannot be a good reason for B to be true of anybody. This
is not usually a promising approach, since most mature arguers
have enough knowledge of human nature to know what counts as good
reasons for something that needs to be explained.

Secondly, we can try to show that B is better explained by
some good reason other than A. In the example we could try to
show that even if it were true that Hitler did not want the
Russians to interfere with his invasion of Poland, there was some
other reason why he signed a treaty with them. Two possibilities
considered at the time were: (a) Hitler wanted to co-exist
peacefully with Russia, and (b) he wanted to buy time until he was
ready to fight the Russians. The first could not have been
Hitler's reason as he considered Russian Communism a great threat
to Europe which would have to be dealt with militarily. The
second might have been true of Hitler at that time, but
indications were that he may have felt himself ready to deal with
the Russians even then, and it was clear to those who watched
German troop movements that an invasion of Poland might be his
major immediate objective. Thus, what was known of Hitler and the
German military in the summer of 1939 favored his wanting to
forestall Russian interference with his Polish plans as the reason
for signing the treaty.

(6) ASSUMPTION EVALUATION. No special considerations apply.

(7) VARIANT VERSIONS. The most common variant on this
pattern is the attempt to explain by citing a cause rather than
some factor that the person took to be a sufficient reason. Here
the possible reasoms will include body states and/or incidents in
the person's background. To prove that being intoxicated or being
sleepy explains something is often easy to do. On the other hand,
proving that a woman dislikes sex because of casual negative
comments her mother made on the subject when she was young can be
difficult. Evidence of such comments would have to be derived
from the mother herself if the daughter cannot recall any such
comments. If the mother is unavailable or cannot recall much
about her early dealings with her daughter it would take a
psychotherapist to amass the evidence for the explanation.

In criticizing arguments that try to prove explanations of
behavior, attitudes, wants, or beliefs by citing unconscious
motives, it may often be most effective to identify conscious
reasons that might be operative. More often than not it is
conscious motives rather than unconscious ones that explain our
behavior, although the existence of the conscious motive itself
may have to be explained in terms of unconscious motives.

101

A second variant arises from the possibility of explaining an action by showing that it is an instance of a regular behavior pattern. For example, in G. B. Shaw's play "The Chocolate Cream Soldier", the soldier was insulted by another soldier and expects an apology. When the other does not apologize a third party explains by saying "he never apologizes". Putting this in argument form we can regard the third party as arguing: "He has a policy of never apologizing. Therefore, his failure to apologize here is explained by his having this policy."

The most common weakness of such arguments is the assumption claiming the existence of a policy. To prove the person has a policy the arguer needs to depict a pattern in previous behavior, or enumerate cases of behavior similar to that which is to be explained. Sometimes, however, people do things such as acting in a condescending manner on a regular basis without being aware of it. In such cases the individual does not have a policy at all. The behavior is unintentional but voluntary, and has to be explained in terms of ignorance, not policy.

(8) EVALUATION OF EXAMPLE: In almost every company there are attractive single women who will not date any of the men who work there. These women have various reasons for their no-date policy but rejection and damaged pride often leads the men to put forward this vicious argument:

"Ms. X has homosexual preferences. Therefore this explains why she will not date any guy in the firm."

Step One: Construct an accurate diagrammatic version of the argument:

A = Ms. X has homosexual preferences.

B = Ms. X won't date any guy in the firm.

Step Two: Evaluate the inference. The inference is satisfactory. If Ms. X does indeed have homosexual preferences then that would explain B better than any other reason a woman might have for refusing to date men she works with.

Step Three: Evaluate the assumption. Support for A would be behavior by Ms. X that points toward homosexuality: she associates only with women when she socializes off the job, she lives with a woman who may be a homosexual, etc. Given the

102

distinct possibility that a female these days may be heterosexual yet not seek the company of men, we have to be careful about relying on public behavior to judge that a woman is a homosexual. The only really conclusive evidence of a publicly accessible kind is a woman's declaring that she is "gay". Given the lack of evidence in this case and the realistic presumption that most persons are heterosexual, we would rate the assumption "X".

Step Four: determine the extent to which the intermediate conclusion is proved. There is none.

Step Five: determine the extent to which the final conclusion is proved. Given an unsupported assumption we can judge the conclusion to be unproved.

Step Six: formulate a response to the arguer. "A homosexual preference may not be the reason for Ms. X's not dating anyone who works here. A lot more evidence is needed to show that she has this preference. She may just not want to get involved with men she has to work with."

EXERCISE 5 - 10

Evaluate each of the following arguments. Each has a behavioral explanation pattern.

1. The football star is turned down when he asks Ethel, the cute coed, for a date. He can't understand this. No one has ever turned him down since he came to college! Then he hears that Ethel was jilted by another guy on the team. He thinks: "She doesn't like football players. This explains why she won't date me."

2. Believe it or not, someone once tried to explain inflation by starting from the maxim that money is the root of all evil. "The Devil encourages people to seek big raises. This explains why we have inflation."

3. "Young adults strive to develop value systems separate from their parents, so this explains why the young adults of the early 70's opposed the Viet Nam war."

103

4. John has gotten the impression that Ms. X., his history professor, is a strong feminist. When he receives a failing grade on his mid-term he says to his parents: "The professor has a feminist bias against men. This explains why I got a low grade."

(5.7) MORAL ARGUMENT. In any society there are rules governing private and public conduct. Rules embodied in laws passed by the government are one kind and moral rules are another. These two overlap at many points: conduct required or prohibited by law is also often prohibited by morality. One important difference between the two kinds of rules is in their origin. Legal rules are in most cases enacted by a body authorized to do so. Moral rules are customary rules, much like rules of etiquette. They tend to develop over time as a result of people coming to see the value of the conduct in question and engaging in it. Moral rules are not enacted by anyone, although sometimes particular individuals are associated with the origins of moral rules because they persuaded their community to adopt a particular pattern of conduct.

Although both moral rules and rules of etiquette are customary in origin, they are importantly different. Etiquette rules are highly conventional in the sense that a variety of kinds of conduct are equally functional but only one pattern is followed. Good etiquette in North America requires holding one's fork with the right hand, but in Britain it is held in the left. Yet people can function effectively using either method. To the observer, it seems that the important thing for those involved is uniformity of behavior, not the utility of the behavior. Uniformity is a goal in the moral sphere also, but there cannot normally be a variety of equally appropriate practices in a particular situation such that one group is required to act one way and another in a different way.

Morality is intended to promote two ideals in our interactions with each other: justice and welfare. The good society has a good measure of both of these and given that human nature is pretty much the same everywhere there is bound to be a great deal of similarity in moral codes.

Moral rules are the basis for moral judgments, judgments about the rightness and wrongness of actions. There are two sorts of rules: those requiring a certain action in certain circumstances and those prohibiting action of a particular kind. Behavior that is neither required nor prohibited is considered permissible. Thus, we are required to come to someone's aid when we will not be inconvenienced, we are prohibited from killing except in special circumstances, and it is permissible to avoid someone's company if we choose.

Several factors enter into the making of moral judgments. First, every act takes place in a set of concrete circumstances. Included in the circumstances are the physical setting in which the act occurs, the desires, values, and other attitudes of those involved, as well as their role status. All moral rules are

105

applicable to a set of circumstances. The action to be judged receives its moral significance from the circumstances in which it occurs. If the two kinds of circumstances do not "match up" in the relevant ways, a moral rule may not be applicable in the circumstances in which the act was done. Because of this, probably all moral rules admit of exceptions. Killing a fellow citizen is normally prohibited, but when it is clear that someone is attempting to kill us we are permitted to kill them in self-defence, if necessary, to save ourselves. Thus, all moral requirements and prohibitions are best expressed by adding the word 'normally': killing a human is NORMALLY prohibited, rendering aid to those in distress is NORMALLY required, etc.

Another factor influencing the making of moral judgments is the relativity of moral rules. Good moral rules promote justice and the welfare (material and non-material) of the members of a society. But as we are all aware the economic and social conditions are differemt in different societies, so a rule that promotes justice and welfare in one society may not do so in another--it may even be harmful. In your society allowing an aged relative to starve to death is morally prohibited, but not so long ago it was permissible among the Eskimos. Different economic conditions account for this. When there is enough food for all it is wrong to allow anyone to die of starvation, but when there is not it may be appropriate for some to go without rather than all perish. The Eskimos chose to sacrifice those who were no longer able to contribute to the survival of the group.

This moral relativity does not imply that what is prohibited in one place can be compulsory somewhere else, only that what is prohibited in one society may be permissible elsewhere. And what is required in one society people may be permitted to refrain from in another. In one society people may be required to share their harvest with others, but in another they are under no such obligation.

To summarize the points you need to be aware of in evaluating moral arguments: (a) moral rules are customary, not enacted, (b) moral rules are supposed to promote the welfare of members of society and justice within it, and are good or bad to the extent that they do so, (c) probably all moral rules admit of exceptions justifiable in terms of some value that is of greater importance than the value the rule promotes, and (d) a moral rule can be a good one in one society and a bad one in another because of differing social and economic conditions.

(5.71) ARGUMENTS FOR RIGHTNESS OF CONDUCT.

(1) INTRODUCTION. We often try to justify favorable moral judgments by citing a moral rule that is supposedly operative in

the society in which an act took place.

(2) TYPICAL EXAMPLE. "We are required to try to return lost property to its owner, so Elmer acted rightly when he turned in the money he found to the police."

(3) BASIC LOGICAL FORM:

X is morally required (or prohibited) in society S.

P did (or refrained from) X in S.

Therefore, P acted rightly.

(4) INFERENCE VALIDITY ANALYSIS. Validity depends on two conditions being met. First, there must be no extenuating circumstances that render the moral rule non-applicable to P's action. Secondly, even though the circumstances of P's action were such that the moral rule applies, the rule may be a bad rule. That is, the rule may be prejudical to the promotion of justice and/or the welfare of the society.

In the example we do not hear of any extenuating circumstances, such as that Elmer would incur great expense or risk in trying to return the money. And the rule itself does seem to be a good one for any society having the institution of private property.

(5) INFERENCE CRITICISM STRATEGY. One way to criticize the inference is to try to show that some extenuating circumstance surrounding P's action prevents the assumptions from proving the conclusion. If there is such an extenuating circumstance that makes the rule non-applicable, you must cite the higher value that justifies the action as an exception.

The other way to criticize the inference is to show that the moral rule is a bad one, that acting in conformity with it does more harm than good, or leads to injustice.

(6) ASSUMPTION EVALUATION. Establishing whether or not X is morally required (or prohibited) in society S is a matter of relying on one's own intuitions if one is a member of S. Sometimes the answer we can provide is clear-cut, sometimes it is not. X need not actually be a moral rule we ourselves follow but our contacts with others will have shown whether X is a rule operative for most members of our society.

When we ourselves are not part of S we can rely on the testimony of those who are part of it, or we can look for clues in their interactions with each other. If X is morally required, failures to do X will incite blame. If people are required to respect other people's desire for quiet, those who play stereos loudly will be criticised by others, and not just those they offend with their music. Similarly, if X is prohibited, doing X will incite blame and criticism.

It is important to remember that we want to establish whether X is operative in S, not whether it is a moral rule of ours.

The issue of whether or not P did (or refrained from) X in S is decidable by the usual criteria for publicly observable phenomena.

(7) VARIANT VERSION. The strategies apply to arguments intended to prove that a person acted wrongly when such arguments have this logical form:

X is morally required (or prohibited) in society S.

P failed to do (or did) X in S.

Therefore, P acted wrongly.

As in the positive version, inference validity depends on the moral rule being defensible and this is a matter of how it promotes justice and welfare in society. If the rule is not defensible then the behavior cannot be proved wrong on other grounds, of course.

In assumption evaluation the weakness is likely to lie in the assumption embodying the moral rule. Whether the rule is indeed operative is to be decided by the attitudes of people to those who commit the act. These attitudes are displayed by their disposition to blame or not blame them, and in their expressed views about acts of this kind.

(8) EVALUATION OF EXAMPLES. Example (a): "In our part of the country white barbershop owners do not cut a black man's hair, so Sam acted rightly when he refused to cut that black tourist's hair."

Step One: construct an accurate diagrammatic version of the argument.

> A = In our part of the country
>   white barbershop owners are
>   morally prohibited from
>   cutting a black man's hair.

B = Sam refused to cut the
    black tourist's hair.

C = Sam acted rightly.

Step Two: evaluate the inference. The inference from A and B to C is invalid because A embodies a bad moral rule. Discrimination in the provision of services on grounds of color is unjust. Thus, we rate the inference "X".

Step Three: evaluate the assumptions. We can suppose both A and B are true since we have no reason to suppose otherwise.

Step Four: determine the extent to which intermediate conclusions are proved. There are none here.

Step Five: determine the extent to which the final conclusion is proved. With the assumptions rated as true and the inference invalid, the conclusion is unproved. The rated argument looks like this:

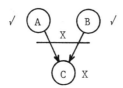

Step Six: formulate a reply to the arguer. A good reply is this: "The fact that barbers do not cut a black man's hair in your part of the country does not prove Sam did the right thing. It is unjust to discriminate on racial grounds in the provision of services to the community, so your rule is a bad one."

EXAMPLE (b): This is an example of a situation many German army officers found themselves in during World War Two when they became military commanders of occupied towns. (Names have been changed.)

"Soldiers are morally required to obey the directions of their superiors, so when Captain Strasser put the Jews of Bellefleur on the train to the concentration camp, as he was ordered, he acted rightly."

Step One: construct an accurate diagrammatic version of the argument.

109

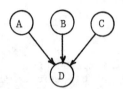

A = Soldiers are morally required to obey the directives of their superiors.

B = Captain Strasser was ordered to put the Jewish people of Bellefleur on the train to the concentration camp.

C = Captain Strasser did as he was ordered.

D = He acted rightly.

Step Two: evaluate the inference. Are there any extenuating circumstances in this case that would make the moral rule (expressed in A) non-applicable? None come to mind. The directive had to do with a military task, the relocation of conquered people. It could be said that the weeding-out of the Jewish people was a political, not a military goal, but the military is an instrument of the government and thus an instrument for political goals.

Is the moral rule being invoked a defensible one? Those who have studied the matter make a distinction between legal and moral obligation and insist that a soldier's obligations are legal ones, ones created by governments. It is generally recognized that moral obligations override legal ones, so that when an order would require a soldier to act immorally, the soldier has an obligation to refuse to carry out the order. If we accept these points we must say that the moral rule cited in A cannot be defended even if it was operative in the German Army at the time. Thus the inference should be rated "X".

Step Three: evaluate the assumptions. We may suppose that B and C are true, but is A true? This would require historical research to decide. In general, the existence of a moral rule is confirmed by seeing the community's reactions to acts that it would have a bearing on if it exists. In particular, if people blame, censure, and perhaps even punish conduct then we can say that it is morally prohibited (or, if ommissions receive this treatment, then the committed behavior is morally required). Also, the use of the words 'right' and 'wrong' in judging conduct is a sign that conduct has moral significance and thus is governed by moral rules. In the example at hand we would need to examine cases in which soldiers had refused to obey orders to see whether the society thought that not obeying orders provoked moral condemnation. We may wish to concede that A is true for the German army in World War Two, and thus avoid the need for research. (The argument already is defective because of the inference.)

Step Four: determine the extent to which intermediate

conclusions are proved. There are none.

Step Five: determine the extent to which the final conclusion is proved. With the ratings we have assigned, the argument fails to prove its conclusion to any appreciable extent. The rated version looks like this:

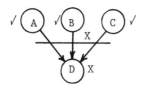

Step Six: formulate a response to the arguer. A good response would be: "Even if the assumptions are true they cannot prove that Captain Strasser acted rightly. The claim that soldiers are morally required to obey their superiors may have been a moral rule in the German army in World War Two but it was a bad rule. Such a rule can lead people to do things that harm others and treat them unjustly, as in this case, and unnecessary harm can never be morally justified. Acting in accordance with a bad moral rule cannot lead to a right action."

EXAMPLE (C). An opponent of abortion speaks on behalf of an American physician who refused to perform an abortion on a young rape victim : "Abortion is morally prohibited in this country so Dr. Roe did the right thing when he refused to perform an abortion on Miss Doe."

Step One: construct an accurate diagrammatic version of the argument. The first assumption, that abortion is morally prohibited in this country, is somewhat vague. Does the speaker mean abortion is normally prohibited, thus allowing exceptions, or is the prohibition extended to all circumstances? Given the conclusion we should probably assume the latter interpretation is intended. On the former interpretation the inference is fairly weak.

A = Abortion is morally prohibited in this country in all circumstances.

B = Dr. Roe refused to perform an abortion on Miss Doe.

C = Dr. Roe acted rightly.

Step Two: evaluate the inference. Is the moral rule expressed in A a defensible one in the U.S.? By being absolute it

111

may lead to unnecssary harm to members of the community (i.e., women who may die from pregnancy, or become psychologically ill). It may also promote injustice, as in this case, by forcing women to give birth against their wishes. We have here a situation in which women's rights and fetus rights are in opposition but in the case of involuntary pregnancy (not the same as "pregnancy by accident") the woman's rights must override the fetus's right not to be destroyed. Certainly this is true in the very early stages of pregnancy when the fetus is not yet a human being. Accepting these points we ought to rate the inference as "X".

Step Three: evaluate the assumptions. With no reason to doubt B, we will accept it as true. Assumption A, however, is probably not acceptable as a moral rule to most Americans. They would not think that a physician performing an abortion, in the circumstances described, ought to be blamed or censured. Thus, we are probably entitled to rate A as "X", although reference to surveys would be desirable to support an intuitive judgment about peoples' views on abortion.

Step Four: determine the extent to which intermediate conclusions are proved. There are none.

Step Five: determine the extent to which the final conclusion is proved. Given the ratings, we should say that the argument does not prove the conclusion to any appreciable extent. The rated version looks like this:

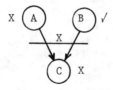

Step Six: formulate a response to the arguer. A fairly good response to the arguer is this: "Abortion is not morally prohibited in this country in all circumstances, as you would find by conducting a survey. But even if it were it couldn't be used to prove that Dr. Roe acted rightly because a rule that leads to the violation of women's rights in this way is a bad one. A much more defensible rule is that abortion is normally morally prohibited."

EXERCISE 5 - 11

Evaluate each of the following arguments. Each is an argument about moral conduct.

1. "Capital punishment is morally prohibited in our society. The

112

Governor granted a stay of execution for Renfield, the hired killer, so the Governor did the right thing."

2. "Reporting cheating by fellow students is morally required. Prudence told the professor that Clyde cheated on the logic test. Therefore, Prudence did the right thing."

3. "In 19th century America physical punishment of even young children for breaches of discipline was morally required. Teachers frequently strapped pupils for coming a few minutes late. Therefore, these teachers acted rightly."

4. "Pre-marital sex is morally prohibited in our society. Joe and Suzy have engaged in sexual activity, so they acted wrongly."

(5.72) ARGUMENTS FOR MORAL RESPONSIBILITY.

(1) INTRODUCTION. When we have acted in a way that is morally wrong we are blameworthy. That is, people are justified in morally censuring us and in punishing us when it seems appropriate. The same holds true when we omit doing something we had an obligation to do.

In blaming us for the consequences of our actions (or failure to act) people are judging us to be morally responsible. (We might also be legally responsible, but these two kinds of responsibility do not always go together.) Our response to such judgments can be one of several kinds. (In what follows I am relying on a paper by Laurence Heintz published in the AMERICAN PHILOSOPHICAL QUARTERLY, volume 18, number 3, entitled "The Logic of Defenses".)

One response to the assignment of blame is to capitulate and admit one's guilt, and ask forgiveness for the harm done.

A second response is to take the offensive and cite a defeasibility factor, of which there are three kinds: (a) Defeating conditions, which are evidence for there never having been an obligation in the first place. For example, I could avoid blame for breaking a promise by showing that no promise was made. (b) Voiding conditions, which are evidence that the obligation once existed but has been terminated for some reason. I could avoid blame for failure to keep a promise to marry someone by showing that the person no longer wants me to marry her. (C) Suspending conditions, which are evidence for the temporary impossibility of fulfilling the obligation. For instance, I could argue that I am not to blame for failing to take an active part in raising my children because I have been wrongly convicted of a crime and sent to prison. When released I would again shoulder this particular responsibility.

A third response is to offer a defence. Rather than try to show that there is not at this time any obligation on my part by citing a defeasibility factor, I admit that the obligation exists but cite some factor that reduces my responsibilitiy for the bad consequence of my action. There are two kinds of factors that can reduce responsibility.

One kind of factor represents a justification. A justification is given by citing reasons why not fulfilling the responsibility was morally right. For example, I have been given a pistol for safekeeping by a friend and when he comes for it I refuse to hand it over because he says he intends to shoot his wife with it. I can show that not fulfilling my obligation is morally right by appealing to a higher-ranking obligation, the

114

obligation to preserve life. This does not mean that I had no obligataion to hand over the pistol. I did, but the higher-ranking one overrides it. When satisfactory justifications are given for not fulfilling an obligation, the persons claiming we are responsible must withdraw their charge. No responsibility is incurred.

The second kind of factor that can serve as a defense is to offer an excuse. In this case it is agreed that there is an obligation and that I am correctly held responsible for any harm arising, but that some factor in the circumstances reduces my responsibility. Responsibility-reducing excuses come in many forms. As Heintz put it: "Excuses may take the form of claims of physical or psychological inability, ignorance, accident, misunderstanding, duress, diminished capacity, deceit, misimpression, illness, inconvenience, present danger, pain, etc. Included in the excuses that could be offered would be the claim, "I thought I had reason to believe that there was a defeating (voiding, suspending) condition present, but I was mistaken" (p. 343). Human beings are remarkably good at producing the best excuse in defense of their behavior. We seem to know intutiively that any of these sorts of factors can be a good excuse in the right circumstances. When we fail to do what we ought to do we almost always know why.

In what follows each of the kinds of offensive and defensive responses will be mentioned in the context of argument evaluation. They are all pertinent to the criticism of arguments trying to prove responsibility for harm arising from failure to fulfill an obligation. Here is a brief summary of the responses described:

(a) Admit guilt.

(b) Cite a defeasibility factor (no obligation in effect):
    (i)   Defeating condition: no obligation ever existed,
    (ii)   Voiding condition: the obligation no longer exists,
    (iii) Suspending condition: the obligation is temporarily not in force,

(c) Offer a responsibility-reducing defence:
    (i)   Justification: meeting obligation would be wrong,
    (ii)   Excuse: legitimate reason for diminished responsibility

(2) TYPICAL EXAMPLE. On the night of June 17, 1972, five men attempted to break into the offices of the Democratic National Committee in the Watergate Hotel in Washington, D.C. Their purpose was to "bug" the office so that the Republicans, including President Nixon, could obtain information during the forthcoming Democratic convention that would give them some sort of edge in the November election. The burglars were arrested and subsequent

115

investigation revealed that members of the White House staff were implicated.

Before it was clear that Nixon himself had approved this operation and other unsavory ones, this argument was used against him: "Nixon had an obligation to ensure that his staff did nothing to subvert the democratic process. He failed to fulfill his obligation, so he has full moral responsibility for the harm resulting from this failure."

(3) BASIC LOGIC FORM:
            P has obligation O.
            P failed to fulfill O.
    Therefore, P is morally responsible for the consequences
            of this failure.

(4) INFERENCE VALIDITY ANALYSIS. Validity depends on there being no factors that can represent an adequate justification for P's failure, and no excuses that warrant a reduced responsibility. Almost always there are some such factors potentially operative, but very often they are not actually operative. Thus the assumptions can seldom guarantee the truth of the conclusion. Circumstances play a large part in determining what potential and actual intervening factors there are.

In the example, given the obligation and the failure to fulfill it, is there some chance that Nixon was not fully responsible? Is there some overriding moral obligation that made it right not to fulfill the obligation mentioned in the argument? Some people, perhaps including Nixon himself, felt that the President's obligation to maintain and promote national security was an overriding factor but this justification is not plausible given the international situation. Not every means towards a morally worthy goal is itself morally acceptable. There do not seem to be any other palusible factors that might have made Nixon's failure to prevent the Watergate operation the right thing to do. Now what about excuses that would reduce Nixon's responsibility? From the list enumerated earlier, perhaps ignorance is the best excuse he could appeal to. He could, and did, argue that he did not know about the Watergate operation. If this were true it would not follow from the assumptions that he should bear the full responsibility he would bear if he did know about the operation.

Thus, inference validity depends on there being no intervening justifications or excuses that could result in the removal of all or some responsibility.

(5) INFERENCE CRITICISM STRATEGY. To criticize the inference try to show that not fulfilling the obligation was the right thing to do by citing some more important obligation that

116

overrode it. If this cannot be done try to identify am excuse that would reduce the amount of responsibility. Most frequently the second approach is best simply because we are not often in a position where one obligation is overridden by another. Usually we simply fail to meet our obligations through lack of resolve.

(6) ASSUMPTION EVALUATION. The assumption that can be troublesome to evaluate in arguments of this kind is the claim that P has obligation O. To refute such claims you need to cite one of the three kinds of defeasibility factors described in the introduction.

Obligations, as we shall see, come from two different sources. They can be imposed on us when we come to occupy a particular role. These obligations are normally long-term and require action on more than one occasion. For example, our obligation to support children must be discharged by continually doing things such as providing food, clothing, and shelter over many years.

Obligations can also be created by freely making promises. These may be such that they require continual action or they may be fulfilled by a single action. For example, if I promise to do the dishes tonight this obligation is fulfilled when I have done the dishes.

Criticism is a matter of deciding whether any one of the three defeasibility conditions apply. First, was there some defeating condition present that prevented the obligation from coming into existence in the first place? If the supposed obligation arose from occupying a role, did the individual (P) adopt the role voluntarily? Some roles are inherited (being a daughter or a sister, for example) so that voluntariness is not a factor. Others are not, but are not voluntarily assumed either. Morally speaking, someone forced to marry does not have any of the obligations that normally go with the role of spouse. If the purported obligation arose from a promise, was there something in the circumstances that prevented the promise from actually being created? Were the promise-making words said under duress, or when the person was not mentally competent (drunk, or insane, for example), or did the promisee mislead the promiser somehow?

Secondly, has a voiding condition arose that has terminated the obligation? A parent has an obligation to provide material support for his/her children, but by the time the child reaches 21 (if not sooner) this obligation is terminated. If I have promised to marry a woman and she no longer wishes me to, then my obligation is terminated.

Thirdly, is there a suspending condition currently in force,

117

so that P does not now have obligation O, although it may come back into effect later? It may be false that Romeo has at this time an obligation to take Juliet dancing on Friday nights because he broke his leg skiing.

(7) VARIANT VERSIONS. None

(8) EVALUATION OF EXAMPLES. A young woman intentionally became pregant and after several visits to her physician it was discovered that she had a serious heart defect that would make it extremely dangerous for her to give birth, either by caesarian section or the normal way. Her physician urged her to have an abortion and she agreed. A militant anti-abortionist argues: "Mrs. X had an obligation to carry the fetus the full term. She failed to fulfill her obligation, so she is morally responsible for the death of her fetus."

Step One: construct an accurate diagrammatic version of the argument.

A = Mrs. X had an obligation to carry her fetus to full term.

B = She failed to fulfill her obligation.

C = She is morally responsible for the death of her fetus.

Step Two: evaluate the inference. It is clear that Mrs. X is causally responsible for the death of the fetus, since without her agreeing to have an abortion it would not have died. But does she have an excuse or an overriding obligation that would reduce her moral responsibility even though this is true? It would seem that she certainly has a good excuse. The development and birth of the fetus would probably have killed her. Thus, she acted in self-defence, and self-defence is a completely exonerating ground for harming others. We might also argue that she had a duty to preserve her life because of her commitments to her husband.

All in all, the conclusion does not follow from the premises so that we can rate the inference "X".

Step Three: evaluate the assumptions. Here the defeasibility considerations are relevant. Assertion A is a general moral principle applied to Mrs. X. Prior to the diagnosis of her heart condition it would be correct to say that she did undertake the obligation because she voluntarily became pregnant, presumably with knowledge of the normal consequences that would follow. Thus, there is no defeating condition which would allow us to say that she never undertook the obligation. Is there some other

118

defeasibility factor operative? Clearly, it could not be a suspending condition, but there may be a voiding condition. Although she undertook the obligation, we can argue that it had been terminated because she found out that her life would be in danger if she tried to fulfill the obligation. We rate A "X".

Assumption B must be rated "√". She did indeed fail to fulfill her obligation, but of course she had a good reason.

Step Four: determine the extent to which intermediate conclusions are proved. There are none.

Step Five: determine the extent to which the final conclusion has been proved. Given the inference and assumption ratings we can say that the final conclusion, C, has not been proved to any significant extent. The rated version looks like this:

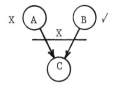

Step Six: formulate a response to the arguer. A good response is this: "Yes, Mrs. X did fail to fulfill her obligation, but she had an excellent excuse. She was entitled to have an abortion in self-defence. Furthermore, she may have had obligations to others, including her husband, that were more important than her obligation to the fetus. Mrs. X cannot be held morally accountable for the death of the fetus."

EXERCISE 5 - 12

Evaluate each of the following arguments for moral responsibility. Number 1 has been answered in the back.

1. In what became known as "the Tarasoff case," a young male student at the University of California apparently confided his intention to kill Tatiana Tarasoff, his former girlfriend, to a U. Cal. psychologist. Neither the psychologist nor anyone else warned the girl in advance and her parents sued the University for failure to take any steps to protect their daughter. The issue in court was whether professional confidentiality was an adequate basis for not disclosing the murderer's stated intention to anyone. This was one argument

brought forward: "The psychologist has an obligation to use reasonable care to protect intended victims from harm at the hands of his client. He failed to warn Tatiana Tarasoff of the danger she was in. Therefore, he is morally responsible for her death."

2. Suzy convinced her parents to give her enough money to get through a year of college, but she hung around with the party crowd. Her father says: "Suzy had an obligation to make a serious attempt to pass courses. She did not make a serious attempt. Therefore, Suzy is morally responsible for returning our money."

3. "People have an obligation to prevent children from suffering, but Mr. and Mrs. X knowingly allowed a child to come into the world who has an incurable medical condition that is continuously painful. Therefore Mr. and Mrs. X are morally responsible for their child's suffering."

4. In California a couple bought their son a high-powered car knowing that he had often in the past engaged in reckless, and possibly dangerous, driving. However, he had promised to reform and they decided to trust him. The son, while speeding, was in an accident that killed a passenger in the car he hit. They were sued by the deceased person's family , which contended that, by giving the man the car, they contributed to the death. One argument used went like this: "Mr. and Mrs. X had an obligation to protect the public from their son's recklessness. They failed to fulfill that obligation. Therefore, they are morally responsible for the emotional suffering caused by our daughter's death."

5. Elmer missed class on Wednesday but he knew Harmon went so he asked him what happened. Harmon said that the Prof. announced a test for the following Wednesday. They both took an "unofficial long weekend" and skipped the next class, on Friday. On Monday morning they find they have to do the test, and both do badly. Elmer says to Harmon: "You had an obligation to give me the correct information or say you did not know. You failed to give me the correct information, so you are responsible for me receiving a poor grade on the test."

(5.73) ARGUMENTS FOR MORAL OBLIGATIONS

(1) INTRODUCTION. One common form of argument for proving that some individual or group has a moral obligation to do something proceeds from the premise that a general obligation exists for people (groups) in the role to do that specific thing. This is one of the simplest forms of moral argument. A somewhat more complex form will be studied in this section. It is more complex because the action description in the conclusion is different from the one in the premise. The action described in the conclusion is intended, however, to be a means of fulfilling the obligation referred to in the premise.

Obligations are acquired in two ways. They can be acquired by adopting a role, either natural or social. A natural role would be that of parent or child, or even human being. Natural roles are so-called here because only physical facts need be used to prove someone occupies such roles. It is, for example, the physical fact of having sired a child that makes a man a father. Social roles, on the other hand, come into being by virtue of social arrangements. Examples include being a wife, a bank teller, a Senator, a college student, and so on.

Every role has some obligations associated with it. They are imposed on us when we accept or assume the role. Sometimes we voluntarily take on roles, but sometimes they are imposed upon us (being a child, for example). Not all of the obligations associated with a role are moral obligations, except perhaps in the case of being a human being. Most obligations are professional or legal. As a citizen we have a legal obligation to avoid parking in a "no parking" zone. As a college student we have a professional obligation to make an effort to benefit from the professor's instruction. All of us occupy many roles and occasionally obligations associated with diffeent roles conflict. Moral obligations override legal and professional ones, of course.

The second way in which obligations can be acquired is by voluntary commitment, i.e., making promises. Wedding vows, contracts, and professional oaths are examples of promise-making. Arguments based on promises will be discussed below as a variant of the basic pattern.

(2) TYPICAL EXAMPLE: "Parents have a moral obligation to ensure that their children are educated. Therefore, the Smiths have a moral obligation to send their children to school."

(3) BASIC LOGICAL FORM:
People in role R have a moral obligation O.
Therefore, person P has a moral obligation to do Y.

121

NOTE: Y is intended to be a means to fulfilling O.

(4)   INFERENCE VALIDITY ANALYSIS.   Inference validity depends on the following conditions being met:

(a)   Y is an effective means of fulfilling obligation O.   The example meets this requirement because attending school is an effective means of acquiring an education.

(b)   Person P occupies role R. In the example the Smiths must actually be parents.

(c)   There are no over-riding obligations. If the Smiths were sure their children would be in real danger by going to school they would not have to meet their obligation by this means.

(d)   There are no defeasibility conditions that relieve P of her/his obligation to do Y.   There are three such conditions: (1) Defeating conditions, ones that prevent the obligation from coming into existence.   This would be a matter of the individual having the role R imposed on them in a morally non-legitimate way, such as by force.   If the Smiths were forced by the government to produce children they could argue that they do not have the obligations that go with being parents, that the government is responsible.   (ii)   Voiding conditions, ones that terminate the obligation after it has been accepted.   If the Smiths are living in dire poverty and have arranged for their children to be adopted they would no longer have an obligation to send them to school. The adopting persons would.   (iii) Suspending conditions, ones that temporarily remove the obligation.   If the Smiths are prosperous and have hired a professional tutor they would have no obligation to send the children to school while they were being tutored.

(e)   There are no adequately effective alternatives to fulfilling O by doing Y. The Smiths have a moral obligation to send their children to school only if they cannot ensure their education in some other way, such as by teaching them at home.

(5)   INFERENCE CRITICISM STRATEGY.   Since inference validity depends on the conditions mentioned above, criticism amounts to showing that one or more of these conditions are not met. When dealing with arguers who are reasonably competent in generating moral arguments the most common inference weakness is failure to meet condition (e).   There are normally several means of fulfilling an obligation so that a criticism takes the form of showing that obligation O could be fulfilled by doing something other than Y.   Whether an alternative to Y is an adequately effective one depends on how it relates to O and what the

situation is. In the example, one alternative to educating by sending to school is to educate at home. But if the Smiths do not have enough education themselves, or are too busy, or do not have the money to hire a tutor for their children, then educating them at home will not be an effective means of ensuring that they are educated.

(6) ASSUMPTION EVALUATION. Whether a role involves a particular obligation is in the first instance a matter of community judgment. But it can be argued effectively sometimes that the community is wrong in thinking that an obligation is attached to a role. For example, in Mexico it seems that young men, apparently with the society's approval, believe they have an obligation to father as many children as possible. But since this practice is harming the society in the ways that population explosions cause harm, it cannot be a moral obligation. On the other hand, in societies where there is a shortage of people for the tasks that must be done, being a man might involve fulfilling such an obligation.

(7) VARIANT VERSION. As noted in the introduction, obligations are acquired by adopting roles, but also by promise-making. Arguments that cite promises as a means of proving the existence of obligations have this basic logical form:

Person P promised to do Y.

Therefore, person P has a moral obligation to do Y.

"Y" can stand for either a one-time action or a continuing effort. Sam might promise to take Sue to the prom--a one-time commitment--or he might promise to take her out every Saturday night.

Inferences in arguments of this form can be shown to be defective by citing some voiding or suspending condition. Perhaps the person to whom the promise was made no longer wishes it to be kept, which voids it. Perhaps Sam promised to take Sue to the prom but does not now have a moral obligation to do so because she has dropped him for another boy. Or perhaps Sam has had a motorcycle accident and is in hospital in a coma. Since he cannot keep his promise for a reason beyond his control, he no longer has an obligation to take Sue to the prom. Suspending conditions are of a similar kind although they are primarily connected with continuing obligations. Sam may have promised to visit his mother every Sunday but if he is temporarily hospitalized his obligation is not in force.

In evaluating the assumption in arguments of this kind we try to identify a defeating condition, one that prevents the promise-making action from becoming a promise. Sam may have said to Sue that he promises to take her to the prom, but if she does not want to go with him then no promise is made. A promise is like a contract. Both parties must agree to what one party intends to do. For the same reason, no promise is created if the promisee does not hear the words being uttered, since in this situation the promisee has not had an opportunity to agree.

Again, no promise is made when the words are said under duress. A forced promise is not made voluntarily so it does not count. Of course compulsion is a matter of degee, so that sometimes it is difficult to tell whether there was enough of it to defeat the promise.

(8) EVALUATION OF EXAMPLES. Example (a): During the last few years legal battles have been waged in several western countries over whether reporters who have published stories disliked by governments and civil servants must reveal the identities of their informants, the people inside or close to government who have "blown the whistle" on what they have regarded as illegal and immoral practices. Some reporters have been convicted of contempt of court for not revealing sources when asked under oath. Arguments such as the following are used to try to justify such judgments: "Those testifying in court have an obligation to answer truthfully all questions whose answers do not incriminate them. Therefore, reporters have an obligation to reveal the identity of their informants when asked to do so on the witness stand."

Step One: construct an accurate diagrammatic version of the argument.

A = Those testifying in court have an obligation to answer truthfully all questions whose answers do not incriminate them.

B = Reporters have an obligation to reveal the identity of their informants when asked to do so on the witness stand.

Step Two: evaluate the inference. Let us apply to this argument the five conditions for validity noted earlier.

(a) Is revealing the identity of their informants a means of fulfilling an obligation to answer all questions truthfully? Clearly it is, since it is a kind of testimony that does not incriminate the reporters themselves.

(b) Are reporters occupying the role of "those testifying in

124

court"? Clearly. yes.

(c) Are there any obligations that would make it right not
to reveal the identity of their informants? There may be. We
will return to this point.

(d) Are there any defeasibility conditions that would mean
they did not have the obligation mentioned in the conclusion?
Since we are concerned with cases in general and no particular
case, there will not be any such conditions.

(e) Are there any effective alternative ways of fulfilling
the obligation mentioned in the assumption? None come to mind.
If the obligation is to answer all questions and one such question
is "Who was your source?", only the provision of the correct name
can fulfill the obligation.

Thus, the inference meets all conditions for validity except
perhaps (c). The reporters could argue that their stories
uncovering immoral and/or criminal activities are an essential
means of maintaining the political moral health of their country.
Their obligation to promote and maintain that health justifies
claiming that they have no obligation to reveal informants'
identities. If it became known that reporters would reveal such
information to the courts, potential informers would not come
forward for fear of losing their jobs, and reporters would no
longer be able to write stories based on inside information. If
we accept the existence of the over-riding obligation then we
should rate the inference "X".

Step Three: evaluate assumptions. Given that we have a
moral obligation to ensure that justice is done, A should be rated
true.

Step Four: determine the extent to which intermediate
conclusions are proved. There are none.

Step Five: determine the extent to which the final
conclusion is proved. Since A has been rated true and the
inference "X", the final conclusion has not been proved to any
significant extent. The argument rating is "X" and the rated
version looks like this:

Step Six: formulate a response to the arguer. A good response is: "Even though people do normally have an obligation to answer truthfully all questions when testifying, this does not prove that reporters must reveal the identities of their informants. This is a justified exception to the general rule, because if people knew that reporters might reveal their names they would not give important information to them and reporters would not be able to serve as watchdogs of government nearly as effectively."

EXAMPLE (b): Herbert and Prudence have been married about ten years and Prudence wants to take a job that would mean she would not be at home during the day. Herbert is against this and reminds her of her wedding vows, vows of the traditional kind that she only agreed to take under pressure from Herbert: "You promised to love, honour, and obey me, so you have an obligation not to take the job".

Step One: construct an accurate diagrammatic version of the argument.

A = Prudence promised to love, honour, and obey Herbert.

B = Prudence has an obligation not to take the job.

Step Two: evaluate the inference. Can we identify a voiding or suspending condition that undermines the inference in this argument? Given that the promise was made, has it been voided during the ten years of marriage? We have no information to show that it has. Neither do we have any to show that the promise has been suspended. We must therefore regard the inference as valid.

Step Three: evaluate the assumptions. Is there any evidence to show that a defeating condition prevented the creation of a genuine promise? There is some, in that we are told that Herbert pressured Prudence into taking the traditional vows that contain the "love, honour, and obey" clause. Given this fact we should probably rate the assumption "?".

Step Four: determine the extent to which intermediate conclusions have been proved. There are none.

Step Five: determine the extent to which the final conclusion has been proved. Given the assumption rating of "?" and the inference rating of "√" we should say that the conclusion has been proved to some extent but not conclusively. The rated version of the argument looks like this:

Step Six: formulate a response to the arguer. A good response is this: "Although your conclusion logically follows it is not proved conclusively because it is not certain that Prudence voluntarily promised to "love, honour and obey," and a promise that is not voluntary is no real promise."

EXERCISE 5 - 13

Evaluate each of these moral obligation arguments. The answer to No. 1 is given in the back.

1. "Parents have an obligation to ensure that their children are safe coming and going to school. Therefore, Mr. and Mrs. X have an obligation to escort their children to and from school."

2. "Students who make appointments to meet a professor have an obligation to keep them, so Joe has an obligation to tell his professor he will not be able to keep their appointment."

3. P woke up with a somewhat sore throat and the sniffles, which she takes to be the sign of a cold coming on. She tells her father she is staying home from classes today. He argues: "Students at university have a moral obligation to try to benefit from instruction provided in their courses. Therefore, you have an obligation to go to class."

4. "The rich nations have an obligation to improve the standard of living in the poor nations, so Mexico has an obligation to lend money to the poor Latin American countries."

5. It is the first class of the term and Professor Bird has not included the date of the mid-term test on the course outline for "Intro. Ornithology." A student says: "Professors have an obligation to give their students adequate advance notice of test dates. Thus Professor Bird ought to tell us the date of our mid-term now."

(5.8)   PRUDENTIAL   ARGUMENTS.   Prudential   arguments   are
intended   to   prove   that   a   certain course of action is the one a
person   ought   to   adopt,   not because it is morally required, but
because   it   is   the   best   (or, at least, a good) means to satisfy
some want that that person has.

Moral   and   prudential   considerations   are   different   logically.
Failure   to   fulfill   a   moral   obligation   subjects   you to blame and
frequent   failure   leads   the   community   to   condemn you as a bad
person.   Failure   to   follow   a   prudentially   prescribed course of
conduct,   on   the   other   hand,   simply   leads others to say you are
foolish or unwise if the conduct prescribed actually would satisfy
your wants.   The contrasts are between good versus bad persons and
wise   versus   foolish   persons.   Being prudent depends upon knowing
how   the   world   (including humans) works, being moral depends upon
knowing what is right and wrong.

The prudent course of action may differ from the moral course
of action.   The moral course of action, if followed, may result in
some   loss   of   benefit   or   even personal harm.   Ibsen's play, AN
ENEMY OF THE PEOPLE, is based on this hard truth.   Although few of
us   are   put   in the position of the doctor in that play, not many
people   can   go through life without facing conflicts between what
is good for them and what is right.

(5.8.)   PRUDENTIAL ARGUMENT TYPE ONE.

(1)   INTRODUCTION.   Sonmetimes   we   prescribe   a   course of
conduct   and   try to justify it by citing a want a person (perhaps
ourselves)   has.   Usually arguments of this type are addressed to
someone   other   than   the   person   (or   group) mentioned in the
argument.   We rely on the arguee's knowledge of what would satisfy
the   person whose wants we are talking about. However, they may be
private arguments, about ourselves.

(2)   TYPICAL EXAMPLE.   For some years there has been military
strife   in   the Middle East, much of it initiated by the Palestine
Liberation   Organization (P.L.O.), which is fighting for territory
that   would provide displaced Palestinians with a country of their
own.   This   argument   has   been   directed at the United States and
others seeking peace in the Middle East: "The U.S. wants peace in
the   Middle   East.   Therefore, the U.S. ought to arrange that some
territory is ceded to the Palestinians."

(3) BASIC LOGICAL FORM:
        Person/group P wants W.
    Therefore, P ought to do M.

(4)   INFERENCE VALIDITY ANALYSIS.   Inference validity depends
partly   on   the   extent   to   which   doing M will lead to the

satisfaction of want W. This must be a means-end relationship. However, there is a moral restriction on the means recommended. People are fond of accusing those who act ruthlessly of following the principle that the end justifies the means. Up to a point it must, but we must operate within a framework of moral rules so that M must be a morally permissible course of action. Given this restriction it is indeed true that the end justifies the means.

(5) INFERENCE CRITICISM STRATEGY. One way to criticize the inference is to argue that the course of action M is not morally permissible. Dealing with the example someone might say that even though the U.S. wants peace in the Middle East, it ought not arrange that some territory is ceded to the Palestines because this would involve taking land from some country that it rightfully belongs to, and this is not morally permissible.

A second way to criticize the inference is to show that M is not a good means to satisfy W regardless of who P is even though M is morally permissible. It might be argued that settling the Palestinians on land of their own will not bring peace to the middle East because the P.L.O. is dedicated to destroying Israel and would not remain peacefully within the bounds of their new country.

A third way, related to the last one, is to try to show that although M may be a way of satisfying W for some individuals, it is not a good way for P. Here we would cite something about P's situation or capabilities that make M an unsuitable means for satisfying the want W. For example, we might try to show that the U.S. is not politically in a good position to arrange that the Palestinians are given territory. Perhaps it would take a United Nations task force to manage it.

A fourth way to criticize the inference is to show that P ought not to do M because M would interfere with the satisfaction of some want that is more important than want W. Everybody has a variety of wants and some of these are incompatible. We may want to earn good grades but we may also want to enjoy ourselves. Sometimes these conflict and we have to make a choice. Often our choice is relatively easy because we rank our wants in order of importance. Should we study for tomorrow's test or go to the movies? If getting a good grade is relatively important then the correct choice is to study. In the example, we might argue that even though the U.S. wants peace in the Middle East, it ought not arrange to get territory for the Palestinians because it wants to honor commitments to Israel which it deems to be more important. (This is probably not true, so it would not make a good inference criticism. But it does show the form such cricitisms must take.) To make a criticism of this kind effective we need to provide good evidence that P does indeed have the conflicting want and that it is more important to P than want W.

A fifth way, and normally one of the most effective, is to point out effective alternatives for satisfying want W.

(6) ASSUMPTION EVALUATION. To establish whether P wants W we ought to consult P. This is normally a reliable approach, although it sometimes happens that people do not really know what they want, in which case both us and the arguer should rate the assumption "?"

Often we cannot consult P directly so we will have to examine their past utterances and behavior patterns to decide if they really want W.

(7) VARIANT VERSIONS. None

(8) EVALUATION OF EXAMPLES. Example (a): Joe College and Suzy Wholesome are talking about Suzy's problems with Introductory Philosophy. Joe did well in it last year and offers to give her one of his papers to submit as hers:

"You want a good grade in the course, so you ought to pass in this "A" paper of mine as your own."

Step One: construct an accurate diagrammatic version of the argument.

A = Suzy wants a good grade in
Introductory Philosophy.

B = Suzy ought to pass in
Joe's paper as her own.

Step Two: Evaluate the inference. The inference rating should be "X" since fraud is both morally and legally impermissible. Furthermore, this may not be an effective means of getting a good grade for several reasons: (a) she may get caught and be given an F, (b) the paper may only be worth a small proportion of the total mark so a good grade on it will not help much overall. Finally, there are other effective ways of getting a good grade, one of which is to get help from the instructor.

Step Three: evaluate the assumption. We can assume that Suzy does indeed want a good grade, since students generally do. Rate A true.

Step Four: determine the extent to which intermediate conclusions are proved. There are none.

Step Five: determine the extent to which the final conclusion has been proved. Given A true and the inference rated "X", the argument ought to be rated "X". The rated version looks like this:

Step Six: formulate a response to the arguer. We could say this to Joe: "Even though Suzy wants a good grade in Introductory Philosophy, that doesn't prove she ought to pass in your paper. Doing that is wrong so the end can't justify the means. Besides, she might get caught and be given an F, and if the paper isn't an important component of the course grade a good grade on it won't help her much."

EXAMPLE (b). Sigmund is a mature young man of average scholastic apitude who wants a career in which he can help people with their personal problems. His father tells him this: "You want to help people with their personal problems, so you ought to try to become a psychiatrist."

Step One: construct an accurate diagrammatic version of the argument.

A = Sigmund wants to help people with their personal problems.

B = Sigmund ought to try to become a psychia-trist.

Step Two: evaluate the inference. In the background information we are told that Sigmund has "average" scholastic aptitude, so it is somewhat questionable to argue that he should try to become a psychiatrist. This program requires about ten years of college including medical school. Admission to medical school is based to a great extent on high grades, something Sigmund may not be able to get. Thus, although this might be a good means to the end for some people, it probably isn't for Sigmund. We should rate the inference as "?". An "X" might be too pessimistic since motivated people can often do well academically through sheer hard work.

131

Step Three: evaluate the assumption. Given the background information we rate A true.

Step Four: determine the extent to which intermediate conclusions have been proved. There are none.

Step Five: determine the extent to which the final conclusion is proved. Given the assumption rating "√" and the inference rating "?", we should rate the argument "?" overall. The rated version looks like this:

Step Six: formulate a response to the arguer. We could say to Sigmund's father: "Given that Sigmund wants to help people, it does not quite follow that he ought to try to become a psychiatrist. The academic program is long and demanding and he may not do well enough to even get into medical school."

Example (c): In the movie "The Graduate", the "hero", played by Dustin Hoffman, has just graduated from college but does not know what career to pursue. He does seem to be sure he does not want to be a businessman as his father and his father's friends are. His parents invite their friends to a party to celebrate his graduation and in one of the brief but funny incidents in the movie, he is taken aside by one of them as if to be told a profound secret. The businessman tells him he has only one word to give him and whispers "Plastics!" in his ear. Our hero looks blank. The argument amounts to this: "You want to be a success in business, so you ought to get into the plastics industry."

Step One: construct an accurate diagrammatic version of the argument.

A = You want to be a success
    in business.

B = You ought to get into the
    plastics industry.

Step Two: evaluate the inference. First of all, there are

probably other ways of being successful in business than by getting into the plastics industry. Perhaps at the time getting into computers was even better advice. Furthermore, our hero probably has wants that are more important than wanting to be a success in business, and "getting into plastics" may be incompatible with those. We can rate the inference as "X".

Step Three: evaluate the assumption. Given the background we can rate A as "X". Of course in the movie the hero did not tell people he did not want to be a businessman. The businessman simply took it for granted that he would want to.

Step Four: determine the extent to which intermediate conclusions are proved. There are none.

Step Five: determine the extent to which the final conclusion is proved. Given A rated "X" and the inference rated "X" the overall rating must be "X". The rated version looks like this:

Step Six: formulate a response to the arguer. The hero could say this to his would-be advisor: "I don't really want to be a business success, but even if I did there are other ways to achieve it, such as getting into computers."

EXERCISE 5 - 14

Evaluate each of the following Type One Prudential arguments. The answer to No. 1 is given in the back.

1. Since graduating from college Emmaline has worked as a teller at a bank. She wants the job of loan officer, which is opening up. Her boss, the manager, has beeen asking her (she is not married) to take weekend trips with him when his wife is away. She has told all this to an acquaintance who says: "You want the loan officer's job, so you ought to accept the manager's invitations."

2. Earl is fed up with the gasoline costs of driving his big Chevy. His business is going well and his partner suggests he consider a Mercedes 300D diesel, which costs $30,000.

However, it can be driven for about 2/3 the cost in fuel. He argues: "You want to cut your fuel costs, so you ought to buy a Mercedes 300D."

3. Mabel is a college freshman who aspires to be a doctor. She is well aware that very good grades are needed to get into medical school. Her friend says: "You want to have good grades for medical school so you should take lots of easy non-science courses.

4. "We don't want a nuclear war with the Soviet Union. Therefore, we should ensure that our weapons systems are superior to theirs."

5. "Americans want better public safety so they ought to give the police geater powers of arrest and detention."

(5.82)   PRUDENTIAL ARGUMENT TYPE TWO.

(1)   INTRODUCTION.   This   pattern differs from the previous
one   in   that, although the conclusion is the same, the assumption
used   to   prove   it   is the claim that the action mentioned in the
conclusion   is an effective means to achieving the satisfaction of
the sort of want in question.

(2)   TYPICAL   EXAMPLE.   "Exercising   is   a   good way to lose
weight, so Sam ought to exercise."

(3)   BASIC LOGICAL FORM:

M is a good means of satisfying want W.

Therefore, P ought to do M.

(4)   INFERENCE   VALIDITY   ANALYSIS.   Validity   depends on a
number   of   conditions.   First,   there   must be no other means to
satisfying   W   that   is   anywhere as effective.   Secondly, doing M
must   be   morally   and   legally permissible. Thirdly, P's situation
must   be   a   normal   one,   so   that   the general claim made in the
assumption   fits   P's   situation.   Fourthly,   doing   M   must   not
interfere   with   P's   pursuit   of more important goals. Fifthly, P
must actually have want W.

(5)   INFERENCE   CRITICISM   STRATEGY. The points of criticism
correspond   to   the   five conditions for validity mentioned above.
The   strategies   will   be   described   in   the   order   the validity
conditions are mentioned.

First,   try   to   show that there are other effective ways for
satisfying   W.   In the example we could point out that dieting is
an   even   better   way of losing weight, so it does not follow that
Sam   ought to exercise.   This form of criticism is usually the one
these arguments are most vulnerable to.

Secondly,   we   can try to show that doing M is either morally
or legally prohibited.   Unless the arguer is of dubious character,
we   will   not   normally   find   it   possible   to   criticize on this
ground.

(6)   ASSUMPTION EVALUATION.   Deciding on whether M is indeed
a good   means of satisfying W is simply a matter of looking at the
record.   Is   exercising   a good way of losing weight? Exercising
does   increase   fitness,   which   is part of good health, but it is
actually   an   inefficient   means   of losing weight. To burn off the
calories   from   an   extra   piece   of   pie   may   take most people a
half-hour   of moderate exercise.   Depending on how busy you are it
may   be   better   to forego the piece of pie in the first place.   It

135

has been said that the best exercise for weight control is pushing yourself away from the table at the right time!

We often leap to the conclusion that the assumption is true or false because in our own case M has been a good (or poor) way of satisfying W. A person may claim that exercise is not a good means of losing weight because it has not worked for them. This is generalizing from a sample of one. A much larger sample is needed.

(8) EVALUATION OF EXAMPLES. Example (a): Professional hockey as played in the National Hockey League (N.H.L.) has for many years involved much more fighting than any other professional sport (except possibly boxing!). Those interested in seeing a "cleaner" brand of hockey often argue this way: "Bigger fines for players who fight is a good way of cleaning up hockey. Therefore the N.H.L. league management ought to levy bigger fines for fighting."

Step One: construct an accurate diagrammatic version of the argument.

A = Bigger fines for players who fight is a good way to clean up hockey.

B = The N.H.L. league management ought to levy bigger fines for fighting.

Step Two: evaluate the inference. Let us go through each of the strategies described above to see how the inference might be criticized.

First, are there other effective ways of cleaning up N.H.L. hockey? At least one approach comes to mind: suspend players for a number of games. Professional hockey is very competitive and players are worried that if they miss games someone else will take over their job. Thus, fear of suspension can be an effective deterrent.

Second, is levying fines immoral or illegal? Neither.

Third, is there some special feature that makes levying fines an ineffective method in the N.H.L.? One possibility is that, since players fight with the support of their team management because intimidation contributes to winning, management may pay the fines for the players "under the table", so the players are not punished at all.

Fourth, will fines interfere with some other goal of those

136

who want hockey cleaned up? Nothing comes to mind here.

Fifth, do those arguing this way on their own behalf really want less fighting? Not all fans do, but these ones obviously do.

For the reasons just mentioned we are entitled to rate the inference "X".

Step Three: evaluate the assumption. As a general policy fines may not result in cleaner hockey at any level, since the team management is often prepared to pay the fines for the players. We should rate A as "?". (This criticism should be backed by testimony from people involved in hockey, but given that the inference is already rated "X" this is enough to condemn the argument.)

Step Four: determine the extent to which intermediate conclusions are proved. There are none.

Step Five: determine the extent to which the final conclusion is proved. Given that the assumption is rated "?" and the inference is rated "X", the conclusion has not been proved to any extent. The overall rating is "X". The rated version looks like this:

Step Six: formulate a response to the arguer. We could respond like this: "It is doubtful that the policy of fines for fighting is an efective way of cleaning up hockey because teams may pay the fines for the players. But even if it was an effective policy, it could not prove that the N.H.L. ought to levy bigger fines. Suspending players may be better. Furthermore, even though fines might work in some leagues the N.H.L. teams might pay the fines for the players."

EXAMPLE (b): Herbert, who earns a modest income working in a bank, is out playing golf with his brother the doctor and one of his brother's colleagues. Herbert mentions that he is thinking of buying a new car. His brother, with his colleague's support tells Herbert: "A Mercedes-Benz is a good car, so you ought to buy a Mercedes."

Step One: construct an accurate diagrammatic version of the argument.

A = A Mercedes-Benz is a good car.

B = Herbert ought to buy a Mercedes-Benz.

Step Two: Evaluate the inference. We can work through each of the strategies to see which might be effective here.

First, are there other effective ways of satisfying Herbert's desire for a new car? Clearly there are, since there are quite a few satisfactory brands of cars.

Secondly, is there anything immoral or illegal about buying a Mercedes-Benz? There is certainly nothing illegal about it. It might be argued that it is somewhat immoral to support the economy of another country when one can support one's own, but at present there is no strong moral requirement to do this.

Thirdly, is there some special feature of Herbert's situation that makes the strategy of buying a Mercedes as a means to getting a good car inappropriate for Hebert? There seems to be. It might be a good strategy for doctors who have high incomes, but since Herbert has a modest income it may not fit his situation.

Fourthly, would buying a Mercedes interfere with the satisfaction of some other wants Herbert has? The cheapest Mercedes is about $25.000., which could make Herbert's payments over $500.00 per month for five years. On a modest salary he will have to operate on a strict budget that will involve doing without some luxuries he enjoys. He may have a good car for traveling but no money to travel!

Fifthly, does Herbert actually want a new car? We hear that he "is thinking of buying a new car", so it would seem that he does.

Given what has been said from applying the first, third, and fourth strategies, we can probably rate the inference as "X".

Step Three: evaluate the assumption. Is it true that the Mercedes-Benz is a good car? The experts and the general public seem to agree that it is. We can rate A true.

Step Four: determine the extent to which intermediate conclusions are proved. There are none.

Step Five: determine the extent to which the final

conclusion is proved. Given the assumption rating of "√" and the inference rating as "X", the conclusion has not been proved to any appreciable extent. We can rate the argument "X". The rated version looks like this:

Step Six: formulate a response to the arguer. Herbert should say this: "I agree that the Mercedes is a good car but that doesn't mean I ought to get one. On my income the payments would be too high and I don't want to lower my standard of living when I buy a car. Anyway, there are other kinds of cars that would meet my needs just as well."

EXERCISE 5 - 15

Evaluate the following Type Two Prudential Arguments. No. 1 is answered in the back.

1. Advertisements from some home computer firms contain this argument: "Acquiring computer skills is a good way to prepare for college, so parents ought to buy their children a home computer."

2. Priscilla has a choice of men to marry: one is a busy physician, the other a writer. Her mother says: "Marrying a doctor is a good way to get financial security, so you ought to marry him."

3. Ten-year Louis is very curious, driving his mother crazy with questions. She tells him: "Reading the paper is a good way to learn about the world, so you ought to do that instead of asking me all these questions."

4. Traditionally, Professor X's university has tried to ensure that professors do not have to go into debt to attend conferences, so it has a policy of supplementing whatever grant money they can obtain with enough to cover the total costs. Professor X has been given enough funds by his university to attend a conference. Afterwards he received a cheque from a research foundation to cover part of his expenses. Should X hand his money over to his university, or keep it for himself? Someone says to him: "The extra money

139

can be used to buy yourself some books, so you ought to keep it."

5. A college junior wants a career in law and has deided to apply to law school prior to her senior year because she found out that people can be admitted without completing their undergraduate degrees. To her surprise she is accepted, but in the meantime she has decided she wants to finish her B.A. The law school will not promise to admit her a year later. To help her resolve her dilemma her boyfriend says: "You may be able to begin your law career by entering law school a year from next fall, therefore, you ought to stay here to complete your B.A."

(5.9)   EVALUATIVE ARGUMENTS.   In judging that something is good, bad, or indifferent we are making value judgments. In what follows four common argument patterns involving valuation will be discussed. These divide into two types, those which involve judgments about particular things, states of affairs, or events, and those arguments that try to prove what qualities a thing (state, or event) must have to count as a good example of that sort. The first type is directly concerned with value, while the second type is concerned instead with the qualities anything must have to be good, bad, or indifferent. Trying to prove that WAR AND PEACE is a great novel involves using criteria for greatness in novels but trying to prove that a great novel must have such-and-such qualities is to argue over criteria.

Actually, judgments about moral rightness and wrongness are evaluative judgments also, but arguments trying to prove such judgments have already been discussed.

(5.91)   TYPE-RELATIVE EVALUATIVE ARGUMENTS.

(1)   INTRODUCTION.   A very common evaluative judgment involves identifying a thing (or class of things) as a member of some class and claiming it is a good, bad, or indifferent member (or sub-class) of that class. To prove such a claim we cite the attributes that this thing has that are attributes that make for goodness or deficiency in things of this kind. This amounts to measuring the thing against the standards of goodness for things of that kind.

(2)   TYPICAL EXAMPLE.   The proud car owner says: "My car gives 30 miles per gallon of gasoline, accelerates from zero to sixty miles per hour in ten seconds, and develops a cornering force of 0.8 g's, so it is a good car."

(3)   BASIC LOGICAL FORM:

x has good-making attributes G1, G2, etc.

Therefore, as an X, x is rated R.

Note: "x" denotes the particular thing (state, or event) and "X" denotes the kind of thing it is being classified as. "R" may denote any positive valuation expression.

(4)   INFERENCE VALIDITY ANALYSIS.   Arguments of this type rely on the good-making attributes mentioned in the premises being collectively sufficient to warrant rating x as it is rated in the conclusion. In our example the attributes mentioned must be a majority of those that a perfect car would have since the owner wants to prove that his car is a "good" car. If he were to try to

141

prove that it is a "very good" car he would have to cite more good-making attributes. It must be realized, of course, that not all such attributes are equally important. In these times giving 30 miles per gallon is probably more important than developing high cornering power even though cornering power is a safety feature.

(5) INFERENCE CRITICISM STRATEGY. There are two different strategies appropriate for different circumstances. Sometimes, although rarely, the rating of x is not apppropriate in the sense that it is not high enough, given the attributes mentioned in the premises. To conclude that someone who has graduated from university with straight A's is "a fairly good student" would be inaccurate. Such a record is sufficient for claiming that this individual is an excellent student. This kind of deficiency is only likely to occur when the arguer is given to understatement or is not aware of the standards of goodness for things of kind X. When it is encountered, try to show that the attributes cited are such that x should receive a more favorable rating.

The most frequent deficiency, of course, is that of assigning an unduly favorable rating, given the attributes that have been cited. Try to show that these attributes, when compared with the good-making attributes for X's, are not jointly sufficient to warrant concluding that x should be rated as R. To do this you need to point to good-making attributes of X's that not have been mentioned. It may be that x does have some of these, but we are concerned here with whether the ones mentioned in the premises are sufficient to warrant the rating assigned by the arguer. It is not unfair in argument evaluation to pretend that evidence not mentioned does not exist since we are trying to evaluate the argument as it has been put forward. It is not unfair because the onus is on the arguer to provide all the evidence at her/his disposal in the first place.

(6) ASSUMPTION EVALUATION. No special considerations are involved in deciding whether a thing has each of the good-making attributes assigned to it, although sometimes vagueness in the terms can make an accurate judgment difficult.

(7) VARIANT VERSION. Often arguers try to prove that an x warrants an unfavorable rating as an X. Normally the arguer will point out one or more good-making qualities of X's that this x lacks. The basic logical form of the argument is this:

x lacks good-making attributes G1, G2, etc.

Therefore, as an X, x is rated R.

To criticize the inference we try to show that x does not

142

warrant the unfavorable rating R. This can be done by showing that the attributes x lacks are not (taken together) important enough. Suppose someone tries to prove that a particular brand of car is not a good car by claiming that it gives less than 25 miles per gallon of gasoline. We could argue that the inference is poor because this criterion is not essential for a good car. This particular brand of car might have enough other good-making attributes to offset this supposed deficiency.

Sometimes arguments to negative ratings do cite essential attributes of a good X, in which case the inference will be satisfactory. For instance, an essential attribute of a good car is that it can provide transportation. It is legitimate to conclude that x is not a good car when it is known that x cannot provide transportation.

(8) EVALUATION OF EXAMPLES. Example (a): Sports writers sometimes exaggerate when evaluating particular athletes. In the winter of 82/83 several presented this argument about Al Oliver, the first baseman of the Montreal Expos baseball team: "In 1982 Oliver won the National League batting championship with a 0.331 batting average. Therefore Oliver had a great year as a National League first baseman."

Step One: construct an accurate diagrammatic version of the argument.

A = In 1982 Oliver won the National League batting championship with a 0.331 batting average.

B = Oliver had a great year as a National League first baseman.

Step Two: evaluate the inference. The class whose good-making attributes we are concerned with is that of National League first basemen. Batting 0.331 meets one standard for greatness in this group as any baseball experts can confirm. Are there other attributes? Obviously, there is an individual's defensive performance, what he does while on the field. To rate as having had a great season as a National League first baseman it would seem that a player would also have to play very well defensively. It does not seem necessary that one would have to be both the top hitting first baseman and the top fielding one to qualify as having a "great year", but a player probably should rate as at least average. Thus, hitting performance does not guarantee a great year.

The inference should be rated as "?" since there is a possibility Oliver did not have a great year even though he led in hitting.

Step Three: evaluate the assumption. Checking the statistics will confirm that A is correct. We rate it true.

Step Four: determine the extent to which intermediate conclusions are proved. There are none.

Step Five: determine the extent to which the final conclusion is proved. Given A rated as "√" and the inference rated "?", the proof rating will be "?". The argument proves its conclusion to some extent but not totally. The rated version looks like this:

Step Six: formulate a response to the arguer. A good response to the sports writers is this: "It is true that Oliver led the league in hitting but that doesn't quite prove he had a GREAT year in 1982. Fielding performance must also be taken into account."

Note: In fact, Oliver's performance at first base was the worst in the League. He led all first basemen with 19 errors.

EXAMPLE (b): An argument implicit in ads for Sony TV's: "Sony TV's are very reliable, so Sony TV's are good TV buys."

Step One: construct an accurate diagrammatic version of the argument. We can probably clarify the conclusion somewhat. They probably mean that Sony's are good value for money, which here would mean cost of operation per hour--including depreciation as well as electricity consumed.

A = Sony TV's are very
    reliable.

B = Sony TV's are good
    value for money.

Step Two: evaluate the inference. The Sony is being measured against the criteria for TV's that are good value for money. It seems clear that reliability is a good-making attribute for TV's that are good value for money. But is this one attribute

144

enough to guarantee that a set is good value for money? In the cost per hour of operation equation, initial purchase price will be a factor as well as service costs, so that if two brands have the same reliability the one that has the lower price tag will be the better value. In fact, high reliability and low cost are incompatible qualities since it is more expensive to build a quality product. Furthermore, nothing has been said about picture quality. Thus, high reliability is not sufficient to guarantee good value for money. We can rate the inference as "?".

Step Three: Evaluate the assumption. On consulting CONSUMER REPORTS, which collect information on such matters we will find that Sony TV's are the most reliable brand so that we can rate A as true.

Step Four: determine the extent to which intermediate conclusions are proved. There are none.

Step Five: determine the extent to which the final conclusion is proved. Given that A is rated "√" and the inference "?", the proof rating is "?". B has been proved to some extent but not conclusively. The rated version of the argument looks like this:

Step Six: formulate a response to the arguer. We could respond to Sony like this: "Even though your sets are reliable this fact by itself does not prove conclusively that they are good value for money. Good value depends also on low initial purchase price and good picture quality."

EXAMPLE (c): Often overheard among students discussing their professors: "Professor X's lectures are boring, so X is a poor professor."

Step One: construct an accurate diagrammatic version of the argument.

A = Professor X's lectures are boring.

B = X is a poor professor.

145

Step Two: evaluate the inference. Professor X is being evaluated by the criteria applicable to college professors in general. How essential is it for being a good professor to give interesting lectures? The professor is there to facilitate learning by the students. This is done by assigning the right reading material, getting input from the students in the form of tests, essays, and other written assignments, and by in-class activity. It seems clear that the "bottom line" is how well the students learn the material, and this standard can be met by an instructor even though he/she is a boring lecturer. Such an instructor could not be rated as excellent but could surely rate as adequate. Thus, giving boring lectures does not by itself warrant rating an individual as poor, although it is some evidence for sayng so. We will rate the inference as "?".

Step Three: evaluate the assumption. We have the testimony of one student that X's lectures are boring. This is hardly enough evidence and we would do well to solicit the opinions of a sample of the class. Consulting about 20% should be sufficient. Let us suppose that most of those asked confirmed the arguer's view and rate A as true.

Step Four: determine the extent to which intermediate conclusions are proved. There are none.

Step Five: determine the extent to which the final conclusion is proved. Given that A is rated "√" and the inference rated "?" we rate the degree of proof as "?". The rated version of the argument is this:

STEP SIX: formulate a response to the arguer. We could say this to the student: "Being a boring lecturer is not by itself enough to prove that X is a poor professor. X may organize his courses well enough so that you learn as much from X's courses as from any of your other ones."

EXERCISE 5 - 16

Evaluate the following type-relative arguments. No. 1 is answered in the back.

146

1. "Nuclear power plants consume no natural resources, are fuel efficient, and give off no atmospheric pollutants. Therefore, as energy sources, nuclear power plants are superior to other energy sources."

2. A benevolent despot is a dictator who acts for the good of his subjects as he/she sees it. This argument used to be given in favor of this form of government: "Benevolent despotism as a form of government is very efficient in arriving at decisions and requires no expensive legislature. Therefore, it is a good form of government."

3. "Lyndon Johnson had more civil rights legislation enacted than any recent President, so he was a great President."

4. In Hardy's TESS OF THE D'URBERVILLES the woman referred to in the title is hanged for killing her husband even though he probably deserved his fate because of the way he treated her. A reader disappointed by the ending says: "A good novel has a satisfying ending so TESS is not a good novel."

5. "Excelsior University has very restrictive admission standards. Therefore, Excelsior gives you a very good education."

(5.92) ARGUMENTS FOR RANKINGS.

(1) INTRODUCTION. The last argument pattern discussed was found in arguments intended to prove that something warranted a certain rating as a member of a class of things. In proving a rating is justified we cite attributes of the thing that are good-making attributes of the kind in question. In this section we are concerned with another way of evaluating things--comparing one to another or to all other members of a class. This is the process of ranking. We might try to prove, for instance, that in 1982 Lendl was a better tennis player than Connors. Or that a Mazda RX7 is a better GT car than a Camaro. In arriving at such judgments we compare the one thing to the other in those respects that represent the good-making qualities of things of that kind. This is the procedure followed by CONSUMER REPORTS in judging consumer products.

In making ranking judgments you should realize that no absolute rating of a thing can be inferred from the claim that it is better than, as good as, or worse than, another. The claim that Lendl was a better player than Connors in 1982 does not provide any information about how good Lendl was. We also need to know how good Connors was on the absolute scale. If we know Lendl was better than Connors AND that Connors was one of the best players then we can infer that Lendl was also one of the best. Thus, rankings can be very informative about the rating of one individual when we know the rating of the one he/she/it is being compared to.

(2) TYPICAL EXAMPLE. The sporty car buyer argues as follows: "The Mazda RX7 handles better than the Camaro, it is built better, and it costs less. Therefore the Mazda is a better sporty car."

(3) BASIC LOGICAL FORM:

x1 is better than x2 in ways B1, B2, etc.

x1 is as good as x2 in ways G1, G2, etc.

x1 is worse than x2 in ways W1, W2, etc.

Therefore, x1 as an X ranks R relative to x2.

(4) INFERENCE VALIDITY ANALYSIS. The whole ranking process can be seen as one of weighing the two things in a balance scale. When the one thing is not superior in all relevant respects, value judgments about the importance of each good-making quality of an X will have to be made. These should conform to what experts would say and not to any eccentric views you yourself may have. The

148

inference will be valid to the extent that all important good-making attributes have been considered and weighted according to their importance. If an arguer was trying to prove that one brand of 19-inch TV was better than another she/he would want to show that one had a better picture, was not as susceptible to electrical interference, and had a better reliability record. Portability, color of cabinet, and country of origin would not be important characteristics because they are not directly relevant to performance.

An additional factor is the ranking x1 is given relative to x2. Is it said to be "much better" or only "better"? Both of these expressions are somewhat vague but 'better' is especially vague. Only a slight superiority is required to qualify as better, so that a ranking of "x1 is better than x2" is easier to prove. Almost all ranking expressions are vague, which makes the evaluation of inference quality uncertain.

(5) INFERENCE CRITICISM STRATEGY. This is simply a matter of weighing up the "weight" (importance) of each attribute mentioned in the premises and deciding whether the ranking claim made in the conclusion is appropriate. As in the case of rating, the ranking may actually be too modest. It would, for instance, not follow that Jimmy Connors' tennis game is "somewhat better" than mine if a complete comparison were made of the facets of our games. His is far superior in every respect. However, it must be remembered that we ignore comparisons not mentioned in the premises since we are trying to decide whether or not the arguer's assumptions can prove the conclusion. Thus, if someone argued "Connors serves a lot better than you, so he is a lot better tennis player than you." Both assumption and conclusion are true, but the former does not prove the latter. There is more to a tennis game than serving and people who serve well can be beaten by someone who playes other facets of the game better.

Perhaps the first step is to decide whether any attribute against which the things are being compared is acually a good-making characteristic for X's. For instance, in the example, we note that the Mazda is said to cost less than the Camaro. Is cost a good-making attribute of sporty cars? It is doubtful because price is not an intrinsic property of cars at all. The conclusion simply ranks the Mazda as "a better sporty car", not a better sporty car for the money.

The next step is to arrive at a judgment as to whether or not, given the favorable comparison of x1 to x2 made in the premises, the ranking in the conclusion is appropriate. To do this we must be aware of all the significant good-making attributes of X's. With this knowledge we can decide in what ways and to what extent x1 must be superior to x2 to warrant the ranking given in the conclusion. Then, if the premises make a much less (or much more) favorable comparison of x1 to x2 we can claim that the inference is not satisfactory. If someone says that Connors is a lot better tennis player than I, on the ground that he is a lot better at serving, I bring to my mind all of the good-making qualities of tennis players. Then I judge that Connors would have to be a lot better at most facets of the game (ground strokes, volleying, positioning, smashes, etc.) to justify saying he is a lot better than I. But since only one good-making quality is mentioned in the premise, this means the inference is poor.

(6) ASSUMPTION EVALUATION. Keep in mind that there are significant and insignificant differences. Normally x1 is not really significantly better than x2 if it is one per cent better, for example.

(7) VARIANT VERSION. A variant of this pattern is the argument that ranks an individual (or type of individual) with respect to a whole class of which the individual is a member. Thus, someone might try to prove that Jimmy Connors was the world's best tennis player in 1982, or that he was one of the top half dozen players. To prove the first claim he would have to be judged as better overall than any of the other top players, which involves comparing him with several others and not just one. The second claim is less ambitious, though he would again have to be compared with the others who might have a claim to such a ranking.

The main difference between this variant and the regular pattern is that the individual has to be compared with more than one other individual to establish a ranking in the class as a whole. The strategies of inference and assumption criticism are the same.

(8) EVALUATION OF EXAMPLES. Example (a): The pop music critic argues: "The Beatles' music is more innovative than the Rolling Stones, so the Beatles were a better rock band than the Stones."

STEP ONE: construct an accurate diagrammatic version of the argument.

A = The Beatles' music is more innovative than the Rolling stones.

B = The Beatles were a better rock band than the Stones.

STEP TWO: evaluate the inference. To be in a position to

150

evaluate we must call to mind the main good-making qualities of rock bands. This is not easy to do. A good band plays good music and provides a certain amount of showmanship. The components of any music are the beat, the melody, and the words but these must form a unity to make a good song. Being successfully innovative can also be regarded as a good-making quality. However, this is only one quality and could not by itself show the superiority of the Beatles over the Stones. We can rate the inference as "X".

STEP THREE: evaluate the assumption. To make a judgment about A we would have to consult the experts' opinions, which can be found in books on the history of rock music, and in encyclopedias on the subject. On doing so you would find that A should be rated true.

STEP FOUR: determine the extent to which intermediate conclusions are proved. There are none.

STEP FIVE: determine the extent to which the final conclusion is proved. Given the assumption and inference rating we rate the argument "X". The rated version looks like this:

STEP SIX: formulate a response to the arguer. We could reply: "The Beatles' music is more innovative than the Rolling Stones but that does not go very far by itself to prove that the Beatles were a better rock band. There is a lot more to being a good rock band than writing and performing innovative music, such as the way the music is played, showmanship, etc. You do not say whether the Beatles were better in these areas too."

EXAMPLE (b). Through surveys asking professors to rate university faculties by prestige in research, the University of California (Berkeley) has recently been chosen number one. This tempts professors and others to give this argument:

"The University of California has the most prestigious faculty, so it is the best university in the United States."

STEP ONE: construct an accurate diagrammatic version of the argument. This is shown on the next page.

A = The University of California has the most prestigious faculty in the United States.

B = It is the best university in the United States.

Step Two: evaluate the inference. Prestige in faculty research accomplishment is certainly one good-making quality for a universiy. Are there others? Well, another important one is teaching effectiveness of the faculty. A third would be physical facilities for students and faculty. A fourth is library holdings. To qualify as the best university in the United States an institution would have to rank well up in each of these good-making characteristics, although it would not have to be tops in each case to be tops overall. Thus, having the most prestigious faculty is good evidence for the conclusion but is not conclusive evidence. We can rate the inference as "?"

Step Three: evaluate the assumption. A is a judgment made by the individuals (peers) in the best position to judge, so we should accept it as true. Prestige is difficult to measure and it is always plausible to claim that a rival, Harvard for example, is just as prestigious by citing other evidence. However, in the absence of a good reason to the contrary we can accept the professors' judgment.

Step Four: determine the extent to which intermediate conclusions have been proved. There are none.

Step Five: determine the extent to which the final conclusion has been proved. With the assumption true and the inference rated "?" we can rate the argument as "?". B is proved to some extent but not conclusively. The rated argument looks like this:

Step Six: formulate a response to the arguer. We can respond by saying "perhaps the University of California does have the most prestigious faculty but that by itself does not quite prove it is the best university. The best university must also excell at teaching effectiveness, facilities, and library holdings. For all we know the University of California may be deficient in one or

152

more of these qualities."

(9) ASSOCIATED FALLACIES. A fallacious argument can be produced by trying to compare two things under some broad general class when they are quite different. This might be called the "apples and oranges fallacy". Attempting to prove that the Beatles produced better music than Beethoven would be an example. Both produced music but very different kinds of music aimed at achieving different effects using different musical instruments. The good-making qualities of music that are common to both are too few to allow us to judge one product as better than another.

EXERCISE 5 - 17

Evaluate each of the following arguments for rankings. No. 1 is answered in the back.

1. A scholarship committee must choose between X and Y. Looking at their academic records one committee member says: "X has a good average with no low or high marks. Y's average is similar but he has some very high grades and some failures. Therefore X is a better student than Y."

2. Baseball fans have argued about the virtues of the grass surface compared to the artifical surface ever since the first major league ballpark had its grass replaced by Astroturf. One former infielder said this: "Artificial surfaces give a more reliable bounce when the ball is hit into the infield, so it's a lot better than grass."

3. Joline is trying to decide whether to go to Enormous State University (E.S.U.) or Cosy College. She thinks: "Cosy is a friendly place with small classes, but E.S.U. has a high-powered faculty and a big choice of courses. So E.S.U. will give me a better education."

4. "The murder rate in the U.S. is about four times that in Canada, so Canada is a better place to live."

5. "The Rolling Stones have been successful over a longer period than any other rock band, so they are the best rock band ever."

153

(5.93) "GOOD-FOR" ARGUMENTS.

(1) INTRODUCTION. Another kind of directly evaluative argument besides those intended to rate and rank things as members of a class is the one that tries to prove that something is good, beneficial, etc., because it satisfied someone's want. Such arguments can be about things, states of affairs ("It's good for England that Prince Charles is married"), or events ("It's good for the country that the recession is ending").

We have in such arguments, then, three main ingredients: a thing, state, or event, a want, and the individual or group whose want it is.

(2) TYPICAL EXAMPLE: "A lot of people want work so it's good that the recession is ending".

(3) BASIC LOGICAL FORM:

X wants W

Therefore, it is good for X that P.

NOTE: X = the individual, W = the want, P = the phenomenon that is supposed to satisfy the want.

(4) INFERENCE VALIDITY ANALYSIS. Validity depends on two conditions being met. First, P must actually contribute to the satisfaction of W. In the example, the conclusion follows from the assumption only if the end of the recession results in a significant rise in employment.

Secondly, P must not, on balance, do X more harm than good. This condition is necessary because of two things: (a) we do not always know what is best for us, and (b) we have a variety of wants and these are often incompatible so that sometimes P may satisfy one want but frustrate a more important one or perhaps several others. An example for each case will make this clearer.

A hiker encounters a footbridge over a gorge he wishes to cross. Unknown to him, the bridge will not carry his weight. He reasons: "I want to cross this gorge, so it's a good thing this bridge is here." Here the conclusion does not follow because the bridge will not serve to satisfy the desire to cross the gorge. Lack of knowledge prevents the hiker from knowing what is good for him.

A touring musician who is relying on amphetamines (pep pills) to help her keep up with the pace of the tour thinks: "I want to perform well through the entire tour so it's a good thing I have

154

these pills available". Here the conclusion may not follow because the musician may also want to remain in good health and continually taking amphetamines can ruin one's health. Even though the pills help satisfy one want they are incompatible with another and if good health is more important to this woman then it is, overall, not a good thing she has the pills available.

(5)   INFERENCE CRITICISM STRATEGY.   Since there are two conditions for inference validity there are two strategies for inference criticism.   One is to try to show that P will not contribute to the satisfaction of want W.   It is not usually on this score that the inference is weak.   More often a better strategy is to try to identify other wants the individual (or group) has, which will be frustrated by P. Preferably, these wants should be ones whose satisfaction is more important to the individual.   Frequently they will be long-term goals while W is relatively short-term.   Short-term and long-term goals often conflict.   The desire to lose ten pounds within a year conflicts with the present desire to eat the apple pie one is facing.

(6)   ASSUMPTION EVALUATION.   Normally the best way of establishing or refuting 'X wants W' is to consult X, although sometimes people do not really know what they want.

(7)   VARIANT VERSION. Besides arguing that something is beneficial we also infer from wants that something harms a person or frustrates their desires.   The type of inference criticism strategy is the same as for the positive version except that we try to show either that P is not really detrimental to X's want W, or that P may actually promote the satisfaction of other wants that X has.

(8)   EVALUATION OF EXAMPLES. Example (a): An example from the world of finance: "The people of this country want our currency to be respected in other countries, so it's good that the dollar is rising against other currencies."

Step   One: construct an accurate diagrammatic version of the argument.

A = The people of this country want our currency to be respected in other countries.

B = It's good that the dollar is rising against other currencies.

Step   Two: evaluate the inference.   First we ask if the rising of the dollar will make our currency respected in other countries. The answer would seem to be "yes". If a foreigner finds that he/she needs more of his/her own money to buy a dollar this creates an impression of value. The inference passes the first test. Now, is the rising of the dollar incompatible with the satisfaction of other wants the arguer may have? There is at least one, our desire to export goods, that is incompatible with a rising currency. As currency rises the item that a foreign customer is buying from us rises in price, so that the product tends to be less competitively priced, which means that export sales drop. This, of course, can mean more unemployment and/or lower wages for workers at home. The effects at home will depend on the proportion of sales that are export sales.

Since a rising dollar can ultimately result in lower sales at home, and the desire for sales is probably more important to satisfy than the desire to have currency respected, we should rate this inference as "?".

Step Three: evaluate the assumption. It is probably true that people want their currency respected by foreigners, since this is one facet of an overall desire to have one's country respected. We can rate A true.

Step Four: determine the extent to which intermediate conclusions are proved. There are none.

Step Five: determine the extent to which the final conclusion is proved. Given A rated "√" and the inference from A to B rated "?", we rate the overall argument as "?". B has been proved to some extent but not conclusively. The rated version looks like this:

Step Six: formulate a response to the arguer. We can respond by saying: "The people of this country probably do want their currency respected in other countries but this does not quite prove that it's good for the dollar to be rising. A rising dollar will mean a loss in export sales and if this is a big enough loss people will lose jobs."

EXAMPLE (b). The militant libertarian argues: "We want as much freedom of choice as possible, so it is unfortunate that a law has been passed to require the use of seat belts while driving."

Step One: construct an accurate diagrammatic version of the argument.

A = We want as much freedom of choice as possible.

B = It is unfortunate that a law has been passed to require the use of seat belts while driving.

Step Two: evaluate the inference. This is the negative variant of the main argument, so we first ask whether the seat belt legislation really does restrict freedom of choice. There seems no doubt that it does. Those who wish to be good citizens and obey the laws will feel compelled to obey this law.

The second test is whether or not there are other goals and desires in the society that are promoted by the legislation. The main one that comes to mind is the desire to prevent unnecessary injury and death. Lots of good studies show that seat belt use significantly reduces injuries and fatalities in accidents and this surely is more important than the small loss of overall freedom that is undesirable. We should probably rate the inference as "X" since most people probably view the loss of freedom as a very small sacrifice. For most it is the inconvenience that they might be unhappy with.

Step Three: evaluate the assumption. The libertarian is probably right about this as stated. How much freedom is possible, however, depends upon what other goods we seek in life that are incompatible with freedom of choice. Rate A true.

Step Four: determine the extent to which intermediate conclusions are proved. There are none.

Step Five: determine the extent to which the final conclusion is proved. With A rated "√" and the inference rated "X", we rate the argument as "X". The conclusion, B, has not been proved to an appreciable extent. The rated argument looks like this:

157

Step Six: formulate a response to the arguer. A suitable response is this: "Yes, we do want as much freedom of choice as possible, but this does not go very far towards proving that the seat belt legislation is a bad thing. We also want to prevent unnecessary injury and death in accidents and this is more important than the loss of freedom resulting from this legislation."

EXERCISE 5 - 18

Evaluate each of the following arguments. No. 1 is answered in the back.

1. "People want the unemployment insurance program to continue, so it is good that money was diverted from the defence budget to finance it."

2. "Students want to be able to earn lots of money during the summer, so it is just as well that the college year is short."

3. The use of the "social pass" (promoting students who fail to achieve a passing standard) has been accepted as a legitimate practice in high school for some years. It is supported by this argument: "Underachieving students want to develop their social skills at the same rate as others their own age. These skills will not develop at the same rate when they are in classes with students several years younger. Therefore, it is desirable to promote underachievers at the same rate as their more successful peers."

4. "Americans want as much personal freedom as possible in choosing what to own. Therefore, it is a good thing that the Second Amendment to the Constitution guarantees the right to own firearms."

5. "Men nowadays want to be married to women they love, so it is good that divorces are not difficult to get."

(5.94)   ARGUMENTS FOR EVALUATIVE CRITERIA

(1)   INTRODUCTION.   In trying to justify an evaluation of something we cite qualities relevant to that evaluative judgment or some want that will be satisfied. We also sometimes try to justify using the qualities we do in making judgments of an evaluative kind.   That is, we try to justify the criteria of evaluation that we rely on in judging particular things.   When two baseball fans cannot agree on who is the best hitter of all time it is probably because they are using different criteria for best hitter.   Until there is agreement on the relevant criteria and their relative importance it is easy to get different individuals selected.

The argument pattern to be discussed here tries to prove that a particular attribute of a kind of thing is a good-making attribute for it by citing the function that sort of thing serves. This pattern is obviously appropriate for dealing with artifacts, things created to serve human purposes.   But it is also appropriate for natural phenomena and even works of art. Thus, we might justify claiming that a good-making attribute of sunsets is vivid color, on the ground that the "function" of a sunset is to be visually impressive. We might argue that a good-making quality of a popular song is a good melody on the ground that one "function" a song can have is to be pleasing to the ear.

(2)   TYPICAL EXAMPLE. "One function of a lecture in a course is to help the student understand the reading material assigned. Therefore, a good-making attribute of a lecture is the discussion of the main points in the reading assignment."

(3)   BASIC LOGICAL FORM:

A function of X's is F.

Therefore, a good-making attribute of X's is G.

(4)   INFERENCE VALIDITY ANALYSIS.   Inference validity depends on two conditions being met.   First, G must contribute to function F.   If discussion of the main points in the reading assignment did not help the student understand the assignment then the inference in the example would be poor.

Secondly, G must be compatible with other functions of X's, at least if those functions are as important as F.   For instance, lectures have other functions such as generating interest in the material and allowing students an opportuntiy to ask questions not related to the assigment, so that using the whole class time for a recitation of the main points in the assignment would mean that this is somewhat dubious as a good-making attribute.   The practice conflicts with other functions that lectures have.

(5) INFERENCE CRITICISM STRATEGY. There are two strategies. The least usable is to try to show that G does not contribute to function F. Normally an arguer is sufficiently knowledgeable not to make this mistake.

The second strategy can be used more frequently. You can try to show that C is incompatible with other functions that X's serve. This involves bringing to mind the functions that X's have. Often, especially in the case of artifacts, a kind of thing will have one dominant function because it has been designed expressly to perform that function. A car, for instance, is designed to provide private ground transportation. It can also be an instrument of aesthetic pleasure by virtue of its driving qualities or its appearance, and there is nothing to stop a person from buying a particular car to serve one of these secondary purposes. Natural objects and natural phenomena are not subject to this primary-secondary function distinction since they are not intentionally designed. In such cases we assign functions, but there can be no intelligible talk of THE function.

(6) ASSUMPTION EVALUATION. In deciding whether F is a function of X's we need to keep in mind the distinction between designed and assigned functions. Artifacts have both kinds of functions. A primary designed function of cars is to provide transportation. A secondary designed function is to provide sensory gratification through appearance and/or performance. Artifacts can also have assigned functions, ones that people actually use them for, but which did not influence the designers. Cars are often used as bedrooms by poor people who are travelling around looking for work and this is clearly an assigned function.

A thing, whether natural or an artifact, can have a wide range of assigned functions and whether we want to accept that a thing has function F seems to be a matter of whether it is frequently used by people for function F.

(7) VARIANT VERSIONS. Sometimes people wish to include in their conclusions a rating of the importance of the good-making attribute they are talking about. They may claim it is "essential", or "important", or just "worthwhile". When it is said to be essential the assumption must state that F is the only function of X's or an essential function, if the inference is to be valid.

(8) EVALUATION OF EXAMPLES. Example (a): An argument many people would use in discussing the role of colleges: "Colleges are supposed to equip their students to be good citizens. Therefore, a good college attribute is the ability to indoctrinate

160

students into the central values of their society."

Step One: construct an accurate diagrammatic version of the argument.

A = Colleges are supposed to equip their students to be good citizens.

B = A good college attribute is the ability to indoctrinate students into the central values of their society.

Step Two: evaluate the inference. Would value indoctrination be a good way of equipping students to be good citizens? Indoctrination is a process of creating belief while ignoring what is to be said for rival points of view and the evidence against the belief one wishes to inculcate. That is, only evidence for the belief is mentioned. It is essentially non-critical in spirit. It is desirable for people to enter the working world with the value convictions the society holds but it is also important to know about alternative values which might be pursued because they are superior. No society is perfect and a critical attitude and broad-mindedness are important attributes if people are to improve the society they find themselves in. Thus, indoctrination equips us only for maintaining the "status quo", but part of being a good citizen is to be able to respond to the challenge to improve the society. Thus, it is dubious that indoctrination serves the function of contributing to good citizenship. Furthermore, it also conflicts with our ideal of what a university should be. That is, an institution in which free intellectual inquiry occurs. Indoctrination is not an example of free intellectual inquiry. Thus, we rate the inference "X".

Step Three: evaluate the assumption. If we consult prominent philosophers of education from Plato to the pesent we find that just about all agree that equipping students to be good citizens is one function of educational institutions. There is disagreement about some proposed functions, but there is general agreement that this is one legitimate function. We can rate the assumption A true.

Step Four: determine the extent to which intermediate conclusions are proved. There are none.

Step Five: determine the extent to which the final conclusion is proved. Given A rated "√" and the inference from A to B rated "X". we can rate the argument as "X". B is not proved to any appreciable degree. The rated argument is shown on the next page.

161

Step Six: formulate a response to the arguer. We can say: "Your conclusion does not follow. Indoctrination involves ignoring alternatives and objections to ones own position and results in naivety, and narrow mindedness, which interfere with being a good citizen. Furthermore, the indoctrination process is contrary to the university ideal of free rational enquiry which allows the university to function as a watch-dog of society."

EXAMPLE (b). An argument from the theory of politics: "The function of elected representatives is to represent the interests of those who elected them. Therefore, a good-making attribute of elected representatives is concentrating exclusively on promoting these interests."

Step One: construct an accurate diagrammatic version of the argument.

A = The function of elected representatives is to represent the interests of those who elected them.

B = A good-making attribute of elected representatives is concentrating exclusively on promoting those interests.

Step Two: evaluate the inference. Let us try the two strategies in succession. First, is concentrating exclusively on promoting the interests of those who elected them a contribution to representing those interests? Given that A says "THE function" is this, it seems that the answer is "yes". So the inference passes this test.

Secondly, does concentrating exclusively on promoting electors' interest interfere with other functions of elected representatives? This may be so, but is not relevant here since the arguer has begun from an assumption that denies the existence of such functions. If the assumption were true, there can be no other functions. The inference passes this test also, so we will rate it valid.

Step Three: evaluate the assumption. Is it THE function of elected representatives to represent the interests of those who elected them? If the word 'the' is meant to be equivalent to 'the only', as it seems to be, the assumption is false. First, representatives have a duty to represent all members of their constituencies, even those who voted for other candidates. Each person has a constitutional right to representation regardless of how he/she votes. Secondly, representatives normally have other functions such as considering the interests of the political unit as a whole. A U.S. Senator has a responsibility for ensuring that the Senate passes legislation that is good for the U.S. as a whole. This obligation to the whole sometimes conflicts, of course, with the obligation to the part he/she represents. We therefore rate the assumption A as "X".

Step Four: determine the extent to which intermediate conclusions are proved. There are none.

Step Five: determine the extent to which the final conclusion is proved. Given A rated "X" and the inference valid we rate the argument "X". The assumption cannot prove the conclusion (B) to any applicable extent because it is false. The rated argument looks like this:

Step Six: formulate a response to the arguer. A good response would be: "Representing the interests of those who elected them is not the only function of representatives. They also have to represent the constituents who voted for others. Also, they have a duty to ensure that the political unit of which their constituency is a part gets good legislation as a whole. Since your assumption is false it cannot prove your conclusion.

EXERCISE 5 - 19

Evaluate each of the following arguments. No. 1 is answered in the back.

1. "Novels are to provide entertainment, so a good novel must be humorous."

163

2. "Beaches are places for swimming, so a good beach has a good surf."

3. "Religions help us deal with life. Therefore, a good religion helps us to accept our circumstances in life."

4. "The legal system is designed to promote justice. Therefore, a good system punishes all who are guilty."

5. "The police are supposed to detect wrongdoing, so any police department worth its salt has lots of sophisticated electronic surveillance gear."

(5.10)   STATISTICAL   ARGUMENTS.   Two   types   of   statistical
arguments   will   be   discussed: those   making an inference from a
sample   to   a   whole population, and those proceeding in the other
direction.   Both of these patterns are commonly used.   There are,
of course, other patterns that can be reliable.

   (5.101) SAMPLE-TO-POPULATION ARGUMENTS.

   (1)   INTRODUCTION.   This pattern is used when we argue from
the   fact   that   a   proportion   of   a   sample   from   a   population
('population' here can refer to any collection of things, not just
to   human   populations) has a property, to the conclusion that the
same proportion of the entire population has that property.

   This   kind of statistical reasoning is very common in social
science.   Making   inferences from samples is a very efficient way
of getting information about very large populations of things.   It
is   impossible to canvass the opinion of every voter, for example,
on   whether   she/he   thinks the present government is doing a good
job.   But   by taking a judicious sample it is possible to reach a
fairly   accurate   judgment.   Statistical techniques thus enable us
to   make   reasonably   accurate   judgments   about   large populations
without   taking the time and expense to examine each member of the
population individually.

   (2)   TYPICAL   EXAMPLE.   The Cadillac owner says: "The five
traffic accidents I've seen this year involved eight cars and five
have been small cars.   Therefore, small cars are more likely to be
involved in accidents."

   (3)   BASIC LOGICAL FORM:

N% of sample x of population X has property P.

Therefore, N% of all X's have property P.

   (4)   INFERENCE   VALIDITY   ANALYSIS.   The   validity   of   a
statistical inference   from a sample (x) depends upon the sample
being   representative   of   the   entire   population   (X)   in   its
characteristics.   There   are   two   ways   of   attempting   to   get
representativeness.   One is to pick a sample in a random way,
using   a   method   of   selection   that has no bearing on whether an
individual   has   or   has   not   the   property   (P)   the   sampler is
interested in.   However,   even if the sample selection procedure
does   not systematically bias the sample it is still possible that
the   sample   will not be representative.   The sampler might simply
be unlucky, just as the gambler may be unlucky.   There is a pretty
good chance that four tosses of a fair coin will yield tails three
times, a 75% proportion, but we can be confident that after 100
tosses the proportion will be much closer to 50%.   In general, the

165

larger the random sample that we examine the more likely it will be representative. How large is large enough? No precise figure can be stated, but proportions between 10% and 30% are often regarded as acceptable.

Besides bad luck, the other problem for sampling is the built-in bias. This occurs when the selection procedure makes it more likely (or less likely) that the sample (x) has the property (P) we are interested in. The biases that can be built into sampling procedures can be difficult to uncover, as those who have used sampling are only too well aware. A classic example was provided by a poll taken by the now-defunct U.S. magazine, the LITERARY DIGEST. In 1936 the magazine used a poll to predict the outcome of the presidential election (Roosevelt vs Landon). They contacted a large number of people by picking names at random out of phone books across the U.S. and asked them which candidate they preferred. They favored Landon, the Republican, by about two-to-one. The sample was large, the magazine was confident, and Roosevelt won!

Where was the bias in the sample? Well, in 1936 the Depression was just coming to an end and so only relatively prosperous people could afford phones. How is this relevant? It turns out that the likelihood that Americans vote Republican is greater for people with higher incomes. So the sample included, because of economic circumstances, a disproportionate number of Republicans. The poorer people, who were more disposed to vote for Roosevelt, were under-represented in their sample. Even if the magazine had canvassed twice as many voters, their selection criterion would have kept them from reaching the right conclusion because it introduced a bias.

To eliminate the sample distortion that can arise from built-in biases, the method of stratified random sampling has been developed. In trying to determine the incidence of a property in a population (X) by studying a sample (x), the sampler tries to identify all of the properties that members of the population have which might influence whether they have the property (P) the sampler is interested in. Not all of the members of the population will have all of these influencing properties so the trick is to get a sample with each of them represented in the same proportion in which they occur in the population. Using the method, the sampler gets a miniature version of the population he/she is interested in.

This is the method the professional pollsters often use because it is possible to work from a relatively small sample. In fact, professional pollsters are able to get good reliability on ascertaining political views using samples of one-thousandth of one per ccent of voting population. A stratified sample is one which is intentionally selected to reflect the characteristics of the whole population. If pollsters want a stratified sample of voters they will ensure that men and women are about equally represented, retired persons will be present in the same proportion that they occur in the voting population, etc. It is more expensive to identify a stratified sample but the cost is offset by the savings in polling costs to be had because a much smaller sample can be used.

Validity of inference, then, depends upon obtaining a representative sample. Representativeness can be ensured by using a fairly large (10% to 30%) sample, the members of which are chosen randomly, or by using stratified sampling which involves getting a cross-section of the population based on factors that might influence whether or not individuals had the property of interest.

(5) INFERENCE CRITICISM STRATEGY. The first step in evaluating the inference is to make sure you have correctly identified the population the conclusion is about. Take the reference to it as broadly as the language entitles you. In the example, take it to be the class of all cars involved in accidents.

There are two sorts of weaknesses that inferences of this type can have. Our example embodies one, the likelihood of sample unrepresentativeness arising from a too-small sample. Each of us only sees a very small proportion of the traffic accidents that occur and it may be that it just happened that the Cadillac owner saw ones involving more small cars. The next five accidents he sees might involve more big cars (perhaps even his own!). Try to show that this weakness is present by finding out the size of the sample relative to the whole population. In the example the conclusion makes a universal claim, so the population will consist of all car accidents for at least the past year. Obviously with this population the sample will be far too small.

The second weakness that sample-to-population inferences can have is unrepresentativeness of sample arising from sample selection bias. Try to establish that an argument has this weakness by identifying the factor that biases the sample. This might not be easy to do but there are certain steps that are useful to take. First, be clear about what the membership of the population is. Secondly, try to think of at least one attribute that is common to the sample members but not common to all the population and that might influence whether or not the members of the sample have the property P being attributed to the population in the conclusion.

In the example, perhaps we would find that all the accidents

167

in the sample occurred in a neighbourhood in which people own a high proportion of small cars, relative to the entire country.

(6) ASSUMPTION EVALUATION. Confirming or disconfirming is simply a matter of checking on the sample.

(7) VARIANT VERSIONS. None.

(8) EVALUATION OF EXAMPLES. Example (a): Your country cousin Virgil doesn't like using seat belts while driving. He studies the accidents that have occurred in his area and confronts you with this argument: "There have been ten fatalities in accidents in this county in the last five years. Half the victims were wearing seat belts and half were not, so you're just as likely to die with your belt on as with it off."

Step one: construct an accurate diagrammatic version of the argument.

A = There have been ten fatalities in accidents in this county in the last five years.

B = Half of the ten accident victims were wearing seat belts and half were not.

C = A person is just as likely to die with their belt on as with it off.

Step Two: evaluate the inference. Is there some factor that might make Virgil's sample unrepresentative of all accidents? Note that his sample membership comes from the county he lives in, and we are led to believe that this is a rural area. Could this have a bearing on the percentage of fatalities in the sample? Definitely. In rural areas cars travel faster, so that when a crash occurs the forces generated are much greater than in ones occurring in urban areas where speeds are lower. Perhaps the accidents in Virgil's sample are cases of cars meeting head-on, or hitting trees or other immovable objects. In these situations seat belts cannot help because of the very high impact levels. But at lower speeds they can and do, and since most accidents occur in urban areas, seat belts can save lives. Their main benefit seems to be that they keep people in the car so that they are not thrown out. This frequently is fatal since head injuries are likely.

The inference in Virgil's argument, therefore, is defective because the sample is not representative. It seems to include only accidents at highway speeds. Seat belts can make a better showing overall because most accidents occur in urban areas with lower speeds. A rating of "X" seems appropriate.

Step Three: evaluate the assumptions. Since we have no way to check on A and B we will accept them as true.

Step Four: determine the extent to which intermediate conclusions are proved. There are none in this argument.

Step Five: determine the extent to which the final conclusion has been proved. Given the ratings of the inference and the assumptions we should rate the argument "X". The rated diagrammatic version looks like this:

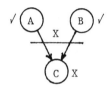

Step Six: formulate a response to the arguer. A good response to Virgil would be: "Even if you are correct about your statistics, your sample is not representative. Most accidents happen in urban areas where speeds are lower than they are out your way. Seat belts are much more effective at city traffic speeds. A sample of accidents occuring in urban areas would probably tell a different story, so your statistics do not go far to proving your conclusion."

EXAMPLE (b): Professors commonly select issues for their students to study that they themselves found interesting and challenging as students. The philosophy professor reasons: "When I was a student I found arguments for God's existence to be interesting, so my students will find them interesting also."

Step One: construct an accurate diagrammatic version of the argument.

A = As a student I found arguments
for God's existence to be interesting.

B = My students will find these arguments
interesting also.

Step Two: evaluate the inference. The argument here might be regarded as a special sub-species of arguments from sample to population. The sample is the professor himself. The population is his philosophy class, including himself. Clearly, the sample size is very small, which entitles us to consider the inference dubious to begin with. Furthermore, the sample may have characteristics not shared by the rest of the population, and which may affect the characteristic being attributed, i.e. an interest in arguments for the existence of God. For instance, the professor may have had a special interest in the intellectual issues of religion that his students do not share. They may think the arguments a waste of time because religion for them is a matter of feeling. Or perhaps they have no intellectual inclinations at all, and wish to consider only issues with a practical payoff such as issues in applied ethics.

Given the fact that the sample is small and the likelihood that the individual comprising the sample is not representative of the whole class we should rate the inference as "X".

Step Three: evaluate the assumption. We can probably accept A as true, although when dealing with autobiographical claims people sometimes have an inaccurate memory of situations. In particular, most of us are inclined to recall selectively, remembering the good and forgetting the bad. This may make life more enjoyable when we "travel down memory lane", but it also means that other people may be more correct about what we experienced than we are.

Step Four: determine the extent to which intermediate conclusions are proved. There are none here.

Step Five: determine the extent to which the final conclusion is proved. Given the rating for A and for the inference from A to B, we judge the argument to not have proved its conclusion to any significant extent. We place an "X" by B. The rated version looks like this:

Step Six: formulate a response to the arguer. We could respond like this: "Your assumption may be true but it does not go very far toward proving that your students will find these arguments interesting. For one thing, your sample (i.e.,yourself) is too small to be reliable in reaching conclusions about a whole class. For another, when you were a student you were probably much more intellectual than the typical student and you probably found philosophical issues more interesting anyway since you chose to become a philosophy professor."

EXERCISE 5 - 20

Each of the following arguments makes an inference about a population from a fact about a sample from it. Complete steps one and two for each. Number 2 and 4 are answered in the back.

1. "The more successful students say they enjoy this course, therefore, the class finds this an enjoyable course."

2. "Recent tests showed football quarterbacks to have above-average intelligence so football players aren't dumb like some people thought."

3. "In a test in which people had to choose which one of three TV's had the best picture, 70% preferred Clairphone's picture. So if you want the set with the picture most people prefer get a Clairphone."

4. Politican on the campaign trail: "Nearly every one at the rally is behind me so it looks like I'll be elected."

5. "There are more left-handed baseball pitchers now so there must be more left-handed people around."

171

(5.102)   POPULATION-TO-SAMPLE ARGUMENTS

(1)   INTRODUCTION.   Arguments of this kind identify an individual or group as a part of a class of things and from this it is inferred that that individual (or group) has a property associated with members of that class.

(2)   TYPICAL EXAMPLE: "Myrtle is a physics major. Therefore, Myrtle is bright."

(3)   LOGICAL FORM:

x is a member of the class X.

Therefore, x has property P.

(4)   INFERENCE VALIDITY ANALYSIS.   Inference quality depends upon how universal the property P is among the members of class X. If all of them have it then x has it too, so the inference is 100% valid. (When the premise 'All X's are P' is added to the argument it becomes a valid syllogism, syllogisms will be discussed in Chapter Six.) When fewer than 100% of X's are P the inference in our argument has a lesser degree of validity. For example, if it turns out that the best we can say is that most physics majors are bright we can only take the assertion that Myrtle is a physics major to be good, but not decisive grounds for saying that she is bright. If only a minority of physics majors are bright then Myrtle's status as a physics major is only fair evidence for her being bright. To ensure validity in arguments of this kind, the conclusion must contain an appropriate "hedging term" when not all members of the class X have the property P. For example, if two-thirds do then the word 'probably' should appear in the conclusion.

(5)   INFERENCE CRITICISM STRATEGY.   Try to show that the proportion of X's that have property P is considerably less than 100%. This will require statistical data. Citing a few examples will not be enough to convince the arguer that the percentage is low enough to make it distinctly possible for the conclusion to be false even if the premise is true.

Inference quality is pretty much proportional to the percentages of X's that are P. Thus, in the example, if you can show by administering an I.Q. test to an adequate sample of physics majors that only half of them scored in the "bright" category, you could infer that only about half of all physics majors are bright. And this is grounds for rating the inference "?", since "?" is used to designate inference quality of this level.

(6)   ASSUMPTION EVALUATION.   No special considerations are

172

involved.

(7) VARIANT VERSIONS. Cautious arguers will usually use a "hedge word" in the conclusion when only a proportion of x's are believed to have property P. In criticising the inference try to show that the hedge words used are not appropriate to the proportion. For example, if the arguer says "Myrtle is a physics major, so Myrtle is very likely bright", you could argue that this does not follow because only half of all physics majors are bright (supposing this is true).

(8) EVALUATION OF EXAMPLE: We see a very tall student walk past and I say: "He is very tall so he is a good basketball player."

Step One: construct an accurate diagrammatic version of the argument.

A = He is very tall.

B = He is a good basketball player.

Step Two: evaluate the inference. If you only have personal impressions to rely on, to the effect that most of the tall male students are good basketball players, and the knowledge that there are a lot of foreign students on campus, you could note that the assumption is fairly good evidence for my conclusion but not conclusive. The student might not be a good basketball player because he never had the opportunity to learn or because he doesn't care to play or because he is not well-coordinated. You can rate the inference "?".

Step Three: evaluate the assumption. Rate A as true, assuming I have correctly described the student's height.

Step Four: determine the extent to which intermediate conclusions are proved. There are none.

Step Five: determine the extent to which the final conclusion is proved. Given that A is rated "√" and the inference is rated "?", we can rate the argument overall as "?". The rated version is shown below.

Step Six: formulate a response to the arguer. You can say to me: "Yes, he is very tall, but that doesn't prove conclusively that he is a good basketball player. He may be a foreigner who never had a chance to learn, or he may not have played much because he doesn't enjoy it, or he may not have good coordination."

EXERCISE 5 - 21

Each of the following arguments make an inference about the individual from a generalization about a population to which that individual belongs. Complete steps one and two for each. Numbers 2 and 4 are answered in the back.

1. "Science majors study long hours. Ken is a science major. Therefore, he studies long hours."

2. "The army is notoriously inefficient. Therefore, we cannot expect Major Jones to do a good job."

3. "The mechanics in this garage have 100 years experience among them, so the guy working on my car really knows what he's doing."

4. "All weapons are prohibited in the Park. Therefore, you must not take your bow and arrow into the Park."

CHAPTER SIX: STRUCTURAL VALIDITY

(6.1) INTRODUCTION: Evidential validity is so-called because the premises of arguments that have it represent, individually, evidence for believing the conclusion. It is a matter of degree--the more evidence for the conclusion the greater the degree of validity. Structural validity contrasts with evidential validity in several ways. As the name implies, validity depends on logical structure, the way elements in the argument relate to one another within assertions and to other assertions. Logical relationships rather than content determine validity of inferences.

In this chapter two sorts of arguments relying on two different sorts of logical relationships will be studied. First, arguments that have validity arising from relationships among the simple propositions contained within the assumptions and conclusions will be studied. This topic is called propositional logic. Secondly, arguments that derive validity from relationships between classes of things mentioned in the assertions will be examined. This topic is syllogistic logic.

To illustrate how structural validity can arise we can examine arguments relying on each of the two kinds of logical relationships. Consider the propositional argument "Either she's a model or she's an actress. She's not an actress, so she's a model." For convenience let's substitute the letter 'A' for 'she's a model', and 'B' for 'she's an actress' so that we can see the structure of the argument more clearly. In its semi-symbolic form the argument looks like this: "Either A or B. Not B, so A".

Clearly, the conclusion of the argument cannot help but be true if the premises are true. We have two possibilities mentioned in one pemise, one is eliminated by the second, and we are left with the other. We can say that it is IMPOSSIBLE FOR THE CONCLUSION TO BE FALSE WHEN THE PREMISES ARE TRUE IN A STRUCTURALLY VALID ARGUMENT. For suppose, in the example, that A is false and that the second premise (not-B) is true. This means B is false. With both A and B false the first premise is false. Suppose instead that the conclusion is false and the first premise is true. For this situation with A false and the first premise true, B itself must be true. But this means that the second premise can't be true. So by assuming the conclusion is false we can only get one premise or the other true, but not both. That is, it is impossible to get both the premises true at the same time that the conclusion is false.

Note that the situation arises for any argument that can be written as "Either A or B. Not B, so A." The reasoning we just went through really didn't involve any discussion of models and actresses. Whatever propositions 'A' and 'B' stand for, it will be impossible to have the assumptions true and the conclusion false. This is why inference validity in propositional logic is independent of propositional content.

Now let's look at an example from syllogistic logic. Syllogisms refer to three classes of things in three assertions. Here is an example: "All sciolists are antinomians. All antinomians are atavistic. Therefore, all sciolists are atavistic." Even if you are unsure what the three classes of things are you may be prepared to believe that the inference in the argument is valid because of the word 'all' and the locations of the different class terms. The argument can be symbolized like this: "All X's are Y's. All Y's are Z's. Therefore, all X's are Z's." Validity can be established using the same approach applied to the previous example.

Suppose that not all X's are Z's, i.e. that some X's aren't Z's. Suppose also that all X's are Y's. This would mean that some Y's are not Z's (= not all Y's are Z's) and if this were true the second assumption could not be true. Thus, with the conclusion false and the first assumption true, the second assumption cannot be true.

Again, suppose the conclusion is false (= some X's aren't Z's) and the second assumption is true (all Y's are Z's). This would entail that some X's are not Y's, but would mean the first assumption could not be true. Thus, with the conclusion false and the second assumption true, the first assumption is false. As in the case of the previous argument, it is impossible to have true assumptions and a false conclusion simultaneously. Thus, the inference is structurally valid, in this case by virtue of the way the class symbols 'X', 'Y', and 'Z' relate to one another. Again, as for the other argument, it does not matter what the symbols actually stand for. This is only relevant when we have to decide whether assumptions are true or not.

These examples illustrate two points about structural validity. First, it is not a matter of degree. An inference will be rated either "√" or "X", never "?". Secondly, since content plays no part in securing validity, all arguments that share the structure of a valid argument will also have valid inferences by the same test. (This does not mean, of course, that an argument will prove its conclusion when it has the same structure as one that does. Assumption truth is required and this is a function of content.)

Let us now move to a discussion of arguments that can be cast in propositional logic and have the potential for structural validity.

(6.2) STRUCTURAL VALIDITY (PROPOSITIONAL): In this section we will see the development of an effective and reasonably simple means of testing the inferences of arguments cast in propositional logic form. Among other things this involves the presentation of a simple symbolic language.

(6.21) THE COUNTER-EXAMPLE TEST FOR VALIDITY. If an argument of a particular logical form or structure is structurally valid, any argument with the same form is also valid. The semi-symbolic version of the example given above is "Either A or B. Not B, so A." Here is another argument with the same form: "Either it will snow or it will rain. It will not rain, so it will snow." Since it has the same logical form we can say that it too is structurally valid.

There is implied here a way of testing arguments for structural validity. Given an argument whose validity or invalidity is not evident, we can reach a decision by trying to invent an argument that has the same form but which has clearly true premises and a clearly false conclusion. Just as all arguments of a given form are valid if one instance is, all arguments of a given form are invalid if one instance is.

Suppose someone argues: "Either Farrah is a model or she's an actress. She's an actress, so she's not a model." The semi-symbolic version of this can be written "Either A or B. B, so not A". Is it valid? To find out we will try to construct another argument having the same form but which has true premises and false conclusion. Here is one attempt.

"Either George Washington was the first U.S. President or he was a general. Washington was a general, so he was not the first U.S. President."

The semi-symbolic version is "Either A or B. B, so not A." This argument has the same structure as the previous one. Is it valid? Clearly not. The first premise is true because a proposition of this form is true when at least one of its parts is true. The second premise (Washington was a general) is also true. The conclusion, however, is clearly false. Thus the inference in the argument must be invalid since in a valid argument the conclusion must be true if the premises are. Now since structural validity is a formal property shared by all arguments of the same form, it will also be true that two arguments of the same form are both invalid if one is. Therefore, the original argument about Farrah is not structurally valid. This can be confirmed to some extent by asking if the truth of the premises guarantees the truth of the conclusion. In this case they don't. Even though Farrah is an actress she might be a model too.

The examples presented illustrate one way of settling the

question of structural validity. In principle, this method can be used to test any argument but it has two serious drawbacks. First, its use can require considerable imagination in the construction of arguments having a common structure but with true premises and false conclusion. Secondly, and more seriously, failure to find such an argument need not show that our argument is valid. It might show merely that we weren't clever enough and imaginative enough to discover a suitable argument.

(6.22) AN IMPROVED TEST FOR VALIDITY. Fortunately, there is a better way of testing inference forms that is based on the method we have been discussing. In the example discussed we produced an argument having true premises and a false conclusion, and which shared the logical form of the other argument. This involved constructing an argument whose two simple propositions were true. Some other combination of truth values might have been required to show the form invalid, and would be for arguments having a different form. Our procedure has essentially been one of finding two simple propositions having truth values such that, when combined in the form of the original argument, they result in an argument that has true premises and false conclusion.

Now, if we assume that it is always theoretically possible to find simple propositions with truth values which would make the argument formed from them invalid, (when the form is invalid) then we need not actually go to the trouble of finding particular simple propositions that would yield the desired result.

We can apply this approach to the example about Farrah which was written semi-symbolically as "Either A or B. B, so not A". Rather than look for particular propositions that 'A' and 'B' could stand for, and which would yield an argument with true premises and a false conclusion, all we need to do is to see if there is a truth value for 'A' and one for 'B' that will yield this. To get the conclusion (not-A) false, A must be true. Also, the second premise (B) must be true. With A and B both true the first premise will be true. Thus, we know that the argument is invalid because any argument of this form that has A and B true will have true premises and a false conclusion. Of course we are assuming that at least one such argument can be found, but it should be obvious that this is a totally safe assumption since it is possible to have an indefinite number of arguments of any particular form and some of these will inevitably have both of their simple propositions true.

The foregoing procedure really just amounts to attempting to show an argument form is invalid by assigning truth values to the various letters that could stand for simple propositions. The surest way to do this is to test the argument form for every combination of truth values that the simple propositions can have. This is the basis of the so-called truth-table method of testing

178

that will eventually be presented.

(6.23) A SYMBOLIC LANGUAGE. The Truth Table method has been designed to operate using a fully symbolic language. Basically, this language simply enables us to replace the English words with symbols in semi-symbolic versions of arguments. Surprisingly, we can have a very complete symbolic language using only four special symbols, plus capital letters that stand for simple propositions, and parentheses (their use will be described shortly). The reason that this simple symbolic language can be adequate is that there actually are few logical concepts in English and most natural languages. These get expressed in a variety of ways, however, and this means that a particular logical relation can be expressed in several (or even many) ways. In the symbolic language of propositional logic, we substitute a single symbol for a variety of different English expressions so that only a few logical symbols are needed for testing all argument forms that can be symbolized by linking simple propositions.

Now let's see what symbols are needed in the language, besides capital letters and parentheses. It was noted earlier that only arguments containing logically compound propositions can have the property of structural validity (of course not all of them do). There are two kinds of logical compounds that we want to represent: conditionals (if ... then, ... only if ..., etc.) and alternations (either ... or ..., ... or ..., etc.). It is also necessary to have a symbol for negation so that we can distinguish, for example, 'She's an actress' from 'She's NOT an actress' without having to assign a different letter to each, since one asserts and the other denies the same state of affairs. We will also need a symbol for conjunction (and, but, etc.).

The symbols to be used, besides capital letters and parentheses are these:

negation	: ∿	∿ X = not X
conjunction	: •	X • Y = X and Y
alternation	: v	X v Y = X or Y
conditional	: ⊃	X ⊃ Y = If X then Y

Each of the above symbols represents a logical concept that is used in reasoning in everyday life and on the basis of the English synonyms for each we can construct a definition for it in terms of its truth properties. That is, we can construct a truth table showing the truth value of a complex proposition created by using it (except in the case of ' ∿ ') to connect two simple propositions, for all the truth value combinations these simple propositions can form.

NEGATION (∿): This symbol is the simplest in its logical

179

behavior. It simply indicates that, whatever the truth value of a proposition, placing the '∿' in front of it yields a proposition with the opposite truth value. Using the letters 'T' and 'F' for 'true' and 'false' respectively we can construct a table to show what happens to '∿X' for the different values of 'X':

X	∿ X
T	F
F	T

You should realize that here, and in the following truth table definitions, the values in the table would remain the same if both occurrences of 'X' were replaced with a complex proposition. For example, supposing we had 'B v C' instead of 'X' and ' ∿ (B v C)' instead of '∿ X', the truth values in the table would remain unchanged.

Of special interest is that the '∿' symbol follows the rule of "two negatives make an affirmative". If we made a column in the truth table for ' ∿ ∿ X' it would have the opposite truth values to ' ∿ X'. That is, its values would be the same as for 'X', so we can say it is logically equivalent to 'X'. This is normally the way negation behaves in English. The proposition 'It is false that she is not an actress', which we would symbolize as '∿ ∿ A' is logically equivalent to 'A', or 'She is an actress'.

CONJUNCTION (•). Someone asserting something of the form 'X and Y' is committed to saying X is true and Y is true. Thus, if we are to assign truth values to 'X • Y' we will want to say it is true only when X and Y are each individually true. Thus, for other truth value combinations of 'X' and 'Y' we will say 'X • Y' is false. Since altogether there are four truth value combinations the truth definition for '•' will be this:

X	Y	X • Y
T	T	T
T	F	F
F	T	F
F	F	F

Commonly in English and many other languages we utter conjunctions that ascribe two properties to a single subject while mentioning the subject only once. For example: "She's a model and an actress", is just a more concise way of saying "She's a model and she's an actress." You should be aware that two distinguishable assertions are being made in these cases because normally different evidence is relevant to whether each property applies to the particular subject.

ALTERNATIONS ('Either X or Y' = 'X v Y'): This form is used when we want to state alternatives. Characteristically, we do this when we are referring to alternatives (even our own) that are a matter of a choice ("Either I will go to the movies or I will go to the play"), or when we want to make an assertion about how things are and we aren't quite sure which of several states of affairs exists ("Either she's an actress or she's a model"). Alternations can state any number of alternatives theoretically. They are logically-compound assertions, which means the propositions within them cannot be thought of as being asserted individually. If I assert something of the form 'X or Y' I am not committed to claiming X is true, I am only committed to claiming that one of the two is true.

To criticize an alternation effectively you must show that none of the alternatives stated is true. If two people at a party notice the arrival of an especially glamorous woman and one says "Either she's an actress or she's a model", the other could refute this by showing that she has never done any acting and that she has never done any modelling. Thus, the alternation is false when both alternatives are false. On the other hand, if either one was true then the whole assertion itself is said to be true. If you say "She is an actress or she is a model" and it turns out she is an actress but not a model your assertion will not be attacked. Indeed someone might say "You are right. She's an actress."

What about when both propositions turn out to be true? We certainly would not want to say you were wrong and if only one proposition needs to be true to make the compound one true we will want to say that 'X v Y' is true when both are true. The truth table definition will therefore be this:

A	B	A v B
T	T	T
T	F	T
F	T	T
F	F	F

181

The concept of 'or' just described is, unfortunately, only one of two that are used in everyday language. This one can be called the "inclusive 'or'", in contrast with the other one which is called the "exclusive 'or'". The truth table for the exclusive 'or' differs from the other one in that when both alternatives are true the compound assertion is FALSE. For the exclusive 'or' the truth of one alternative excludes the truth of the other so that when both are true 'X or Y' cannot be true. Here is an example: "Either the earth is a sphere or it is a cube." Obviously both alternatives cannot be true at the same time. If one is true then the other is false, although theoretically both could be false in which case the whole assertion would be false. Now if someone says "Either the earth rotates or it goes around the sun" and THEY regard the 'or' as an exclusive 'or' we will want to say that their assertion is false. Since both alternatives are in fact true it is false that the truth of either one excludes the truth of the other.

The exclusive 'or' could be given a symbol of its own but we will not use one because an assertion containing an exclusive 'or' can be translated as '$(X \vee Y) \cdot \sim (X \cdot Y)$'. This symbolic sentence means 'Either X or Y and not both X and Y', which conveys the meaning of exclusive 'or' correctly using symbols we already have.

CONDITIONALS ('If X then Y'): It will be convenient to be able to refer to the propositions within a conditional separately so we will say that in 'If X then Y', 'X' is the ANTECEDENT and 'Y' the CONSEQUENT.

The most logically important thing about conditionals is that the truth value of the conditional itself is independent (in all but one case) of the truth values of its constituent propositions. This is somewhat analogous to the way in which the properties of water, a fluid, are quite different from the properties of the gases (oxygen and hydrogen) that are chemically combined to produce it. The truth value behavior of the logical "molecule" is radically different from that of its separate logical "elements", the antecedent and consequent. Specifically, assertions of the form 'If X then Y' do not commit the assertor to saying that X is true and that Y is true. Thus, conditionals are logically compound assertions. For example, if a baseball fan, waiting for a game to start, says "If the umpire thinks it's too wet then the game will be postponed", he/she is not asserting that the umpire thinks it's too wet, nor is he/she asserting that the game will be postponed. If both of these were being asserted then the conditional would be logically equivalent to 'A and B'. But the fact is that a true conditional can contain two false propositions. In the example, the conditional assertion remains true even though, on this occasion, the umpire doesn't think it is too wet and the game will not be postponed. On the other hand, 'A and B' would be false on such an occasion.

Another proof that 'If X then Y' is not logically like 'X and Y' is this: a conditional can be false when its antecedent and consequent are both true. Here is an example: "If New York is more than 10 miles from Boston then New York is more than 12 miles from Boston". Here the antecedent is true and so is the consequent but the conditional itself is false because the truth of the antecedent does not guarantee the truth of the consequent. There is the possibility, not excluded by the truth of the antecedent, that New York is between 10 and 12 miles from Boston. We know this isn't so but the antecedent does not guarantee that it isn't, and that is what counts here.

Think of conditionals as assertions of guarantees. The truth of the antecedent is being said to guarantee the truth of the consequent although the antecedent is not itself being claimed as true. A common source of fallacious reasoning is to treat conditionals as biconditionals, regarding 'X ⊃ Y' as saying that 'if X then Y and if Y then X'. However, this is incorrect as an example will show.

The conditional "If Boston is more than 100 miles from New York then Boston is more than 10 miles from New York" can be written semi-symbolically as "If A then B". This conditional is true because the truth of A guarantees the truth of B. But obviously the truth of B does not guarantee the truth of A since Boston might be 50 miles from New York for all that we can tell given only that it is more than 10 miles from it. This example functions like all true conditionals. The truth of the consequent does not guarantee the truth of the antecedent. The truth guarantee is a one-way guarantee, we might say. Therefore, do not think of 'X Y' as also saying 'Y ⊃ X.'

There is, however, a guarantee from consequent to antecedent in true conditionals. It is a falsehood guarantee to the effect that if 'X ⊃ Y' is true, the falsity of 'Y' guarantees the falsity of 'X'. In the example just discussed, if Boston was not more than 10 miles from New York then Boston would not be more than 100 miles from New York.

Conditionals explicitly assert truth guarantees. The assertion of such a truth guarantee requires that, when 'X ⊃ Y' is true we cannot have X true and Y false. This means that in the truth table definition 'X ⊃ Y' must be false when X is true and Y is false. However, it is possible for 'X ⊃ Y' to be true for each of the other three truth value combinations for X and Y. Unfortunately it is also possible to have conditionals that are false for each of these other three combinations, so that we cannot say for sure what truth value a conditional has unless we

183

know its antecedent is true and its consequent is false. It is the content of the two propositions that determines the truth value of the conditional itself.

Nevertheless, it is important to assign a value (T or F) to make use of the test procedure to be presented. Accordingly, we adopt this as the truth table definition of 'X ⊃ Y':

X	Y	X ⊃ Y
T	T	T
T	F	F
F	T	T
F	F	T

The general idea of the procedure is to assign values to letters that yield true premises and a false conclusion. It turns out that we need to allow for conditionals being true when they are premises for the three combinations of X and Y shown on lines 1, 3, and 4. And since it is in fact possible to get true ones for these combinations that is all we need to make the procedure work.

PARENTHESES. The Truth Table definitions for the logical connectives have now been given, but there is one more "symbol" needed in our symbolic language and this is a set of parentheses. Parentheses take the place of commas and certain words that are used in natural languages to eliminate syntactical ambiguity (ambiguity arising from the way in which words are arranged in sentences).

The need for parentheses can be shown by attempting to symbolize this sentence: 'She is rich and either she is an actress or she is a model.' We might immediately write 'A • B v C' as a symbolization, but this is logically ambiguous. When we have a mixture of logical connectives in a sentence in English one of them is always the main connective, with the others being grouped together. In the example above, the word 'either' tells us that the two propositions following it are grouped together, so that the 'and' is the main connective. However, the symbolic version offers us no clue as to which connective is the main one. It could be translated back in at least two different ways:

(1) Either she is rich and she is an actress or she is a model.

(2) She is rich and either she is an actress or she is a

184

model.

The second one is the same as the original but the first is different from it. If someone uttered (1) he/she would be held to have said something true if the girl is a model but not rich and not an actress. That is how 'either ... or ...' assertions work. For (2) to be a true assertion when the girl is a model it would ALSO have to be true that she is rich, because BOTH propositions in a conjunction must be true for the whole to be true.

Translations (1) and (2) from 'A • B v C' do not mean the same thing, then, since their truth conditions are different. IF A SYMBOLIC SENTENCE IS TO BE A CORRECT TRANSLATION OF AN ENGLISH ONE IT MUST, WHEN TRANSLATED BACK, GIVE ONE THAT MEANS THE SAME AS THE ORIGINAL ENGLISH ONE. If it allows two different ones the symbolic sentence is ambiguous and therefore unsuitable.

To eliminate ambiguities we must introduce parentheses into our language. They enable us to reproduce in the symbolic sentence the grouping of simple propositions that exist in complex English sentences. Thus we write the example as 'A • (B v C)'. In this case the parentheses tell us that ' • ' is the main connective, which is the correct state of affairs. In dealing with very complex sentences we use as many sets of parentheses as we need.

(6.24) TRANSLATING INTO THE SYMBOLIC LANGUAGE. To make use of the method developed for validity testing we must translate the English (or other) version of the argument into the fully symbolic form. The first point about translating is that each symbol for a logical connective has a variety of English equivalents. In Chapter Eight you will become acquainted with these and with other matters that make translation difficult sometimes. In this chapter the arguments you will be asked to translate are worded using a single expression for each connective.

To be sure of getting the correct symbolic version of an argument you should first write it in a semi-symbolic form. This is done by simply assigning the letters A, B, C, etc. to the simple propositions and rewriting the argument with the letters replacing the simple propositions. Retain all punctuation because punctuation often serves to make sentences unambiguous. Given a semi-symbolic version of a sentence you can usually rely on it to show you where parentheses should go. You add the parentheses, then rewrite the sentence replacing the English version of the logical symbols with our symbolic ones. Here is an example for translation:

"If water boils then its temperature is 212 degrees Fahrenheit and the vapor presssure is less than 29.92 inches of mercury."

185

Step 1.: we write a semi-symbolic version, letting 'A' stand for 'water boils', 'B' for 'its temperature is 212 degrees Fahrenheit', and 'C' for 'the vapor pressure is less than 29.92 inches of mercury':

"If A then B and C."

Step 2: we superimpose on this version the parentheses needed to give the correct meaning. In most logically complex sentences there is a main connective at which point the sentence is split by putting pairs of parentheses around the right and left parts. In English a sentence that begins with an 'if' will normally represent a conditional so that the sentence will be split into antededent and consequent. In the example being discussed, the word 'then', which splits the antecedent and consequent, is the main connective point so that we want parentheses thus:

"If (A) then (B and C)."

It is not necessary to put parentheses around 'A' here since there is no possibility of ambiguity with only one simple proposition as the antecedent, so we can symbolize the sentence like this:

"A ⊃ (B · C)"

Two more examples will further illustrate the procedure and also serve to warn of a common error.

Suppose we have the sentence:

"It is not true that if Virgil absconds then Elvis will be arrested."

Step 1: we let 'A' stand for 'Virgil absconds' and 'B' for 'Elvis will be arrested,' and write this semi-symbolic version:

"It is not true that if A then B."

Step 2: we decide where to put the parentheses, and put them in the semi-symbolic version. Here the 'it is not true that' indicates that the whole conditional is being denied, because 'if' comes after it. So we have:

"It is not true that (if A then B)."

Step 3: we replace the English expressions with symbols, leaving:

" ∿(A ⊃ B)"

186

The next example looks like the last one in some ways:

"If it is not true that Virgil absconds then Elvis will be arrested."

Step 1: using the same letter assignment we get this semi-symbolic version:

"If it not true that A then B."

Step 2: notice that, unlike the previous sentence, the 'if' occurs before 'it is not true that'. This indicates that the denial applies to the 'A', not to the entire conditional, so we have this situation:

"If (it is not true that A) then B."

Step 3: we write the final version:

"($\sim$ A) ⊃ B"

Following this procedure should help you get accurate symbolic translations of English sentences. Having mastered this skill we will apply it to arguments, which after all are only collections of sentences, having logical relations to each other. The difference requires little change to the foregoing procedure.

EXERCISE 6 - 1

Write each sentence in semi-symbolic form then in full symbolic form, using letters A, B, C, etc. in sequence as needed. Nos. 1, 3, 6, and 10 have been answered in the back.

1. Either Alonzo absconds or Basil will not be impeached.

2. It is not true that both Alonzo absconds and Basil will be impeached.

3. It isn't true that either Alonzo absconds or Basil will not be impeached.

4. Either Alonzo absconds and Basil will be impeached or it is false that both Chloris will be outraged and Dudley will be disgraced.

5. Either Alonzo absconds and Basil will be impeached or either Chloris will be outraged or Dudley will be disgraced.

6. Alonzo absconds and either Basil will be impeached or both

Chloris will be outraged and Dudley will be disgraced.

7. If Alonzo absconds then Basil will be impeached and Chloris will be outraged.

8. If Alonzo absconds then if Basil will be impeached then Chloris will be outraged.

9. Either Alonzo absconds or if Basil will be impeached then Chloris will not be outraged.

10. It's false that if Alonzo absconds then Basil will not be impeached and Chloris will be outraged.

(6.25) INTERIM SUMMARY. In a structurally valid argument the logical relations between the simple propositions in the argument (the ones symbolized by letters A, B, C, etc.) make the truth of the premises guarantee the truth of the conclusion. The actual content of these simple propositions is not a factor. Only arguments containing a conditional or an alternation (or something logically equivalent to these) can have structural validity.

The first approach to detecting structural validity was that of trying to invent an argument of the same structure as the one to be evaluated, but which had clearly true premises and a clearly false conclusion. If such an argument could be invented then the original argument is invalid because, since structural validity is a matter of structure, all arguments of a given structure are invalid if one is.

Since the basic approach just described represents a search for a set of truth values for the letters that can stand for simple propositions rather than for any particular single propositions, we can test an argument simply by assigning truth values to the letters. We can assume that it is possible to get propositions with any particular combination of truth values. Now to show invalidity we only have to assign truth values to the leters that will result in true premises and a false conclusion. If it is not possible to do this then the argument is valid.

To use the new method effectively a propositional logic language was introduced, consisting of capital letters to represent simple propositions, parentheses to disambiguate symbolic translations, and a set of special symbols to stand for 'not', 'and', 'or', and 'if...then...'. These special symbols were defined in terms of their logical behavior using truth tables. Truth tables for the various symbols follow.

X	$\sim$X
T	F
F	T

NEGATION

X	Y	X $\cdot$ Y
T	T	T
T	F	F
F	T	F
F	F	F

CONJUNCTION

X	Y	X v Y
T	T	T
T	F	T
F	T	T
F	F	F

ALTERNATION

X	Y	X $\supset$ Y
T	T	T
T	F	F
F	T	T
F	F	T

CONDITIONAL

The definition for negation is easy to remember, the others less so. Here is a slogan to cover each of them. You should memorize these,

189

- Conjunctions are TRUE ONLY WHEN ALL conjuncts ARE TRUE.

- Alternations are FALSE ONLY WHEN ALL alternates ARE FALSE

- Conditionals are FALSE ONLY WHEN THE ANTECEDENT IS TRUE AND THE CONSEQUENT IS FALSE.

The above definitions make it possible to construct truth tables for the premises and conclusions of arguments once they are symbolized in the new symbolic language. In the truth tables we can test an argument for every truth value combination that the simple propositions could have, so that we can know for sure if there is any combination that shows the inference to be invalid.

(6.26) THE TRUTH TABLE TEST. You have now been furnished with definitions of the logic symbols used in the symbolic language and with some information on how to translate arguments from English into the symbolic language. The next step is to learn how you can test arguments for structural validity once they are written in the symbolic language. It was suggested earlier that the problem of showing invalidity was one of inventing an argument with a given argument form that has all its premises true and its conclusion false. It was further suggested that, by assuming that an argument could always be found that would have propositions with whatever truth values we want, we could show validity or invalidity simply by assigning truth values to the proposition letters. A systematic way to search for a set of values that would yield true premises and a false conclusion is to establish premise and conclusion truth values for every combination of simple propositional truth values. This can be done by constructing a truth table for the argument, of the kind we have used to define the logic symbols.

Suppose we have this argument and want to know whether it has a structurally valid inference: "If George Washington was a general then he was a soldier. He was a soldier. Therefore, he was a general." The semi-symbolic version of the argument is: "If A then B. B. Therefore A." The fully symbolic version is:

"A ⊃ B / B // A" (NOTE: in future single slanted lines will be used to separate premises and double slanted ones will be used to separate the conclusion from the premises, as shown here).

To show this argument to be invalid we need to get truth values for 'A' and 'B' that make the premises true and the conclusion false. If the argument is valid it will not be possible to do this. We will test for all truth value combinations. There are four.

190

A	B	A ⊃ B	B	A
T	T	T	T	T
T	F	F	F	T
F	T	T	T	F
F	F	T	F	F

The first premise truth values are given in column three, the second in column four, and those of the conclusion are in the last column. What we are looking for is a line in which there is a "T" for each premise and an "F" for the conclusion. The third line meets this requirement. It shows that with A false and B true the premises will be true and the conclusion false. It is possible, therefore, to construct an argument with a proposition A false and another (B) true that will be invalid. It is not necessary to actually construct an argument but here is one that meets the logical requirements:

"If Boston is ten miles from New York then Boston is more than eight miles from New York. Boston is more than eight miles from New York. Therefore, Boston is ten miles from New York."

This argument has the same form as the other one. It has true premises and a false conclusion, so that it must be invalid. Since it is invalid any argument of the same form is invalid, so that the original argument is invalid.

If you thought the argument was valid it was probably because the premises and the conclusion are all true. An argument that proves its conclusion must have true premises AND a valid inference. This one does not. Its conclusion is true for reasons other tha the ones given.

The argument just tested is somewhat similar in structure to this one: "If Washington was a general then he was a soldier. He was a general. Therefore he was a soldier." Is this argument valid? The fully symbolic version looks like this: "A ⊃ B / A // B".

Notice that in the truth table for the argument pattern shown on the next page, B (the conclusion) is false on lines two and four but on line two the first premise is false and on line four the second premise is false. Thus, there is no combination of truth values for A and B that would yield an argument that has both premises true at the same time that the conclusion is false. This means there can be no argument that is a counter-example to the claim that arguments of this form are valid, which in turn means that our argument is valid. Furthermore, since the premises

191

are true they prove the conclusion true.

A	B	A ⊃ B	A	B
T	T	T	T	T
T	F	F	T	F
F	T	T	F	T
F	F	T	F	F

This argument form is a very common one, and is called "Modus Ponens". It may look like the fallacious form previously tested but it is different in a crucial way. That is, the second premise is A rather than B and the conclusion is B rather than A. This has turned out to make the difference between validity and invalidity. The simple propositions in the two arguments are the same but their structures are different. One reason that people commit the fallacy of Affirming the Consequent, which is what the second-last argument is an instance of, seems to be that they confuse the argument with Modus Ponens. The confusion is caused by the fact that the two argument forms are slightly similar. By writing an argument in fully symbolic form it is much easier to tell which kind of argument it is.

Theoretically, truth tables can be constructed for argument forms having any number of different simple propositions. Here is a table proving that 'A ⊃ B / B ⊃ C // A ⊃ C' has a valid inference. Since there are three propositional letters there are eight truth value combinations for A, B, and C taken together.

A	B	C	A ⊃ B	B ⊃ C	A ⊃ C
T	T	T	T	T	T
T	T	F	T	F	F
T	F	T	F	T	T
T	F	F	F	T	F
F	T	T	T	T	T
F	T	F	T	F	F
F	F	T	T	T	T
F	F	F	T	T	T

Notice in this table that there is no line on which 'A ⊃ B' and 'B ⊃ C' are true and on which 'A ⊃ C' is false. The truth table shows the form is valid. Note also how the combinations of truth values for A, B, and C were written. They were not combined in random sets of three values because it is difficult to ensure that all combinations have been found if it is done randomly. A pattern was used that yields all combinations automatically. Here is how it is done: (1) find the total number of combinations of truth values for the simple propositions by the formula "2 raised to the power of n", where 'n' stands for the total number of propositional letters (four combinations for two letters, eight for three, 16 for four, etc.), this will be the number of lines in the truth table; (2) make columns with the correct number of lines for each letter; (3) for the letter to the right ('C' in the above table) write "T", then "F", then "T", alternating until you come to the end of the column (the last entry will be an "F" if it has been done correctly); (4) in the column to the immediate left of this one (the one for 'B' in the truth table above) write "T", "T", "F", "F", "T", "T", etc. alternating two "T's" and two "F's" after beginning with two "T's"; (5) for the next column to the left enter four "T's", then alternate with four "F's". This method can be used to construct truth tables of any length. In a 32-line one you simply add another column to the left and write twice as many entries for each column using the pattern described for each column. The farthest column to the left in this case will have eight "T's", then eight "F's", etc.

(6.27) THE SHORT TRUTH TABLE TEST. The fact that the length of a Truth Table doubles each time a new letter is added to an argument does make the Truth Table method cumbersome when there are more than three letters. Constructing tables of 16 lines (four letters) is slow going and the great number of entries that have to be made increases the likelihood of errors. Unfortunately, with this method a single error can lead to the wrong answer. If there is one line in a table on which the premises all seem to be true and the conclusion is false we say the argument is invalid. However, if we have made a slip and one of the premises should be "F" instead of "T" then in fact the argument is valid. Therefore, extreme care is needed in constructing truth tables and when they must be large it would be better to use a shorter method.

A shorter method is available and it is based on the truth table approach. In fact, it really represents the truth table method used in reverse. You will recall that earlier we tried to test for structural validity by constructing an argument that had true premises and a false conclusion, and which had the same form as the argument we wanted to evaluate. The first improvement on this approach was to pretend we had simple propositions by simply assigning truth values to the individual letters which were to be regarded as standing for different propositions than the letters

193

in the original argument. Then the truth table method was introduced to provide a mechanical means of testing all the possible truth value combinations for the letters to see if there was a combination that yielded true premises and a false conclusion. Now we find that this mechanical approach has practical limitations.

To overcome the limitations of the truth table method we simply try to discover one line of the truth table that has true premises and a false conclusion. To do this we begin with the result we want, not with letter values. We try to assign values to the letters that will yield true premises and a false conclusion. If there is a line in the complete truth table that meets these requirements then we will have found it without writing the whole table. An example will clarify things.

Suppose we want to evaluate for validity an argument whose fully symbolic form is "B v C / A ⊃ B // A ⊃ C". We could construct an eight line truth table to do it, but instead we will work backwards to see if there is a line in it that shows it is invalid. If there is such a line then 'A ⊃ C' will be false on that line, so that 'A' will be true and 'C' false. We can write these truth values under the argument form like this:

$$
\begin{array}{ccccc}
\text{B v C} & / & \text{A} \supset \text{B} & // & \text{A} \supset \text{C} \\
& & & & \text{T F F} \\
& & & & \text{2 1 3}
\end{array}
$$

Notice the "F" for 'A ⊃ C' is placed under the connective and the values which the letter must have are placed under them, and that the order of truth value entry is numbered. Now we can put these values under all other letters since these letters must have these values if the conclusion is to be false in the truth table. We now have this:

$$
\begin{array}{ccccc}
\text{B v C} & / & \text{A} \supset \text{B} & // & \text{A} \supset \text{C} \\
\text{F} & & \text{T} & & \text{T F F} \\
\text{5} & & \text{4} & & \text{2 1 3}
\end{array}
$$

Remember that we are striving to get values for the letters that yield true premises and a false conclusion. We have a false conclusion. We need the premises true so let us assign "T" to the first premise. This means that B must be true since C is false already. We also write "T" under the 'B' in the second premise, and with A and B both true, A ⊃ B is true. When all this has been entered we have:

$$
\begin{array}{ccccc}
\text{B v C} & / & \text{A} \supset \text{B} & // & \text{A} \supset \text{C} \\
\text{T T F} & & \text{T T T} & & \text{T F F} \\
\text{7 6 5} & & \text{4 9 8} & & \text{2 1 3}
\end{array}
$$

194

By making A true, B true, and C false we were able to get true premises and a false conclusion. The argument is therefore invalid.

To show how efficient the short truth table method really is for inference testing we will test the preceding argument pattern by constructing a complete truth table. The table contains six columns and eight lines, for a total of 48 truth value entries. It is shown below. The line revealing invalidity is the second one. We were able to identify the line by working backwards. Making the conclusion false allowed us to infer values for A and C. Making B v C true with C already false allowed us to infer that B must be true. With each letter having a value we must make the second premise true, we are not at liberty to do otherwise.

A	B	C	B v C	A ⊃ B	A ⊃ C
T	T	T	T	T	T
T	T	F	T	T	F
T	F	T	T	F	T
T	F	F	F	F	F
F	T	T	T	T	T
F	T	F	T	T	T
F	F	T	T	T	T
F	F	F	F	T	T

The short method can be thought of as doing a truth table line in reverse because more often than not we infer values for propositional letters from values for premises and conclusions that are more complex assertions.

A second example: "A ⊃ (B ⊃ C) / A ⊃ (C ⊃ D) // A ⊃ D". Here the truth table would be 16 lines long and quite laborious to construct. To use the short method we begin with an assertion that yields truth values for some letters. In this case it is the conclusion which yields values for A and D. We now have this:

```
A ⊃ (B ⊃ C) / A ⊃ (C ⊃ D) // A ⊃ D
T              T          F     T F F
5              4          6     2 1 3
```

Since we have values for two letters in the second premise, we deal with it next. We set the premise true by writing "T"

195

under the main connective, which means that we must make C ⊃ D true and with D false, C must be false. We now have this:

```
A ⊃ (B ⊃ C) / A ⊃ (C ⊃ D) // A ⊃ D
T          F   T T  F T F    T F F
5          10  4 7  9 8 6    2 1 3
```

Now we have values that make the second premise true and the conclusion false. What about the first premise? The same kind of reasoning applies that we used for the second premise. We set the premise true (Step 11), which entails that B ⊃ C must be true. This in turn means that B must be false. Finally we have this:

```
A ⊃ (B ⊃ C) / A ⊃ (C ⊃ D) // A ⊃ D
T T  F T F    T T  F T F     T F F
511 131210    4 9  7 8 6     2 1 3
```

With A true and each of the others false we found that the premises will be true and the conclusion false. The argument is invalid.

The arguments so far evaluated using the short method have turned out to be invalid. When they are valid things go differently. Let us test the Hypothetical Syllogism:

"A ⊃ B / B ⊃ C // A ⊃ C"

We must begin with the conclusion because that is the only assertion in the argument whose letters have predetermined truth values. After making the appropriate entries we have this:

```
A ⊃ B / B ⊃ C // A ⊃ C
T         F     T   F
4         5     2 1 3
```

Next we look at premise two. Making it true forces us to make B false. We make the appropriate entries and now have this:

```
A ⊃ B / B ⊃ C // A ⊃ C
T F F   F T F    T F F
4 9 8   7 6 5    2 1 3
```

We now have the second premise true and the conclusion false, but notice that with the values needed the first premise is false, not true. If we had dealt with the first premise before the second one we would have had to make B true to get it true, but then the second one would have ended up false. Either way we cannot have the conclusion false and both premises true. This, of course, shows that the argument form is valid. The short test method amounts to trying to show an argument is invalid. Failure to do so shows that the argument is valid.

(6.28) SHORT TRUTH TABLE PROCEDURE: There are a total of 37 basic "moves" that are permissible in using the short truth table method, although only 31 are really different. They are based on the truth-table definitions of the various logical connectives. It may be convenient to present those definitions here, in a format that has not been previously used. In this format the truth values of the complex assertions are shown under the connective symbols. You may find this way of writing the definitions more useful in doing short truth table tests.

∿ X	X v Y	X • Y	X ⊃ Y
F T	T T T	T T T	T T T
T F	T T F	T F F	T F F
	F T T	F F T	F T T
	F F F	F F F	F T F

(6.281) SHORT TRUTH TABLE MOVES: The following table presents and comments on each of the 37 basic moves authorized by the truth table definitions of the connectives. THE DERIVED VALUES ARE THE ONES IN PARENTHESES.

(1) ∿ X   From line 2 of the table for '∿'. Given "It is
    T (F)   true that grass is not red" (∿X) we can infer
                  "It is false that grass is red" (X).

(2) ∿ X   From line 1 of the table. Given "It is false
    F (T)   that grass is not green" (X) we can infer
                  "It is true that grass is green" (X).

(3) ∿ X   From line 2 of the table. Given "It is false
    (T) F   that grass is red" (X) we can infer "It is
                  true that grass is not red" (∿X).

(4)   ∿ X   From line 1 of the table. Given "It is true
    (F)T   that grass is green" (X) we can infer "It is
                  false that grass is not green" (∿X).

(5) X v Y   From lines 1 and 2 of the table. Note that Y
    T(T)   is true on line 1 and false on line 2 so we
                  cannot enter a value for Y. Given "It is true
                  that grass is green" (X) or we can infer
                  "It is true that either grass is green or Y".

(6)   X v Y   From lines 1 and 3. Essentially the same
     (T)T   move as #5.

197

(7)	X v Y (F)F(F)	From line 4. When an alternation is false each alternate is false. Given "It is false that X or Y" we can infer "It is false that X and it is false that Y".
(8)	X v Y F T(T)	From line 3. For an alternation to be true at least one of its alternates must be true. Given "It's true that either grass is red (X) or Y" we can infer "Y is true".
(9)	X v Y (T)T F	From line 2. Essentially the same move as #8.
(10)	X v Y F F(F)	From line 4. When an alternation is false each alternate is false. Given "It's false that either grass is red (X) or Y" we can infer "Y is false".
(11)	X v Y (F)F F	From line 4. Essentially the same move as #10.
(12)	X v Y T(T)T	From line 1. When both alternates are true the whole alternation is true. Given "Grass is green" (X) and "Snow is white" (Y) we can infer "It is true that either grass is green or snow is white".
(13)	X v Y T(T)F	From line 2. One true alternate makes an alternation true. Given "Snow is white" (X) and "Grass is red" we can infer "It is true that either snow is white or grass is red".
(14)	X v Y F(T)T	From line 3. Essentially the same move as #13.
(15)	X v Y F(F)F	From line 4. An alternation is false when each of its alternates is false. Given "Snow is blue" (X) and "Grass is red" (Y) we can infer "It's false that either snow is blue or grass is red".
(16)	X · Y (T)T(T)	From line 1. When a conjunction is true all of its conjuncts are true. Given "It's true that both X and Y are true" we can infer "X is true" and "Y is true".
(17)	X · Y F(F)	From lines 3 and 4. One false conjunct makes a conjunction false regardless of the truth value of other conjuncts. Note that on line 3 of the table Y is true and on line 4 it is false. Because of this we cannot infer a value

198

for Y. Given "It is false that grass is red"
(X), we can infer "It is false that both grass
is red and Y".

(18)   X • Y   From lines 2 and 4. Essentially the same
         (F)F   move as #17.

(19)   X • Y   From line 1. When a conjunction is true each
         T T(T)   conjunct is true. Given "It is true that both
                   grass is green (X) and Y", we can infer
                   "Y is true".

(20)   X • Y   From line 1. Same as move #19.
         (T)T T

(21)   X • Y   From line 2. A false conjunction must have
         T F(F)   at least one false conjunct. Given "It is false
                   that both grass is green (X) and Y are true,"
                   we can infer "Y is false".

(22)   X • Y   From line 3. Same as 21.
         (F)F T

(23)   X • Y   From line 1. When all conjuncts are true the
         T(T)T   whole conjunction is true. Given "Snow is white
                   and "Snow is cold", we can infer "It is true
                   that both snow is white and snow is cold".

(24)   X • Y   From line 2. A conjunction is false unless
         T(F)F   all conjuncts are true. Given "Snow is white"
                   (X) and "snow is hot" (Y) we can infer "It is
                   false that both snow is white and snow is hot
                   are true".

(25)   X • Y   From line 3. Same as move #24.
         F(F)T

(26)   X • Y   From line 4. A conjunction is false when one
         F(F)F   or more of its conjuncts are false. Given
                   "Grass is red" and "Grass is metal" we can
                   infer "It is false that both grass is red and
                   grass is metal are true."

(27)   X ⊃ Y   From lines 1 and 3. Note that on line 1 X is
         (T)T   true but that on line 3 it is false, so no
                   definite value for X can be inferred when Y is
                   true, even though the whole assertion is known
                   to be true.

199

(28)   X ⊃ Y   From lines 3 and 4. Note that on line 3 Y is
       F(T)   true but on line 4 it is false, so no definite
                   value for Y can be inferred, even though the
                   whole assertion can be said to be true.

(29)   X ⊃ Y   From line 2. When a conditional is false its
       (T)F(F)   antecedent is true and its consequent is false.

(30)   X ⊃ Y   From line 1. When a conditional is true, the
       T T(T)   truth of its antecedent guarantees the truth
                   of its consequent.

(31)   X ⊃ Y   From line 2. When a conditional is false its
       T F(F)   consequent is false.

(32)   X ⊃ Y   From line 4. When a conditional is true and
       (F)T F   its consequent is false, the antecedent must
                   also be false. If the antecedent were true the
                   the whole conditional would have to be false
                   instead of true. Given "If this plane figure
                   is a triangle then it has three sides" and "It
                   is false that this figure has three sides", we
                   can infer "It is false that this plane figure
                   is a triangle".

(33)   X ⊃ Y   From line 2. When a conditional is false, its
       (T)F F   antecedent must be true.

(34)   X ⊃ Y   From line 1.
       T(T)T

(35)   X ⊃ Y   From line 2. Conditionals are false when
       T(F)F   their antecedents are true and their
                   consequents are false.

(36)   X ⊃ Y   From line 3.
       F(T)T

(37)   X ⊃ Y   From line 4.
       F(T)F

     (6.282) SOME HINTS FOR TESTING. The key to successful use of
the short test method is to identify the assertion that provides
the best starting point. Depending on how complex the assertions
are, any of the following make good starting points:

     (1) premises and conclusions with single letters;

     (2) premises that represent conjunctions--each conjunct must
be true;

     (3) conclusions that are alternations--each alternate must
                                200

be false;

(4) conclusions that are conditionals--the antecedent must be true and the consequent false;

(5) premises that are negated alternations--for instance: if '~(A v B)' must be true then A v B must be false and thus A and B must each be false;

(6) premises that are negated conditionals--for instance: if '~(A ⊃ B)' must be true then A ⊃ B must be false, which means that A must be true and B false;

(7) conclusions that are negated conjunctions--for instance: if ' ~(A • B)' must be false then A • B must be true, which means that A must be true and B must be true.

Some further points are worthwhile noting. Remember that the idea is to derive truth values for the letters that will result in true premises and a false conclusion, so begin with assertion truth values and derive letter values as was done in the examples. Also remember that because of the truth table definitions for the connectives we can often know the truth value of a complex expression without knowing the truth value of all the letters contained in it. A ⊃ B is true when B is true regardless of what A is, A ⊃B is also true when A is false regardless of what B is, A v B is true when only one disjunct is true, and A • B is false when only one conjunct is false. All this means that sometimes we can get a decision on an argument form without getting values for all letters. Here is an example:

```
A ⊃ B / C ⊃ D / A ⊃ D // B v C
F T F    F T      F T      F F F
8 7 6    4 5      9 10     2 1 3
```

In this example we have found the argument form to be invalid without getting a value for D. This just means that D can be either true or false, which is to say that there are two lines in the truth table for the argument form that show it to be invalid.

EXERCISE 6 - 2

Establish the validity or invalidity of each of the following argument forms using the short test method. Write T's and F's under each symbol, recording the order in which you write each under it. Remember, if you can give values to the letters that result in true premises and a false conclusion you have shown the form to be invalid. This is what you should try to do. If you find you cannot do this then the form is valid. Some can be done more than one way. Nos. 1, 4, 7, 10, 13, and 16 are answered in the back. Here is an example that proves to be invalid:

```
A v B / A // ∿ B
T T T   T    F T
6 4 3   5    1 2
```

1. A ⊃ ∿ B / B ⊃ ∿ A // ∿ A

2. (A v B) ⊃ C // (A • B) ⊃ C

3. (A ⊃ B) • (C ⊃ D) // (A • C) ⊃ (B v D)

4 A ⊃ B / A ⊃ C // B v C

5. A ⊃ B / C ⊃ D / A ⊃ D // B v C

6. (∿ A v ∿ B) ⊃ (∿ C) / D ⊃ (C • ∿ B) // ∿ D

7. (A • ∿ B) ⊃ ∿ C / C // ∿ A v (A • B)

8. A ⊃ B / B ⊃ C // C ⊃ A

9. A ⊃ (B ⊃ C) / A ⊃ B // A ⊃ C

10. A ⊃ (B • C) / (B v C) ⊃ ∿ A // ∿ A

11. (A ⊃ B) • (C ⊃ D) / A v C // B v D

12. A ⊃ (B ⊃ C) / (B ⊃ C) ⊃ D // A ⊃ D

13. A ⊃ B / C ⊃ ∿ D / D ⊃ A // ∿ B ⊃ C

14. A ⊃ (B v C) / B ⊃ (D v E) / A ⊃ ∿ E // ∿ (A • ∿ D)

15. ∿ A v ∿ (B ⊃ C) / (A • C) v (D • E) / (∿ D ⊃ ∿ E) ⊃ ∿ B /
    A • F // F ⊃ ∿ B

16. ((A v B) • C) ⊃ D / (C ⊃ D) ⊃ (E ⊃ F) / E // A ⊃ F

202

(6.283)   A COMPLICATION.   A difficulty in using the short
test method is that it is not always possible to infer values for
enough letters by setting the premises true and the conclusion
false.   Sometimes we can get values for some but sometimes we
cannot even make a start. In such cases we assign a value to some
letter and see if we can infer values for all the rest. Here is an
instance of such a case:

"(A v B) ⊃ (A • B) // (A ⊃ B) • (B ⊃ A)"

To establish that this is invalid we must begin by assigning
a value to some letter. To get the conclusion false we need to
get at least one part of the conjunct false. Let us make A false,
which makes A ⊃ B true.   We need B ⊃ A false to get a false
conclusion so we know B must be true. Making all appropriate
entries we have the following situation. Notice that the assigned
value has been circled. This helps us remember later which value
was assigned.

(A v B) ⊃ (A • B) // (A ⊃ B) • (B ⊃ A)
 F T T F F F T   F T T F T F F
 810 9 14 111312   1 2 7 4 6 5 3

With A false and B true the conclusion is false but so is the
premise.   Does this show the argument to be valid? Unfortunately,
it is not a conclusive test. After all, we did assign a value to
A to get started. Perhaps if we had made it true instead of false
we would have been able to get the premise true as well as the
conclusion false.   To be certain it is valid we have to test the
possibility.   What we have proved is that the argument cannot be
shown to be invalid with A false. If there is one (or more) line
in the full truth table showing the argument to be invalid it must
be a line with A true. Thus we enter A as true everywhere it
occurs.   Now B ⊃ A will be true in the conclusion, so to get the
conclusion false we must make B false to get A ⊃ B false. After
making all appropriate entries we have this result:

(A v B) ⊃ (A • B) // (A ⊃ B) • (B ⊃ A)
 T T F F T F F   T F F F F T T
 4 13 12 14 3 11 10   1 7 8 6 9 5 2

Again the premise turns out false. Thus, with either A true
or A false we cannot get a true premise and a false conclusion.
We can now be sure the argument is valid. There are no other
values A could be assigned. THE POINT TO REMEMBER WHEN WE ASSIGN
A TRUTH VALUE TO A LETTER AND DO NOT END UP WITH TRUE PREMISES AND
A FALSE CONCLUSION IS THAT WE MUST TEST THE ARGUMENT AGAIN USING
THE OPPOSITE TRUTH VALUE FOR THAT LETTER. Then, if we again fail
to get true premises and a false conclusion we know the argument
is valid.   However, if on the second try we do get true premises
and a false conclusion then the argument is actually invalid.

(6.284) STRATEGIES FOR VALUE CHOICE.

(1) Don't assign a value to a letter until you have to; otherwise, you will have to test the argument form a second time if it appears to be valid.

(2) Assign a value that allows you to infer values for other letters. This may involve acting somewhat counter-intuitively in the following way. Supppose you are considering making a value assignment for the premise A v B. You want this premise to be true so you will be tempted to make A true, perhaps. But this is not as fruitful as making A false because then B will have to be true, whereas making A true does not allow us to infer a value for B. So in deciding whether to make a letter true or false, use the value that will entail a value for another letter within the assertion, so long as the choice will allow the overall assertion to have the truth value desired. One more example: given a conclusion A • B it is best to make one letter true because then the other one must be false given that we want the whole conclusion false.

(3) In general, choosing values for letters that occur in several assertions in the argument is more fruitful in yielding values than choosing values for ones that occur in fewer assertions.

EXERCISE 6 - 3

Establish the validity or invalidity of each of the following argument forms using the short test method. Each of these requires assigning a value to some letter. Put a circle around the value assigned so that you can remember to test with the opposite value if the form is not shown invalid on the first assignment. Remember that the form is only shown to be valid if invalidity is not found for both values a letter can be assigned. Make no more than ONE value assignment, in addition to premise and conclusion assignments. Nos. 1 and 4 have been answered in the back.

1. A ⊃ B / C ⊃ D / A v C // (A • B) v (C • D)

2. (A ⊃ B) v (C ⊃ D) / A v C // B v D

3. (A v B) ⊃ C / C ⊃ (A   B) // (A v B) ⊃ (A • B)

4. (A v B) v (C ⊃ D) // (A v C) ⊃ (B v D)

5. A ⊃ (B v C) / ∿(A • B) // C

6. ∿(A • B) / (∿A • ∿B) ⊃ (C • D) / D ⊃ C // C

204

(6.285) SUMMARY. In the first part of the chapter you were introduced to a method of testing inferences for structural validity that relied on the attempt to produce a counter-example to show that a given argument was invalid. The shortcomings of this method were pointed out and it was used as the basis for developing a purely formal method called the truth table method. Since the truth table method can be most effectively employed on arguments written in a symbolic language, such a language was introduced. Then the truth table method was illustrated.

The truth table method, although it gives the correct decision on whether an argument is valid, proves to be cumbersome when arguments contain four or more simple propositions. To get around this the short truth table method was introduced. To use it we try to get truth values for the individual letters that will result in the premises being true and the conclusion false. This could best be done by inferring values for the letters from the conclusion and each premise. If, by inferring values, we are not able to get all premises true and the conclusion false at the same time, then we know the argument is valid. Sometimes we are not able to infer values for all letters and we are forced to assign values. If we cannot get all premises true and the conclusion false after assigning a value, we are not yet entitled to conclude that the argument is valid. We must give the letter to which a truth value has been assigned the opposite truth value and repeat the test procedure. If it is still not possible to get true premises and a false conclusion then we know the argument is valid.

EXERCISE 6 - 4

Test using the short test method. Some of these may require a value assignment. Make no more than one, exclusive of premise and conclusion assignments. Nos. 1 and 3 have been answered in the back, but remember that each can probably be done in several ways that are equally correct.

1. A ⊃ B / B ⊃ (A ⊃ (C v D)) / C ⊃ D / ∿(C • D) //∿ A

2. A ⊃ F / (F v G) ⊃ B / C ⊃ (D • E) / A v C // B v D

3. A v ∿B / ∿(∿C • D) / ∿(∿A •∿ D) // ∿B ⊃ C

4. (A • B) ⊃ (C • D) / ∿E ⊃ (A ⊃ B) / (E ⊃ A) ⊃∿C

    // ∿ (A ⊃ D) • E

5. A ⊃ (B v C) / B ⊃ (D v E) / E ⊃ F /∿ (F v D) //∿ A

6. (B v C) ⊃ A / ⊃(A • B) // C

(6.29)   SOME COMMON ARGUMENT FORMS WITH POTENTIAL STRUCTURAL VALIDITY: There are a number of argument patterns commonly used that are put forward as having structural validity. In this section we will examine some of them and evaluate examples using the short truth table test for inference validity.

(6.291) MODUS PONENS

(1)   INTRODUCTION.   Every argument with a single inference can be put forward in the modus ponens pattern simply by including as an extra assumption the claim that the other assumptions guarantee the truth of the conclusion. For example, instead of saying "A, therefore B", the arguer can say "A. If A then B. Therefore B". This move is simply a way of making explicit the claim that the inference in "A, therefore B" is valid.

(2)   TYPICAL EXAMPLE: "If logical skills are useful then this book is useful. Logical skills are useful. Therefore, this book is useful."

(3)   BASIC LOGICAL FORM: If A then B. A. Therefore B.

(4)   INFERENCE VALIDITY ANALYSIS.   The inference in the argument of this pattern is valid. When A guarantees the truth of B and A is true, B will be also.

(5)   INFERENCE CRITICISM STRATEGY. Perform a short truth table test.

(6)   ASSUMPTION EVALUATION. The conditional assumption can be evaluated by trying to show that B is false even though A is true, or that the truth of A is compatible with the falsity of B.

(7)   VARIANT VERSIONS. None.

(8)   EVALUATION OF EXAMPLE. "If punishment should fit the crime then murderers should be executed. Punishment should fit the crime. Therefore, murderers should be executed."

Step One: construct an accurate diagrammatic version of the argument.   The semi-symbolic version is: "If A then B. A. Therefore B." The symbolic version is "A ⊃ B / A // B."

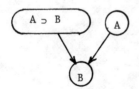

A = Punishment should fit the crime.

B = Murderers should be executed.

206

Step Two: evaluate the inference. A short truth table test shows the inference is valid:

A ⊃ B / A // B
F T F   F   F
4 3 2   5   1

Step Three: evaluate the assumptions. A can be given a true rating since it is entailed by a generally accepted principle of justice. (Of course, in practice there are often disagreements about what counts as fitting punishment for a particular crime.)

The other assumption, A ⊃ B, raises the issue of fittingness. The arguer is obviously exposing the eye-for-an-eye standard of fittingness, but there is another conception that is at least as defensible. This version holds that punishment need not be equal in severity to the crime but must be proportional. Thus, as murder is considered more serious than other crimes, the punishment is greatest for it, whereas theft is considered less serious and is punishable by a lesser sentence.

The proportionality conception of fittingness has enough in its favor to induce most people to rate A ⊃ B "?". There is a distinct possibility that B is false even though A is true.

Step Four: determine the extent to which intermediate conclusions have been proved. Not applicable.

Step Five: determine the extent to which the final conclusion has been proved. Since both assumptions are essential to prove B and we have accepted A as true the argument rating must reflect the rating of A ⊃ B. The rated diagrammatic version is shown below:

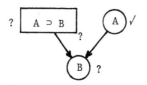

Step Six: formulate a response to the argument. "Since the principle of punishment fitting the crime may not entail the eye-for-an-eye view, the argument falls short of proving that murderers should be executed. The proper moral view of fittingness may be that punishment should be proportional to the crime, in which case murderers should receive the severest punishment of any offence, but not necessarily death.

(9) ASSOCIATED FALLACIES: Affirming the Consequent, the next argument pattern to be discussed.

(6.292) AFFIRMING THE CONSEQUENT.

(1) INTRODUCTION. This argument form gets its plausibility from its similarity to Modus Ponens.

(2) TYPICAL EXAMPLE. "If a fetus is a human being then it consists of human cells. A fetus does consist of human cells. Therefore, a fetus is a human being."

(3) BASIC LOGICAL FORM: If A then B. B. Therefore, A.

(4) INFERENCE VALIDITY ANALYSIS. The inference in arguments of this pattern is not valid. Given B, A would be proved true only if B guaranteed the truth of A. But the first assumption is not equivalent to this.

(5) INFERENCE CRITICISM STRATEGY. Perform a short truth table test.

(6) ASSUMPTION EVALUATION. The conditional assumption can be evaluated by trying to show that B is false even though A is true, or that the truth of A is compatible with the falsity of B.

(7) VARIANT VERSIONS. None.

(8) EVALUATION OF EXAMPLE. The example given above serves as a good example.

Step One: construct an accurate diagrammatic version of the argument. The semi-synbolic version is: "If A then B. B. Therefore A." The symbolic version is: "A ⊃ B / B // A."

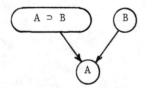

A = A fetus is a human being.

B = A fetus consists of human cells.

Step Two: Evaluate the inference. A short truth table test shows the inference is not valid.

208

```
A ⊃ B / B // A
F T T   T   F
2 5 4   3   1
```

Step Three: evaluate the assumptions. Both assumptions are clearly true if it is understood that we are talking about human fetuses, which the arguer evidently is.

Step Four: determine the extent to which intermediate conclusions are proved. Not applicable here.

Step Five: determine the extent to which the final conclusion has been proved. With the assumptions true and the inference invalid the conclusion is not proved to any significant extent:

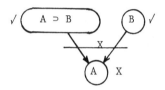

Step Six: formulate a response to the argument. We can respond: "Your assumptions are true but the conclusion does not follow from them. If it is to be proved that a fetus is a human being, given that it consists of human cells, the other assumption must claim that consisting of human cells guarantees that a thing is a human being. Yours claims the reverse."

(6.293) MODUS TOLLENS.

(1) INTRODUCTION: This is a fairly common pattern.

(2) TYPICAL EXAMPLE: "If this university is seriously concerned with course quality then students are given the opportunity to evaluate their courses. Students are not given the opportunity to evaluate their courses. Therefore, this university is not seriously concerned with course quality."

(3) BASIC LOGICAL FORM: If A then B. Not B. Therefore, not A.

(4) INFERENCE VALIDITY ANALYSIS. The inference is structurally valid. If the truth of A guarantees the truth of B but B is false then of course A is also false.

209

(5)   INFERENCE   CRITICISM   STRATEGY.   Perform   a short truth table test.

(6)   ASSUMPTION   EVALUATION.   The conditional assumption can be evaluated by trying to show that B is false even though A is true, or that the truth of A is compatible with the falsity of B.

(7)   VARIANT VERSIONS.   None.

(8)   EVALUATION OF EXAMPLE.   An argument often put forward by the philosophically naive: "If morality is objective then people agree in moral judgments. People do not always agree in moral judgments. Therefore, morality is not objective."

Step   One: construct an accurate diagrammatic version of the argument. The semi-symbolic version is: "If A then B. Not B. Therefore, not A." The symbolic version is "A ⊃ B / ∿B // ∿A".

The conditional assumption is somewhat vague because of its antecedent. What does the arguer mean by the proposition 'morality is objective'? In particular, what is meant by 'objective'? This word is notoriously vague and ambiguous. In the context of this argument it is likely that the arguer would say that claims about the material world (e.g., "grass is green") are objective. That is, the truth or falsity of such claims is independent of us, the perceivers. Providing that two people meant the same by the words, a disagreement about a proposition about the material world could be resolved by appeal to procedures and standards that are shared. In the argument at hand the arguer would probably say that 'morality is objective' means that the truth or falsity of a moral claim is independent of particular persons and that any two people could come to agree about its truth value.

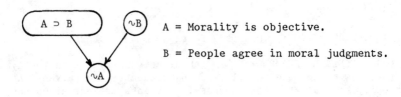

A = Morality is objective.

B = People agree in moral judgments.

Step   Two: evaluate the inference. A short truth table test shows the inference is valid.

```
A ⊃ B / ∿ B // ∿ A
T T T   F T    F T
3 4 5   7 6    1 2
```

Step Three: evaluate the assumptions. The assumption that people do not agree in moral judgments is clearly true. Young people often have disagreements with their parents about the rightness or wrongness of particular kinds of practices. Usually moral disagreement consists in one person insisting something is wrong and the other insisting it is permissible.

The conditional assumption is clearly false, given the concept of objectivity that we have imputed to the arguer. Even if the truth or falsity of a moral claim is independent of any particular individual and there are standards and procedures that can lead to a definitive answer, this could not guarantee that people will always agree about the claim. One party may not be relying on the correct standards of judgment, or possibly the two are not equally aware of the facts of the case. Either of these factors can result in a disagreement.

Step Four: determine the extent to which intermediate conclusions are proved. Not applicable here.

Step Five: determine the extent to which the final conclusion has been proved. With each assumption essential to proving the conclusion, the argument rating can be no better than the weakest assumption. Thus the conclusion is not proved to any great extent.

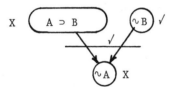

Step Six: formulate a response to the argument. We can respond: "Your argument does not prove morality is not objective because your conditional assumption is false. If morality was objective it could still happen that there was disagreement in moral judgments. Some people may have incorrect standards of judgment or there may be disagreement arising from lack of knowledge of the facts of a particular case."

(6.294) DENYING THE ANTECEDENT.

(1) INTRODUCTION. This argument form gets its plausibility from its similarity to Modus Tollens.

(2) TYPICAL EXAMPLE. "If punishment subsequently deters

211

those who have committed crimes from further crime then punishment of offenders is morally justified. But punishment does not deter those who have committed crimes from further crime. Therefore, punishment of offenders is not morally justified."

(3) BASIC LOGICAL FORM: If A then B. Not A. Therefore, not B.

(4) INFERENCE VALIDITY ANALYSIS. The inference in arguments of this pattern is not valid. Given not-A, not-B would be proved if the other assumption was "if B then A", but the assumption relied on is the inverse of this.

(5) INFERENCE CRITICISM STRATEGY. Perform a short truth table test.

(6) ASSUMPTION EVALUATION. The conditional assumption can be evaluated by trying to show that B is false even though A is true, or that the truth of A is compatible with the falsity of B.

(7) VARIANT VERSIONS. None.

(8) EVALUATION OF EXAMPLE. The example given above provides a suitable instance.

Step One: construct an accurate diagrammatic version of the argument. The semi-symbolic version is: "A ⊃ B /∿ A //∿ B". The diagrammatic version is:

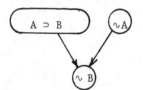

A = Punishment subsequently deters those who have committed crimes from further crime.

B = Punishment of offenders is morally justified.

Step Two: evaluate the inferences. A short truth table test shows the inference is not valid.

```
A ⊃ B /  ∿ A //  ∿ B
F T T    T F     F T
6 7 3    4 5     1 2
```

Step Three: evaluate the assumptions. Given that deterrence can justify punishing, the conditional assumption is acceptable. The other assumption is dubious, although the percentage of those returning to prison is significant it is not great enough to establish the claim that punishment does not subsequently deter those who have committed crimes before.

212

Step Four: determine the extent to which intermediate conclusions are proved. Not applicable here.

Step Five: determine the extent to which the final conclusion has been proved. Given the ratings, the conclusion has not been proved to any great extent:

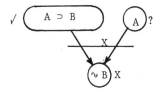

Step Six: formulate a response to the argument. We can respond: "Your argument does not prove that punishment of offenders is not morally justified. It is dubious that punishment does not subsequently deter those who have committed crimes, although a majority are not deterred. But even if this assumption were true, the conclusion would not be proved since it does not follow from the assumption. It would follow only if the conditional assumption was the reverse of what it is. But this assumption would be false."

(6.295) DISJUNCTIVE SYLLOGISM.

(1) INTRODUCTION. Since this pattern does not appear to be a syllogistic form it is inappropriately named. It is, however, a fairly common pattern.

(2) TYPICAL EXAMPLE. "Either you should marry for love or you should marry for money. You should not marry for money. Therefore you should marry for love."

(3) BASIC LOGICAL FORM: Either A or B. Not B. Therefore, A.

(4) INFERENCE VALIDITY ANALYSIS. The inference is valid. Given two possible alternatives and then excluding one we must say the other is true.

(5) INFERENCE CRITICISM STRATEGY. Perform a short truth table test.

(6) ASSUMPTION EVALUATION. In arguments of this type the alternation may be the weak point because it may ignore other alternatives. We should try to identify a third alternative that

213

may be true. This amounts to treating the alternation as equivalent to 'either A or B AND ONLY A or B' but this is probably the arguer's meaning.

(7) VARIANT VERSIONS. None.

(8) EVALUATION OF EXAMPLE. The example given above is suitable for discussion.

Step One: construct an accurate diagrammatic version of the argument. The semi-symbolic version is: "Either A or B. Not B. Therefore, A." The symbolic version is: "A v B / ∿ B // A." The diagrammatic version is:

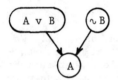

A = You should marry for love.

B = You should marry for money.

Step Two: evaluate the inferences. A short truth table test shows the inference is valid.

```
A v B / ∿ B // A
F F F   T F     F
4 6 5   2 3     1
```

Step Three: Evaluate the assumptions. The claim that one should marry only for love or money is dubious because of other possible alternatives. What about marrying for happiness, which seems to be distinct from the other two? What about marrying for convenience, which might involve no financial benefit and nothing more than mild affection?

The other assumption, that one shouldn't marry for money, is also dubious. Money may not guarantee happiness but may provide opportunities to acquire it.

Step Four: determine the extent to which intermediate conclusions are proved. Not appropriate here.

Step Five: determine the extent to which the final conclusion has been proved. Given that both assumptions are dubious and that both are crucial, we should rate the argument "X".

Step Six: formulate a response to the argument. We can

214

respond: "Your conclusion is not proved because both assumptions are dubious. Love and money are not the only resons for marrying. One might marry for happiness or convenience. Also, it is not clear that one should not marry for money. Money may provide opportunities for happiness."

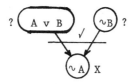

(6.296) ASSUMED EXCLUSION

(1) INTRODUCTION. This pattern is so called because it contains an assumption that is regarded as an exclusive 'or' by the arguer.

(2) TYPICAL EXAMPLE. A college student reasons: "Either I should go to medical school or I should get married. I should go to medical school. Therefore, I shouldn't get married."

(3) BASIC LOGICAL FORM. Either A or B and not both. A. Therefore, not B.

(4) INFERENCE VALIDITY ANALYSIS. The inference is structurally valid.

(5) INFERENCE CRITICISM STRATEGY. Perform a short truth table test.

(6) ASSUMPTION EVALUATION. The alternation needs to be examined to determine if it actually is exclusive. Try to show that both alternatives can be true at once.

(7) VARIANT VERSIONS. None

(8) EVALUATION OF EXAMPLE. The example given above is suitable.

Step One: construct an accurate diagrammatic version of the argument. The semi-symbolic version of the argument is: "Either A or B. A. Therefore, not B." Since the arguer evidently regards the alternatives A and B as incompatible, the full symbolic version is this: "(A v B) • $\sim$ (A • B) / A // $\sim$B".

The diagrammatic version looks like this:

215

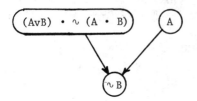

A = I should go to medical school.

B = I should get married.

Step Two: evaluate the inference. A short truth table test shows the inference is valid.

$$(A \vee B) \quad \bullet \quad \sim (A \bullet B) \;/\; A \;//\; \sim B$$
$$\begin{array}{ccccccc} \text{F} & \text{F} & \text{T} & \text{T} & \text{T} & \text{T} & \text{F} & \text{T} \\ 8 & 7 & & 5 & 6 & 4 & 3 & 1 & 2 \end{array}$$

Step Three: evaluate the assumptions. To determine whether A is true or not we would need detailed knowledge of the arguer's aspirations, abilities, and financial situation. Lacking this and realizing that the arguer is an authority in her/his own case, we should regard A as true.

The alternation appears to be dubious because A and B do not clearly exclude each other. Lots of people have married before going to medical school and found that it helped rather than hindered them.

Step Four: determine the extent to which intermediate conclusions are proved. There are none.

Step Five: determine the extent to which the final conclusion is proved. With a dubious, but crucial, assumption the final conclusion is proved to some extent but not conclusively. The rated argument looks like this:

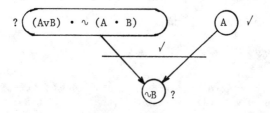

Step Six: formulate a response to the argument. We can respond: "Your reasoning doesn't fully prove you should not get married, since going to medical school does not automatically exclude getting married."

216

(6.297) HYPOTHETICAL SYLLOGISM.

(1) INTRODUCTION. The name of this pattern is somewhat
misleading because it does not have the form of a standard
syllogism. However, the logical chain that the pattern follows is
often encountered. Each conditional represents a link in a chain
forming a connection between the antecedent of the first
conditional and the consequent of the last. The chain can have
two or more "links".

(2) TYPICAL EXAMPLE. "If the human fetus has a human
genetic makeup then it is a human being at all stages of
development. If it is a human being at all stages of development
then it has a right not to be killed. Therefore, if the human
fetus has a human genetic makeup then it has a right not to be
killed."

(3) BASIC LOGICAL FORM. If A then B. If B then C.
Therefore, if A then C.

(4) INFERENCE VALIDITY ANALYSIS. The inference is valid
providing the propositions occur in the correct sequence. If, for
example, the second assumption was 'if C then B' the inference
would be invalid.

(5) INFERENCE CRITICISM STRATEGY. Perform a short truth
table test.

(6) ASSUMPTION EVALUATION. Apply the usual criteria for
evaluating the conditionals.

(7) VARIANT VERSIONS. None.

(8) EVALUATION OF EXAMPLE. The above example will be
evaluated.

Step One: construct an accurate diagrammatic version of the
argument. The semi-symbolic version is: "If A then B. If B then
C. Therefore, if A then C." The symbolic version is: "A ⊃ B /
B ⊃ C // A ⊃ C".

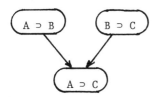

A = The human fetus has a human
    genetic makeup.

B = The human fetus is a human being
    at all stages of development.

C = The human fetus has a right not
    to be killed.

217

Step Two: Evaluate the inference. A short truth table test shows the inference to be valid:

$$
\begin{array}{ccc c c c}
A \supset B & / & B \supset C & // & A \supset C \\
T\ T\ T & & T\ F\ F & & T\ F\ F \\
5\ 6\ 7 & & 8\ 9\ 4 & & 2\ 1\ 3
\end{array}
$$

Step Three: evaluate the assumptions. The assumption B ⊃ C can be regarded as true. The differences between human beings in the womb and ones outside it, e.g., that the latter obtain oxygen by breathing rather than through an umbilical cord, do not seem to be relevant to the issue of the right not to be killed. We must recognize, however, that the right not to be killed is a presumptive right, a right that can be overridden by the rights of others or other fetus rights. For example, the mother's right to life can override the fetus's right where a choice must be made between lives.

The other assumption, A ⊃ B, is much more dubious, depending on the stage of fetal development. Here it is being claimed that having human genetic makeup guarantees that the fetus is a human being even when it is merely a fertilized egg. This very ambitious claim is false because a fertilized egg does not have enough of the attributes that count toward a thing being a human being. At the minimum, a thing with human genetic makeup must be an organism to count as a human being, and a single egg cell is not an organism. The assumption is false.

Step Four: determine the extent to which intermediate conclusions are proved. There are none.

Step Five: determine the extent to which the final conclusion is proved. With a crucial premise (A ⊃ B) false we rate the argument "X".

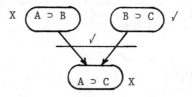

Step Six: formulate a response to the argument. We can respond: "Your conclusion hasn't been proved because there is a false assumption. Having human genetic makeup does not guarantee that the fetus is a human being at all stages of development. It starts out as a fertilized egg cell and a cell is not an organism. To be a human being a thing must be an organism."

218

EXERCISE 6-5

Using the six step procedure with the short truth table test for inference validity, evaluate each of these arguments. No. 1 has been answered in the back.

1. An old argument intended to prove the existence of God relies on evidence of the regularity of behavior of material objects such as the movement of the planets in our solar system. This regularity is regarded as unexplainable except as being the work of a designer. "There is design in the world. If there is design in the world then there is a cosmic designer. Therefore, there is a cosmic designer."

2. Since its beginnings social science has been deeply concerned with the issue of "nature or nurture". To what extent are humans "moldable" by their societies? Are human personalities changed by experience or are they a given, something unalterable? The behavior of reared-together and reared-apart identical twins has been regarded as a way of settling the issue. This argument relies on data showing that intelligence in twins is affected by their being reared apart. "If intelligence is wholly hereditary and identical twins have the same heredity, then raising twins in separate households will not reduce the similarity of intelligence between them. Raising twins in separate households does reduce the similarity of intelligence between them. Identical twins have the same heredity. Therefore, intelligence is not wholly hereditary." (From Pospesel, ARGUMENTS: DEDUCTIVE LOGIC EXERCISES, Prentice-Hall Inc.)

3. A Volkswagen ad shows a photo of a street of identical houses. In front of each is parked a red-and-white Volkswagen station wagon. "If the world looked like this, and you want to buy a car that sticks out a little then you shouldn't buy a Volkswagen Station Wagon. The world doesn't look like this. So if you want to buy a car that sticks out a little, then you should buy a Volkswagen station wagon." (From Pospesel)

4. "If abortion on demand were permitted, abortion will become more widespread; if it becomes widespread, respect for human life will weaken; if respect for human life weakens, our form of civilization will be jeopardized. But surely we don't want to jeopardize our form of civilization. (= Our form of civilization will not be jeopardized.) Therefore, abortion on demand will not be permitted."

219

(6.3) SYLLOGISTIC LOGIC: INTRODUCTION. In Section (6.2) we found that certain arguments, if they contained at least one logically compound assertion, had the property of structural validity. This kind of validity was found to arise from the way the propositions within the argument are related to each other.

It is also possible to have structural validity in arguments that contain assertions about classes of things. These assertions have traditionally been regarded as being of four types, the types being labeled "A", "E", "I", and "O":

A: All X's are Y's

E: No X's are Y's. (= All X's are not Y's)

I: Some X's are Y's

O: Some X's are not Y's

In the I and O types other expressions can occur in place of 'some', for example: 'nearly all', 'most', 'a few', and 'many'. Obviously, these are not synonymous with 'some' but the validity of arguments remains unchanged when any of these expressions are substituted in place of 'some' in ALL occurrences in an argument. In this chapter the word 'some' will be used exclusively in discussing validity, but it must be understood that these other expressions can also occur legitimately.

Singular assertions, those that refer by name or description to a single individual, can be counted as A-type assertions. "Socrates is a philosopher", for example, can count as an A-type assertion because we can think of the word 'Socrates' as denoting a class containing a single individual. Thus, the assertion can be interpreted as saying that "All members of the class of things referred to as Socrates in this assertion are philosophers." This may appear very artificial but treating the assertion this way enables us to correctly apply the test procedures to be presented in this chapter.

(6.31) SYLLOGISMS. Historically, the most common type of argument that contains assertions about class membership is the syllogism.

A typical syllogism is this one (Example One):

All humans are organisms.

All children are humans.

Therefore, all children are organisms.

In this argument we have three kinds of things mentioned

220

(humans, organisms, and children) with each assertion claiming that there is a logical relation between two of the kinds. The first premise, for instance, asserts that all humans belong to the class of organisms. It is an A-type assertion, as are all three assertions in the argument. The argument, typically, uses two distinct class-relation assertions as premises for concluding that a third class relation exists. Since in a genuine syllogism there are three pairs of terms (class names) and only three different terms, it turns out that there is always one term that appears in both premises and that common term is missing in the conclusion. The common term, in a sense, provides a link between the two. In Example 1 the common term is 'humans', which "ties" the other two terms together in the conclusion.

Every genuine syllogism has the properties just described. They must consist of three assertions, each expressing a class relation. They must have exactly three terms, with each assertion expressing a relation between a different pair.

Study of the syllogism was initiated by, and nearly completed by, the Greek philosopher Aristotle. He tried to discover which syllogistic patterns are valid and which are not, and to formulate the principles that could be used for testing them for validity. These were not easy tasks because there are 256 legitimate syllogistic forms, and some that look valid are not and vice versa. Some examples will help you appreciate the problems.

EXAMPLE 2:

All Communists are Socialists.

All Leninists are Communists.

Therefore, all Leninists are Socialists.

EXAMPLE 3:

All Communists are Socialists.

All Leninists are Socialists.

Therefore, all Leninists are Communists.

Example 2 has a valid inference. It is valid because of where the terms 'Communist', 'Socialist',and 'Leninist' occur in the three assertions. No matter what terms (class names) occurred

221

in an argument having this pattern it would have a valid inference. So long as the form of the argument is 'All X's are Y / All Z's are X // All Z's are Y' it is valid. You should find this intuitively plausible.

Example 3 might also seem to have a valid inference but it does not. You may have been misled because each of its assertions is true. But as has been stressed a number of times, an argument is a proof only if the given premises guarantee conclusion truth. It is not a proof merely because the conclusion is true. Furthermore, because validity depends on structure, all arguments that have the same form as Example 3 will also be invalid.

In what follows you will be shown a method for distinguishing valid from invalid syllogisms that is derived from a device called the "Venn Diagram", after the British logician who invented it.

(6.32) VENN DIAGRAMS. In Venn diagrams we have a circle representing each of the three things or properties mentioned in the syllogism. The circles are drawn so that each overlaps the other two. Each circle is conceived of as "containing" all things of a particular kind. For instance, no X's can be outside the X circle. If 'X' stands for 'Communists' the X circle is thought of as containing all Communists, if there are any. When the three circles are drawn so that they overlap in the required way we can identify seven different "cells".

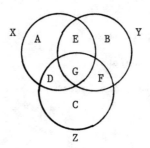

The contents of each cell is as follows:

CELL	POSSIBLE CONTENTS
A	X's only
B	Y's only
C	Z's only
D	X's and Z's
E	X's and Y's
F	Y's and Z's
G	X's, Y's, and Z's

222

This table shows that the circles arranged in this way can represent all possible combinations of three different kinds of things. This makes it possible to represent any assertion whatever that can occur in a syllogism. Thus, if we let 'X' represent 'Communists' and 'Y' represent 'Socialists', the assertion "All Communists are Socialists" can be symbolized as "All X's are Y's." In terms of the diagram this amounts to saying that there are no X's in cells A and D. To express this more formally we write it as 'It is false that there is something in Cell A and it is false that there is something in Cell D'. Now if we let 'A' stand for 'There is something in Cell A' and 'D' stands for 'There is something in Cell D', we can symbolize the Venn-equivalent assertion as '∿A • ∿D'. (We will follow the same convention for all the cells.)

Perhaps you think that 'All X's are Y's' should refer to Cells E and G, since any X's that exist must be in these two cells. However, it is best to think of the assertion as NOT entailing that there are X's in existence. It is better to think of A-assertions as disguised conditionals, assertions that can be written as: 'If something is an X then it is a Y'. This last assertion form, of course, does not entail that there are X's.

If we do not think of 'All X's are Y's' as a disguised conditional we will have logical problems with assertions about empty classes. If we regard, for example, 'All dodos are birds' as entailing that 'There are dodos' then we must say that the first is false because of the fact that the latter is. However, there is something odd about saying that 'All dodos are birds' is false. To do so in normal circumstances would imply that some dodos are not birds.

It is better, then, to treat A-type assertions as neutral so far as the actual existence of things in a class is concerned. What is guaranteed by 'all X's are Y's' is that there are no X's that are not Y's, which is to say that the assertion guarantees, if true, that cells A and D are empty. This is why we write the Venn-equivalent as '∿A • ∿ D'.

E-type assertions are treated in the same way. 'No X's are Y's' is regarded as leaving open the question of whether there actually are any X's or not. These assertions can best be seen as disguised conditionals also, because of this. 'No X's are Y's' is equivalent to 'If something is an X then it is not a Y.' Thus, it tells us that Cells E and G are empty and we can symbolize this as '∿E • ∿ G'.

I-type assertions such as 'Some X's are Y's' have a different logical status. We regard them as entailing the existence of things the assertion is about. If someone claims that some dodos

223

are over three inches high, we are entitled to infer that the assertor believes there are dodos. Thus we will want to regard 'Some X's are Y's' as equivalent (on the Venn diagram) to saying 'either there is something in Cell E or there is something in Cell G and perhaps there are things in both.' This gets symbolized as 'E v G'.

O-type assertions are like I-type ones in that 'Some X's are not Y's' is taken as entailing 'There are X's'. In the Venn diagram 'Some X's are not Y's', is equivalent to 'Either there is something in Cell A or there is something in Cell D and perhaps there are things in both.' This last assertion is symbolized as 'A v D'.

We can, then, express each of the four types of assertion that can occur in syllogisms in terms of assertions about Venn diagrams. The Venn diagram assertions can be symbolized using the symbolic language presented earlier. For things X and Y the Venn-equivalent assertions are as follows:

TYPE	SEMI-SYMBOLIC FORM	VENN-EQUIVALENT FORM
A	All X's are Y's.	$\sim$ A $\cdot$ $\sim$ D
E	No X's are Y's.	$\sim$ E $\cdot$ $\sim$ G
I	Some X's are Y's.	E v G
O	Some X's are not Y's.	A v D

Obviously there are Venn-equivalents for assertions mentioning X's and Z's and for those mentioning Y's and Z's. For instance, 'No Z's are Y's' says that there is nothing in cell F and nothing in cell G, which is symbolized as '$\sim$F $\cdot$ $\sim$ G'.

EXERCISE 6-6

Write the Venn - Equivalent version of each semi-symbolic assertion. Nos. 1 and 2 are answered in back.

1. All Y's are X's.

2. Some Z's are not X's.

3. All Z's are not Y's.

4. Some Y's are X's.

5. All Z's are X's.

6. Some Y's are not Z's.

(6.33) TESTING SYLLOGISMS. Since it is possible to write a Venn-equivalent assertion for each assertion in a syllogism, we can construct argument forms equivalent in logical structure to syllogisms in Venn diagram terms. Then, if the Venn-equivalent of the syllogism proves to be structurally valid we can also say that the syllogism is valid. And of course if the Venn-equivalent argument is invalid so is the syllogism.

We already have at our disposal methods for testing Venn-equivalent arguments. We could use the truth-table method but this would be too cumbersome because most syllogisms have Venn-equivalent versions containing four propositional letters. The short test method, on the other hand, is quite adequate for our purposes. Now let's look at some examples.

Consider this argument: "All men are animals. No woman is a man. Therefore, no woman is an animal." Is this valid?

The first step in syllogism evaluation is to put the argument in semi-symbolic form by substituting X, Y and Z for the names of the three classes mentioned in the argument. In this example let X = man, Y = animals, and Z = women. The semi-symbolic version will be: "All X's are Y's. No Z is X. Therefore, no Z is Y."

Next, we look at the Ven diagram (shown below) to determine how each assertion is symbolized as a Venn-equivalent.

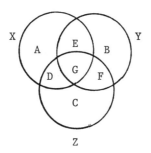

The Venn-equivalent for the argument is this:

All X's are Y.   : $\sim$ A $\cdot$ $\sim$ D
No Z is X.   : $\sim$ D $\cdot$ $\sim$ G
Therefore, no Z is Y. :   Therefore, $\sim$ G $\cdot$ $\sim$ F

To test this argument form we will use the short truth table method.

The result is as follows:

225

```
∿ A  •  ∿ D / ∿  D •  ∿ G // ∿ G •  ∿ F
  T  F  T  T  F   T  FT T  F    T F F F T
 14 15 13 12 11   9 10 1 2 3    5 4 6 7 8
```

In effect, the test shows that, given that there is something in A, D, and G, this does not guarantee that there is nothing in both G and F. The premises guarantee that there is nothing in G but not that there is nothing in F. Therefore, the syllogism has been shown to be invalid.

One more example: "All men are animals. No animals are women. Therefore, no woman is a man." The semi-symbolic version is: "All X's are Y's. No Y's are Z's. Therefore, no Z's are X's". Symbolically, we write: "∿ A • ∿ D / ∿ G • ∿ F // ∿ D • ∿ G." It is not really necessary to go to the trouble of testing this argument form. We can see that D and G both appear in the premises in such a way tht if the premises are true the conclusion will be also. When all three assertions in a syllogism are conjunctions this will always be true if the syllogism is valid. If it is not valid then there will be a proposition appearing in the conclusion that does not appear in the premises. The second-last example is in this category.

One final example: "All men are chauvinists. Some hair-dressers are men. Therefore, some hairdressers are chauvinists." This can be written as "All X's are Y's. Some Z's are X's. Therefore, some Z's are Y's." The symbolic version is: "∿ A • ∿ D / D v G // G v F". This form tests out to be valid, as you might verify for yourself.

EXERCISE 6 -7

Using the propositional Venn equivalents, symbolize and test each of the following syllogisms given in semi-symbolic form. Nos. 1, 6 and 7 have been answered in the back.

1. Some X is not Y / No X is Z // Some Z is not Y

2. Every X is Y / Every Z is X // Every Z is Y

3. Every X is Y/ Some Z is Y // Some Z is X

4. No X is Y / Some Y is Z // Some Z is not X

5. Some X is Y / Some Z is X // No Z is Y

6. No X is Y / Every Z is Y // Some Z is not X

7. Some X is not Y / Every X is Z // Some Z is not Y

8. No X is Y / Every X is Z // No Z is Y

226

(6.34) TRANSLATIONS. It should be no surprise to learn that the A, E, I, and O assertions can be expressed in a variety of ways other than the standard forms presented at the beginning of section 6.3. A few commonly encountered stylistic variations should be noted.

(1) Syllogisms are about classes of things, but many assertions attribute a predicate to a subject: 'All men are assertive', 'No human being is ten feet tall', etc. These should be understood as having the form 'All men are THINGS THAT are assertive', 'no human being is A THING THAT is ten feet tall', and so on. In the first example we have the class of men and the class of things that are assertive and it is being said that the members of the former class all belong to the latter. You should be aware, therefore, that many sentences forming parts of syllogisms are about classes of things even if they are attributing a property to members of a class.

(2) A similar point is applicable to sentences in which a verb is applied to a class of things. For instance, 'Some turtles run' can be thought of as saying 'Some turtles ARE THINGS THAT run.'

(3) It has already been pointed out that singular assertions can form parts of syllogisms. 'Socrates is mortal' can be regarded as saying that 'ALL THINGS THAT ARE Socrates are mortal,' 'Mount Everest is a high mountain' can be reworded as 'ALL THINGS THAT ARE Mount Everest are high mountains.'

(4) Some assertions that can belong to syllogisms are best thought of as being about occasions. For example, 'Borg always beats Connors at tennis' can be thought of as saying that 'All occasions on which Borg plays Connors at tennis are occasions on which Borg beats Connors at tennis.'

(5) Generalizations without explicit qualifiers such as 'some', 'most', etc., can be dealt with in syllogisms but they are somewhat tricky. They can be treated as if they do contain a particular qualifier, or as being about all the typical or normal individuals of the kind. For example,'Bears are omnivorous' can be regarded as equivalent to 'Most bears are omnivorous' or 'Some bears are omnivorous', which would make it an I-assertion, or it could be seen as equivalent to 'All typical bears are omnivorous.' If the latter is chosen as appropriate, it would be necessary to regard all references to bears in the syllogism as applying to typical bears only.

Finally, here is a list of some English sentences and their standard-form equivalents. Several of these are deceptive in that they seem to be written the wrong way around. Verify them by writing Venn-equivalent versions of the ones in the left column.

227

Every X is a Y	:	All X's are Y's
Any X is a Y	:	All X's are Y's
Everything X is a Y	:	All X's are Y's
Nothing except X is Y	:	All Y's are X's
Only X's are Y's	:	All Y's are X's
Nothing is X if it is Y	:	No X is Y

(6.35) SOME COMMON SYLLOGISMS. As in the propositional logic field, certain syllogism patterns are used more frequently than others. In this section several of the more common ones will be discussed and examples evaluated. Some have valid patterns, some have not.

(6.351) PATTERN #1 (UNDISTRIBUTED MIDDLE)

(1) INTRODUCTION. This pattern often occurs. It is so-called because of the position of the Y term in the assumptions.

(2) TYPICAL EXAMPLE. "All good Americans are supporters of school prayer. All members of the Moral Majority are supporters of school prayer. Therefore, all members of the Moral Majority are good Americans."

(3) BASIC LOGICAL FORM. All X's are Y's. All Z's are Y's. Therefore, all Z's are X's.

(4) INFERENCE VALIDITY ANALYSIS. A Venn-equivalent version of the pattern is: $\sim A \cdot \sim D / \sim C \cdot \sim D // \sim C \cdot \sim F$. A test shows the inference is not valid:

```
∿ A • ∿ D / ∿  C • ∿ D // ∿ C  •  ∿  F
T F T T F    T  F T T F    T  F  F  F  T
2 3 1 4 5    9 10 8 7 6    12 11 13 14 15
```

Premises are true when A, C, and D are empty, but this does not exclude something being in cell F, so that the conclusion can be false. Whatever is in cell F is a Z but not an X.

(5) INFERENCE CRITICISM STRATEGY. Use a short truth table test of a Venn-equivalent version. Then, if the inference is invalid, create a counter-example argument such as this: "All dogs are animals. All cats are animals. Therefore, all cats are dogs."

(6) ASSUMPTION EVALUATION. Each assumption can be refuted

by producing solid counter-examples. Try to refute 'all X's are Y's' by identifying an X that is not a Y. Try to refute 'all Z's are Y's' by identifying a Z that is not a Y.

(7) VARIANT VERSIONS. None.

(8) EVALUATION OF AN EXAMPLE. The example given above is suitable for discussion.

Step One: construct an accurate diagrammatic version of the argument.

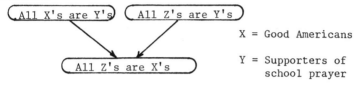

X = Good Americans

Y = Supporters of
    school prayer

Z = Members of the
    Moral Majority

Step Two: Evaluate the inference. We write and test the Venn-equivalent version:

$\sim$ A $\cdot$ $\sim$ D / $\sim$ C $\cdot$ $\sim$ D // $\sim$ C $\cdot$ $\sim$ F

T F T T F T F T T F   T F F F T

2 3 1 4 5 9 10 8 7 6 12 11 13 14 15

With the premises true, the conclusion can be false when cell F is occupied. That is, the premises allow for there being persons who support school prayer and are members of the Moral Majority but who are not good Americans. The inference is rated "X".

Step Three: evaluate assumptions. The assumption "all good Americans are supporters of school prayer" is certainly dubious and probably false, depending on what the arguer regards as being a "good American." A person can be a model citizen in every respect but be opposed to school prayer for a variety of reasons. Perhaps one is a follower of a non-Christian religion (Judaism, for example), or perhaps one regards prayer in school as violating the principle of separation of church and state institutions. Of course, if the arguer thinks that being a good American requires religious worship we can attack the assumption on the ground that this is at least debatable as a good-making characteristic of the American citizen. Religious involvement does not seem to be a civic duty like voting and obeying the law. In either case we can rate the assumption "X".

The other assumption, that all members of the Moral Majority are supporters of school prayer, can be accepted in the absence of any knowledge of possible counter-instances. It is likely that there are at least some individuals who can serve as counter-examples, but we need not take the trouble to identify them since the argument already merits an "X" proof rating.

Step Five: determine the extent to which the final conclusion is proved. Given that the inference is invalid and one assumption is rated "X" the final conclusion is rated "X".

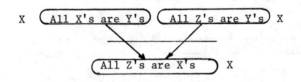

Step Six: formulate a response to the argument. We can respond as follows: "You have not proved to any appreciable extent that all members of the Moral Majority are good Americans. For one thing, there are surely people who count as good Americans even though they are opposed to school prayer. A Jewish person might be, or someone who wishes to follow the example of Thomas Jefferson and other "founding fathers" who believed in separation of church and state. For another thing, even if your assumptions were both true they could not prove the conclusion, since the reasoning is the same as in this argument: "All dogs are animals. All cats are animals. Therefore, all cats are dogs."

(6.352) PATTERN #2 ("BARBARA")

(1) INTRODUCTION. In the middle ages logic students had to memorize all the valid syllogistic patterns (there were 19 recognized ones). Someone developed a name for each that could be incorporated into a "rhyme". The pattern to be examined here was labeled "Barbara" because it consists of three A-type assertions. The vowels in the names correspond to the types of assertions in syllogisms.

(2) TYPICAL EXAMPLE. "All supporters of school prayer are members of the Moral Majority. All good Americans are supporters of school prayer. Therefore, all good Americans are members of the Moral Majority."

(3) BASIC LOGICAL FORM. All X's are Y's. All Z's are X's.

230

Therefore, all Z's are Y's.

(4) INFERENCE VALIDITY ANALYSIS. A Venn-equivalent version of the pattern is:

$\sim$ A $\bullet$ $\sim$ D / $\sim$ C $\bullet$ $\sim$ F // $\sim$ C $\bullet$ $\sim$ D.

The pattern is valid because for the premises to be true $\sim$C and $\sim$ D must both be true.

(5) INFERENCE CRITICISM STRATEGY. Use a short truth table test of a Venn-equivalent version.

(6) ASSUMPTION EVALUATION. Try to refute by identifying good counter-examples.

(7) VARIANT VERSIONS. None.

(8) EVALUATION OF EXAMPLE. The example given above is suitable for discussion.

Step One: construct an accurate diagrammatic version of the argument.

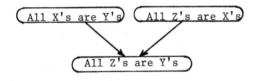

X = supporters of
    school prayer

Y = members of the
    Moral Majority

Z = good Americans

Step Two: evaluate the inference. The test shows the inference is valid:

$\sim$ A $\bullet$ $\sim$ D / $\sim$ C $\bullet$ $\sim$ F // $\sim$ C $\bullet$ $\sim$ D

T F T T F   T F T T   F   T   F   T   T   T

2 3 1 4 5   7 8 6 9 10   12 11 15 14 13

Step Three: evaluate assumptions. The assumption "all good Americans are supporters of school prayer" was evaluated in connection with the previous argument pattern. Reasons were given for regarding it false.

The assumption "all supporters of school prayer are members of Moral Majority" can easily be shown to be false by identifying

231

someone who is a counter example. Most of us can probably find someone we know who "fits the bill." After all, the Moral Majority is not all that large in terms of membership.

Step Four: determine the extent to which intermediate conclusions are proved. There are none.

Step Five: determine the extent to which the final conclusion is proved. Given that both assumptions are rated "X" the argument rating will be "X".

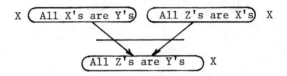

Step Six: formulate a response to the argument. We can respond by saying: "Your conclusion is not proved to any great extent since both assumptions are false. There are bound to be people who support school prayer but who are not members of Moral Majority. Most Roman Catholics who support school prayer would not be members. The other assumption, that all good Americans are supporters of school prayer, is false too. A person could be a model American citizen in every respect but still be against school prayer. Perhaps one is a member of a non-Christian religious group, or believes in the complete separation of church and state as the "founding fathers" did.

(6.353) PATTERN #3 (ILLICIT MINOR)

(1) INTRODUCTION. This pattern is another invalid one that gets its credibility from its similarity to "Barbara". It differs in that the second assumption is 'All X's are Z's' rather than 'All Z's are X's'.

(2) TYPICAL EXAMPLE. "All Marxists are Communists. All Marxists are Socialists. Therefore, all Socialists are Communists."

(3) BASIC LOGICAL FORM: All X's are Y's. All X's are Z's. Therefore, all Z's are Y's.

(4) INFERENCE VALIDITY ANALYSIS. A Venn-equivalent version of the pattern is: $\sim A \cdot \sim D / \sim A \cdot \sim E // \sim C \cdot \sim D$. A test

232

shows the inference is not valid:

∿ A • ∿ D / ∿ A • ∿ E // ∿ C • ∿ D

T F T T F   T F T T F   F T F T F

2 3 1 4 5   7 6 8 9 10   14 15 13 12 11

Assumptions are true when cells A, D, and E are empty but this does not exclude the conclusion being false, which can occur when cell C is occupied. This will happen when there is something that is Z but not X or Y.

(5) INFERENCE CRITICISM STRATEGY. Use the short truth table test of a Venn-equivalent version. Then create a counter-example argument such as this: "All cats are furry. All cats are animals. Therefore, all animals are furry."

(6) ASSUMPTION EVALUATION. Try to refute the assumptions by producing counter-examples or arguing for the improbability of their being true based on general knowledge.

(7) VARIANT VERSIONS. None.

(8) EVALUATION OF AN EXAMPLE: The example given above is suitable.

Step One: construct an accurate diagrammatic version of the argument.

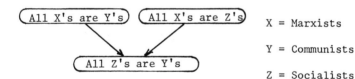

X = Marxists

Y = Communists

Z = Socialists

Step Two: evaluate the inference. A Venn-equivalent version is:
"∿ A • ∿ D / ∿ A • ∿ E // ∿ C • ∿ D"
A test shows the inference is not valid:

∿ A • ∿ D / ∿ A • ∿ E // ∿ C • ∿ D

T F T T F   T F T T F   F T F T F

2 3 1 4 5   7 6 8 910   14 15 13 12 11

233

Step Three: evaluate the assumptions. Is it true that all Marxists are Communists? On consulting THE ENCYCLOPEDIA OF PHILOSOPHY (volume 2, p. 162) we find (surprisingly) that Marx dissociated himself from communist ideas which stressed the commune as a social unit. Thus, at least one Marxist is not a Communist in the original literal sense. The term 'Communism' was used by Lenin instead of 'Marxism', although the former term had a prior meaning that would not really allow Lenin's system to count as an example. The other assumption, that all Marxists are Socialists, is relatively defensible.

Step Four: determine the extent to which the intermediate conclusions are proved. There are none.

Step Five: determine the extent to which the final conclusion has been proved. With one false assumption and an invalid inference the conclusion has not been proved to any satisfactory degree.

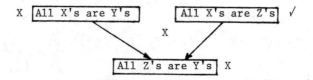

Step Six: formulate a response to the argument. We can respond: "You haven't proved that all socialists are Communists, because it is not true that all Marxists are Communists. Marx himself did not regard himself as a Communist in the literal sense of the term. Furthermore, even if this assumption were true the conclusion would not follow. The argument has the same pattern as this one, and it has a false conclusion; "All cats are furry. All cats are animals. Therefore, all animals are furry."

(6.354) PATTERN #4 ("DARII").

(1) INTRODUCTION. This is a valid pattern used when a non-universal claim must be used as an assumption.

(2) TYPICAL EXAMPLE. In recent years philosophers have been examining the concept of personhood, which means identifying the attributes an individual might have that would count toward that individual being correctly regarded as a person. One attribute that seems important is that of being able to function as a moral

234

agent, to be able to make correct moral judgments and to be able to act in such a way that one can be held morally responsible for one's actions. Some argue that being a moral agent is sufficient to qualify an individual as a person. This argument proceeds from that conviction:

"All moral agents are persons. Some extra-terrestrial individuals are moral agents. Therefore, some extra-terrestrial individuals are persons."

(3) BASIC LOGICAL FORM. All X's are Y's. Some Z's are X's. Therefore, some Z's are Y's.

(4) INFERENCE VALIDITY ANALYSIS. Testing a Venn-equivalent of the pattern shows it is valid:

$\sim$ A • $\sim$ D / D v G / F v G

F F T   T T F   F F F

9 8 7   6 5 4   2 1 3

(5) INFERENCE CRITICISM STRATEGY. Use a short truth table test of a Venn-equivalent version.

(6) ASSUMPTION EVALUATION. Try to refute the universal assumption by producing examples of X's that are not Y's, or arguing in general terms for the likelihood of there being such cases.

The second assumption, 'some Z's are X's', is difficult to refute. We can only do so by proving that no Z's are X's.

(7) VARIANT VERSIONS. Another valid pattern arises when the terms in the second assumption are reversed. That is, by changing 'some Z's are X's' to 'some X's are Z's' and retaining the other assertions we have a valid syllogism. This is because the altered assertion and the original one are logically equivalent. The truth conditions of 'some cows are brown' and 'some brown things are cows' are the same.

(8) EVALUATION OF AN EXAMPLE. Let us test the example given above.

Step One: construct an accurate diagrammatic version of the argument. (The diagram is shown on the next page.)

X = moral agents

Y = persons

Z = extra-terrestrials

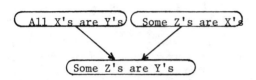

Step Two: evaluate the inference. Testing the Venn-equivalent version shows the inference is valid:

∿ A • ∿ D / D v G // F v G

    F F T   T T F   F F F

    9 8 7   6 5 4   2 1 3

Step Three: evaluate assumptions. Are all moral agents persons? This is a difficult philosophical question, and this is not the place to go into it at length. Some think that one needs to be a human being to count as a person and typical humans are more than moral agents. One might be a non-human and a moral agent but perhaps not count as a person because one cannot have emotional responses (e.g. Mr. Spock in Star Trek). Let us rate the assumption "?" pending further investigation.

The other assumption, 'Some extra-terrestrials are moral agents', is not known to be true at this time since we have no conclusive evidence that there actually are extra-terrestrials, much less any evidence about their capabilities. On the other hand we do not know the assumption is false. Rate it "?", giving the arguer some benefit of doubt.

Step Four: determine the extent to which intermediate conclusions are proved. There are none.

Step Five: determine the extent to which the final conclusion is proved. With a valid inference and two assumptions rated "?" let us rate the argument "X". The conclusion has not been proved to a significant extent.

Step Six: formulate a response to the argument. We can respond: "The conclusion has not been proved because both assumptions are questionable. An individual may have to have more attributes than being a moral agent to qualify as a person. They might, for example, have to be capable of emotional responses. As to whether some extra-terrestrials are moral agents, we are not (right now) in a position to know, although given the number of

236

habitable places in the universe there is a definite chance that
there are."

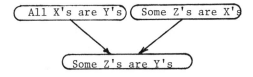

EXERCISE 6 - 8

Evaluate each of the following syllogisms following the
method used in this chapter. Nos. 1 and 2 have been answered in
the back.

1. "No persons in fox-holes are atheists. No Christians are
    atheists. Therefore, some persons in fox-holes are
    Christians."

2. "Some college students are lazy, but no college student who
    studies more than 25 hours per week is lazy. Therefore, some
    college students do study more than 25 hours per week."

3. "Some football stars are quiche eaters. All quiche eaters are
    sissys, so some football stars are sissys."

4. It was once revealed that former Lost Angeles Rams defensive
    lineman Roosevelt Greer did needlepoint for relaxation. This
    is pretty impressive when one realizes that Greer has hands
    the size of encyclopedia volumes: "R. Greer does needlepoint.
    R. Greer is not to be trifled with. Therefore some people who
    do needlepoint are not to be trifled with."

5. "Every man who admires feminine beauty is a sexist. Some
    admirers of beauty are men who admire feminine beauty. So
    some admirers of beauty are sexists."

CHAPTER SEVEN: SUPPLYING MISSING ASSUMPTIONS

(7.1) INTRODUCTION: In this chapter a different approach to argument evaluation will be presented. Instead of evaluating each inference and assumption individually and using the resulting ratings as a basis for deciding the extent to which conclusions are proved, this alternative approach involves attributing assumptions that result in valid inferences and then basing our judgement of the degree of proof on the ratings of the assumptions. This approach is an effective one because most people can understand criticisms of assumptions better than criticisms of inferences.

In Chapter Five it was pointed out that evidential arguments are most adequately expressed in the form 'P, therefore C unless U.' 'U' stands for plausible factors that would prevent C from being true when P is true. Let us suppose there is one such factor and that it warrants rating the inference as "?". Suppose also that P warrants a true rating. We then have the situation shown in Figure (a). Now let us use the new approach. This involves adding an assumption that entails the falsity of the U-factor claim. This can often be equivalent to 'not-U'. Having added this assumption, C now follows validly from 'P' and ' U'. If P is a good reason for C and U is a plausible rival to C then there will be some doubt about the truth of 'not-U', so we would want to rate it "?". This is the situation in Figure (b).

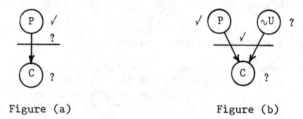

Figure (a)   Figure (b)

Notice in the above rated arguments that the overall rating is the same. This can be explained in terms of probabilities.

The argument in Figure (b) can be written as "P / ∿ U// C." The inference is '(P , ∿ U) ⊃ C', which is logically equivalent to 'P ⊃ (∿U ⊃ C)'. The latter can, in turn, be written as 'P ⊃ (U v C)'. Thus an equivalent to the argument would have P as the sole assumption, with 'U v C' as the conclusion. The inference would be valid since the original one was. Now suppose that, given P, C has a probability of 0.6. This means that U has a probability of 0.4 since the probability of U v C is 1, given a perfectly valid inference and the truth of P. From this it follows that ∿ U has a probability of 0.6 since p(∿ X) = 1 - p(X). Thus, with a 0.6

probability we would rate the assumption U as "?". Furthermore, returning to Figure (b), with the inference valid the probability of C is $p(P) \times p(\sim U)$, which is 0.6, since $p(P) = 1$. The upshot of all this is that the overall rating of the argument is the same in both Figure (a) and Figure (b) versions, since the probability of C being true with P being true is 0.6 in both cases.

The phenomenon of "conservation of overall degree of proof" applies to the procedures that will be followed in supplying missing premises for both evidential and propositional arguments. There is one important difference in that the assumption in propositional arguments will be logically equivalent to the claim that the inference is valid. That is, the added assumption will be equivalent to 'P ⊃ C'.

It is important to realize that, although we are improving the inference quality by adding assumptions, we are not doing so by providing new evidence for the conclusion. If we were to do this we would have to give the revised argument a better overall rating. The assumptions we do add are ones the arguer is committed to because of his/her claim that the inference from P to C is valid. As we noted, this is often correct only when all plausible U-factors are eliminated. So the arguer is always committed to denying that there are any plausible U-factors. When there are some he/she is committed to denying that they are operative and this amounts to relying on extra assumptions.

The treatment required by abbreviated syllogisms (Section 7.4) is somewhat different. When an argument amounts to the conclusion and one assumption of a syllogism it has an invalid inference, but sometimes another assumption can be added that converts it into a complete syllogism with a valid inference. When this happens the overall rating of the argument depends on the ratings of the assumptions, as in the case of the other two argument types.

(7.2) EVIDENTIAL ARGUMENTS. As pointed out in Chapter Five, most evidential argument paterns can be seen as following a cause-to-effect direction or an effect-to-cause direction. When they follow the cause-to-effect direction, inference criticism involves identifying plausible "I-factors", factors that would prevent the conclusion from being true even though the premises are true. When they follow the effect-to-cause direction, criticism involves identifying "A-factors", factors that represent alternatives to the conclusion as producers of premise truth. Together I-factors and A-factors were called "U-factors".

In identifying missing assumptions we try to first identify all plausible U-factors. Then we formulate one or more assertions that, if true, would entail that the plausible U-factors are not

239

present. In other words, the assumptions are incompatible with the U-factor.

Note that missing assumptions are not new evidence for the conclusion. They are claims to which the arguer is already committed in maintaining that the inference is valid. That is, the arguer must agree that the plausible U-factors are not operative if he/she wishes to say that the inference is valid.

In what follows examples of each of the argument patterns presented in Chapter Five will be evaluated using the new approach. Since the strategy is different, the procedure first set out in Chapter Four must be changed. The revised procedure follows.

STEP ONE: construct an accurate diagrammatic version of the argument.

STEP TWO (a): identify the plausible U-factors.

STEP TWO (b): formulate the most defensible assumption(s) that exclude the plausible U-factors.

STEP TWO (c): add the assumptions to the diagram and rate each inference valid.

STEP THREE: evaluate each of the original assumptions and each of the added ones and assign ratings to them.

STEP FOUR: determine the extent to which each intermediate conclusion is proved. Enter the rating by the conclusion.

STEP FIVE: determine the extent to which the final conclusion is proved. Enter the result by the conclusion. This is the overall rating of the argument.

STEP SIX: formulate a response to the argument.

Only Step Two (b) is really new and in need of special comment. It is best to try to formulate a single assumption that will exclude all plausible U-factors, but often this cannot be done because these factors are too logically different. For example, one may report a psychological state and another a physical state. There is no logical need to strive for one assumption, but simplicity has persuasive advantages. Arguers may be prepared to agree that they have made one assumption, but may not be so ready to accept a second or third as a commitment.

Ideally the missing assumptions should be general enough to exclude the U-factors identified at Step Two (a), but they should

240

not be less defensible than necessary. Otherwise, the arguer can deny being committed to assuming what you have attributed. An example will illustrate this delicate problem.

Suppose someone says "Marlon is an actor so Marlon is probably a womanizer." We could make the inference in this argument valid by adding the assumption 'All actors are womanizers', since this excludes the possibility that Marlon is one actor who is not a womanizer. Our response to the arguer would be: "You're assuming that all actors are womanizers but this is untrue because there are some who have been faithfully married to one woman for many years, so your conclusion has not been proved." Unfortunately, the arguer could reply by saying: "I'm not assuming that ALL actors are womanizers, only that most are, and you haven't said anything to disprove that." The arguer would be on solid ground in making this reply because the conclusion contains the "hedge word" 'probably'. We would have done better in the first place to have noticed this word and attributed the assumption 'Most actors are womanizers' since by adding this the inference will warrant a valid rating. (A "√" rating in evidential arguments does not signify 100% validity, but between 75% and 100%.

To summarize the point illustrated: make the attributed missing assumptions adequate to exclude plausible U-factors, but no more logically ambitious than required to bring the inference rating up to "√".

One further point before we proceed to deal with actual arguments: note that in Step Two (c) the inferences are rated "√" after the missing assumptions are added. It is important, of course, that each inference does warrant this rating. It is always good practice before assigning the "√" rating to re-examine each inference to be sure that it is of adequate quality. If you still think of a U-factor that prevents rating an inference "√", then you must add an additional assumption to exclude it.

In the remainder of section 7.2 an example corresponding to each of the patterns presented in Chapter Five will be partially evaluated using the new approach. Only steps 1 through 2(b) will be performed. If you wish, you can complete each evaluation yourself. In the case of Exercises 7 - 1 through 7 - 20 recommended assumptions are given in the back for number one in each set.

(7.21)   ARGUMENTS FROM EFFECT TO CAUSE (see 5.51).

(1)   BASIC LOGICAL FORM:

E has occurred.

Therefore, C has occurred.

(2)   EXAMPLE: The irate houseowner has noticed a small round hole in his picture window, the sort of hole made by a pellet fired by a pellet gun. He reasons: "My window has a small round hole in it, so someone has fired a pellet gun at it."

(3)   EXAMPLE EVALUATION.

STEP ONE: construct an accurate diagrammatic version of the argument.

A = My window has a small round hole in it.

B = Someone has fired a pellet gun at it.

STEP TWO (a): identify all plausible factors undermining the inferences. This being an effect-to-cause pattern we seek alternative causes. Here are the most plausible:

1.   Someone fired a BB gun at the window.

2.   A pellet struck the window accidentally.

3.   A BB struck the window accidentally.

4.   A flying stone struck the window.

STEP TWO (b): formulate the most defensible assumptions that exclude these factors. The alternatives noted above are of two kinds. The first one is similar to the conclusion in that it alleges someone intentionally fired a weapon at the window. The other three allege the hole was made accidentally. Given this difference it is probably best to add two missing assumptions:

C = A BB gun was not fired at the window.

D = The hole was not made accidentally.

242

Evaluate each of the following effect-to-cause arguments after supplying the missing assumptions.

1. After the election in the Province of Quebec of a government whose declared intent was separation from Canada the birth rate among English-speaking residents of Quebec dropped significantly. A newspaper noted this and gave this argument: "The birth rate among English-speaking Quebeckers dropped after the Parti Quebecois was elected. Therefore, the political climate made them less romantic."

2. A professor was heard to say: "I get a lot of poorly written essays from freshmen, so the high schools do a poor job of teaching English composition." (Hint: what else affects writing performance besides skill level?)

3. "Most college athletes playing varsity sports don't do well academically, so playing their sport interferes with their study time."

(7.22)   ARGUMENTS FROM CAUSE TO EFFECT (see 5.52)

(1)   BASIC LOGICAL FORM:

C has occurred.

Therefore, E will occur.

(2)   EXAMPLE:

STEP   ONE: construct an accurate diagrammatic version of the argument.

A = Thunderclouds are coming.

B = We will have a thunderstorm.

STEP TWO (a):   identify all plausible factors undermining the inferences. Since this is a cause-to-effect pattern, we should try to formulate factors that would interfere with B coming true when A is true. Here are the most plausible ones:

1.   The thunderclouds will be blown "off course" and not reach us.

2.   Conditions within the clouds will not be right to result in a thunderstorm by the time they arrive.

STEP TWO (b): formulate the most defensible assumption that excludes these factors.   The two factors noted are sufficiently different so that there does not seem to be a single assumption that would exclude both. We need to supply two assumptions:

C = The clouds will reach us.

D = The clouds will be ready to produce a thunderstorm by the time they reach us.

EXERCISE 7 - 2

Evaluate each of the following cause-to-effect arguments after supplying the missing assumptions.

1.   "Most members of the Rolling Stones band are in their forties now, so the band will probably stop performing soon."

244

2. "U.S. business schools have been studying Japanese management methods in recent years, so graduates from these schools will be able to successfully apply these methods in American business ."

3. "More and more people are quitting smoking. Therefore, tobacco sales will drop to a low level."

(7.23) THE METHOD OF AGREEMENT (see 5.54)

(1) BASIC LOGICAL FORM:

Cases 1, 2, 3, etc., are cases of phenomenon E and have phenomenon C in common.

Phenomenon C preceded (or occurred at the same time as) phenomenon E.

Therefore, C is the cause of E.

(2) EXAMPLE. The farmer argues: "Every autumn when the full moon is visible there is a frost. So the full moon can cause frost."

(3) EXAMPLE EVALUATION

STEP ONE: construct an accurate diagrammatic version of the argument.

A = Every autumn when the full moon is visible there is a frost.

B = The full moon can cause frost.

STEP TWO (a): identify all plausible factors undermining the inferences. This argument has an effect-to-cause pattern. In undermining the inference we try to identify other factors besides C that might be common to all cases and which could be the cause of E. In this case we need to identify phenomena other than the full moon that are common to autumn nights when there is frost. One comes to mind: extra cooling caused by the absence of cloud cover. (The sky will frequently be clear when the moon is visible.).

STEP TWO (b): formulate the most defensible assumption that excludes this factor. Since there is only one factor identified a simple denial of it is a satisfactory assumption:

C = Absence of cloud cover does not affect surface temperature.

246

EXERCISE 7 - 3

Evaluate   each of the following method-of-agreement arguments after supplying their missing assumptions.

1. The   compulsive   crammer   says: "I usually do better on exams when   I   study late the night before.   So the extra study must be very useful."

2. Dr. X is a general practitioner but a frustrated medical researcher.   He gives aspirin to his patients who have flu, telling   them   it   is a new wonder drug for flu. Almost all of them   report   that   their   flu   went   away   more   quickly.   He reasons: "I gave 10 flu patients aspirin.   Nearly all of them say   they   recovered   more   quickly.   Therefore, aspirin is an effective cure for influenza."

3. A novice   car   test driver needs to establish the top speed of the   car   he is testing.   (The manufacturer claims a top speed of   110   m.p.h.)   He   picks a long stretch of road and drives along   it   three   times: "On   three runs the car just barely exceeded   100   m.p.h.   each time. Each time there was a slight wind   facing   me.   So   the   low   top   speed was caused by the wind."

(7.24)   METHOD OF DIFFERENCE (see Section 5.55)

(1)   BASIC LOGICAL FORM:

Cases 1, 2, 3, etc. differed from cases a, b, c, etc., in respect C.

Cases 1, 2, 3, etc. differed from cases a, b, c, etc., in having outcome E.

Phenomenon C preceded (or occurred at the same time as) E.

Therefore, C is the cause of E.

(2)   EXAMPLE. An argument in support of vitamin C tablets as cold preventatives: "Each time I have noticed the onset of cold symptoms and have done nothing, I have gotten a cold. The last time I noticed symptoms I took a large daily dose of vitamin C tablets and did not get a cold. Therefore, vitamin C tablets prevented my cold."

(3)   EXAMPLE EVALUATION

STEP ONE: construct an accurate diagrammatic version of the argument.

A = Each time I have noticed the onset of cold symptoms and have done nothing I have gotten a cold.

B = The last time I noticed symptoms I took a large daily dose of vitamin C and did not get a cold.

C = Vitamin C tablets prevented my cold.

STEP TWO (a): identify all plausible factors that could undermine the inference. These factors will be differences other than C between the two sets of cases, factors which might cause E. In this example such factors might be other things the individual did that are effective in warding off colds. Also, the individual's physical condition may have been extra-good so the body could fight off the cold bacteria.

STEP TWO (b): formulate the most defensible assumptions that exclude these factors. These assumptions are satisfactory:

D = No other special steps were taken to ward off the cold.

E = My state of health preceding the onset of the cold

248

symptoms was no better than it normally is.

Evaluate each of the following method-of-difference arguments after supplying their missing assumptions.

1. "Working women are paid less for the same work as men. Therefore, gender discrimination is the cause of the discrepancy."

2. This is a true medical story. A man whose daughter was being treated for leukemia by radiation therapy had to ensure that she took a zinc tablet each day. At some stage the child refused to swallow the tablets anymore and took to sucking them instead. At that time she was coming down with a cold, but he noticed that it did not develop as expected. He wondered if sucking the zinc tablets was responsible, so he decided to try them himself when he noticed a cold coming on. He noticed a difference and reasoned thusly: "In the past my colds ran their course over about a week. I sucked zinc tablets the last three times I contracted colds. My last three colds have been of shorter duration than usual. Therefore, zinc is responsible for shortening my colds."

3. A professor finds that his current class in Freshman English is not doing so well as previous ones, even though he has introduced (what he takes to be) a better text and is offering the class at a better time. He thinks: "In past years the average mid-term grade has been "B". This class had an average of "C" and seems less well-prepared. So poorer student preparation is the cause of the lower mid-term grades."

(7.25)   METHOD OF CONCOMITANT VARIATION (see Section 5.56)

(1)   BASIC LOGICAL FORM:

E varies when C varies.

Therefore, C is the cause of E.

(2)   EXAMPLE.   The harassed homeowner gives us this argument as he cuts his grass for the third time this spring: "The more often I cut the grass, the faster it grows.   So frequent cutting must cause grass to grow faster."

STEP ONE: construct an accurate diagrammatic version of the argument.

A = The more often I cut the grass, the faster it grows.

B = Frequent cutting causes grass to grow faster.

STEP TWO (a):   identify all plausible factors that could undermine the inferences.   If C is a controlled variable we need to identify factors other than C which are also varying and which are potential causes of E.   If C is not a controlled variable we can consider whether E is really the cause of C or whether the concomitant variation of C and E is coincidental, resulting from two separate causes or some third factor causing both.

In this example C is a controlled variable so we need to identify other variables that might be the cause of E.   One factor qualifies here: the soil is warming up, which causes the grass to grow.

STEP TWO (b):   formulate the most defensible assumptions that exclude these factors.   The assumption needed is:

C = The temperature of the soil does not affect grass growth rate.

EXERCISE 7 - 5

Evaluate each of the following concomitant variation arguments after supplying their missing assumptions.

1.   Sociologists have noted that as the legal system becomes more responsive to rape victims the number of reported rapes

250

increases. This argument has been heard: "When the legal system supports rape victims, rape complaints increase. Therefore, support for rape victims causes rape to increase."

2. Student course questionnaires have been in use at some universities as a basis for evaluating the teaching performance of professors. A researcher finds that there is a positive correlation between average course grade and overall course rating. She reasons like this: "Generally speaking, the higher the average course grade, the higher the overall course rating. Therefore, students rate courses higher because they get better grades."

3. A student notices that Professor A has more books in her office than Professor B, and Professor C has fewer books than B. Professor A is also known to have published more than Professor B, and B has published more than C. She reasons: "Amount published correlates positively with the number of books in a professor's office. Therefore, book ownership promotes research activity."

(7.26) METHOD OF RESIDUES (See 5.57).

(1) BASIC LOGICAL FORM:

C is the cause of E.

C1 (a part of C) is the cause of E1 (a part of E)

Therefore, C2 is the cause of E2 (the rest of E).

(2) EXAMPLE. The house-plant lover has the habit of talking to her plants much like some of us talk to our pets. The extraordinary health of the plants prompts her to reason as follows: "Environmental factors cause plant health. Natural environmental factors (soil nutrients, sun, water, temperature) cause normal health in plants. Therefore, the abnormal health of my plants is caused by my talking to them."

STEP ONE: construct an accurate diagrammatic version of the argument.

A = Environomental factors cause plant health.

B = Natural environmental factors cause normal health in plants.

C = The abnormal health of my plants is caused by my talking to them.

STEP TWO (a): identify all plausible factors that could undermine the inferences. Relevant factors are unnoticed potential causes of E2 or part of E2. In this example three factors come to mind:

1. The natural environmental conditions for her plants are better than normal since she is more conscientious than most plant owners.

2. Some single environmental factor is especially superior in her house. Perhaps her plants thrive best at a 60 degree F temperature and she is one of the few people who keep their house at this relatively low temperature.

3. She is very good at picking out good plants so that hers are genetically superior to most.

STEP TWO (b): formulate the most defensible assumptions that exclude these factors. Two distinct assumptions are needed:

D = The natural environment of the plants is not abnormally

252

good.

E = The plants are not genetically superior.

EXERCISE 7 - 6

Evaluate each of the following method-of-residues arguments after supplying their missing assumptions.

1. A man who moves to a warm climate for a long vacation finds he has gained ten pounds in a month: "Half of the weight is due to eating more lunch, some of it is a result of the warmer climate, so the rest must be due to less worry about my job."

2. Someone who holds the view that a child must be born before counting as a full-fledged human being is asked which differences between the born and the unborn make the difference: "Well, if we subtract the fact that a new-born is in a public environment, that doesn't suffice to withdraw the term 'human' being. The other factor is that new-borns breathe, so that must make the difference between being human and not being human.

3. The family notices that mom's apple pie is unusually sweet. She reflects thusly: "The amount of sugar the recipe calls for wouldn't make it over-sweet, so the apples themselves must have been unusually sweet."

(7.27)   ARGUMENTS   FROM ACTIONS TO PSYCHOLOGICAL STATES (see 5.61)

(1)   BASIC LOGICAL FORM:

N did X.

Therefore, N believes/wants/has the attitude/ has policy Y.

(2)   EXAMPLE.   "Lavinia is trying to get into medical school. Therefore, she wants to make a lot of money after college."

(3)   EXAMPLE EVALUATION

Step   One: construct an accurate diagrammatic version of the argument.

A = Lavina is trying to get into medical school.

B = She wants to make a lot of money after college.

STEP   TWO   (a):   identify   all   plausible factors that could undermine   the   inferences.   The inferences in these arguments are like   an   effect-to-cause   pattern   so we need to identify alternatives   to   the   conclusion   that   could   be potentially the reason for N doing X: (1) Lavinia wants to help fight disease, (2) she wants good job security.

STEP TWO (b):   formulate the most defensible assumptions that exclude   these   factors.   Since   the   two   explanations are quite different   we   will   need   two   assumptions,   one to exclude each. These can be:

C = Wanting to fight disease is not her main goal.

D = She is not merely interested in job security.

These   assumptions are phrased in the way they are because it is   possible   that   Lavinia wants each of the two things mentioned even   though   she   also   wants to make a lot of money.   The arguer does   not   need   to deny that she has these other wants, only that these are not her main goal.

254

EXERCISE 7 - 7

Evaluate each of the following arguments after supplying their missing assumptions.

1. A foreigner continually encounters people in the U.S. who ask about her health, even though they are total strangers. She thinks: "People here ask about a stranger's health, so they are more concerned about the health of their citizens then people in most countries."

2. A concerned citizen writes to the Governor of his state giving advice to solve a social problem. A reply from the Governor's secretary reads: "The Governor will take your suggestion under advisement." The citizen says to his wife: "The Governor's secretary says he will consider my suggestion, so he is clearly a man interested in what the voters have to say."

3. A man meets a young woman in a bar wearing an unusual outfit and enquires where she got it, explaining that he is a fashion designer. She says she made it herself and has designed other things. He asks if he can go to her place to see them. She thinks: "He is interested im my designs, so he wants to help me get established in the fashion business."

255

(7.28) BEHAVIOR PREDICTION ARGUMENTS (see Section 5.62).

(1) BASIC LOGICAL FORM:

A

Therefore, N will do X.

(2) EXAMPLE. Supporters of generous foreign aid policies sometimes use this argument to incite support for a larger aid effort by the government. "The third world countries are envious of our prosperity. Therefore they may take from us what we don't give them."

(3) EXAMPLE EVALUATION

STEP ONE: construct an accurate diagrammatic version of the argument.

A = The third world countries
    are envious of our pros-
    perity.

B = They may take from us what
    we don't give them.

STEP TWO (a): identify all plausible factors that could undermine the inferences. We can think of this argument form as following a cause-to-effect pattern, so that the factors we seek are ones that might prevent the conclusion from becoming true when the assumption is true. These are ones that, given A, might lead N to not do X or do something else. In this example two factors meet our requirements:

1. Third world countries may lack the power to take anything from us.

2. They may gain prosperity through our aid and their own efforts.

STEP TWO (b): formulate the most defensible assumptions that exclude these factors. Since the factors are logically different we need a separate assumption to exclude each. This pair is satisfactory:

C = Third world countries have the power to take things from us.

D = Third world countries cannot attain prosperity

256

independently of us.

EXERCISE 7 - 8

Evaluate each of the following behavior-prediction arguments after supplying their missing assumptions.

1. A TV news story in the spring of 1984 about Ronald Reagan's attempts to win the women's vote noted that his administration had spent much less than Jimmy Carter on fightng court battles in sex discrimination cases. This argument emerged: "Women realize Reagan is not fighting sex discrimination in the courts, so they will not vote for him in the next election."

2. In many places university funding is proportional to enrolment. It is known that there will be a drop in the number of people reaching university entrance age in the late 80's and some people argue as follows: "The number of students applying for university entrance will drop in the late 1980's. Universities depend on enrolment for funding, so there will be a lowering of admission standards in the near future."

3. The use of a nuclear deterrent to maintain peace depends on using purely offensive weapons that harm the other side. Some people are arguing for the replacement of these with short-range, purely defensive weapons: "Purely defensive weapons are no threat to the other side, so we should adopt them in place of purely offensive ones, since we will still be safe and the other side will feel safe in eliminating their offensive weaponry."

(7.29)   BEHAVIOR EXPLANATION ARGUMENTS (See 5.63)

(1)   BASIC LOGICAL FORM:

A.   Therefore, A explains why B.

(2)   EXAMPLE: Western nations, and especially the U.S., have been striving to get the U.S.S.R. to agree to arms reduction in Europe.   Here is one argument for an explanation of the uncooperativeness of the U.S.S.R.: "The U.S.S.R. expects an attack by N.A.T.O. countries. This explains why it won't agree to arms reduction in Europe".

(3) EXAMPLE EVALUATION:

Step One: construct an accurate diagrammatic version of the argument.

A = The U.S.S.R. expects an attack by N.A.T.O. countries.

B = The U.S.S.R. won't agree to arms reduction in Europe.

STEP TWO (a): identify all plausible factors that could undermine the inference. First, is A the sort of factor that might explain B? Definitely. Secondly, is there any other possible reason for B? One may be that the U.S.S.R. plans to attack N.A.T.O. forces. This is clearly compatible with A. Perhaps the other reasonably plausible reason is that the U.S.S.R. thinks N.A.T.O. forces have an edge in strength. If this is their belief then they could hardly be expected to agree to equal reductions, which would probably be what the western powers are seeking.

STEP TWO (b): formulate the most defensible assumptions that exclude the U-factors. We need separate assumptions here. These are satisfactory:

C = The U.S.S.R. does not intend to attack N.A.T.O. forces.

D = The U.S.S.R. does not regard its forces in Europe as inferior to N.A.T.O. forces.

EXERCISE 7 - 9

Evaluate each of the following behavior explanation arguments after supplying their missing assumptions.

1. On visiting a bookstore you will notice quite a few books on

investing. You might think this argument is plausible: "Successful people want to share the secrets of their success with the rest of us. This explains why there are books on investing."

2. A professor who uses multiple-choice tests to test for comprehension of his text says: "College freshmen do not read well. This explains why so many do poorly on my tests".

3. Auto workers in Japan are paid about two-thirds as much as their American counterparts, and this has led some labor union people to say: "Japanese workers are paid less. This explains why their cars are better value for money than ours are".

(7.30)   ARGUMENTS FOR RIGHTNESS OF CONDUCT (See 5.71)

(1)   BASIC LOGICAL FORM:

X is morally required (or prohibited) in society S.

P did (or refrained from) X in S.

Therefore, P acted rightly.

(2)   EXAMPLE   "In our part of the country white barbershop owners do not cut a black man's hair, so Sam acted rightly when he refused to cut the tourist's hair."

(3)   EXAMPLE EVALUATION

STEP   ONE: construct an accurate diagrammatic version of the argument.

A = In our part of the country white barbershop owners are morally prohibited from cutting a black man's hair.

B = Sam refused to cut the tourist's hair.

C = Sam acted rightly.

STEP TWO (a): identify the plausible U-factors. Two sorts of factors are important: (1) extenuating circumstances that make the moral rule contained in A inapplicable to P's action; (2) factors that make the rule a bad rule so that complying with the moral prohibition does not result in right action.

In this example we have no basis for assuming that the rule should be waived in his specific case.   The other sort of situation does seem to have a bearing. Sam could have acted rightly   unless   the   rule   was   a   bad   one.   Relative to the conclusion, the claim that the rule is a bad one is much more plausible.

STEP TWO (b): formulate the most defensible assumptions that exclude the U-factors. Here we simply need the assumption that the rule is a morally acceptable one. We do not want the opposite of the U-factor, i.e., that the prohibition mentioned in A is a good one.   That would be less defensible. An acceptable one is this:

D = Prohibiting white barbershop owners from cutting a black man's hair is morally acceptable.

EXERCISE 7 -10

Evaluate each of the following rightness-of-conduct arguments after supplying their missing assumptions.

1. In the last 10 years there have been a number of high-school teachers fired because they were convicted of possession of marijuana for personal use. The action is usually defended by an argument like this: "Marijuana use is morally wrong. Teachers who act in immoral ways set bad examples for their students. Therefore, it is right to fire such teachers."

2. In 1983 and 1984 a group of British women picketed American bases in England where Cruise missiles are stored. They believed that storing them there put England at greater risk of destruction in a nuclear war. Some of them, however, went to the extreme of cutting open the fence of one of the bases and entering the base. Someone argued: "It's wrong to trespass, so the women acted wrongly when they entered the airbase."

3. "Disciplining their children is a moral obligation for parents. Therefore, people who use physical punishment are acting correctly."

(7.31) ARGUMENTS FOR MORAL RESPONSIBILITY (see 5.72)

(1) BASIC LOGICAL FORM:

P has obligation O.

P failed to fulfill O.

Therefore, P is morally responsible for the consequences.

(2) EXAMPLE. A young married woman voluntarily became pregnant and after several visits to her physician it was discovered that she had a serious heart defect that would make it extremely dangerous for her to give birth, either by caesarian section or in the normal way. Her physician urged her to have an abortion and she agreed. A militant anti-abortionist argued: "Mrs. X had an obligation to give birth to her child. She failed to fulfill her obligation, so she is morally responsible for its death."

(3) EXAMPLE EVALUATION

STEP ONE: construct an accurate diagrammatic version of the argument.

A = Mrs. X had an obligation to give birth to her child.

B = Mrs. X failed to fulfill her obligation.

C = Mrs. X is morally responsible for her child's death.

STEP TWO (a): identify the plausible U-factors. This pattern has a cause-to-effect form, so that U-factors will be ones that interfere with C being true when A and B are true. One kind of factor is the existence of a more important obligation that would override the obligation stated in A. A second kind of factor is the existence of a good excuse that reduces moral responsibility.

In this example Mrs. X does have a good excuse, she acted in self-defence. Self-defence is a good excuse even when the other party, by whom one is threatened, does not intend harm. This factor is not contentious at all relative to the conclusion. A second factor may be the existence of overriding obligations to others, to whom she has commitments. This factor, that Mrs. X's obligations to others (including her husband) override her obligation to her child is perhaps about as dubious as the conclusion and should count as a plausible U-factor. There are, then, two plausible U-factors: (1) the excuse of self-defence, and (2) overriding obligations to others.

STEP TWO (b): formulate the most defensible assumptions that exclude the U-factors. Since the U-factors are logically different, two assumptions are needed:

D = Mrs. X was not entitled to defend her life against the fetus.

E = Mrs. X's obligations to others do not override her obligation to give birth.

EXERCISE 7 - 11

Evaluate each of the following moral responsibility arguments after identifying their missing assumptions.

1. In discussions of what to do to help the millions of people who are starving in the third-world countries this argument is sometimes made: "People have an obligation not to create children they cannot support. Many parents in third-world countries fail to fulfill this obligation. Therefore, they are responsible for the suffering of their children."

2. The notion that a woman might be raped by her own husband has come to our attention in recent years. Courts sometimes say this when they discover a woman has not filed charges against her husband: "Women have a moral obligation to report sexual assaults upon their person. Mrs. R. failed to report an assault by her husand, so she is morally responsible for encouraging him to commit further sexual assaults on her and others."

3. "Crib death" is the term applied to those unfortunate cases in which a sleeping baby simply stops breathing for no reason that can be ascertained afterwards. In one case this happened while the baby was in the care of a sitter. The distraught mother argued: "Sitters have an obligation to look after children in their care. You failed to keep my baby alive, so you are responsible for its death."

(7.32) ARGUMENTS FOR MORAL OBLIGATIONS (See 5.73)

(1) BASIC LOGICAL FORM:

People in role R have moral obligation O.

Therefore, person P has a moral obligation to do Y.

(2) EXAMPLE. The Smiths are philosophically opposed to the educational system used in their local schools. They themselves are well educated and wish to teach their children themselves. The local principal says: "Parents have a moral obligation to ensure that their children are educated. Therefore, the Smiths have a moral obligation to send their childen to school."

(3) EXAMPLE EVALUATION

STEP ONE: construct an accurate diagrammatic version of the argument.

A = Parents have a moral obligation to
    ensure that children are educated.

B = The Smiths have a moral obligation to
    send their children to school.

STEP TWO (a): identify the plausible U-factors. In Section 5.73 inference validity was said to depend on five conditions. Each of these is a basis for a U-factor, of which there will be five kinds:
(a) Y is not an effective means of fulfilling O.
(b) Person P does not occupy role R.
(c) There are overriding obligations.
(d) There is a defeasibility condition (defeating, voiding, or suspending).
(e) There are effective alternatives to Y for fulfilling obligation O.
Let us identify a U-factor for the example based on each of these.
First, could it be said that sending children to school is not an effective means of educating them? This claim seems to be not nearly as plausible as the conclusion itself, given assumption A.
Secondly, do the Smiths occupy the role of parents? Yes.
Thirdly, are there any overriding obligations? There could be, although we are not told of any.
Fourthly, is there a defeasibility condition present? Again, we are not given any information that would point to one.
Fifthly, are there effective alternatives to sending the

264

Smith children to school? One possibility is that the children could get an education through correspondence courses. Another is that they could be taught at home by the parents or a tutor. Normally children cannot enroll in a correspondence program if they are able to attend local schools. The other possibility is a plausible one, though.

We have been able to identify one U-factor: "The Smith children could be taught at home."

STEP TWO (b): formulate the most defensible assumptions that exclude the U-factors. The U-factor identified could be excluded by this assumption:

C = The Smith children could not be taught at home by their parents or a tutor.

EXERCISE 7 -12

Evaluate each of the following moral obligation arguments after identifying their missing assumptions.

1. "Teachers have a moral obligation to set a good example for their students. Therefore, Mr. S, our physics teacher, has an obligation to marry the woman he is living with."

2. Ralph is upset because Eunice has casually mentioned that she had happened to encounter Alfred, his pal, on the street and they had lunch together. He says: "Wives have an obligation to tell their husbands who they keep company with, so you ought to have told me you had lunch with Alfred."

3. An engineer is involved in a hardware development program his company has contracted with the government to carry out. He knows that the program is having serious problems that the chief engineer has shielded from the government by falsifying test results. He feels a duty to "blow the whistle" on the program but knows he would probably be fired, and jobs in his speciality are difficult to find. He reasons: "As the wage-earner in my family I have a moral obligation to hold on to a job. Therefore, I ought to keep quiet about the deception."

265

(7.33)   PRUDENTIAL ARGUMENT TYPE ONE (see 5.81)

(1)   BASIC LOGICAL FORM:

Person (or group) P wants W.

Therefore, P ought to do M.

(2)   EXAMPLE.   "The U.S. wants peace in the Middle East.
Therefore, the U.S. ought to arrange that some territory is ceded
to the Palestinians."

(3)   EXAMPLE EVALUATION

STEP   ONE.   construct an accurate diagrammatic version of the
argument.

A = The U.S. wants to promote
peace in the Middle East.

B = The U.S. ought to arrange that some
territory is ceded to the Palestinians.

STEP   TWO   (a):   identify the plausible U-factors. There are
five sorts of U-factors associated with this argument pattern: (1)
the   course   of action recommended (M) is not morally permissible;
(2)   M   is   not in general an effective means of satisfying W; (3)
although   M   is an effective means in most cases, it is not for P;
(4)   M would conflict with some want that is more important than W;
and   (5)   there   are other reasonably good means for satisfying W.
Let us apply this list to the example.

First,   is the course of action, arranging for some territory
to   be   ceded   to the Palestinians, morally impermissible? It need
not   be and it is not likely that the U.S. would try to do this in
an objectionable way.

Secondly,   is it   plausible to hold that ceding territory to
displaced peoples will not promote peace in the area in which they
now   live?   It   would   not   seem   to   be   when   these   people are
themselves the source of much discord.

Thirdly,   is it plausible to hold that some special feature of
the current Middle East situation prevents the ceding of territory
from   being   a   way   of promoting peace in this case? It does not
seem   to   be, although the P.L.O. may be so hostile to Israel that
they   would   continue   to   fight even after they have a country of
their   own.   This   factor   probably   needs   to   be excluded by an
assumption.

Fourthly, is it plausible that ceding territory to the Palestinians would conflict with some more important goal that the U.S. has? A goal that comes to mind is the goal of maintaining the state of Israel. However, it is not likely that Israel will be endangered so long as the territory allotted to the Palestinians is not part of the territory originally given to the Israelis.

Fifthly, is it plausible that there are other good ways of securing peace in the Middle East that the U.S. can use? Perhaps the best alternative is to arrange to have the United Nations play a more active part by supplying a much larger peace-keeping force. However, this requires the consent of the countries that would host the force, and may not be obtainable. Since the last alternative is not very effective compared with providing the Palestinians with their own country, this factor need not be excluded by an assumption.

There seems to be one U-factor that needs to be excluded: the Palestinians will continue hostilities against Israel even when they have their own territory.

STEP TWO (b): formulate the most defensible assumptions that exclude the U-factors. This single assumption will be suitable:

C = The Palestinians will cease hostilities against Israel when they have a country of their own.

EXERCISE 7 - 13

Evaluate the following type one prudential arguments after supplying their missing assumptions.

1. "America wants a lasting peace with the U.S.S.R. Therefore, it should eliminate all of its offensive weaponry that threatens the U.S.S.R."

2. Joe College's roommate notes that Joe is worried about the psychology exam he has tomorrow. He tells Joe: "You want to pass that exam, so you should read the text all the way through between now and tomorrow morning."

3. Pat and Mike are away on a business trip. Mike picks out a present for his wife, but hesitates because of the price. Pat says: "Since you want to get this for your wife, you ought to charge it to your expense account as a travel expense.

(7.34)   PRUDENTIAL ARGUMENT TYPE TWO (see 5.83).

(1)   BASIC LOGICAL FORM:

M is a good means of satisfying want W.

Therefore, P ought to do M.

(2)   EXAMPLE.   Herbert, who earns a modest income working in a bank, is out playing golf with his brother the doctor and one of his brother's colleagues. Herbert mentions that he is thinking of buying a new car.   His brother, with his colleague's support, tells Herbert: "A Mercedes-Benz is a good car, so you ought to buy one of them."

(3)   EXAMPLE EVALUATION

STEP ONE: construct an accurate diagrammatic version of the argument.

A = A Mercedes-Benz is a good car.

B = Herbert ought to buy one of them.

STEP TWO (a):   identify the plausible U-factors.   There are five sorts of U-factors that are associated with this argument pattern:

(1)   There are good alternative means of satisfying the want.

(2)   M is morally and/or legally prohibited.

(3)   There is an exceptional circumstance that makes M inappropriate for P.

(4)   M will interfere with P's pursuit of more important goals.

(5)   P does not actually have want W.

In this example factors of kinds (1), (3) and (4) may be operative.   There are good alternatives to the Mercedes-Benz as a car, quite a few even if one wants a luxury car.   There is an exceptional circumstance in Herbert's case too: he may not earn enough to afford a Mercedes.   Also, since his income is limited, Herbert may find that the payments on a Mercedes prevent him from having other things he values more than a car.

STEP TWO (b): formulate the most defensible assumptions that exclude the U-factors. Two assumptions can exclude the three U-factors:

C = There are no other cars that would suit Herbert.

D = Herbert could maintain his current lifestyle if he bought a Mercedes.

EXERCISE 7 - 14

Evaluate the following type-two prudential arguments after supplying their missing assumptions.

1. Joe College is financially hard-pressed. He is trying to finish university without taking a part-time job. A fellow student says: "Selling cocaine to business people allows you to make good money with a minimum of time invested. You ought to get involved."

2. An advertisement in a travel agency: "Come to Florida. It is the best value for fun in the sun."

3. Maisie wants to study acting, but her father does not think this is a good idea: "Becoming a courtroom lawyer is a good way of satisfying a need to perform. So you ought to study law."

(7.35)   TYPE-RELATIVE EVALUATIVE ARGUMENTS (see Section 5.91)

(1) BASIC LOGICAL FORM:

x has good-making attributes G1, G2, etc.

Therefore, as an X, x is rated R.

(2) EXAMPLE. Sports writers sometimes exaggerate when evaluating athletes. In the winter of 82/83 many sportswriters said this about Al Oliver, the first baseman for the Montreal Expos, a National League baseball team: "In 1982 Oliver won the National League batting championship with a 0.331 batting average. Therefore, Oliver had a great year as a National League first baseman."

(3) EXAMPLE EVALUATION

STEP ONE: construct an accurate diagrammatic version of the argument.

A = In 1982 Al Oliver won the National League batting championship with a 0.331 average.

B = Oliver had a great year as National League first baseman.

STEP TWO (a): identify the plausible U-factors. In arguments of this kind the conclusion may be prevented from being true because of an inappropriate set of good-making attributes being mentioned in the premises. Here the issue is one of how many and what attributes one needs as a National League first baseman to qualify as great, and whether a league-leading batting average is sufficient. Here, we could say "P, therefore C unless Oliver was deficient in some quality a first baseman must have to be great." The most plausible U-factor is lacking at least a very good performance on the field. There does not seem to be any other factor nearly as plausible.

STEP TWO (b): formulate the most defensible assumption that excludes the U-factors. In this case a suitable assumption is:

C = Al Oliver had at least a very good year playing first base.

Evaluate each of the following type-relative evaluative arguments after supplying their missing assumptions.

1. "The late Rocky Marciano was capable of absorbing a lot of punishment in a fight and he was never defeated as a professional fighter. Therefore, he was the greatest heavyweight champion."

2. "Professor Barnum is friendly to his students and provides entertaining classes. We can conclude that he is a pretty good professor."

3. "A great TV series lasts a long time, so obviously M.A.S.H. was a great series."

(7.36) ARGUMENTS FOR RANKINGS (see 5.92)

(1) BASIC LOGICAL FORM:

x1 is better than x2 in ways B1, B2, etc.

x1 is as good as x2 in ways G1, G2, etc.

x1 is worse than x2 in ways W1, W2, etc.

Therefore, x1 as an X, ranks R relative to x2.

(2) EXAMPLE. Professors across the U.S. were surveyed and it was found that the faculty of the University of California (Berkeley) was considered to have the most prestige in research. This leads people to argue: "The University of California (Berkeley) has the most prestigious research faculty, so it is the best university in the United States."

(3) EXAMPLE EVALUATION.

STEP ONE: construct an accurate diagrammatic version of the argument.

A = The University of California (Berkeley) has the most prestigious research faculty in the U.S.

B = It is the best university in the U.S.

STEP TWO (a): identify the plausible U-factors. The primary factor that might prevent the conclusion from being true in the arguments is that x1 is only as good as or worse than x2 in important ways. In this example, Berkeley might be worse than several other universities in important ways, the most important of which is teaching effectiveness. Physical facilities and library holdings are also important, but less so.

STEP TWO (b): formulate the most defensible assumptions that exclude the U-factors. In the example we can cover the three good-making qualities mentioned above using this assumption:

C = Berkeley is at or near the top in teaching effectiveness, library holdings, and physical facilities.

EXERCISE 7 - 16

Evaluate each of the following ranking arguments after supplying their missing assumptions.

1. "More people drink Coke than Pepsi. Therefore, Coke is a better cola than Pepsi."

2. "Chris Everett is the best base-line player but Navratilova is the best net player, so Navratilova is the best female tennis player."

3. Jock argues that the Red Sox are a better ball team than the Dodgers: "The Dodgers have better pitching but the Red Sox have better hitting and better defence. So they are a better team overall."

(7.37) "GOOD FOR" ARGUMENTS (see 5.93).

(1) BASIC LOGICAL FORM:

X wants W. Therefore, it is good for X that P.

(2) EXAMPLE. An example from the world of finance: "The people of this country want our currency to be respected in other countries, so its good that the dollar is rising against other currencies."

(3) EXAMPLE EVALUATION.

STEP ONE: construct an accurate diagrammatic version of the argument.

A = The people of this country want our currency to be respected in other countries.

B = It's good that the dollar is rising against other currencies.

STEP TWO (a): identify the plausible U-factors. Two sorts of U-factors are associated with arguments of this kind:

(1) P does not contribute to the satisfaction of W.

(2) P, overall, does X more harm than good.

For this example the particular U-factors are:

(1) The dollar rise does not contribute to the satisfaction of the desire to have our currency respected in other countries.

(2) Overall, the dollar rise does the people of this country more harm than good.

The first factor does not seem to be very plausible. When foreigners convert their currency into ours and find that they must pay more to get ours they will be given the impression that ours is valuable and those who know a bit about international finance will realize that higher value reflects economic strength.

The second factor is at least as plausible as the conclusion, for the following reasons. A rise in our currency value makes goods purchased from us by foreigners more expensive, which makes us less competitive in international markets. This, in turn, results in loss of sales, which may result in loss of jobs, especially in industries that have a high percentage of foreign sales.

STEP TWO (b): formulate the most defensible assumptions that exclude the U-factors. The plausible U-factor noted above can be excluded by this assumption:

C = The rise in the dollar does not do more harm than good overall to the people of this country.

EXERCISE 7 - 17

Evaluate each of the following "good for" arguments after supplying their missing assumptions.

1. "Most people want an emotionally satisfying marital relationship, so it's a good thing that divorce and remarriage are no longer legally difficult."

2. "Julia wants to make a lot of money, so she is lucky to have been accepted in law school."

3. "Canadians want to be economically independent of the U.S. Therefore, it must be a good thing for them that Americans are pulling their investment money out of Canada."

(7.38)   ARGUMENTS FOR EVALUATIVE CRITERIA (see 5.94)

(1) BASIC LOGICAL FORM:

A function of X's is F.

Therefore, a good-making attribute of X's is G.

(2)   EXAMPLE. "Colleges are supposed to be able to equip their students to be good citizens. Therefore, a good college attribute is the ability to indoctrinate students into the central values of their society."

(3)   EXAMPLE EVALUATION.

STEP ONE: construct an accurate diagrammatic version of the argument.

A = Colleges are supposed to equip their students to be good citizens.

B = A good college attribute is the ability to indoctrinate students into the central values of their society.

STEP TWO (a): identify the plausible U-factors. In arguments of this kind there are two potential kinds of U-factors: (1) G does not contribute to function F, and (2) G is incompatible with other functions that X's serve.

The particular version associated with the example are:

(1) The ability of colleges to indoctrinate their students into the central values of their society does not make them able to equip their students to be good citizens.

(2) The ability of colleges to indoctrinate their students into the central values of their society is incompatible with other functions colleges serve.

The first factor is not very plausible. An important part of being a good citizen is accepting the values of the society. Indoctrination is not the best way of inculcating values, but it is one way of performing an essential task. Indoctrination tends to erode respect for the unbiased search for truth, but it may be better to indoctrinate initially and then invite people to scrutinize the values they have accepted, as happens sometimes in religion.

The second factor is more plausible. Indoctrination is

276

incompatible with one of the main ideals colleges and universities uphold, the ideal of free inquiry. This involves looking at the evidence for and against a view, as well as what can be said for other rival views. Thus, the ability to indoctrinate is incompatible with an essential ideal and function of higher education institutions.

STEP TWO (b): Formulate the most defensible assumptions that exclude the U-factors. Only one assumption is needed since only the second U-factor is plausible: C = Indoctrination is compatible with the other functions of colleges.

EXERCISE 7 - 18

Evaluate each of the following evaluative criteria arguments after supplying their missing assumptions.

1. "Schools are supposed to prepare children for life as adults. Religion helps people cope with adult life. Therefore, good schools teach religion."

2. "Flight attendants should make flights enjoyable for the passengers, so good flight attendants are physically attractive people."

3. A currently-popular theme in beer commercials: "Beer should be refreshing but not filling. Therefore, a good beer is light-tasting."

277

(7.39) SAMPLE TO POPULATION ARGUMENTS (see 5.101)

(1) BASIC LOGICAL FORM:

N% of sample x of population X has property P.

Therefore, N% of all X's have property P.

(2) EXAMPLE. The Cadillac owner says: "The five traffic accidents I've seen this year involved eight cars and five have been small cars. Therefore, small cars are more likely to be involved in accidents."

(3) EXAMPLE EVALUATION

STEP ONE: construct an accurate diagrammatic version of the argument.

A = The five traffic accidents I've seen this year involved eight cars and five were small cars.

B = Small cars are more likely to be involved in accidents.

STEP TWO (a): identify the plausible U-factors. Two sorts of U-factors are associated with arguments of this kind:

1. The sample is too small to be reliable.

2. The sample is unreliable because of a selection bias.

Specific U-factors for this example are:

1. A sample of five traffic accidents is too small to be reliable.

2. The sample is unreliable because of a selection bias.

The first of these is quite plausible. In urban areas there are hundreds of accidents every year. With a sample of five there is too much possibility of coincidence.

The second is not very plausible because it seems that the accidents in the sample are there by chance. It may be that the Cadillac owner observed all of them in a suburban area where there is a high proportion of small cars used as second cars, but we are not told anything that would indicate there is such a bias.

STEP TWO (b): formulate the most defensible assumptions that

278

exclude the U-factor: C = The sample is large enough to be reliable.

Evaluate each of the following sample to population arguments after supplying their missing assumptions.

1. A woman wrote to a newspaper arguing against legislating the use of seat belts: "My seat-belt release once jammed so seat belts can prevent you from escaping from your car when you have an accident."

2. Intellectually gifted students can qualify as National Merit Scholars. A study of their conception of a good teacher led to this inference: "National Merit Scholars check 'allowing time for classroom discussion' as one of the outstanding characteristics of the teachers who contributed most to their desire to learn. Therefore, college students in general think classroom discussion is important."

3. The young woman who frequents singles bars and discos laments the lack of seriousness in the men she meets there: "Men are naturally shallow individuals, because none that I meet want to develop a serious relationship."

(7.40) POPULATION TO SAMPLE ARGUMENTS (see 5.102)

(1) BASIC LOGICAL FORM:

x is a member of class X. Therefore, x has property P.

(2) EXAMPLE: We see a very tall student walk past and I say:
"He is very tall so he is a good basketball player."

(3) EXAMPLE EVALUATION

STEP ONE: construct an accurate diagrammatic version of the
argument.

A = He is very tall.

B = He is a good basketball player.

STEP TWO (a): identify the plausible U-factors. There is
only one U-factor type associated with this kind of argument:
that the proportion of members of class X that have property P is
considerably less than 100%. For this example, then, we have one
potentially plausible U-factor: the percentage of very tall
people who are good basketball players is considerably less than
100%. This is reasonably plausible since many tall people do not
grow up where they can learn to play basketball. Furthermore,
there are probably quite a few tall people who are not gifted
athletically.

STEP TWO (b): formulate the most defensible assumptions that
exclude the U-factors. In this case the plausible factor is
excluded by this assumption: C = Nearly all very tall people are
good basketball players. This assumption does not make the
inference 100%, but puts it in the range above 75%.

EXERCISE 7 - 20

Evaluate each of the following population to sample arguments
after supplying their missing assumptions.

1. "He is a computer design expert, so he is a good computer
    programmer.

2. "Brooke Sheilds is a movie star. Therefore, she must be a
    good actress."

3. "College professors are highly-educated people, so they must
    be very rational."

280

(7.3) MISSING ASSUMPTIONS IN PROPOSITIONAL ARGUMENTS: We have seen that in identifying missing assumptions in evidential arguments we were identifying factors that could result in true premises and a false conclusion, then we created assumptions that would exclude the more plausible of the U-factors, as they were called. This approach is not appropriate in supplying missing assumptions for propositional arguments. Here validity depends on the argument having a suitable logical structure, so that when an inference is invalid a premise must be added to create structural validity. One way to do this is to simply add a premise which asserts that the given premises entail the conclusion. In the simplest case when the argument is "A, therefore B", we can add the assumption "If A then B" and get structural validity. Unfortunately, it is not normally effective to leave it at this. The arguer will readily admit to claiming the inference is valid, as "If A then B" asserts. What is usually needed is to find some assertion that is logically eqivalent to the assertion that the conclusion follows from the premises, but which is simpler and which the arguer can see, or be persuaded to see, is false. An example will clarify the strategy.

"If God loves all humans then he does not love only one. If he loves only one, then God does not love all humans. Hence, He does not love all humans." (Pospesel) The semi-symbolic version is:

"If A then not B. If B then not A. Hence not A."

The full symbolic version is:

"A ⊃ ∿ B / B ⊃ ∿ A // ∿ A"

The inference is invalid when A is true and B is false. To get a valid inference we need an assumption that excludes these possibilities. We can get it by denying their conjunction:

∿(A • ∿B)

This expression happens to be logically equivalent to A ⊃ B.

Now it turns out that when ALL combinations of truth values that yield true premises and a false conclusion are excluded by creating the negation of each combination, the resulting expression is logically equivalent to the original inference claim. This can be shown for the example by constructing a truth table for the inference claim, as shown below. Note that its truth table, given in the right-hand column, is the same as that for 'A ⊃ B'. This shows the two assertions are logically equivalent, so that the inference claim can be replaced by 'A ⊃ B' in the argument without changing its logical properties.

A	B	∿B	A⊃∿B	∿A	B⊃∿A	(A⊃∿B)•(B⊃∿A)	((A⊃∿B)•(B⊃∿A))⊃∿A
T	T	F	F	F	F	F	T
T	F	T	T	F	T	T	F
F	T	F	T	T	T	T	T
F	F	T	T	T	T	T	T

When all combinations of letter truth values that show inference validity are excluded the assertion expressing this will be logically equivalent to the inference claim, so it can be substituted for it as the missing assumption to which the arguer is committed. Almost invariably this expression will be simpler than the inference claim. This is an important consideration because we are trying to identify a version of the assumption that will be accepted by the arguer as a commitment she/he must make. Complexity makes for unclarity, which lessens the likelihood of acceptance.

You may be wondering what happens when a letter can be either true or false in an invalidity demonstration. No real difficulty arises, as the following example shows:

A ⊃ B / B ⊃ C // C ⊃ A

The short truth table test yields this result:

```
A ⊃ B / B ⊃ C // C ⊃ A
F T       T T     T F F
4 5       7 6     2 1 3
```

We cannot derive a value for B and since the premises are true and the conclusion false with A false and C true, B can be either true or false. So there are two lines in the truth table showing invalidity. So long as the missing premise excludes the combination of A false and C true, both of these lines are excluded. Our assumption is simply '∿(∿A • C)'. In effect, B does not appear at all.

Sometimes when values assigned show invalidity, it will happen that there are two distinct sets of values. Usually, in such cases, it is best to treat these as giving rise to two separate assumptions. Two relatively simple assertions are preferable to one complex one.

The overall procedure for producing missing assumptions is

this:

(a)   Perform a short truth table test on the fully symbolic version of the argument. If it cannot be invalidated then the inference is valid and no missing assumption needs to be added. If a set of variable values can be found that show the inference is invalid, go to step (b);

(b)   Form a conjunction of the invalidating values. For example: '∿ A • B • ∿ C'.

(c) Negate the conjunction, e.g., '∿ (∿ A • B • ∿ C)'.

(d)   Use the logical equivalences '∿ (p • ∿ q) = p ⊃ q' and '(p • q • r) = p • (q • r)' to get a conditional assertion that is appropriate for the argument.   For the example, there are six initial forms to choose from, each logically equivalent to the other:

(1) ∿ A ⊃ ∿(B • ∿ C)
(2) B ⊃ ∿ (∿ A • ∿ C)
(3) ∿ C ⊃ ∿ (∿ A • B)
(4) (∿ A • B) ⊃ C
(5) (∿ A • ∿ C) ⊃ ∿ B
(6) (B • ∿ C) ⊃ A

Which of the foregoing is most suitable will depend on the content of the argument, but it should be noted that the equivalence   '∿ (∿ p • ∿ q) = p v q' can be used to get conditionals that are simple and often appropriate. Number 2 from the above list, for example, can be written as 'B ⊃ (A v C)'.

Now let's look at an example.   Number 3 from exercise 6 - 7 reads as follows: "If the world looked like this, and you want to buy a car that sticks out a little then you shouldn't buy a Volkswagen Station Wagon.   But the world doesn't look like this. So if you want to buy a car that sticks out a little, then you should buy a Volkswagen Station Wagon."

The semi-symbolic version is:

"If A and B then not C. But not A. So if B, then C."

The symbolic version is:

(A • B) ⊃ ∿ C / ∿ A // B ⊃ C

Perform a short truth table test on the argument:

$(A \cdot B) \supset \sim C \; / \; \sim A \; // \; B \supset C$

```
(A • B) ⊃ ∿ C  /  ∿ A  //  B ⊃ C
 T T   F    T F     T F F
 6 5   4    7 8     2 1 3
```

The inference is invalid so we move to step (b).

Step (b): form a conjunction of the invalidating values. The inference is shown invalid with A false, B true, and C false so we write:

$\sim A \cdot B \cdot \sim C$

Step (c): negate the conjunction to get the assumption:

$\sim (\sim A \cdot B \cdot \sim C)$

Step (d): the "raw" assumption has the form just used as an example, so we can look at the six possibilities that were set out, in seeking a version that would be congenial to the arguer. Since the arguer is trying to persuade us to buy a Volkswagen the best version would have C as a consequent of a conditional. It will not normally be appropriate to have anything that looks like an assumption in its own right as a consequent. With this in mind, number 4 on the list seems to be the best choice: $'(\sim A \cdot B) \supset C'$. In English this reads: "If the world is not like this and you want to buy a car that sticks out a little then you should buy a Volkswagen Station Wagon." This sounds like something the arguer would be happy to accept. Of course, while the addition of this assumption makes the inference valid, the assumption itself is false since several other cars could satisfy one's desire to have a car that sticks out a little.

EXERCISE 7 - 21

For each of the following arguments determine the assumption that must be added to produce validity and express it as conditional, with the consequent shown. Nos. 2 and 4 are answered in the back.

1. $A \supset B \; / \; B \; // \; A$. Consequent is A.

2. $A \supset B \; / \; \sim A \; // \sim B$. Consequent is $\sim B$.

3. $(B \lor C) \supset A \; / \sim (A \supset B) \; // \; C$. Consequent is C.

4. $A \supset B \; / \; B \supset C \; // \; C$.   Consequent is C.

5. $A \supset B \; / \; A \supset C \; // \; B \lor C$. Consequent is B ∨ C.

(7.301)　　EVALUATION　PROCEDURE.　The procedure to follow is the original one set out in Chapter Four, except that Step Two must be modified. The revised procedure is this:

STEP　ONE:　　construct an accurate diagammatic version of the argument.

STEP　TWO　(a):　　perform a short truth table test on each inference having a potential for structural validity. Rate each valid inference "√". For evidential inferences follow the procedure set out previously for them.

STEP　TWO　(b):　for each invalid inference having a potential for structural validity form a conjunction for each set of invalidating variable values.

STEP　TWO　(c):　　negate each inference conjunction to create the missing assumptions in their "raw" form.

STEP　TWO　(d):　　put each assumption into the most suitable form.

STEP TWO (e):　add the missing assumptions to the diagram and rate the inference "√".

STEP　THREE:　evaluate all assumptions and assign a rating to each.

STEP　FOUR:　determine the extent to which each intermediate conclusion is proved.

STEP　FIVE:　determine the extent to which the final conclusion is proved.

STEP SIX:　formulate a response to the arguer.

The same procedure applies to all arguments that have inferences with a potential for structural validity. A few sample evaluations will illustrate the procedure.

(7.302)　SAMPLE EVALUATION ONE: "If God loves all humans then He does not love only one. If He only loves only one, then God does not love all humans. Hence He does not love all humans."

STEP　ONE:　construct an accurate diagrammatic version of the argument.

The semi-symbolic version is:

"If A then not B. If B, then not A. Hence not A."

285

The symbolic version is: "A ⊃ ∿ B / B ⊃ ∿ A // ∿ A." The diagram version is this:

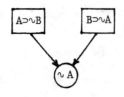

A = God loves all humans.

B = God loves only one human.

STEP TWO (a): perform a short truth table test on each inference having a potential for structural validity:

```
A ⊃ ∿ B / B  ⊃ ∿ A // ∿ A
T T T F    F  T F T    F T
5 6 7 8    9 10 4 3    1 2
```

The inference is invalid with A true and B false.

STEP TWO (b): for each invalid inference having a potential for structural validity form a conjunction for each set of invalidating variable values:

A • ∿ B

STEP TWO (c): negate each inference conjunction:

∿(A • ∿ B)

STEP TWO (d): put each assumption into the most suitable conditional form. There are two possibilities here. 'A ⊃ B' reads 'If God loves all humans then He loves only one.' '∿ B ⊃ ∿ A' reads 'If God does not love only one human then He does not love all humans.' Neither of these would be very congenial to most people, so let's take the first because it is simpler.

STEP TWO (e): add the missing assumption to the diagram and rate the inference "√".

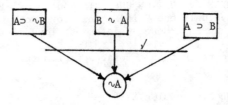

STEP THREE: evaluate all assumptions and assign a rating to

286

each. The first assumption, A ⊃ ∿ B, is clearly true. If God loves all humans then God does not love only one. The second assumption, B ⊃ ∿ A, is also true. The third one, A ⊃ B, is false. If God loves all humans then it cannot be true that God loves only one human.

STEP FOUR: determine the extent to which each intermediate conclusion is proved. There are none.

STEP FIVE: determine the extent to which the final conclusion is proved. Since A ⊃ B, an essential premise, is false, the argument can be rated "X".

STEP SIX: formulate a response to the argument. We can respond by saying: "For the conclusion to follow you must add an assumption logically equivalent to 'If God loves all humans then God loves only one.' But the assumption is false, so the conclusion is not proved to any significant extent."

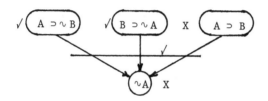

(7.33) SAMPLE EVALUATION TWO. Tobacco company spokesmen used to argue: "Lung cancer is more common among male smokers than among female smokers. If lung cancer is more common among male smokers than among female smokers then cancer is caused by something in the male makeup. It follows that lung cancer is not caused by smoking." (From Pospesel)

STEP ONE: construct an accurate diagrammatic version of the argument. The semisymbolic version is: "A. If A then B. It follows that not C."

The symbolic version is: "A / A⊃ B // ∿ C." The diagram version is:

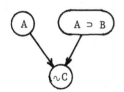

A = Lung cancer is more common among male smokers than among female smokers.

B = Cancer is caused by something in the male makeup.

C = Lung cancer is caused by smoking.

287

Step Two (a): perform a short truth table test on each inference having a potential for structural validity:

```
A / A ⊃ B // ∿ C
T   T T T     F T
3   4 5 6     1 2
```

The inference is invalid.

STEP TWO (b): for each invalid inference having a potential for structural validity, form a conjunction for each set of invalidating variable values:

A • B • C

STEP TWO (c): negate each inference conjunction:

∿ (A • B • C)

STEP TWO (d): put each assumption into the most suitable form. One suitable equivalent is a conditional with the conclusion as consequent:

(A • B) ⊃ ∿ C

STEP TWO (e): add the missing assumptions to the diagram and rate the inferences "√".

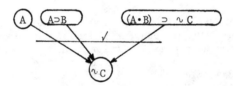

STEP THREE: evaluate all assumptions and assign a rating to each.

The added assumption is "If lung cancer is more common among male smokers than among female smokers and lung cancer is caused by something in the male makeup then lung cancer is not caused by smoking." This seems to assume that lung cancer cannot be caused by both factors, that is, by male susceptibility and smoking. Rate the assumption "?".

Is A ⊃ B true? Does a higher incidence of lung cancer in male smokers entail that something in the male makeup causes lung cancer? At most it could entail that males who smoke are more susceptible to lung cancer than are females. This leaves open the possibility that the smoke is the causal factor. The arguer is relying on Mill's Method of Difference (see Section 5.55). How would non-smoking men compare with smoking men in lung cancer incidence? Rate the assumption "?".

What about A? Making a judgement would require sophisticated research surveys. In one sense A is true. There are more male smokers who have gotten lung cancer than female smokers. But it turns out that the INCIDENCE of lung cancer is about the same for both sexes.

The difference between these claims arises because there are more male smokers. To make their argument work the tobacco people need to talk about incidence, not absolute numbers. And if we interpret A in this way, it can be shown to be false.

STEP FOUR: determine the extent to which each intermediate conclusion is proved. There are none.

STEP FIVE: determine the extent to which the final conclusion is proved. Given the assumption ratings we can rate the argument "X" since A, an essential assumption, is false and both of the other assumptions are dubious.

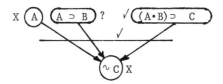

STEP SIX: formulate a response to the argument. We could say to the tobacco people: "For the conclusion to follow you need another assumption: 'If lung cancer is more common among male smokers than among female smokers and cancer is caused by something in the male makeup then lung cancer is not caused by smoking.' This assumption is dubious because male susceptibility does not exclude smoking as a cause. However, your first assumption has been shown to be false when the INCIDENCE of lung cancer among male and female smokers is compared. So your conclusion is not proved."

289

EXERCISE 7 - 22

Evaluate each of the following structural arguments after supplying their missing assumptions. No. 2 is answered in the back.

1. "If men have sexist biases then women are treated unfairly in the business world. Women are treated unfairly in the business world. Hence, men do have sexist biases."

2. "There will be a nuclear war only if the Russians attack us. But we know there won't be a nuclear war so the Russians won't attack us."

3. "If either there will be a nuclear war or there will be a lasting peace then America will survive. That there will be a nuclear war and America will survive cannot both be true. Thus there will be a lasting peace."

(7.4) SYLLOGISTIC ARGUMENTS. Unlike evidential and propositional arguments with a potential for structural validity, syllogisms are not open-ended in the sense that extra assumptions can be added to a normal syllogism. They contain exactly three assertions and mention exactly three classes of things (counting individuals as classes of one). Sometimes, however, people produce arguments that are, in effect, syllogisms with one assumption missing. For example: "All men are male chauvinists, so all men are jerks."

This argument, if tested using the syllogism testing procedure, will be found to have an invalid inference:

"All X's are Y's, so all X's are Z's."

In symbolic form we have:

" ~A • ~ D // ~ A • ~ E"

Testing the argument we get:

```
~ A • ~ D // ~ A • ~ E
T F T T F    T F F F T
2 3 1 4 5    7 6 8 9 10
```

Now there is a possibility that by adding another assumption mentioning Y and Z (X already has been mentioned twice and in a valid syllogism no class is mentioned more than twice) a valid inference can be created.

Table One shows that there are six candidates for the missing assumption role:

TABLE ONE

SEMI-SYMBOLIC	SYMBOLIC
All Y's are Z's	~ B • ~ E
All Z's are Y's	~ C • ~ D
No Y's are Z's. (= No Z's are Y's)	~ F • ~ G
Some Y's are Z's. (= Some Z's are Y's)	F v G
Some Y's are not Z's	B v E
Some Z's are not Y's	C v D

One way to identify the correct assumption (if there is one) is to add each assertion to the argument in turn and test for validity. A more efficient approach is to examine the original argument to see what might be needed. On doing so we notice that if the conclusion (~ A • ~ E) is to be guaranteed true, E must appear in the assumption so that ~ E will be guaranteed true.

291

There is only one candidate that might quAlify: All Y's are Z's.
If we add this assertion as an assumption we will find that the
argument has a valid inference.

```
∿ B • ∿ E / ∿ A • ∿ D // ∿ A • ∿ E
T F T T F   T F T T F    T F T T F
2 3 1 4 5   910 81112   141315 7 6
```

Thus, we could respond to the original argument in part by
pointing out that the arguer needs to assume that all male
chauvinists are jerks in order to have the conclusion follow
validly.

In using this procedure we follow the usual pattern of
assigning 'X' to the first class, 'Y' to the second, and 'Z' to
the third. This means that there are only two sets of possible
assumptions, those mentioning Y and Z (Table One) and those
mentioning X and Z. The table for X and Z is this:

TABLE TWO

SEMI-SYMBOLIC	SYMBOLIC
All X's are Z's	∿ A • ∿ E
All Z's are X's	∿ C • ∿ F
No X's are Z's (= No Z's are X's)	∿ D • ∿ G
Some X's are Z's (= Some Z's are X's)	D v G
Some X's are not Z's	A v E
Some Z's are not X's	C v F

As suggested above, the approach is a trial and error one
that can be shortened by performing a short truth table test on
the abbreviated syllogism. In the example just discussed we can do
this:

```
∿ A • ∿ D // ∿ A • ∿ E
T F T T F    T F F F T
2 3 1 4 5    7 6 8 910
```

This partial test tells us we need E false when A and D are
false to have the assumption true and avoid having the conclusion
false, so that ' ∿ B • ∿ E' is a promising candidate for the second
assumption because it can be true when E is false. At this point
it will be helpful to deal with some examples, so that you should
complete Exercise 7 - 23.

292

Using Tables One and Two, determine whether each of the following partial syllogisms can be completed with an assumption that makes the inference valid. Nos. 1 and 3 are answered in the back.

1. Every X is Y // Some X is not Z.

2. Every X is Y // Some Y is not Z.

3. Some X is Y // No X is Z.

4. Some X is Y // Some Y is not Z.

5. Some X is Y // Some X is Z.

6. No X is Y // Some Y is not Z.

(7.41)   EVALUATION PROCEDURE

STEP ONE: construct an accurate diagrammatic version of the argument using the semi-symbolic version of each assertion.

STEP TWO: using Table One or Table Two as appropriate (the one that does not mention the letter occurring twice in the argument), try to identify an assertion that could, as an assumption, make the inference valid. If there is none, go to Step Two (b), if there is one go to step (c).

STEP TWO (b): produce a counter-example version of the argument and rate the inference "X".

STEP TWO (c): add the missing assumption to the diagram and rate the inference "√".

STEP THREE: evaluate both assumptions and assign a rating to each.

STEP FOUR: determine the extent to which each intermediate conclusion is proved.

STEP FIVE: determine the extent to which the final conclusion is proved.

STEP SIX: formulate a response to the argument.

(7.42)   SAMPLE EVALUATION ONE. A version of an argument overheard in a public drinking place: "Some 'Women's Lib' supporters are men, so some 'Women's Lib' supporters are homosexuals."

STEP ONE: construct an accurate diagrammatic version of the argument. The semisymbolic version is: "Some X's are Y's, so some X's are Z's."

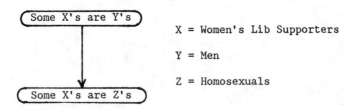

X = Women's Lib Supporters

Y = Men

Z = Homosexuals

STEP TWO (a): A fully symbolic version of the argument is:

E v G // D v G

294

Since 'X' occurs twice, we need an assertion that does not contain it. Therefore, Table One is where we look. We discover that by adding assumption '∿ B • ∿ E' we get a valid inference:

```
∿ B  • ∿ E / E v G // F v G
F F T    T T F    F F F
9 8 7    6 5 4    2 1 3
```

STEP TWO (b): produce a counter-example version and rate the inference "X". Not applicable here.

STEP TWO (c): add the missing assumption to the diagram and rate the inference "√". The assumption equivalent to '∿ B ∴ ∿ E' is 'All Y's are Z's.'

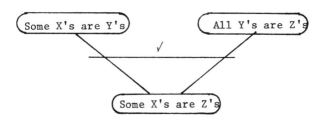

STEP THREE: evaluate both assumptions and assign a rating to each. Is it true that some Women's Lib supporters are men? Only the most militant female feminists would deny it, and not on the basis of evidence either. Rate the assumption "√". The added assumption is: "All men are homosexuals." Clearly false. Rate it "X".

STEP FOUR: determine the extent to which the intermediate conclusions are proved. There are none.

STEP FIVE: determine the extent to which the final conclusion is proved. Given that one essential assumption is false we rate the argument "X".

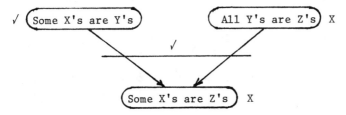

STEP SIX: formulate a response to the argument. We can say to the bigoted "gentleman": "It is true that some Women's Lib supporters are men, but that can't prove they are homosexuals. For this conclusion to follow logically you must depend on the assumption that all men are homosexuals, but you yourself are living proof that this assumption is false....aren't you?"

(7.43) SAMPLE EVALUATION TWO: "Some politicians are dishonest, so no politician is above suspicion."

STEP ONE: construct an accurate diagrammatic version of the argument.

The semi-symbolic version is:

"Some X's are Y's, so no X is Z."

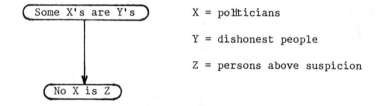

X = politicians

Y = dishonest people

Z = persons above suspicion

STEP TWO (a): a fully symbolic version of the argument is: E v G // ∿ D . ∿ G. Using Table One we are unable to discover any assertion that could be added as an assumption to yield a valid inference.

STEP TWO (b): produce a counter-example version and rate the inference "X". A suitable counter-example is this: "Some animals are cats, so no animal is a dog."

STEP TWO (c): not applicable.

STEP THREE: evaluate each assumption and enter its rating on the diagram. It is regrettably true that some politicans are dishonest. Rate it "√".

STEP FOUR: determine the extent to which the intermediate conclusions are proved. There are none.

STEP FIVE: determine the extent to which the final conclusion is proved. With the assumption rated "√" and the inference rated "X", the argument merits a rating of "X".

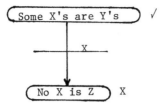

STEP SIX: formulate a response to the argument. We can respond: "Although some politicians are dishonest, this can't prove that no politicians are above suspicion. You might as well argue that some animals are cats proves no animals are dogs."

EXERCISE 7 - 24

Evaluate each argument according to the procedure just presented. No. 2 is answered in the back.

1. "Some art films are pornographic because some of them are erotic."

2. "Not all men accept the double standard of sexual fidelity, so some men are enlightened"

3. "All good-looking girls are conceited. So some conceited people are loved."

CHAPTER EIGHT: ARGUMENT ANALYSIS

(8.1) INTRODUCTION: Up until now we have been concerned with the development of argument evaluation skills. The arguments you have worked on have been provided in a clear standardized form with the assumptions and conclusions being easily identifiable. Unfortunately, arguers rarely present their arguments in such a clear way. For instance, conclusions frequently are presented before assumptions, and there is often logically extraneous material included.

In this chapter the aim is to develop your ability to distinguish argument structure in passages occurring in everyday situations. The examples and exercises will be arguments that are logically untidy and often more complex than those you have dealt with before. In a way, the materials are intended to improve one facet of your reading skill--argument comprehension.

(8.2) IDENTIFYING ARGUMENTS: ARGUMENT INDICATORS. The first step in the process is to improve your ability to distinguish passages that contain arguments from those that don't. This is a matter of being able to tell when an inference is being made. Most of the time there will be one or more special terms used to indicate these. Natural languages each have a variety of these terms and, not only do they signify that an inference is being made, they each enable us to tell what assertion is being inferred from what. The English language has several dozen of these "argument indicators".

The information about argument structure contained in these terms can be made clear by using them to express argument forms having one premise and one conclusion. Since these forms represent arguments, both the premise (P) and the conclusion (C) are being asserted, C being asserted on the basis of P. The terms are of two kinds: (1) those which in normal use have the premise BEFORE the conclusion, (2) those which in normal use have the premise AFTER the conclusion.

ARGUMENT INDICATORS: PREMISE BEFORE CONCLUSION

ACCORDINGLY
P. Accordingly, C.

AS
As P, C.
(Except when 'while'
is meant, e.g. "as I
ran, he followed")

CONCLUDE
P. I conclude that C.
From P I conclude that C.

HENCE
P. Hence, C.

CONSEQUENTLY
P, consequently C.

SO
P, so C.

LEADS
That P leads me
to believe that C.

PROVE
P proves that C.

SHOW
P, which shows that C.

DEMONSTRATE
P, which demonstrates that C.

ENTAIL
P, which entails that C.

FOLLOW
P. It follows that C.
(Except when 'follows in time'
is meant, e.g., "thunder
follows lightning".)

IMPLY
P, which implies that C.

INDICATE
P, which indicates that C.

SUGGEST
P suggests that C.

THEREFORE
P, therefore C.

THUS
P, thus C.

You should be aware that almost all the preceding terms can be used to state arguments with P following C. With some this is done using the passive voice, for example, instead of 'P shows that C' we can write 'C is shown by P' and say the same thing. In other cases we can just switch the words around. Instead of 'As P, C' we can write 'C, as P'. However, in the next list we have expressions that, in the active voice, normally have C preceding P. Be on guard for these. They are relatively common.

ARGUMENT INDICATORS: CONCLUSION BEFORE PREMISE

BECAUSE
C because P.
(Except when an
explanation is
being given.)

REASON
C, for the reason that P.
(Except when 'cause' is meant.)

INFER
C, which may be inferred from P.

FOR
C, for P.
(Where 'for' is
short for 'for
the reason that'.)

SINCE
C since P.
(Except when 'since the time'
is meant, e.g. 'I have
graduated since I met you'.)

DERIVE
C, which may be
derived from P.

DEDUCE
C, which may be deduced from P.

The logical vocabulary just covered is the part of English vocabulary used to indicate that an argument is being uttered, and what the logical structure of that argument is. You should understand the meaning of each of the expressions so that you can exploit the information they represent in the argument.

It is important to be clear about the difference between the statement of an argument and the statement of a conditional. All of the above forms are forms of argument statement. They can be thought of as having three ingredients: (1) the assertion of a premise, (2) a (often unstated) claim that if the premise were true then the conclusion would be true, and (3) the assertion of the conclusion based on the truth of the first two. A conditional really only represents the second claim, so that the best way of making sure you have an argument statement rather than a conditional is to see if the propositions mentioned are actually being asserted themselves. If they are then an argument is being stated rather than just a conditional. For example, in the statement form 'A because B' both 'A' and 'B' are being asserted, whereas in 'If A, B' neither one is being categorically asserted. Thus the first one is an argument and the second is a conditional.

You have now been introduced to most of the argument-indicating expressions used by speakers and writers of English. This is the first step in learning to identify arguments and understand their logical structure. The next stage in learning to discern structure is to get the argument in a semi-symbolic form. That is, in a form in which only the logically significant words appear and the propositions have been replaced by letters. Unfortunately you will frequently find that passages containing arguments are not logically tidy. They contain more than the logically significant words and the propositions these words are supposed to connect. In this chapter you will be introduced to some techniques and be given some advice on how to deal with logically untidy argument passages.

(8.3) BRACKETING. One handy device for arriving at the semi-symbolic version of an argument is to bracket off the propositions that are logically a part of it, and underline the logically significant words. Then the bracketed propositions can be labeled A, B, C, etc. In doing this do not include the logically significant words within brackets if you can avoid it.

We will apply this technique to this argument: "There was frost on my car windshield this morning, which shows that the temperature was below 32 degrees F. last night." Here we have two assertions constituting an argument. The indicator words 'which shows that' tell us this. We leave these words outside the two sets of brackets we use because they are the link between premise and conclusion rather than a part of either one. Furthermore, since the indicator words are valuable clues to the structure of an argument, they should be underlined so that they will be more noticeable. This is especially useful when they occur inside a bracketed assertion. Also underline instances of 'and' and its logical equialents ('but', etc.) when they indicate that a sentence contains two or more distinct assertions.

Having bracketed the argument properly and followed the other steps just mentioned, you should next assign a letter to each assertion, making the first one "A" and labeling the following ones in order, alphabetically. Write the letter in front of, or above, the left-hand bracket like this: A[ ].

Having followed these steps the above argument will look like this:

A[There was frost on my car windshield this morning], which shows that B[the temperature was below 32 degrees F. last night].

Now we write the semi-symbolic version of the argument using the letters instead of the actual propositions, while retaining the words underlined:

"A, which shows that B."

The semi-symbolic version of the argument displays its "logical skeleton" and, as often happens, we can see the entire logical structure of the argument in this version.

Sometimes we can discern the entire logical structure of very complex arguments from semi-symbolic versions of them, and almost always the semi-symbolic version will help us in constructing our structural diagrams because they help prevent us from getting distracted by the content of the argument. The content will have to be relied on sometimes, of course, because not all argument passages contain enough logical clues to show us how the assertions are related.

The foregoing example is a straightforward case of getting semi-symbolic versions of arguments by using bracketing. There are many ways of presenting arguments that make the use of bracketing less straightforward. Three particular complications deserve special mention.

(8.4)   ARGUMENTS CONTAINING ABBREVIATED ASSERTIONS: The bracketing approach to picking out the propositions of an argument is a labor saving device, since it is easier than writing out each premise and conclusion. However, because of certain ways we construct sentences in English it will not always be satisfactory to bracket only strings of words which can represent whole sentences. Sometimes we will fail to identify part of the argument if we do this. For instance, this sentence occurred in a passage of argument: "A statement which is irrelevant to any experience is not an empirical hypothesis, and accordingly has no factual content."

It seems clear that there is an argument here and that, judging by the word 'accordingly'. The part before the comma represents the premise and should be bracketed as such. But the expression after 'accordingly', which would have to be the conclusion, would not be a sentence standing alone. However, it can be seen that we have a contracted sentence because we can change the wording after 'accordingly' to read "A STATEMENT OF THIS KIND has no factual content." We see that this is permitted because it more full expresses the meaning of the original. In the original the writer simply left out the subject expression and left it to us to "read it in" when we read the sentence. This sort of thing is frequently done so WE HAVE TO BE PREPARED TO BRACKET EXPRESSIONS THAT CANNOT STAND AS SENTENCES, BUT WE SHOULD ONLY DO SO WHEN ADDING WORDS TO PRODUCE A SENTENCE WOULD NOT CHANGE THE MEANING OF THE OVERALL SENTENCE IN WHICH THE PART-SENTENCE OCCURS.

The example, then, would be bracketed like this: "A[A statement which is irrelevant to any experience is not an empirical hypothesis], and accordingly B[has no factual content]." The semi-symbolic version will be: "A, and accordingly B."

(8.5)   BRACKETING ARGUMENTS WITH "NESTED" LOGIC TERMS: As it

302

happens, the English language does not require us to place our inference-indicating terms between the propositions in an argument. We are permitted to put them in the middle of a proposition sometimes: "Only demented people believe the earth is flat. Leo is President of the Flat Earth Society. Leo, therefore, is demented."

This position for 'therefore' presents no problem. We simply underline the word and put brackets around each sentence. And since 'therefore' could, without changing the meaning, be placed at the front of the sentence, the semi-symbolic version would be "A. B. Therefore C."

(8.6) BRACKETING ARGUMENTS WITH "NESTED" ASSERTIONS: One further difficulty arising from the flexibility of the English language is this: sometimes a reason for an assertion will be embedded in the assertion itself, or vice versa. In such cases we simply put each of the four brackets in its appropriate place, which means that one set of brackets is within the other. No confusion need arise from this. Here is an example of how to do it:

"It follows, therefore, that A[Barrymore, since B [only this window would serve his purpose], must have been looking out for something or somebody upon the moor]."

The semi-symbolic version of the argument is: "It follows, therefore, that A, since B."

(8.7) BRACKETING AND TRANSLATING COMPOUND ASSERTIONS: Compound assertions such as conditionals, alternations, and complex negations must have their logical connective terms (if . . . then, or, not) preserved in the semi-symbolic version of the argument, so while these are whole assertions we should not represent each of them by a single letter. Instead, we assign letters to the propositions that are contained within the compound assertions. For example, 'If Ewart is healthy then Ewart is alive' should not be symbolized as 'A'. It should be written as 'If A then B'. As a single assertion, of course, we want to put it within a single circle in the argument diagram. For brevity and other reasons it is best to translate such compound assertions into the symbolic language and include them in the diagram in the forms we saw in Chapter Six.

In bracketing compound assertions we will follow the practice of using square brackets to "surround" whole assertions that must appear in a separate circle on the diagram and parentheses "( )" to surround propositions within single compound assertions.

Furthermore, since negations are significant for structural

303

validity we will need to label the negative version of any proposition that appears also in positive form as 'not-A' or 'not-B', etc. When only one or the other appears we can label it with a single letter. Some examples will illustrate these conventions.

"If Ewart is healthy then Ewart is alive. But Ewart is not alive, so Ewart is not healthy."

Here we need to use 'not' in two places in labeling propositions, since a positive version of each also occurs:

"[If A(Ewart is healthy) then B(Ewart is alive)]. But not-B[Ewart is not alive], so not-A[Ewart is not healthy]."

The semi-symbolic version is: "If A then B. But not B, so not A."

Suppose now we have this argument: "If Ewart is not alive then Ewart is not healthy. But Ewart is healthy, so Ewart is alive." Here we would start off by labeling 'Ewart is not alive' as 'A', but when we encounter the conclusion we would label it 'A' because it contradicts 'Ewart is not alive' and is the more positive of the two. We would now relabel 'Ewart is not alive' as 'not-A'. The same would be done with the other propositions.

The procedure for dealing with negations, then, is this: USE A SINGLE LETTER TO LABEL THE FIRST OCCURRENCE OF A PROPOSITION WHETHER IT IS POSITIVE OR NEGATIVE, BUT IF THE OPPOSITE VERSION APPEARS LATER USE THAT SINGLE LETTER TO LABEL THE POSITIVE VERSION.

Unfortunately, just as there are a variety of terms besides 'therefore' and 'so' which serve to indicate that an argument is being made, there are also a variety of ways of representing the logical connectives besides using 'not', 'and', 'or' and 'If . . . then'. Obviously, it is essential to be able to recognize words that are logically equivalent to these if we are to be able to represent in detail arguments that contain them. You will find that the logically equivalent expression to be listed as symbolized by a common symbol do not all mean quite the same thing. For example, 'A and B' and 'A although B' both are symbolized as 'A   B'. However, they don't quite mean the same because 'A although B' suggests that A and B are slightly incompatible, whereas 'A and B' does not. When both are translated the same way, then, we lose some of the significance of 'A although B' because that part is not relevant to the project of determining whether an argument containing such a premise is valid or not. Like "A and B", "A although B" asserts A is true and that B is true, and this is what is important here. The same considerations apply for other terms.

In the next few pages there are tables showing how to translate a variety of English logical connective terms into our symbolic language.

FORMS TRANSLATED AS 'A • B':

A and B	A however B
A but B	not only A but B
A although B	A despite B
Although A, B	A while B (not when 'during which time' is meant)
Both A and B	A yet B
A even though B	A now that B
A whereas B	A in spite of the fact that B

FORMS TRANSLATED AS 'A v B':

> Either A or B
> A or B
> A or else B
> Either A or else B.

FORMS TRANSLATED AS '∿ A • ∿ B' or '∿ (A v B)':

> Neither A nor B.

FORMS TRANSLATED AS '(A v B)• ∿(A• B)': Earlier it was pointed out that we have two different senses of 'or' in English. These were called the inclusive sense (symbolized by 'v') and the exclusive sense, which implies that both alternatives cannot be true at the same time. When this is what is meant by an alternation we translate it as 'A v B' and add '∿(A• B)' to indicate that not both of them are true. Any of the expressions listed under 'A v B' can be used to utter an exclusive alternation. To decide which way to translate we have to decide whether or not both alternatives can be true at the same time. If they can, then use 'A v B'. If not, use '(A v B) • ∿ (A• B)'.

There are at least two terms that you must always treat as exclusive or's : 'unless' and 'otherwise'. If I say to you "The car will start unless the battery is dead", this can be thought of as equivalent to "Either the car will start or the battery is dead, but not both." Always translate 'A unless B' and 'Unless A, B' as '(A v B) • ∿ (A • B)'. Roughly the same is true for 'A otherwise B'.

FORMS TRANSLATED AS 'A⊃ B' or 'B ⊃ A': Previously only the expression 'if . . . then' was used to express conditionals.

Unfortunately for anyone trying to analyze arguments, there are quite a few ways of expressing conditionals in English. Even worse, many of them require us to regard the first proposition in the sequence as the consequent of the conditional. That is, the logical order is the opposite of the grammatical order in these cases! For instance, although 'If A, B' is symbolized as 'A ⊃ B', 'A if B' is symbolized as 'B ⊃ A.' Perhaps you cannot see any reason for translating them differently but there is one. Recall that one way of thinking of 'A ⊃ B' is to think of the truth of A guaranteeing the truth of B. 'A if B', on the other hand, suggests that if B is true then A is true. That is, the truth of B guarantees the truth of A so that we must symbolize the assertion as 'B ⊃ A'.

Some conditionals have forms which stress that the falsity of one proposition guarantees the falsity of another. For example 'A only if B' tells us the falsity of B guarantees the falsity of A so we can symbolize the conditional as '∿ B ⊃ ∿ A'. The truth table for this assertion is the same as that for 'A ⊃ B' so it is logically equivalent to 'A ⊃ B'. Thus, after writing the symbolic version in the falsehood-guarantee form you can rewrite it in the 'A ⊃ B' form. All true conditionals (not the false ones) have this property: the truth of the antecedent guarantees the truth of the consequent AND the falsity of the consequent guarantees the falsity of the antecedent. Most state one of these guarantees more explicitly than the other, so we can classify them on this basis:

TRUTH OF 'A' GUARANTEES TRUTH OF 'B': A ⊃ B
If A then B   Given that A, B
If A, B   A implies that B
A entails B   A means that B
When A, B.

FALSITY OF 'B' GUARANTEES FALSITY OF 'A': ∿B ⊃ ∿ A (= A ⊃ B)
A provided that B
A assuming that B
A on condition that B
A only if B

TRUTH OF 'B' GUARANTEES TRUTH OF 'A': B ⊃ A
A if B   A is inferrable from B
A when B   A is implied by B
A whenever B   A follows from B
A is entailed by B

FALSITY OF 'A' GUARANTEES FALSITY OF 'B': ∿ A ⊃ ∿ B (= B ⊃ A)
    Only if A, B.   A is a necessary
                           condition for B

306

Almost all of us have trouble identifying the antecedent and consequent in some of the English language conditionals. There is even some difficulty in distinguishing conditionals and conjunctions. The best way of distinguishing conditionals and conjunctions is to rely on this fact: in a conjunction each proposition is being asserted, but in a conditional neither one is. Thus, given "A yet B" we ask ourselves "Is A being asserted here?", "Is B being asserted?" The answer is "yes" to both questions, which shows that 'A yet B' is a conjunction, not a conditional.

People have trouble deciding whether a conditional should be symbolized as 'A ⊃ B' or 'B ⊃ A' for a variety of reasons. Almost all of them are intuitively classifiable as stressing a truth guarantee rather than a falsehood guarantee, or vice versa. For example, 'A provided that B' strikes most people as predominantly expressing a falsehood guarantee, i.e., that the falsity of B guarantees the falsity of A. To them it is not so clear that it means that the truth of A guarantees the truth of B, although it does. We can take advantage of our instincts in this matter in the following way. About each conditional we can ask four questions:

1. Does the truth of A guarantee the truth of B?

2. Does the truth of B guarantee the truth of A?

3. Does the falsity of A guarantee the falsity of B?

4. Does the falsity of B guarantee the falsity of A?

When faced with a puzzling one, a "yes" answer will often seem more appropriate to one of these questions than to the others. Most people's linguistic programming is reliable enough to warrant claiming that that particular interpretation is the correct one. As an exercise, you might apply this test to each of the ones presented in the above table. Chances are that you will agree with the classification given there ...in most cases. Where your intuitions do not guide you correctly you should "plug in" some sample propositions ('This is colored' and 'This is red' are a good pair.) and study the resulting conditionals.

EXERCISE 8 - 1

Write each sentence in semi-symbolic form then in full symbolic form. Nos. 2, 4, 6, and 8 have been answered in the back.

1. Either Alonzo absconds or Basil will not be impeached provided that Chloris will not be outraged.

307

2. Alonzo absconds while Basil will be impeached if Chloris will be outraged.

3. Alonzo absconds means that Basil will not be impeached only if Chloris will not be outraged.

4. If Alonzo absconds then Basil will be impeached when either Chloris will be outraged or Dudley will be disgraced.

5. Alonzo absconds even though if Basil will be impeached, Chloris will be outraged.

6. Alonzo will not abscond on condition that Basil will not be impeached.

7. Alonzo will not abscond now that Basil will be impeached, but Chloris will be outraged.

8. Alonzo will abscond otherwise Basil will be impeached.

9. Alonzo will abscond only if either Basil will be impeached or Chloris will be outraged.

(8.8) ARGUMENTS CONTAINING COUNTER PREMISES: Anyone
seriously interested in arriving at the truth about something does
not start with a conclusion and try to find reasons for believing
it. What we do is try to gather evidence both for and against the
assertion we are interested in. Similarly, when trying to
persuade others to believe something we believe, we ought to tell
them about any evidence "pointing the other way." In philosophy,
where argument is the primary activity, this is commonly done.
One of the greatest and earliest philosophers, Aristotle, set a
very high standard for the subject in this respect. He would not
only give reasons for not accepting his personal view, he would
also examine the other positions that might be taken on a topic.

In most areas of endeavor that require the use of argument we
seem to follow, for good or ill, the law court model known as the
adversary system. In criminal court the prosecuting lawyer will
put forward only the evidence that indicates the guilt of the
defendant. The defendant's lawyer will, on the other hand, put
forward only the evidence indicating that the defendant did not
commit the offence. Each lawyer tries to "disarm" the evidence put
forward by the other. The rationale for this system seems to be
that it ensures that the court will reach the right conclusion
because the competition between sides will result in all of the
relevant evidence being brought out. In practice the system has
defects. For one thing, one lawyer may know something relevant
that the other doesn't. The defence lawyer may, for example, know
something his client has told him that is damaging to the client
and it may be impossible for the prosecuting lawyer to find it
out. Thus, some of the evidence does not get brought before the
court.

Outside the courts we also tend to leave the arguee to
discover evidence against the conclusion we are arguing for, and
this attitude is responsible for much deception when the person
presenting the argument knows more about the topic than the
arguee. We can only defend ourselves from being duped by being
informed and reflective about the topics that concern us.

In argument passages where the arguer presents contrary
evidence these assertions are usually not difficult to identify.
They are often preceded by some expressions suggesting contrast
with other evidence, such as: 'on the other hand', 'even though',
'despite this'. Frequently the author will introduce them by
assigning them to a would-be critic using expressions such as 'a
critic might object that . . .', 'it could be objected that . .
.', etc. Here is an example of such an argument.

"A[It is wrong to kill newly conceived fetuses by abortion],
because B[they are human beings], even though C[they do not look
human]. D[They have the genetic makeup of human beings.]"

309

Semi-symbolically this is written as: "A because B, even though C. D." Here D is supposed to outweigh C which, as the expression 'even though' indicates, is thought by the arguer to count against B.

In this example and in most others where objections are mentioned, the arguer will introduce what he/she takes to be evidence that refutes the objection. This is almost always done because an argument will be less persuasive if counter-evidence is presented and not dealt with. Most people are not disposed to make unfavorable facts known when they cannot counter them. Occasionally you will see objections mentioned coupled with confessions that the arguers do not know how to deal with them, but this will only happen when the desire for truth is stronger than the desire to convince others.

For purposes of argument evaluation WE CAN TREAT ITEMS OF COUNTER-EVIDENCE AS SOMETHING TO BE BROUGHT FORWARD IN CRITICIZING THE INFERENCE AND ASSUMPTIONS. Thus, we will not include them in constructing the diagrammatic version of the argument. In the example given above we would construct the diagram based on assertions A, B, and D. The diagram would look like this since B is a reason for A, which is the conclusion, and D is a reason for B:

Now C (fetuses do not look human) is regarded as counting against B (fetuses are human beings), but since D is intended to prove B we can regard C as part of an inference criticism directed against the inference from D to B.

(8.9) FROM SEMI-SYMBOLIC FORM TO DIAGRAM FORM: The bracketing technique helps us to derive a semi-symbolic version of an argument. The semi-symbolic versions enable us to discern the structure of the argument so that we can illustrate it in the structural diagram format. The diagrams are the logical pictures of the arguments they represent. Their construction from the original passage and the semi-symbolic version of it is the final step before we undertake the evaluation procedure. It is probably the most critical step in the whole process because a mistake will result in a picture of an argument different from the one to be evaluated. The evaluation, then, will be more or less inaccurate. What follows is advice of a general sort, to be followed by detailed advice on how to diagam arguments that are logically untidy in various ways.

First of all, and this is important, DO NOT TREAT THE ARGUMENT AS A MERE COLLECTION OF ASSERTIONS THAT YOU ARE TO ARRANGE IN THE LOGICAL ORDER YOU THINK IS BEST. THE STRUCTURAL DIAGRAM YOU ARE TO CONSTRUCT IS THE ONE THE ARGUER WOULD CONSTRUCT, because it is that arguer's argument you will ultimately be evaluating. That argument might not always be the strongest one that can be made from these assertions, but it is the one to be citicized.

The arguer's intentions are reflected in the indicator words used. Therefore, your diagram must be compatible with the way they are used in the argument. Suppose someone argues like this: "The sun is out so the sky is blue." This would be bracketed as: "A[The sun is out] so B[the sky is blue]", and the semi-symbolic form is "A so B". Now if you think about how A and B might be logically related you might conclude that A follows from B. After all, the sun's being out does not prove the sky is blue. The sun might just be shining through a hole in the clouds. Yet if you diagrammed the argument that way you would not have a diagram of the arguer's argument. The use of 'so' clearly shows that for the arguer B is the conclusion. Arranging the assertions this way results in an argument with a weaker inference but that is irrelevant.

The second main point has to do with the beginner's inclination to draw more inference lines between the assertions than warranted. Link two assertions only if one is being given as a reason (as evidence) for the truth of the other. IF YOU ARE TEMPTED TO DRAW AN ARROW FROM A TO B ASK YOURSELF: DOES IT MAKE SENSE TO SAY "A, THEREFORE B"? A point to remember is this: circles often have more than one arrow coming to them but will very, very seldom have more than one arrow going away from them. This is simply because assertions are usually supported by several reasons but a reason is usually only given as a reason for one conclusion.

The most fundamental concept for analyzing arguments is that of a reason. Most of us have a good intuitive grasp of this notion which enables us to see when one assertion is being given as a reason for another. The indicator words help confirm intuitions.

Once having decided that a passage contains an argument you

311

must try to discern its structure. The first thing to do is to establish the final conclusion. ASK YOURSELF: "WHAT IS THE MAIN POINT THE ARGUER IS TRYING TO PROVE?"

Having identified the main conclusion, try to isolate the assumptions, the premises that are not being argued for. For each assertion other than the conclusion ask yourself: IS ANY ASSERTION BEING GIVEN AS A REASON FOR THIS? There will always be at least one assertion for which the answer is "no" if there is an argument present.

Next, connect the intermediate conclusions to either the final conclusion or the assumptions.

Finally, finish tying the diagram together by adding arrows in the places where they are needed to make the diagram into a single unit.

(8.10) SOME EXAMPLES OF DIAGRAMMING: Now let's diagram several arguments, following the steps and advice provided.

"Since A[you hold that nothing is self evident], B[I will not argue with you] for C[it is clear that you are a quibbler and are not to be convinced]."

Having identified the indicator words 'since' and 'for', and bracketed the distinct assertions we next write a semi-symbolic version of the argument:

"Since A, B for C."

The indicator words tell us that A is a reason and so is C. B is not a reason so it must be the conclusion. C seems to be a reason for B, so part of our diagram will be as shown below:

What do we do with A? The word 'since' tells us it is a reason. Is it an assumption or not? Either A or C or both are assumptions. Are they logically related in this argument? It seems that they are. The arguer is taking the fact that someone holds that nothing is self-evident as showing that he is a quibbler. Thus, A is a reason for C. The final diagram looks like this:

312

The above structure is one of two that arguments containing three propositions can have. The other structure is the one possessed by this argument: "A[She is a model] and B[she's an actress] so C[she earns a lot of money]." The semi-symbolic form is "A and B so C". The structural diagram looks like this:

This is the most common of the two structures that a three-assertion argument can have. In such arguments there are two assumptions rather than just one. Neither premise is put forward as a reason for the other, even though in some cases the two might be logically related and this has not been noticed.

The notation adopted for "picturing" the logical structure of arguments can be applied to arguments of any complexity. In practice you are not likely to encounter arguments containing great complexity unless you are studying philosophy, perhaps. We will now work through an example of medium complexity whose structure is logically 'transparent'. That is, there are enough indicator words to almost allow us to construct the diagram from the semi-symbolic version of the argument.

"It seems clear first of all that A[the Russians have only begun to test MIRV missiles]. Secondly, since B[U.S. surveillance systems for monitoring missile tests can discriminate tests of MIRV's], and since C[the Russians are hardly likely to manufacture and emplace an untested system], D[the U.S. can in effect monitor compliance with a ban on production and deployment by verifying the cessation of testing]; therefore E[no on-site inspection is necessary]". (From Thomas, PRACTICAL REASONING IN NATURAL LANGUAGE

(Prentice-Hall).)

The semi-symbolic version is this: "It seems clear first of all that A. Secondly, since B, and since C, D; therefore E."

The final conclusion of the argument is clearly E, as indicated by 'therefore'. The use of the words 'first' and 'secondly' suggest that A and B are both reasons for the same conclusion, and the wording prior to C suggests it is one more reason for that conclusion. Even from the semi-symbolic version it seems plain that D is the conclusion being drawn from A, B, and C. Both the content and the word 'therefore' indicate that E is being concluded from D, so we have this for a diagram:

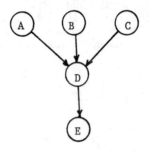

The above argument is fairly easy to structure once written in semi-symbolic form because the arguer has provided enough clues to his/her intentions in the form of argument indicator words. Sometimes it is impossible to construct the diagram by relying solely on these words simply because not enough of them are used. In this case we must rely on the content of the assertions.

Here is an example from THE WATCHTOWER:

"Seeking first God's kingdom and His righteousness can contribute toward security even in an indirect way. A person who applies Bible principles in his life becomes more diligent in his work. Employers will often be reluctant to dismiss or lay-off such a worker."

The semi-symbolic version of this ("A. B. C") is not very useful since there are no inference indicators or logical connectives. Obviously in cases like this we must rely on content. It should be clear that this is an argument because the author is trying to justify an assertion--the first one. If you understand the three assertions you can see that the second and third represent reasons for the first. (For a 'thought

314

experiment' you might try thinking of the first and third
assertions as reasons for the second, then thinking of the first
and second as reasons for the third. Do this by saying the two
assertions to yourself, then say 'therefore' and then the other
one. You should find that the word 'therefore' sounds quite out
of place.) This example also shows that ASSERTION ORDER IS NOT A
RELIABLE GUIDE TO ARGUMENT STRUCTURE. More often than not,
conclusions are given first.

(8.11) ARGUMENTS LACKING STATED CONCLUSIONS: It is a
psychological fact that persuasion can be most effective when the
arguer lets the arguee infer the conclusion independently. The
arguee then feels a need to accept the conclusion probably because
he has the impression of having created the argument himself.
This device is used a lot in advertisements where the ultimate
conclusion has the form 'You ought to buy product/service S.' The
ultimate conclusion is almost never given since everyone involved
knows what the purpose of advertisements is. But many ads also
leave out the conclusion that serves as a premise for the ultimate
conclusion. Here is a TV ad for Burger King:

"A[The bigger the burger the better the burger]. B[The
burgers are bigger at Burger King]". (From Thomas, PRACTICAL
REASONING...)

Obviously neither of these assertions is put forward as a
conclusion. They are supposedly reporting two logically
independent facts. What conclusion are we being invited to infer?
You should be able to see that the conclusion is: "The burgers are
better at Burger King". You should also find the inference in the
argument to be a valid one. If A and B were true they would make
the conclusion true. Ads that rely on the audience to make
inferences generally have clearly implied conclusions, ones that
almost everybody is able to infer. If only a few people could
supply the intended conclusion the ad would be ineffective. Of
course, this does not mean that the ads prove their conclusions.
To do that they must start from true premises. In the Burger King
example assumption B may be true but we do not know that it is.
To check we would have to buy a number of burgers from each of the
various burger chains and weigh them, but even that might not
settle the question. Does the word 'burger' in the ad refer to
only the hamburger patty, or that plus the roll and trimmings?
Burger King might have the biggest complete burger but it might
have less meat than McDonald's Big Mac, for example.

Assumption A might be questionable depending on what 'burger'
refers to. If bigness is achieved by having more roll, more
lettuce, and more onions, there comes a point at which bigger is
not better.

When arguers do not state their conclusions it is usually
315

easy enough to identify them, applying the principle of charity which tells us we should draw the conclusion that is strongest but which logically follows from the premises.

EXERCISE 8 - 2

Bracket each passage and write the semi-symbolic version. Nos. 1, 4, 8, and 11 have been answered in the back.

1. "The postal clerks must be underpaid since they strike frequently."

2. "There must be simple substances because there are composites, for a composite is just a collection of simple substances." (From Thomas.)

3. "Studying logic teaches one how to argue but people argue too much now so I'm not going to study logic."

4. "Garbage collectors should be paid more. Physicians are well paid, and both groups provide essential health services."

5. "Because Hindu villagers will never slaughter a cow, the only cattle available for eating are those that die naturally. Eating beef thus amounts to eating carrion." (From Thomas.)

6. "The most valuable of all soil invertebrates to man is probably the earthworm; these animals break down much of the plant debris reaching the soil. They also aerate it by turning it over. Accordingly, pesticide residues in soil that appreciably reduce the number of earthworms are a particularly serious matter." (From Thomas.)

7. "Matter is activity and therefore a body is where it acts: and because every particle of matter acts all over the universe, each body is everywhere." (From Thomas.)

8. "Since happiness consists in peace of mind, and since durable peace of mind depends on the confidence we have in the future, and since that confidence is based on the knowledge we should have of the nature of God and the soul,, it follows that knowledge is necessary for true happiness." (From Copi, INTRODUCTION TO LOGIC (MacMillan).)

9. "At bottom I did not believe I had touched that man. The law of probabilities decreed me guiltless of his blood for in all my small experience with guns I had never hit anything I had tried to hit and I know I had done my best to hit him." (Mark Twain)

316

10. "All propositions which have factual content are empirical hypotheses, and the function of empirical hypotheses is to provide a rule for the anticipation of experience. And this means that every empirical hypothesis must be relevant to some experience, so that a statement which is not relevant to any experience is not an empirical hypothesis, and accordingly it has no factual content." (From Thomas.)

11. "If Cain married his sister, their marriage was incestuous. If he didn't marry his sister, then Adam and Eve were not the progenitors of the entire human race. It follows that Adam and Eve were the progenitors of the whole human race only if Cain's marriage was incestuous." (Pospesel, DEDUCTIVE ARGUMENTS...)

EXERCISE 8 - 3

Construct a diagrammatic version of each of the arguments in Exercise 8 - 2. Answers are given in the back for 1, 4, 8, and 11.

(8.12)   LOGICALLY OPAQUE ARGUMENTS: The argument about
missiles previously discussed can be successfully structured by
relying entirely on indicator words.   The argument from THE
WATCHTOWER had no indicator words but could be diagrammed from
content,   but   some   arguments   are   more   troublesome in that not
enough indicator words are present and the content itself does not
provide a final criterion for constructing the structural diagram.
This situation is the fault of the arguer and if it is convenient
we should ask her/him to restate the argument more clearly.
Sometimes, especially when the argument is in printed form, we do
not have direct access to the arguer so that we must try to sort
the argument out ourselves if we wish to evaluate it. Here is an
example from a newspaper editorial.

In late 1974 the former long-time Liberal Premier of
Newfoundland, Joey Smallwood, had hinted he might try a comeback.
The St. John's Newfoundland EVENING TELEGRAM argued that he should
not:

"The Liberal party, which was almost wrecked by his going,
may well be destroyed by his attempt to regain control of its
machinery.   It is an affront to a whole new generation of
Newfoundlanders that they should be thought ready to embrace a
septuagenarian who was holding the reins of office before they
were born." (Quoted in R. H. Johnson and J. A. Blair, LOGICAL
SELF-DEFENCE.)

The conclusion, not itself stated, is that Smallwood should
not try to regain control of the party (A). The reason given for
it is that "The Liberal party may well be destroyed by his attempt
to regain control of its machinery" (B). Now what about the clause
between the commas in the first sentence? It represents the
assertion that the Liberal Party was almost wrecked by Smallwood's
retirement (C). Is it merely a parenthetical remark here, an
aside, or is it a reason for accepting B? And what about the last
sentence, assertion D we will call it? It is not argued for so it
must be an assumption, if anything. If it is a premise it would
seem to be a reason for B because we can make out a causal link to
the effect that the younger voters will resist Smallwood's attempt
and perhaps be reasonsible for a split in the party.

If we regard each part of the passage as part of the argument
we would have to diagram the argument as follows, since C and D
are independent assumptions:

318

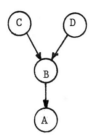

Whether or not this structure corresponds to the Editor's intentions is something only he could tell us. If we regard C as a reason for B we are entitled to say it is not a very good one. Given that Smallwood's retirement nearly wrecked the party, is that any reason to believe that his return would do the same? Indeed, it might be a reaon to believe the opposite, that his return might help the party. A letter to the Editor criticizing this aspect of the argument as structured above might be met by the complaint that this is an unfair criticism since C was not put forward as a reason for B. But the Editor really would have little ground for complaint because it is his own fault for expressing himself as he did.

This suggests a principle that we may rely on when content and indicators do not clearly show us what the structure of an argument is. It is a principle of charity by which WE OUGHT TO MAKE THE MOST LOGICALLY SOUND INTERPRETATION WHEN WE CANNOT DECIDE ON OTHER GROUNDS. This is based on the presumption that most mature arguers have some competence in argument. The presumption is one to be wary of, however. We are safe in presuming it where newspaper editors are concerned, but it is often risky.

Using the principle of charity we should perhaps delete C from the structural diagram, although we are logically entitled to include it until the arguer informs us that it is not to be included.

In general, we structure a logically opaque argument in the most logically adequate form that is compatible with the arguer's intentions, as shown by the use of indicator words.

(8.13) UNTIDY ARGUMENTS - REDUNDANCY: So far we have considered arguments containing only the assertions constituting premises and conclusions and argument indicator expressions, which might be called "logically tidy" arguments. More often than not a passage containing an argument will contain extraneous material of various kinds. These might be called "logically untidy" passages. One kind of untidiness is redundancy, when a premise or conclusion

319

is repeated in the passage.

We will adopt the practice of bracketing every assertion that is part of the argument, so when an assertion is repeated we will label it with the same letter used for the first occurrence. Thus, the following argument is bracketed as shown:

"It seems that A[the will of God is changeable.] For B[the Lord says (Genesis VI.7): It repententh me that I have made man.] But C[who-ever repents of what he has done, has a changeable will.] Therefore, A[God has a changeable will.]"

The semi-symbolic version is this: "It seems that A. For B. But C. Therefore A."

The conclusion of the argument has been asserted twice, so it is included twice in the semi-symbolic version. However, in the structural diagram it makes only one appearance:

Writers often state their conclusions at both the beginning and the end of the argument so that the reader can more easily understand what is being argued for. Stating it at the beginning is especially valuable to the reader because knowing what is being argued for enables him/her to judge more quickly whether the premises lead to that conclusion.

Another occasion on which you will encounter redundancy is when the writer provides a clarification of a prenmise or conclusion. For example:

"A[Thoughts and brain events cannot be identical] since B[the two kinds of things differ in spatial properties.] That is, B[brain events but not thoughts have a location.]"

Strictly speaking, the two assertions labeled "B" do not mean the same. We can tell this because the second version entails the first but not the other way around. Even so, it would be a mistake to label them differently. That would lead us to draw a diagram with a conclusion and two premises when the arguer only thinks of the argument as having one. We can think of the second version as superceding (for the arguer) the first since it is more

320

specific. The expression 'that is' tells us this.

We have to be careful about assigning the same letter to two assertions when they do not quite have the same meaning. Sometimes these can have the relation of premise to conclusion in the argument even though it might look as if one proposition is only a more specific form of the other. Whether we treat one as superceding the other depends upon the arguer's intentions. If the arguer's indicator words show he/she regards one proposition as a conclusion to be drawn from the other then our diagram must reflect that fact.

(8.14) UNTIDY ARGUMENTS - IRRELEVANCIES: Often writers will, in the course of presenting an argument, include background information, explanations, comments on the argument itself, and other extraneous matter. Here is an example containing such an irrelevancy:

"All censorships exist to prevent anyone from challenging current conceptions and existing institutions. All progress is initiated by challenging current concepts, and executed by supplanting existing institutions. Consequently, the first condition of progress is the removal of censorships. There is the whole case against censorships in a nutshell." - G. B. Shaw.

In this passage the second last sentence contains the conclusion of the argument. The last sentence, however, is not part of the argument. It is merely the writer's appraisal of his own argument, so in diagramming the argument we do not bracket the sentence at all.

(8.15) UNTIDY ARGUMENTS - RHETORIC: In an effort to persuade us, people often utilZe a variety of logically illegitimate devices, such as the use of flowery language and emotive language intended to gain our sympathy. Those devices tend to obscure the content and structure of an argument. Here is an example:

"Like an armed warrior, like a plumed knight, James G. Blain marched down the halls of the American Congtess and threw his shining lances full and fair against the brazen foreheads of every defamer of his country and maligner of its honor.

For the Republican Party to desert a gallant man now is worse than if an army should desert their general upon the field of battle." - Robert Ingersoll

This passage is part of a speech made by Ingersoll at the

321

Republican National Convention in 1876 on behalf of Mr. Blain. Even in political contexts we seldom carry rhetoric this far in our time. Just as well, you might say. Now, what about the argument? The conclusion is to be inferred from the context and can be worded thusly: 'You (the delegates) ought to nominate Blain.' What about premises? It is clear that Ingersoll is trying to give reasons for the conclusion, but it would not be useful to simply bracket either of the sentences given. It is better to paraphrase them, dropping out the rehetoric, since in criticizing the argument we are not concerned with the appropriateness of his similies and metaphors. We are interested in the message rather than the words used.

What is the message of the first sentence? Isn't he trying to tell us, in a high-flown way, that Blain has actively defended the country's policies in Congress? In the second, he is only asserting that not supporting Blaine's candicacy would be morally wrong. If we call the first paraphrased assertion 'A', the second 'B', and the conclusion 'C', how should we diagram the argument? 'A' is certainly a basic premise here. Is 'B' independent of it or logically related in the writer's mind? It seems to be intended to follow from 'A' so that we will construct the diagram like this:

Whenever the passage containing an argument is so logically untidy that we must paraphrase the arguer, opinions may differ over what the assertions represented in the structural diagram should be. This is to be expected to a certain degree because flowery language tends to obscure meaning. This is why a clear and concise statement of your argument is what the arguee prefers and is entitled to.

EXERCISE 8 - 4

Construct a structural diagram for each of the following arguments, writing down what each proposition stands for. Not all of the material in these is relevant and in some cases paraphrasing rather than bracketing may be the best approach.

Nos. 2 and 3 are answered in the back.

1. "On examining the apparent solid shell of a hen's egg, one may wonder how the egg can absorb the oxygen necessary to sustain the life and development of the embryo inside it. Obviously the shell must be permeable to oxygen, it must therefore have holes that are large enough to allow oxygen molecules to enter." (From Thomas.)

2. "One conception of logic is approximately as follows: logic is the account of the most universal properties of things, the account of those properties which are common to all things: just as ornithology is the science of birds, zoology the science of all animals, biology the science of all living things, so logic is the science of all things, the science of being as such. If this were the case, it would remain wholly unintelligible whence logic derives its certainty. For we surely do not know all things. We have not observed everything and hence we cannot know how everything behaves." (From Thomas.)

3. "The moose season has been closed during 1975 and 1976 to allow a build-up of the herd. Information gathered at moose check stations last year showed a closed season does not help to increase the herd. Lands and Forest Department big game biologist Art Patton reported that since the legal hunters did not shoot the moose, other factors such as illegal hunting must be preventing the population from building up. Therefore a legal hunting opportunity for resident hunters seems the most logical and best use of our moose resources, Mr. Patton said." (From the HALIFAX MAIL-STAR.)

4. "It is wrong to think that education should encourage independent thinking. If students had to think things out independently of all we know from the great thinkers of the past, they would have to rediscover everything the great thinkers already have discovered. We don't want them to think for themselves, we want them to think rightly. Thus, their thinking must be dependent upon the great thinkers." (From Thomas.)

EXERCISE 8 - 5

Evaluate each of the following extended arguments, using the evaluation procedure. Step One has been done. No. 2 is answered.

1.

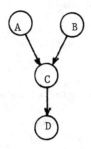

A = Some students here get good grades without working hard.

B = Some students here work hard and don't get good grades.

C = Grades don't reflect how much work students do.

D = Our grading system does not give reliable results.

2.

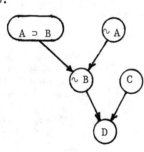

A = Some text books are useful.

B = All useful things are valuable.

C = Some text books are valuable.

D = Some valuable things are expensive.

E = Some text books are expensive.

3.

A = The moon is made of cheese.

B = The moon has a high protein content.

C = There is no plant life on the moon.

D = The moon is not nutritious.

EXERCISE 8 - 6

Evaluate the arguments contained in each of the following passages using the six-step procedure. Nos. 2 and 4 are answered in the back.

1. "Since the world exists, it must have come into existence. But only God can create something from nothing. So the Christian God exists."

2. This argument is intended to show the absurdity of action at a distance: "Matter is activity and therefore a body is where it acts. And because every particle of matter acts all over the universe, every body is everywhere." (From Thomas.)

3. A problem about the theory of the origins of humanity as given in the Book of Genesis: "If Cain married his sister, the marriage was incestuous. If he didn't marry his sister, then Adam and Eve were not the progenitors of the entire human race. It follows that Adam and Eve were the progenitors of the whole human race only if Cain's marriage was incestuous." (From Pospesel, ARGUMENTS: DEDUCTIVE LOGIC EXERCISES).

4. When his legislature was debating a bill that would make use of seat belts in cars mandatory, a citizen wrote this to a local paper: "The current attempt by the government to pass a law requiring use of seat belts is another attempt to restrict our freedom of choice. It is the right of each of us to decide whether we wish to take the risk of not wearing a seat belt. This law would remove our freedom of choice."

5. A student who saw himself pretty much forced to take a logic course in which this text is used said this to a fellow student: "I shouldn't have to learn this logic stuff. I'll never use these diagrams outside this course, so it's a waste of time learning to make them. I'd rather take accounting!"

Evaluate the argument contained in each of the following passages. These are less tidy than the ones in Exercise 8 - 6. Nos. 1 and 3 are answered in the back.

1. "An argument is invalid when its premises are true and its conclusion is false. So no invalid arguments have true conclusions, right?"

2. From the 27 October 1981 HALIFAX MAIL-STAR: "More and more [women] are pursuing high-powered careers. The stress this new lifestyle places on marriage can be calculated: census figures show the divorce rate for women earning more than $25,000.00 per year is double the national average. The rate leaps to four times the national average for women in the $50,000-plus bracket."

3. "The belief that it is mostly European and non-white men who abuse their wives and girl-friends has been proven false. Wife battering occurs in all cultures and in all social classes . . . ."

4. "If ever there was a time for women to stand up for their rights to stay home and be a good wife and mother to their children, it is now. Is that really the right of woman? Sure it is. Let us look at the example of nature. Every species in God's creation follows an order and almost without exception has the mother home in the den protecting and nurturing the young while poppa tracks the forest looking for the family bacon. Man, as of late, seems to be the only one insisting on breaking out of the mold."

5. The belief that the earth is spherical goes back a lot earlier than the Rennaisance. Aristotle argued for it this way: "The evidence of the senses further corroborates this: How else would eclipses of the moon show segments shaped as we see them? As it is, the shapes which the moon itself shows are of every kind--straight, convex, and concave--but in the eclipses the outline is always curved. And since it is the interposition of the earth that makes the eclipse, the form of this line will be caused by the form of the earth's surface, which is therefore spherical."

(8.16) WORD PROBLEMS.   As we all know, discerning what
other people are actually saying is made difficult sometimes by
their choice of words. Some words are ambiguous, having at least
two distinct meanings.   Some are vague, so that we have difficulty
sometimes in deciding whether they apply or not. Some words are
both ambiguous and vague. Unfortunately, it is the more abstract
terms that tend to be troublesome in these ways, and these terms
stand for ideas that are very important in our culture ('justice',
'love', 'democracy', etc.).

Some words can be troublesome for another reason: they have
connotations that evoke emotional responses from us that can make
us more readily disposed to accept or reject the claims in which
they occur. These connotations embody value judgments.   For
example, the slang term 'wop' is used to refer to Italians or
people with Italian forebears, and we can normally infer that a
person who uses the term dislikes Italians, probably without good
reason.

In this section we will discuss strategies for dealing with
these word problems that can help in arriving at accurate
diagrammatic versions of arguments.

(8.161) AMBIGUITY.   Some words seem to denote things or
phenomena that differ sufficiently to lead us to mentally separate
them into two or more classes.   The Greek philosopher Aristotle
was very perceptive in discerning differences that could be used
to distinguish two or more meanings of a term.   In discussing the
terms 'justice' and 'injustice' he says: "Now 'justice' and
'injustice' seem to be ambiguous, but because their different
meanings approach near to one another the abiguity escapes notice
and is not obvious as it is, comparatively, when the meanings are
far apart . . . "(Nicomachean Ethics, Book V). He goes on to
analyze the terms and concludes that there are two kinds of
justice:" . . . one kind is that which is manifested in
distributions of honor or money . . . and one is that which plays
a rectifying part in transactions between man and man . . .".
These two senses have been labeled "distributive" and
"retributive" justice, respectively.   People who talk of social
justice are talking about distributive justice, bringing about a
fair distribution of the advantages of society.   Those who talk of
legal justice are talking about the redressing of wrongs by
appropriate amount of compensation to a wronged party, or about
making punishment fit the crime.   Notice that the two meanings are
related. Both are concerned with equality, but in different ways.

Although many words and expressions can be regarded as having
more than one meaning, this does not often lead to unclarity
because linguistic context rules out all but one meaning. For
example, when someone says "To ensure that justice is done we must

327

give longer prison terms," we know they are talking about retributive justice, not distributive justice. Sometimes, though, context is not adequate to disambiguate. Then we need to consult the arguer to find out what interpretation is intended. If he/she is not available we are forced to evaluate two versions. It is always desirable to substitute synonyms for the expression generating the ambiguity. This helps to prevent confusion.

Here is a comical example of ambiguity from the TV comedy "Welcome Back Kotter": In trying to prove to Mr. Kotter that shool should not be required Horshack says: "Education molds young minds but who wants a moldy mind?"

The argument can be provisionally diagrammed like this:

A = Education molds young minds.

B = No one wants a moldy mind.

C = Education ought to be avoided.

This is a typical example of the use of an ambiguous term ('mold') to create a meaning shift from one assertion to another. In B Horshack is using 'moldy' to refer to "a wooly or furry growth of minute fungi" (Concise Oxford Dictionary). We are disposed to accept this as true, supposing it is possible. We are also disposed to accept A as true, but only because we take 'molds' as a synonym for 'shapes'.

To secure a valid inference Horshack needs to take A as equivalent to 'Education causes young minds to become moldy', but of course the conclusion cannot be proved in this version of the argument because A is false. Minds are not physical objects and cannot, therefore, be subject to mold.

If, on the other hand, A is taken as equivalent to 'Education shapes young minds', A will be true but then the inference will be invalid. So again the conclusion is not proved.

More frequently, interpretation problems arise from a single occurrence of an expression in an argument. For example, here is a classic case. The college student has just handed in her term paper. The professor assures her that he "will waste no time reading this paper." She infers that he is keen to read it:

"Dr. No says he will waste no time reading my paper. so he

328

must be anxious to read it."

The student has interpreted Dr. No as meaning "I will read your paper right away." However, there is the distinct possibility that the professor meant "Reading your paper would be a waste of my time." If the first version is correct the inference is warranted, but on the second interpretation it is not.

One source of ambiguity are relative terms such as 'large', 'small', 'big', 'little', etc. These have different meaning when attributed to different things. Consider this argument: "Mickey is a big mouse. Mice are animals. Therefore, Mickey is a big animal." Here the premises may be true but the inference is invalid because 'big' has different meanings in the two assertions. A big mouse could be held in a cup, but lots of animals are larger than that. To decide whether one is a big animal we use the standards applicable to the entire class of animals. This latter class includes whales and elephants, of course.

To summarize the strategy for dealing with ambiguous assertions in arguments: (1) try to determine which meaning is appropriate by relying on the linguistic context, (2) if this fails try to consult the arguer, (3) if this cannot be done, construct two diagrammatic versions and test each.

EXERCISE 8 - 8

Evaluate each of the following arguments after dealing with the ambiguity in an appropriate way. Nos. 2 and 4 are answered in the back.

1. The expression 'better than' is transitive in the sense that if X is better than Y and Z is better than X, then Z is better than Y. This feature is being relied on in this argument intended to show that hamburger is better than filet mignon. "Nothing is better than filet mignon, but hamburger is better than nothing. So hamburger is better than filet mignon!"

2. "Studying logic teaches one how to argue, but people argue too much already. Therefore, I'm not going to study logic."

3. "Coke adds life, so we should have dying people drink it."

4. "Heterosexuality is a law of nature. Homosexuals should be punished because they violate this law."

(8.162) VAGUENESS. Many terms used to name and describe
features of the material world have clear meanings but it is not
always clear when they can be correctly used. The word 'tall',
for example, means 'above average in height'. The word can be
correctly applied to almost all professional basketball players,
and clearly does not apply to midget wrestlers. However, since
humans can be either short or tall or in between there is an
interval of height within which we have difficulty deciding
whether an individual is tall or not. In North America a man is
definitely short if he is less than five foot eight inches and
definitely tall if he is over six feet two inches. But is a man
of six feet really tall? If we say he is, what about someone five
feet eleven? The farther we move downward from six feet two the
more reluctant we are to say a man is tall, but we are likely to
differ among ourselves about the point at which a man is not tall.
This indeterminacy shows that the word 'tall' is vague. It is
vague not because of what it means but because of what it refers
to. Heights vary on a continuum from short to tall and we have
not adopted a linguistic convention that draws a line between the
two at some point. In this respect 'tall' differs from terms such
as 'speeding' which has a stipulated meaning laid down by law.
Where the speed limit is 30 m.p.h you are speeding when driving at
any speed over 30 m.p.h., and not speeding at 30 m.p.h. or less.
'Speeding' in this case is a precise term in that we can always
say when it is applicable.

Besides vagueness arising from a "gray area" of application
adjacent to a clear area, there is a more troublesome kind often
associated with more abstract terms. These terms can be created
and get used with very little consistency or precision. For
example, rock music fans will be aware of the adjective 'funky'
but just about nobody can say what it means in any accurate way.
It is probably not even possible to get much consensus on whose
music actually is funky. Thus, 'funky' seems to have a relatively
indeterminate meaning as well as having an indeterminate area of
application. It is not totally indeterminate, though. Operatic
arias and tunes played by Lawrence Welk do not have a funky sound,
we can all agree on that.

A common variety of vagueness occurs in the use of
quantitative expressions. This can be illustrated by an
(imaginary) example from advertising, where this sort of vagueness
is often used to advantage.

Alvin is in the market for a small car. He sees a newspaper
advertisment for a new small car, the Hara Kiri. The
advertisement reads: "The new Hara Kiri will give up to 20% better
mileage than the best-selling car in its class!" Alvin reasons:

"I want a car in the Hara Kiri's class and I also want top

330

fuel economy. The Hara Kiri gives up to 20% better mileage than the best-selling car in its class. Therefore, I ought to buy a Hara Kiri."

The problem in evaluating this argument centers on the assumption Alvin got from the advertisement. Even if we are sure that the Hara Kiri manufacturers are comparing their car with ones actually in its class we still have a problem with the expression 'up to 20% better mileage'. Just what is the manufacturer commited to in using this expression in this context?

A strategy for clarifying such vague assertions is this: formulate in relatively precise terms the least ambitious claim that is being made and substitute it for the original version. The least ambitious claim is the most defensible interpretation that cannot be regarded as grossly misleading.

What reformulation is appropriate for the example? Clearly, the Hara Kiri people are not claiming that all, or even most, drivers will get 20% better mileage. They seem to be committed to claiming, at the minimum, that SOME drivers will get 20% better mileage. Any less ambitious interpretation would seem to make the original quite misleading. The second assertion in Alvin's reasoning, then, should be replaced by "The Hara Kiri gives some drivers up to 20% better mileage than the best-selling car in its class."

EXERCISE 8 - 9

Formulate the least ambitious non-misleading claim that is being made in each of the following assertions. Nos. 1 and 3 are answered in the back.

1. "Our tomatoes are days fresher!"

2. A restaurant ad: "Children dine free on Sundays."

3. A Maoist exhortation for the distribution of wealth: "Soak the rich!".

4. "Logic teaches you to think."

EXERCISE 8 - 10

Which of the following expressions are relatively vague? Consult a dictionary if necessary. Nos. 1, 2, 7 and 8 are answered in the back.

1. bald

2. gold

3. dusk

4. daughter

5. as soon as possible

6. newspaper

7. recession

8. argument

9. dentist

10. socialist

(8.163) EMOTIVE CONNOTATIONS. People who wish to make their arguments more appealing to us often exploit the emotive connotations that some terms have. Words can have negative connotations, positive connotations, or be relatively neutral. As noted in the introduction the term 'wop' is used to designate people from Italy or those with Ialian forebears. However, unlike the word 'Italian', its use normally implies that the user has a negative attitude towards the people designated. If you share their attitude then you are susceptible to the use of the term in argument, in that you may be more easily convinced by an argument than you should be. For example: "Wops develop links with organized crime, so we should restrict the number of immigrants we accept from Italy."

It is a cultural fact that some words tend to acquire connotations that are publicly shared. Many words have connotations for particular individuals because of their personal experience. For you the term 'college' may come to have either positive or negative connotations depending on how you view your college experience. Terms that acquire negative or positive connotations that are widely shared usually are ones that stand for things that have attributes (or attributes themselves) about which we take value positions. For example, 'ice cream' has positive connotations, but 'garbage' has negative connotations. For this reason, people do not mind being called ice cream vendors when they sell ice cream, but are not happy with being called garbagemen when they collect garbage.

In our society there is considerable effort expended to generate euphemisms, terms with neutral connotations that are intended to replace others with negative connotations. Thus, in some towns the garbageman is officially titled a "sanitary engineer". Recall how many euphemisms there are for 'toilet': washroom, bathroom, heads (navy term), restroom, loo (British), mens' room, ladies' room, etc.

Sometimes euphemisms are dangerous because they lead us to accept states of affairs we would not otherwise tolerate. This can happen either because we do not know what the euphemism stands for, or because the expression does not evoke the appropriate reaction. The Central Intelligence Agency, during the Viet Nam war, used the phrase 'terminate with extreme prejudice.' This turned out to be synonymous with 'assassinate'! Anyone not aware of this might suppose that the action was less drastic, of course, and thereby be misled. Furthermore, even if one did know what the euphemism meant, the moral connotations are not as strong, so that we may be inclined to overlook this sort of activity more readily. The main function of euphemisms, then, seems to be to make the unpleasant sound less so. This was the function of the expression 'the final solution to the Jewish question' as used by high Nazi officials in the early 1940's. It really meant 'the extermination of the Jews'. When Pearl Harbor was attacked by the Japanese in December, 1941, it was called a "sneak attack" by our side, but when such things are done by nations friendly to us they are called "pre-emptive strikes", as when the Israelis attacked Egyptian airfields on June 6, 1967, and pretty much destroyed their airforce. (Egyptians no doubt called this action a sneak attack!)

There is a humorous side to the emotive connotation phenomenon. Someone once noted that certain concepts can be emotively "declined", as in "I am firm, you are stubborn, he is pig-headed." Here is one more: "I give due regard to the alternatives, you are indecisive, he is a ditherer." With a good vocabulary anyone can play this game.

Do not get the impression that all use of emotively-charged terms is questionable practice. In literature these terms are very useful in conveying the impressions writers wish to give. One character's attitude to another can be very efficiently conveyed to us by having the former use emotive terms. Again, when we wish to exhort others to act on their convictions (which is different from trying to influence their convictions) emotive language is a legitimate and valuable resource. The use of such language is normally illegitimate in argument, but even there it is sometimes appropriate.

The strategy for dealing with assertions that have emotive connotations that may interfere with the accurate appraisal of arguments is to "translate" such assertions into emotively neutral language. As the emotive declension game referred to above suggests, it is almost always possible to do this. A thesaurus is particularly useful in finding non-emotive equivalents.

EXERCISE 8 - 11

Create an emotively neutral "translation" for the capitalized expression in each of the following assertions. Nos. 1 and 3 are answered in the back.

1. "WETBACKS are a serious political issue in the southwest U.S."

2. Anti-abortion groups often say that "This MURDERING of unborn human babies must stop."

3. A proposal to provide better living conditions in a prison led a local politician to react by saying "CODDLING prisoners at public expense is a scandal".

4. The appearance of A.I.D.S. (Acquired Immunity Deficiency Syndrome) in San Francisco in 1982 led a clergyman to say "God is giving QUEERS their comeuppance!"

5. "THE RUNNING DOGS OF THE YANKEE IMPERIALISTS must be driven out of Taiwan."

EXERCISE 8 - 12

Replace the euphemism capitalized in each sentence with the expression (of one word or more) for which it is a euphemism. Nos. 1 and 3 are answered in the back.

1. The gangster speaking of a rival: "I'm going to have him WASTED."

2. Marilyn Monroe in a movie: "I want to MAKE LOVE."

3. When it appeared that White House representatives had lied about their role in the Watergate hotel break-in the Press Secretary announced to newsmen that "All previous White House statements about the Watergate case are INOPERATIVE."

4. Governments sometimes admit they are involved in hostilities in other countries by acknowledging the presence of MILITARY ADVISORS in the countries.

5. Elroy's wife comes into the living room wearing a new hat, which appears to him to be a bowl of plastic fruit worn on the head. She asks him how he likes it. He is aware of the value of diplomacy in marriage so he replies: "Well, its INTERESTING!"

6. A college student was accused by a professor of USING AN UNAUTHORIZED INFORMATION SOURCE during an exam.

7. As fans of M.A.S.H. are aware, the soldiers in Korea were engaged in a POLICE ACTION.

8. A brochure describes winter in Alaska as "INVIGORATING".

CHAPTER NINE: SOME COMMON FALLACIES

(9.1) INTRODUCTION: In the preceding eight chapters you have
been exposed to material that is intended to develop your ability
to analyze arguments and evaluate the extent to which they prove
their conclusions. General guidelines have been provided to help
you criticize arguments effectively. In this final chapter you
will be shown some of the ways in which arguments can be
defective. Defective argument patterns are called "fallacies".
Logicians have been identifying and classifying fallacies for
several thousand years now and probably more than one hundred
fallacies have been identified and given names. In this chapter
you will be exposed to 33 of the most common ones. If you can
remember the faults that each one has you will be better equipped
to spot weaknesses in arguments directed at you, but this
compendium of faults is only intended to supplement the general
guidelines given earlier. For convenience the fallacies have been
classified, but are numbered consecutively.

(9.2) FALLACIES OF RELEVANCE. These defective arguments are
so-called because one or more of the premises relied on are
irrelevant to the conclusion that is drawn.

(1) AD HOMINEM (ABUSIVE)

TYPICAL FORM: STRUCTURE AND RATING

A[I asserts that P]

But B[I is F]

So C[we have no reason to
believe I is correct].

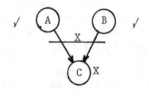

DEFECT.   The inference is invalid. The assumption B asserts
correctly that I has some unacceptable personal attribute, but I's
personal attributes are not relevant to whether I's assertion that
P is true.

COMMENT.   It is easy to be persuaded that someone ought not
to be believed when you don't like them, but even the worst villan
in the world is capable of saying something true. Like many of
these fallacious forms, this one has an exception. When B asserts
that I frequently lies there is some degree of proof to the
argument although we cannot give it a " " rating.

EXAMPLE.   A[Professor Quagmire says that many students do not

336

do enough academic work]. But B[Quagmire himself is lazy]. So C[we have no reason to believe that Professor Quagmire is correct about the students].

CRITICISM OF EXAMPLE. Granted that Professor Quagmire is lazy and should practice what he preaches, it still does not follow that we should dismiss his opinion about students. After all, few people have a better opportunity to judge student effort than the students' professors.

(2) AD HOMINEM (VESTED INTEREST)

TYPICAL FORM: STRUCTURE AND RATING

A[You assert that P].

But B[it is in your interest
to reject P as false].

So C[you ought to reject P
as false].

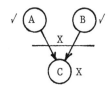

DEFECT. The inference is invalid. Assumption B is irrelevant to C. That a person would benefit from not believing P does not have a bearing on whether or not they should, as logical individuals, regard P as true.

COMMENT. Appeals to personal benefit to get us to change our minds is a kind of pressure that is difficult to resist. It takes a lot of logical integrity to resist this argument when we have a lot to gain by giving in.

EXAMPLE. A[You assert that there is no God]. BUT B[you will feel more secure in life by believing the opposite]. SO C[you ought to stop believing there is no God].

CRITICISM OF EXAMPLE. The conclusion does not follow because personal benefits do not count as evidence against the view that there is no God.

337

(3) AD HOMINEM (Well poisoning)

TYPICAL FORM: STRUCTURE AND RATING

A[K asserts that P]

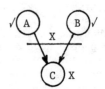

But B[K would benefit from our
believing P].

So C[K's asserting P is no reason
to believe that P is true].

   DEFECT: An individual may be telling the truth even though
he/she   would   benefit if the proposition were generally believed,
and   may   even   be in a better position than others to know the
facts.

   COMMENT.   This practice is called "well poisoning".   It
involves   trying   to   show   that   an individual is not a reliable
source   because   of   some   special   interest that he/she has. This
special   interest   is   seen   as "tainting" any claim the individual
makes that is related to the special interest.

   EXAMPLE: "Professor Quagmire says that college classes are
too   large.   But his job would be easier with smaller classes.   So
his   testimony   is   no   basis   for believing that classes are too
large."

   CRITICISM.   True,   the   Professor's job would be easier with
smaller classes but he probably knows what he is talking about.   A
person   need   not   be   lying   just because they might benefit from
being believed.

(4) TU QUO QUE (You too)

TYPICAL FORM: STRUCTURE AND RATING

A[You say not to do N].

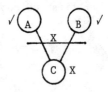

But B[you do N yourself].

So C[I can ignore your advice
not to do N].

   DEFECT.   Invalid inference.   Assumption B is not relevant to
whether   the   individual's advice is well grounded. In fact, those
who   indulge   in   a   practice may be in the best position to give
sound advice about its bad consequences.

COMMENT. This argument relies on the assumption that actions speak louder than words. The arguer is implying that the advice giver does not really believe that doing N is wrong. He/she would refrain if it was.

EXAMPLE. "You tell me not to smoke. But you yourself smoke. So I can ignore your advice not to do it."

CRITICISM OF EXAMPLE. The advice giver should say that he/she regards the advice as sound but is unable to take it himself/herself because he/she does not have the strength of will.

(5) APPEAL TO FAIRNESS

TYPICAL FORM: STRUCTURE AND RATING

A[I did n].

But B[K did n and wasn't criticized or punished].

So C[I should not be critized or punished for doing n].

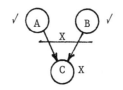

DEFECT. Invalid inference. Assumption B is not relevant to C. Failure to criticize or punish K does not commit the arguee to refrain from criticizing or punishing the arguer. At most the arguee only has to admit he/she was negligent in not dealing properly with K.

COMMENTS. The argument is used by people who have done something morally improper. It is most effective when there are lots of people who have done the act in question and gotten away with it. The persuasiveness of the argument comes from its implicit appeal to the arguee's sense of justice. That is, the arguer is implying that he/she is being singled out for special unfair treatment.

EXAMPLE: Young boy to his mother: "I did take the candy without paying, but you didn't punish my brother when he did. So you shouldn't punish me."

Mother's response: "I should have punished him too. Just because I didn't does not mean I should let you off."

(6) FALSE REFUTATION (IGNORATIO ELENCHI)

TYPICAL FORM   STRUCTURE AND RATING

A[K asserts that P]

B[P is false because Q].

So C[K is wrong].

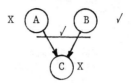

DEFECT. A is false. K really asserted something that appears similar to P but is more defensible than P and Q does not prove K's actual assertion false.

COMMENTS. Point out that K actually supports a different position so that the "refutation" of P is illusory. This might not be possible at the time so you should beware of accepting the refutation as legitimate until you can check on K's precise view.

EXAMPLE. A[Senator Forthright says that government spending is excessive in all departments]. B[This is false because everyone knows that old people do not receive pensions they can live on]. So C[Senator Forthright is mistaken].

EXAMPLE CRITICISM. A is false so the argument does not prove the Senator is mistaken. He said that spending was excessive in NEARLY all departments.

(7) RED HERRING.

TYPICAL FORM. K is arguing against some proposition (P) the arguer accepts. The arguer uses this argument to divert K:

A[Discussing topic T is more   STRUCTURE AND RATING
urgemt/important than deciding
about P].

So B[K should be discussing
T instead of P].

DEFECT. Inference is invalid. The arguer is relying on an unstated assumption, i.e., that the more urgent or important topic should be dealt with first. Apart from any difficulties in ranking topics on a scale of urgency or importance, we are not often obliged to discuss topics in order of urgency or importance. When immediate action is required we may need to do this but we are not frequently in such a situation when people use this argument.

COMMENTS. This argument is used to divert discussion when the arguer feels threatened by an attack on a position he/she has a commitment to. It is used most effecively by choosing a topic T that is a potential source of embarassment to K. The fallacy is named after the English fox-hunting practice of dragging a smoked herring across the fox's trail to divert the dogs in pursuit -- so that the fox can be hunted again another day.

EXAMPLE. Senator Bafflegab has proposed a gasoline rationing scheme for the country and Senator Forthright has been trying to show that it will not work: Bafflegab says: "Discussing the plight of the unemployed is more urgent than getting a rationing plan, so we should be discussing that instead."

EXAMPLE CRITICISM. Senator Forthright can say: "While I agree that unemployment is a serious problem and needs to be solved, it is not relevant to the merits and demerits of the gasoline rationing scheme Senator Bafflegab supports. Senator Bafflegab is trying to change the subject. Perhaps he feels threatened!"

(8) APPEAL TO POPULARITY

TYPICAL FORM: STRUCTURE AND RATING

A[Everyone believes that P].

So B[P must be true].

DEFECT. Unless most people are legitimate authorities about the subject to which P belongs, the fact that many people believe that P is not evidence for the truth of P. Thus, A is irrelevant to the conclusion so the inference is invalid.

COMMENTS. This argument can be difficult to resist because it invokes peer group pressure. The fallacy is not committed when P is something that ordinary people are in a position to know about. For example, if the local people in an area tell you that the water in their area is too cold for swimming in the summer it is safe to infer that it is. This argument usually shows up in discussing matters of taste.

CRITICISM. Point out that the premise may be true but it doesen't prove the conclusion because it is possible that everyone may be wrong. They may be short on good evidence and there may be knowledgeable people who believe the opposite.

EXAMPLE: A critic talking to Christopher Columbus in 1492 before he headed west to find the Indies: "Everyone believes the earth is flat. So it must be true."

EXAMPLE CRITICISM. Columbus could have responded by saying: "Maybe everyone does believe the earth is flat but that doesn't guarantee that it's true. Most people don't have enough evidence and some learned men, such as Aristotle, believe the earth is a sphere."

(9) APPEAL TO TRADITION

TYPICAL FORM   STRUCTURE AND RATING

A[We've always done it this way].

So B[this must be the best way].

Therefore C[you should do it this way too].

(B is part of the argument but is not usually stated).

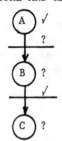

DEFECT: The inference from A to B. The length of time a practice has been followed is some evidence for its superiority but of course it is often possible with a bit of creativity to improve on anything.

COMMENT. The argument relies on the assumption that withstanding the test of time is the best test of the superiority of a practice. But if everyone who has followed it since it was first invented has adopted it without thinking about whether or not it could be improved on, then there is a good chance it is not the best way to get the job done. Generally B is not stated, but is skipped over.

CRITICISM. Point out that the fact that it has always been done this way does not guarantee that this way is the best way. Maybe no one has seriously tried to develop a better method.

EXAMPLE: A political campaign organizer talking to the candidate who has suggested they do more TV appearances: "We've always had our candidates go out door-to-door, so you should campaign this way too."

EXAMPLE CRITICISM: The candidate can say: "You're implying that the traditional way is the best way, but has anybody tried

342

anything new lately? Times change and many voters are best reached through TV."

9.3 CAUSAL FALLACIES: These defective arguments involve some mistake in reasoning from cause to effect, or the other way around.

(10) POST HOC ERGO PROPTER HOC

TYPICAL FORM: STRUCTURE AND RATING

A [Event Y usually follows event X].

So B[X is the cause of Y].

DEFECT. That one event usually follows another does not guarantee that the earlier one is the cause of the later one. It is possible that both events are caused by some third one, or that we are wrong about the sequence of events.

CRITICISM. Point out that the inference is dubious because X and Y may be efects of some third factor Z. Try to identify Z if there is such a factor. If there isn't, try to show that it is a coincidence that Y follows X by showing that they each have a different cause. If neither of these can be done, argue that the inference is dubious by presenting an example such as this: spring always follows winter but winter doesn't cause spring, the movement of the earth around the sun causes both.

EXAMPLE. The unscientific farmer argues: "A frost usually follows a full moon so a full moon causes frost."

EXAMPLE CRITICISM: It's true that frost follows a full moon sometimes but that does not prove the moon causes frost. The absence of an insulating cloud cover allows the earth to cool more overnight, bringing frost, and this also makes it possible to notice that the moon is full.

(11) CAUSAL SLIPPERY SLOPE

TYPICAL FORM: STRUCTURE AND RATING

A[If we do W then X will
follow].

B[If X happens then Y will
follow].

But C[we do not want Y to
happen].

So D[we should not do W].

DEFECT.   Either A or B (perhaps both) is false. They form a
causal chain but the chain has a weak link.

COMMENT: The argument is so-called because it pictures us
stepping onto a 'slippery slope' when we do W, so that we no
longer control what happens and end up with Y occuring, something
we don't want. The arguer does not approve of W and the arguer
does, so the arguer is trying to prove that, regardless of W's
intrinsic merits or demerits, it leads to something (Y) that both
of them find undesirable. The persuasiveness of the argument
depends on how inevitable the slide down the slippery slope to Y
looks.

CRITICISM.   Try to show that either A or B is false or
dubious, that X need not happen just because W does, or that Y
need not happen if X does. Point to some factors that might
intervene to break the chain of causality.

EXAMPLE.   "If we permit abortion then we will lose respect
for human life. If we lose respect for human life then we will
permit the killing of newborns. But we don't want the killing of
newborns. So we should not permit abortion."

EXAMPLE CRITICISM. The first premise is false. Respect for
human life has not suffered from permitting abortion in other
countries.

344

(12) THE GAMBLER'S FALLACY

TYPICAL FORM: STRUCTURE AND RATING

A[Result X has not happened in
many turns lately].

So B[X is more likely than any
alternative to happen next].

So C[X is the 'best bet'].

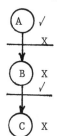

DEFECT.   The inference to B from A is invalid IF outcomes are
totally random.   Since   each   turn   or   trial   is   independent of
previous ones the odds on getting result X do not change from one
turn to another.

COMMENT.   Persuasive because we know that, with no biases, a
particular   outcome   tends   to come out in a certain proportion of
the trials depending on the random odds of its occurrence. For
example,   a fair (unbiased) wheel of chance that has 10 numbers on
it will   tend to have each outcome show up 10% of the time over a
great many trials.   This evening-out tendency disposes us to think
that when a long run of trials occurs in which X does not occur, X
must have an increasing chance of occurring to even out to its
proper proportion.   But the evening-out is a matter of chance, it
is not a causal factor itself. This fallacy is most commonly
committed by gamblers, hence the name.

CRITICISM. Try to remember that each trial is independent and
if the game is fair, what has happened before has no bearing on
what happens next.

EXAMPLE.   Zeke and Virgil are tossing a fair coin and betting
on the outcome.   Virgil reasons: "Heads has not come up in the
last five tosses so it is more likely to come up next time. So
I'm going to call heads."

(9.4) CONCEPTUAL CONFUSION FALLACIES.

There   are a variety of these. Here only two common ones are
described.   They arise from the way we conceptualize certain
aspects of reality.

345

(13) IS-OUGHT FALLACY

TYPICAL FORM   STRUCTURE AND RATING

A[People in fact do X].

So B[people ought to do (be
allowed to do) X].

DEFECT. The inference is invalid. What people ought to do
(or be allowed to do) is determined by other factors than what in
fact they do, such as the tendency of the action to cause benefit
or harm.

COMMENT. Peruasive only when X is something society thinks
is not harmful. The argument seems to assume that an existing
practice is a defensible one.

CRITICISM. Point out that the fact that people actually do
something is no basis for concluding they ought to do it or be
allowed to do it. Actually doing X cannot be a justification for
doing X.

EXAMPLE. "People do own handguns, so they ought to be
allowed to own handguns."EXAMPLE CRITICISM. The conclusion
doesn't follow. It would follow only if we assume that owning
handguns has more good consequences than bad ones, but that needs
arguing.

(14) "SMALL DIFFERENCE IS NO DIFFERENCE"

TYPICAL FORM   STRUCTURE AND RATING

A[No single small change in
X makes it become Y],

So B[saying X has become Y
at some point is totally
arbitrary].

So C[X cannot justifiably be
said to become Y].

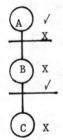

346

DEFECT. Inference from A to B is invalid. Things often change their properties as a result of a SERIES of small changes, even though one single change isn't enough. The problem with the argument is best brought out by an example: "No single change in visibility during a 5-minute interval takes us from day-light to dark. So saying we change from daylight to dark at some point is totally arbitrary. So it cannot justifiably be said that there is ever a change from daylight to dark." This example cannot be sound because the conclusion is false. The initial assumption is true so there is an inference problem, which arises with the first inference. In fact, certain points are much more appropriately chosen as ones at which daylight becomes dark. A half-hour after sunset is a better choice by far than one hour before sunset or two hours after. At that point it is not really dark but not really broad daylight either, so that if we are forced to pick a time, some time around there is appropriate.

COMMENT. This fallacy is only persuasive when we are dealing with concepts that are somewhat vague. It is often called the "bald man" fallacy. If we imagine a man with a full head of hair and remove all his hairs one at a time there is no prticular hair that, when removed, marks the transition from not being bald to being bald. Yet at the beginning he is not bald and at the end he is. We find it difficult to reconcile these facts, but we can do it by specifying an interval in which the change occurs, or by picking some point in the interval somewhat arbitrarily. But picking a point arbitrarily within the appropriate interval is not choosing totally arbitrarily.

CRITICISM. Point out that even though a small change doesn't transform X into Y, it doesn't follow that no point is more justifiable thn any other as a choice for the transition. Give the daylight-to-dark example in support.

EXAMPLE. The anti-abortionist argues: "Fetuses are humans just before birth and if we start counting backwards from there, no single day in the development of the human fetus marks its transition from being a human to not being one. So saying it becomes a non-human at some point is totally arbitrary. So fetuses are humans from conception onward.

EXAMPLE CRITICISM. It does not follow that it is totally arbitrary to say a fetus does not count as a human at some point. Clearly it counts after about five months because it has all organs present and looks like a human baby. But clearly, also, it can't count during the first weeks when it is only a clump of cells. So it is not totally arbitrary to say it becomes a human somewhere around three months.

(9.5) SEMANTIC FALLACIES These rely on the fact that many

347

words have more than one meaning. Sometimes the meanings are
related but reasonably distinct so that a thing could qualify as
an instance under one definition but not under another. Fallacies
of this type are most common with fairly abstract concepts, such
as 'democracy', 'socialism', 'war', etc., because these are more
likely to have a variety of meanings.

(15) AMBIGUITY

TYPICAL FORM:

None, although the assertion
that has more than one meaning will be an assumption.

STRUCTURE AND RATING
(Simple Versions)

Arguee's   Arguer's
Version   Version

DEFECT. Because some expression has more than one meaning,
the assumption can be regarded as representing two different
assertions. The argument will be defective when the assumption is
given the meaning the arguer intends, but the defect may be either
in the assumption or in an inference.

COMMENT. Typically the argument is most persuasive when one
verison of the assumption is acceptable to the arguee, but when
the ambiguous (equivocal) expression is given this sense the
inference is likely to appear invalid. When the expression is
given the meaning the arguer wants to give it the inference is
likely to be valid but the assumption will seem dubious to the
arguee. (See the diagrams above).

CRITICISM. Point out, by rewording the sentence so that the
differences are obvious, that an assumption can be interpreted as
having two different meanings because of some ambiguous
expression, then get the arguer (if available) to specify which of
the re-worded versions he/she intended. Then criticize the
resulting version of the argument. When the arguer is not
available to specify his/her preferred version, criticize both
versions.

EXAMPLE. "The United States is not and never has been a
democracy. So it is in no position to criticize forms of
government in other countries."

EXAMPLE CRITICISM. The word 'democracy' has several

meanings. One requires that a state is governed directly by all the citizens. That is, the executive and legislative branches consist of all citizens of mature age. This was the sort of system existing in the city-states of ancient Greece about 2,500 years ago. But the founders of the U.S.A. did not intend to establish a democracy in this sense. They established a system in which citizens could choose representatives to speak for their interests and who would be responsible to them for their conduct. In such a system, the representatives are chosen democratically so the U.S. has representative democracy rather than the full participatory kind.

If the arguer's assumption can be formulated as "The U.S. is not and never has been a full participatory democracy" then it will be true, but then the inference is not valid because the premise does not require the U.S. to refrain from criticizing other countries so long as it does not criticize them for not having full participatory democracies.

On the other hand, if the arguer's assumption can be formulated as "The U.S. is not and never has been a representative democracy", then we can regard it as false, so that the conclusion cannot be proved even though the inference has some validity in this case.

Here are diagrams and ratings for the two arguments:
A1= The U.S. is not and has never been a representative democracy.
A2= The U.S. is not and has never has been a full participatory democracy.
B= The U.S. is in no position to criticize forms of government in other countries.

ARGUEE VERSION

ARGUER VERSION

(16) EQUIVOCATION

TYPICAL FORM:

None. The argument relies on the existence of two occurrences of an expression with more than one meaning.

349

DEFECT. May be either in assumptions or in inferences.

COMMENT. Arguments that commit this fallacy rely for their persuasiveness on the arguee failing to notice that some expression occurring more than once is being used by the arguer in different ways. The ambiguous expression may occur in two different premises or in the conclusion and a premise. The use of the ambiguity results in the two assertions both being acceptable to the arguee.

CRITICISM. Re-formulate the assertions containing the ambiguous expression so that the ambiguity disappears. Then criticize the argument in the normal way.

EXAMPLE. Here the assertions containing the ambiguous expression 'laws' are both premises:

A[A code of laws indicates the existence of a law-giver].

B[There are laws governing the material world].

Therefore, C[there is a law-giver for the material world--God].

CRITICISM. In A, 'laws' refers to the kind of thing that gets enacted by legislatures. These are a species of the rule requiring us to do something or prohibiting us from doing something. Here 'laws' can be replaced by 'statutes.'

In B, a law is a formulation of an observed regularity in the behavior of material bodies. An example is Newton's law of gravitational attraction, which describes the force of attraction between two bodies of given mass. The equation does not represent a statute or say that material bodies (stones, pencils, etc.) are prohibited from behaving differently. The equation merely asserts that there is a universal regularity in this respect. However, B cannot simply be replaced by 'Material bodies exhibit regularities in their behavior patterns'. The arguer means more than this, implying that material bodies do not deviate from the patterns we find them following. So B can be better replaced by 'Material bodies follow regular patterns of behavior from which they do not deviate'. The argument can now be stated this way:

A[A code of statutes indicates the existence of a law-giver].

B[Material bodies follow regular patterns of behaviour from which they do not deviate].

Therefore, C[there is a law-giver for the material

350

world--God].

In this revised version the premises are again acceptable, but the inference canbe seen to be seriously defective. In particular, premise A no longer seems relevant to the conclusion.

Another approach to dealing with this argument is to point out that the inference is valid only if the term 'laws' is replaced by 'statutes' in premise B. This is the meaning the term must have but of course the proposition 'There are statutes governing the material world' seems absurd. A rock cannot, in falling to the ground when we let go of it, be said to be conforming to a statute. Only conscious entities can be said to obey or disobey legislation. In this version of the argument the inference is valid but premise B is false, so the conclusion is again not proved.

(9.6) "No Progress" Fallacies. These are so-called because they fail to meet a requirement for good argument, that is, that it proceed from better-known assertions to less well-known ones.

(17) QUESTION BEGGING.

TYPICAL FORM:

A, so B

DEFECT. The acceptance of A depends upon also accepting B, the conclusion, so A cannot prove B to someone who finds B dubious or false, nor can it prove it to someone who does accept A since B needs to be accepted in advance.

COMMENT. Persuasive only when the arguee fails to notice that A involves accepting B as well. In accepting A one does not make any progress toward proving B.

CRITICISM. Point out that the argument does not prove its conclusion even if A is true because A is not better known than B.

EXAMPLE. "The Bible says that God exists. The Bible is the word of God. So God exists."

EXAMPLE CRITICISM. The truth of the second premise requires accepting that God exists, otherwise the Bible couldn't be God's word. So the premises can't prove the conclusion because they depend on it being true.

(18) CIRCULARITY

TYPICAL FORM: STRUCTURE

A, so B, so A

DEFECT. B can't prove A when B
itself is intended to be proved by A.

COMMENT. It's persuasiveness depends on the arguee not
noticing that circularity is present. Usually this is not as easy
to spot as it might be, because the arguer first tries to prove A
using B, then when B is challenged he/she gives A in support of
B.

CRITICISM. Point out, after the arguer has responded to the
criticism of B by using A as a reason for it, that A is the
original conclusion so no progress has been made in proving A.

EXAMPLE.:

Virgil: "Our souls are immortal because they can't be
destroyed like the body."

Zeke: "Why do you think they can't be destroyed? Most
things can."

Virgil: "Because they are immortal."

EXAMPLE CRITICISM

Zeke: "You can't use this as support because it's what
you're trying to prove."

(9.7) PSYCHOLOGICAL FALLACIES: These arguments exploit in
various ways our desire to be rational.

(19) LOGICAL SLIPPERY SLOPE

TYPICAL FORM:

If A[you regard X as permissible] then B[you must regard Y as

352

permissible]. And if B[you regard Y as permissible] then C[you must regard Z as permissible].

But not-C [you cannot regard Z as permissible].

So not-A [you can't regard X as permissible].

SEMI-SYMBOLIC VERSION: STRUCTURE AND RATING

If A then B.

And if B then C.

But not C.

So not A.

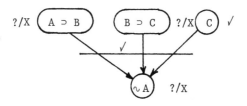

DEFECT.   Valid inference but one or both of the conditional assumptions is dubious or false.

COMMENT.   Argument exerts pressure by appealing to arguee's desire to be consistent, by claiming that whatever principles enable the arguee to accept X also justify accepting Y, so to fail to accept Y is to be inconsistent.   Or: the principles that warrant accepting Y requires accepting Z if one is to be consistent.

To be most effective there should be little difference between X and Y, and Y and Z, yet the differences are large enough that the arguee accepts X as permissible, but not Z. The arguer also needs to know that the arguee does not want to accpt Z.

CRITICISM.   Point out that accepting X does not require accepting Y because there is some important difference between them   such that one's reasons for accepting X do not cover Y.   Or, if the first premise is acceptable, do the same for the second one.

(29) FALLACY OF COMPROMISE

TYPICAL FORM: STRUCTURE AND RATING

A[Positions X and Y are far apart].

B[Position Z is a mean between the two].

So C[we should compromise and adopt position Z].

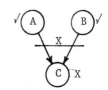

353

DEFECT. The inference is invalid. That Z is a mean between X and Y is no good reason to accept it. X may in fact be the best position, Y the worst, and Z the second-worst. The argument assumes that X and Y will be the same "distance" on either side of Z, but this is often not so.

COMMENT. The argument is often used by people involved in negotiations when there are conflicting interests, especially by those who think of themselves as peacemakers. The approach has something to recommend it when, irrespective of the merits of positions X and Y, a compromise acceptance of Z enables the parties in conflict to 'save face', and this may be important in future dealings. However, someone once said that a compromise is when both sides don't get what they want!

CRITICISM. Point out that one shouldn't adopt a position just because it is a compromise. Urge that Z be examined to see if it is the best solution based on its merits.

EXAMPLE. "Mom wants to go to the seashore on our vacation. Dad wants to go to the mountains. Going to a lake in the hills is an intermediate position, so we should compromise and do that."

EXAMPLE CRITICISM. Perhaps going to a lake in the hills won't satisfy either of them. Let's find out and if it's true then we can go to one place this year and the other place next year.

(21) FALSE PRECISION

TYPICAL FORM: None. The fallacy involves citing figures that give the impression of being accurate because they give lots of apparently significant digits.

DEFECT. The number of digits or decimal places gives the impression that A has been reliably arrived at so that it cannot be refuted, when in fact the numbers in A may be quite inaccurate.

CRITICISM. Point out that the figure quoted in A suggests an accuracy that cannot in fact be obtained.

EXAMPLE: "48,132,000 American women support the Equal Rights Amendment. You ought to too."

EXAMPLE CRITICISM. How could anyone know that 48,132,000 women support E.R.A., without asking all of them? Using sampling techniques there will be a measurement error that makes it pointless to mention the 132,000. Accuracy of 5% would be as good as we could expect, so the correct figure could deviate from the given figure by a couple of million!

(9.8) EVIDENCE FALLACIES. These arise from a mishandling of the concept of evidence.

(22) NEGATIVE PROOF FALLACY

TYPICAL FORM: STRUCTURE AND RATING

A[There is no conclusive
evidence against P].

So B[we are entitled to
believe that P].

DEFECT. Invalid inference. That P hasn't been disproved is no basis for concluding that we are entitled to believe P. We are only so entitled when the evidence FOR P outweighs the evidence AGAINST it.

COMMENT. The argument tends to assume that we would have conclusive evidence against P if it was false, but this is absurd. Perhaps P is false but we do not have access to the evidence that could show it. In such a situation we may have no evidence in favor of P and some against, with P actually being false. We would have no reason whatever for believing P to be true.

EXAMPLE: "There's no conclusive evidence that we don't survive bodily death, so we are entitled to believe that we do."

EXAMPLE CRITICISM. That it hasn't been disproved is no reason to believe that we do survive the death of our bodies. We may never have conclusive evidence against it but we may perish with our bodies anyway.

(23) "NO RIGHT ANSWER" FALLACY

TYPICAL FORM: STRUCTURE AND RATING

A[There is evidence for P].

B[There is evidence against P].

So C[we can believe whatever
we like about P].

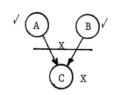

355

DEFECT: Persuasiveness relies on the erroneous belief that there can only be positive evidence for a true proposition and negative evidence for a false one. This leads people to think that when there is evidence for and against a proposition then it is somehow true for anyone who believes it and false for anyone who does not. However, on almost any complex issue there is evidence for and against.

CRITICISM. Point out that the conclusion does not follow, that we must, to be rational, be guided by the relative strength of evidence for and against.

EXAMPLE. "There is evidence for immortality and evidence against it. So we can believe whatever we like about it."

EXAMPLE CRITICISM. The conclusion doesn't follow. What follows is that we should either withhold judgment or take the negative view since there seems to be more empirical evidence against it than for it. Specifically, scientific evidence indicates we rely on our brains for perceiving and thinking. Thus, the destruction of the brain following death results in our ceasing to function as thinking beings, which amounts to our ceasing to be persons.

(9.9) STATISTICAL FALLACIES. It has been said by the nineteenth century Englishman Benjamin Disraeli that "There are lies, damn lies, and statistics." Statistical claims have as much chance of being true as any other kind of claim. Yet because of the technical complexity involved in processing and presenting statistical data, statistical techniques can easily be used to mislead. The only sure way to protect yourself against being misled is to be aware of how statistics work, but if this is not possible then you should at least ask whether the arguer has something to gain by misleading you. Using this criterion you can be confident that figures compiled by the government are reliable, whereas those supplied by an advertiser to persuade you to buy a product should be viewed with suspicion. Few ads these days contain outright statistical lies but many are misleading because of what they don't tell us. One further point: don't be so cynical as to regard all statistical data as dubious, like those people who, when confronted with statistical evidence, dismiss it by saying "statistics can prove anything". This just isn't true. Statistical data can often be the best evidence available, but you have to know how to interpret it.

(24) MISLEADING AVERAGES

TYPICAL FORM: STRUCTURE AND RATING

A[The mean value of X for the
population is Y].

So B[with regard to the property X,
all individuals in the population
are near value Y].

DEFECT. The inference is invalid. Mean values are calculated by adding up values of X for each individual and dividing by the number of individuals. Some individuals may have very low values and others very high ones. The most misleading use of mean figues occurs when one or a small percentage of the individuals in a population distort the result. In this situation most individuals may be quite far from the mean value. For example, suppose we are told that the mechanics at a garage "have an average of ten years experience," when in fact here are three mechanics, one of whom has 28 years experience, and each of the others has onlyone year. In the circumstances we would be misled if the claim led us to infer that whoever worked on our car had about ten years experience.

CRITICISM. Point out that the calculation of means leaves open the possibility that some individuals may be far from the mean value of X on either side and indeed that there may be no individual actually near the mean. Perhaps use the example described above to make the point.

EXAMPLE. "Our mehanics have an average of ten years experience, so your car is in good hands with us."

EXAMPLE CRITICISM. Point out that given the truth of the assumption it is still possible for the majority of them to be relatively inexperienced if a small proportion are very experienced.

(25) UNREAL DIFFERENCES

TYPICAL FORM: STRUCTURE AND RATING

A[X has increased/decreased by N%].

SO B[things are getting
better/worse].

357

DEFECT. There is a margin of error in all measurement, including statistical measurement. Perhaps phenomenon X can only be reliably measured within 5%, so a report of an "increase" from 37% to39%, say, may not really represent an increase since the original value might have been 39% because of error. Indeed, the original value (unknown to anyone) may have actually been 40%, so we may have a decrease rather than an increase.

COMMENT. Most persuasive with those people who do not realize that measurement error can be relatively large. These people are optimistic about the capabilities of statistics-gathering.

CRITICISM. Point out that measurement error can account for the change of N% so there may have been no change at all.

EXAMPLE. "The government's figures show the cost of living rose by one per cent last month, so we're all a little worse off than we were."

EXAMPLE CRITICISM. It is highly unlikely that the government can measure cost of living increases that accurately. They can probably detect yearly trends with accuracy but not monthly ones. What they can only mean is that BASED ON THE DATA GATHERED, the cost of living rose by one percent. Their data may be more in error than one per cent.

(26) MISLEADING PERCENTAGES

TYPICAL FORM: STRUCTURE AND RATING

A[X has increased/decreased by X%]

So B[there has been a major change for the better/worse in X].

DEFECT. The inference is invalid when the initial values of X are small, because a small change will be represented as a large percentage difference.

COMMENT. Persuasive to people who are not inclined to "look behind" numbers.

CRITICISM. Point out that if X's initial value is small even a small change will present a large percentage change.

EXAMPLE. "Murders increased last year by 100% in the next

358

town so violence is getting out of hand there."

EXAMPLE CRITICISM. The conclusion doesn't follow, maybe they only had two murders last year and one the year before. That's a 100% increase, but one murder isn't a big increase even in a small town.

(9.10) FALLACIES OF LOGICAL STRUCTURE. The arguments given in this section are fallacies because they are structurally invalid.

(27) FALLACY OF ASSUMED EXCLUSION

TYPICAL FORM: STRUCTURE AND RATING

A v B / B // ∿ A

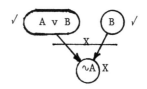

DEFECT.   Inference is invalid. When an assertion of the form 'A or B' is symbolized correctly by 'A v B', it is possible for A to be true when B is. Error arises from confusing the inclusive 'or' and exclusive 'or'.

COMMENT.   Most persuasive to those who are unaware that some 'or's' are not exclusive.

CRITICISM.   Point out that the 'A or B' assertion allows for both propositions being true at once, so that we cannot be sure that A is false when B is true.

EXAMPLE.   "Either Boston is more than 1,000 miles from New York or it is more than 100 miles from it. Boston is more than 100 miles from New York, so Boston is not more than 1,000 miles from New York."

EXAMPLE CRITICISM.   The conclusion doesn't follow because Boston could be both more than 100 miles from New York and more than 1,000 miles from it. It might, for example, have been 1,001 miles from New York. The premises do not exclude this possibility.

(28) FALSE REFUTATION OF CONDITIONAL

TYPICAL FORM: STRUCTURE AND RATING

A // ~(A ⊃ B)

DEFECT. Invalid inference. To disprove a conditional by the factual method we need A TRUE and B false.

COMMENT. Persuasive to those who do not understand that the truth of conditionals is independent of the truth value of their antecedents. That is, 'A ⊃ B' can be true when A is true or false.

CRITICISM. Point out that a conditional is proved false when its antecedent is true and its consequent false.

EXAMPLE. "The moon is not made of cheese, so it's false that if the moon is made of cheese then it contains protein."

EXAMPLE CRITICISM. The premise merely contradicts the antecdeent ("The moon is made of cheese") of the asserted conditional but since the antecedent is not being said to be true the premise is irrelevant. To disprove the conditional, it must be shown that the antecedent, if it was true, could not guarantee that the consequent is true. The fact that something is cheese just about guarantees that it contains protein, so the conclusion is true and no assertion can disprove it.

(29) AFFIRMING THE CONSEQUENT

TYPICAL FORM: STRUCTURE AND RATING

A ⊃ B / B // A

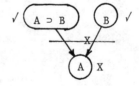

DEFECT. Invalid inference. 'A ⊃ B' asserts that the truth of A guarantees the truth of B, but not that the truth of B guarantees the truth of A.

COMMENT. Persuasive to those who think that 'If A then B',

360

'A only if B', etc., involve a reciprocal truth guarantee. That is, that the truth of A guarantees the truth of B AND VICE VERSA. Conditionals do not work this way. No one who asserts that "If A is true then B is true" is committed to asserting "If B is true then A is true."

CRITICISM. Point out that, given the truth of B, A would be proved only if the other premise was 'B ⊃ A', which it isn't.

EXAMPLE. "If the thief entered this way then there are tracks in the flower bed. There are tracks in the flower bed, so the thief entered this way."

EXAMPLE CRITICISM. There may be tracks in the flower bed but they could have been made by someone else, someone cleaning the windows perhaps. The conclusion would follow logically only if the first premise was "If there are tracks in the flower bed then the thief entered this way", but this is not what it says.

(30) FALSE CONVERSION

TYPICAL FORM: STRUCTURE AND RATING

A[All X's are Y's].

So B[all Y's are X's].

DEFECT. Invalid inference. Involves thinking that 'X' and 'Y' stand for the same class of things. Sometimes they do (e.g. 'bachelor' and 'unmarried man') but there is no guarantee.

COMMENT. Most persuasive when 'X' and 'Y' appear to stand for the same things.

CRITICISM. Point out that the truth of the premise does not guarantee the truth of the conclusion. Give an example such as "All dogs are animals, but it does not follow that all animals are dogs."

EXAMPLE. "All communists are socialists, so all socialists are communists."

EXAMPLE CRITICISM. The inference isn't valid because there could be socialists who are not communists and in fact in Western Europe there are many of them.

(31) UNDISTRIBUTED MIDDLE

TYPICAL FORM: STRUCTURE AND RATING

A[All X's are Y's]

B[All Z's are Y's]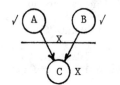

So C[all Z's are X's]

DEFECT. The inference is invalid.
The Venn-equivalent of the argument is:

∿A • ∿D / ∿D • ∿C //∿ C • ∿F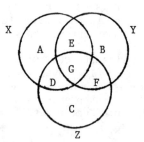

The premises do not guarantee that
cell F, which can contain Z's that
are not X's, is necessarily empty.

    COMMENT.   This   argument   is   persuasive   because   of   our
propensity   to   commit   the   False   Conversion   fallacy   (#30).   If
assertion A was 'All Y's are X's' the argument would be valid.

    CRITICISM.   Point   out   that   the   conclusion isn't guaranteed
true   because   the   premises   do   not   exclude   the   possibility that
there   are   Z's   that   are   Y's   but   not   X's.   Use   a   counter-example
argument   such   as this   one: "All dogs are animals.   All cats are
animals.   So' all cats are dogs."   This example is clearly invalid
because the premises are true and the conclusion is false.

    EXAMPLE.   "All communists are socialists.   All Swedish people
are socialists.   So all Swedish people are communists."

    EXAMPLE CRITICISM.   The   argument   does   not   have   a   valid
inference   because   it   does   not exclude the possibility of there
being   Swedes   who   are   socialists   but not communists. The first
premise   does   not exclude this possibility because it does not say
that all socialists are communists.

(32) ILLICIT MAJOR

TYPICAL FORM: STRUCTURE AND RATING

A[All X's are Y's]

B[No Z's are X's]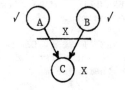

So C[no Z's are Y's]

362

DEFECT. The inference is
invalid. The Venn-equivalent
of the argument is:

'∿A • ∿ D / ∿ D• ∿ G // ∿ F • ∿ G.'

The premises do not guarantee that
cell F is empty.

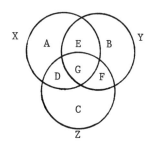

COMMENT. The fallacy is so named because what is called the
major term in syllogistic theory is Y, and the conclusion asserts
something about all Y's even though neither of the premises does.
The fallacy is persuasive because of our inclination to confuse
'All X's are Y's' and 'All Y's are X's' (False Conversion,
fallacy #30). If the first premise was the latter the inference
would be valid.

CRITICISM. Point out that the premises don't exclude the
possibility of there being Z's that are Y's but not X's. Give a
counter-example such as "All dogs are animals. No cats are dogs.
So no cats are animals."

EXAMPLE. "All communists are socialists. No Swedes are
communists. So no Swedes are socialists."

EXAMPLE CRITICISM. The inference is invalid. The premises
do not guarantee that there are no Swedes who are socialists, only
that there are no Swedes who are socialists AND communists.

(33) ILLICIT MINOR

TYPICAL FORM: STRUCTURE AND RATING

A[All X's are Y's].

B[All X's are Z's].

So C[all Z's are Y's].

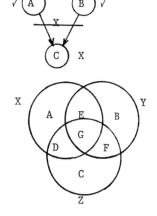

DEFECT. The inference is
invalid. The Venn-equivalent
of the argument is:

'∿ A • ∿ D / ∿ A • ∿ E // ∿ C • ∿ D'

The premises do not guarantee
that cell C is empty.

363

COMMENT. The fallacy is so named because of the minor term 'Z'. In the conclusion an assertion is made about all Z's but no premise refers to all Z's. The fallacy is persuasive because we are inclined to commit the False Conversion fallacy (#30), taking B to be 'All Z's are X's.'

CRITICISM. Point out that the premises do not guarantee that there are no things that are Z and not X's or Y's. Give a counter-example argument to show invalidity, such as: "All swans are white. All swans are birds. So all birds are white."

EXAMPLE. "All sexist people are males. All sexist people are prejudiced. So all prejudiced people are males."

EXAMPLE CRITICISM. Inference is invalid because premises allow for there being prejudiced people who are neither sexist nor male. For example, female racists.

ANSWERS TO SELECTED EXERCISES

EXERCISE 2 - 1

1. Choice (c) is best since it compares reasonably large samples of performance in a fairly representative dexterity test. Choice (a) is not too good because it relies on a very small sample (two). Choice (b) relies on a small sample and deals with only one facet of hand dexterity.

3. Choice (a) is best, since we can reasonably construe the original assertion to be about the typical student. Choice (b) relies on a sample, whereas (a) does not. Choice (c) is not a good criticism since it is about only good students whereas the original is about students in general or typical students.

EXERCISE 2 - 2

1. The definition covers all things that count as universities but does not cover only universties since junior colleges (for example) are also covered.

4. The definition does not cover all possible instances of plagiarization since we count the presentation of paraphrases of extended passages as plagiarization also.

8. The definition does not cover all possible cases because the law does not require the actual use of force as essential. The THREAT of force to obtain consent is regarded as sufficient.

EXERCISE 2 - 3

1. (a) does not disprove it since it does not contradict the secomd alternative.

1. (b) disproves the alternation because neither alternative is true if (b) is true.

1. (c) does not disprove the alternation because it only contradicts the second alternative.

4. (a) disproves the alternation because it contradicts both alternatives provided that preparedness refers to study skills.

365

4. (b) does not disprove the alternation since it contradicts only the second alternative.

4. (c) does not disprove the alternation because it is irrelevant to the truth of both alternatives.

EXERCISE 2 - 4

1. (a) does not disprove the conditional since it simply contradicts the antecedent--the Royals are also in the American League.

1. (b) disproves the conditional because it asserts the antecedent and denies the consequent of the conditional.

1. (c) denies that the consequent is true but does not affirm the antecedent so that it does not clearly disprove the conditional.

3. (a) does not disprove the conditional because it simply contradicts the antecedent.

3. (b) does not clearly disprove the conditional even though it contradicts the consequent, since it does not comment on the antecedent.

3. (c) disproves the conditional because it affirms the antecedent but contradicts the consequent.

EXERCISE 4 - 1

2. Assuming the questionable assumption is an essential one, C rating is "X".

4. C is rated "X", because of inference rating. D is rated "X", because of rating of intermediate conclusion C.

EXERCISE 4 - 2

2.

4.

EXERCISE 5 - 1
1. Last month was a dry month.
   + My well went dry.
   + There was no rain after the middle of the month.
   - There was a big rain storm on the fifth of the month.
   0 There was as much rain as in the month before that.
   + Normally it is dry this time of year.
   0 We're getting plenty of rain this month.

3. England was a happier place in Victorian times.
   + No major war was fought during this period.
   - The mortality rate for children was many times higher than it is now.
   + In those days people knew their place.
   + The British Empire was at its peak.
   0 Queen Victoria had no sense of humor.

EXERCISE 5 - 2

2.

A = The postal clerks strike frequently.

B = They must be underpaid.

Inference is poor. Plausible alternatives to B are: (a) poor working conditions, (b) inadequate fringe benefits, (c) lay-off policies.

4.

A = In the last ten years food prices have risen more quickly than other prices.

B = Supermarket chains have increased their profits more than most other businesses.

Inference is poor. A plausible alternative to B is increases in wages and prices given the producers, transport, and distribution people.

EXERCISE 5 -3

1.

A = The trends indicate that more beer and
liquor will be sold this Christmas than was
purchased last Christmas.

B = Holiday drunkenness will increase again
this year.

Inference is only somewhat valid. One plausible U-factor is that the
are more people drinking. The "baby-boomers" are coming of drinking
age, and more women are consuming alcohol. Thus, the per capita leve
of consumption might increase.

3. Step One:

A = The unemployment rate has increased from
September to November.

B = We must expect an economic depression soon.

Step Two: The inference is invalid. An increase in unemployment
in the autumn is normal because outdoor work ends for the winter.

EXERCISE 5 - 4

1. Step One: Construct an accurate diagrammatic version of the
argument.

A = Sometimes I get really worried before
an exam.

B = When I get really worried I always do
poorly.

C = Worry is the cause of my poor
performance.

Step Two: Evaluate the inference. The student has observed
a positive correlation between worry and poor performance. This is
a classic case of two phenomena having a common cause. Lack of
preparation is probably the cause of both worry and poor
performance, although the worry itself may aggravate the
situation. We rate the inference "?".

Step Three: Evaluate the assumptions. We may suppose the
student is correct about A. B, on the other hand, may be dubious
because the student's memory may be selective. He/she may not
ALWAYS do poorly when really worried. However, since we have no

368

evidence available to support this doubt we should consider B true.

STEP FOUR: determine the extent to which intermediate conclusions are proved. Not appropriate here.

Step Five: Determine the extent to which the final conclusion is proved. Given the above ratings we rate the argument "?".

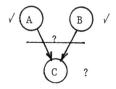

Step Six: formulate a response to the argument. We can respond thusly: "You haven't proved conclusively that worry is the cause of poor performance. It is quite possible that both the worry and the poor performance are the result of lack of preparation."

EXERCISE 5 -5
Step One:

A = The weather people started reporting temperatures in Celcius two years ago.

B = Since then the weather has been very unsettled.

C = The change to Celcius caused the weather to become unsettled.

Step Two: Evaluate the inference. It should be clear that almost any alternative is a more plausible cause of weather changes than a change in measuring systems. Weather instability can have a variety of causes, including volcanic activity (ash blocks sunlight), shifts in jet stream currents, etc. The inference can be rated "X".

Step Three: Evaluate the assumptions. A is true. We may "for the sake of argument" accept B, although it may be noted that people's perceptions of how the weather has been are notoriously inaccurate.

Step Four: Determine the extent to which intermediate conclusions are proved. Not appropriate here.

Step Five: Determine the extent to which the final

conclusion is proved. Given the ratings, the argument can be rated "X".

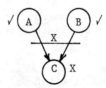

Step Six: Formulate a response to the argument. We can respond: "Your evidence cannot prove your conclusion. Measuring system changes have no causal connection with the weather. You might as well suggest that distances are affected by changing from miles to kilometers."

EXERCISE 5 - 6
1. Step One:

A = When I quit smoking my weight goes up.

B = When I take up smoking my weight drops.

C = Smoking consumes calories.

Step Two: evaluate the inference. Is there an alternative explanation for the changes reported in the assumptions? Indeed there is: smoking reduces appetite. This seems more plausible than C, since it is apparent that smoking does not take a great deal of energy. The inference should be rated "X".

Step Three: Evaluate the assumptions. We may suppose that this individual is telling the truth and rate both assumptions true.

Step Four: Not applicable.

Step Five: Given the ratings the argument rating is "X".

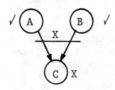

Step Six: formulate a response to the argument. We can respond: "These weight fluctuations do not prove smoking consumes calories. It is obvious that smoking does not take the physical

370

effort that would account for calories being consumed. It is much more likely that smoking kills the appetite, so that smokers eat less."

EXERCISE 5 - 7

1. Step One: Construct an accurate diagrammatic version of the argument.

A = They got the support of their faithful 40%.

B = The support from the uncommitted segment put them ahead of us.

Step Two: evaluate the inference. Is there some other way of accounting for the 12% party X got, assuming that A is true? They may well have gotten eight-tenths of the undecided vote but this is a very large proportion given that the parties were roughly equally favored in the poll and in the election. It is more likely that the balance was tipped in favor of X by voters "defecting" from party Y, even though party Y officials may not care to admit it. We rate the inference "?".

Step Three: Evaluate the assumption. Whether X got the support of all those who said they favored it AND took the trouble to vote, it is difficult to say. But since they started as slight underdogs and won, it is probable that they did. We rate A true.

Step Four: Determine the extent to which intermediate conclusions are proved. Not applicable here.

Step Five: Determine the extent to which the final conclusion is proved. Given the ratings, the argument should be rated "?".

Step Six: formulate a response to the argument. We can respond: "Perhaps X did get the support of "their faithful 40%", but that does not conclusively prove they got the extra support from the uncommitted. Given the results they would need to get eight-tenths of the uncommitted vote but this is unlikely because people seem to favor each party about equally. It is very likely

371

that some of the extra support came from defections from party Y."

EXERCISE 5 - 8

1. Step One:

A = He changed my tire even though he was a stranger.

B = He is one of those people who help people in need.

Step Two: Evaluate the inference. This is an inference to the existence of a policy from a single event, which makes it somewhat shaky. It may be that the man's policy is to be chivalrous, helping "damsels in distress" but not men or older women. Perhaps he was just in a generous mood and was not being inconvenienced by helping, whereas on most occasions he would not have stopped. These possibilities warant rating the inference "?".

Step Three: Evaluate the assumption. We may take it that A is true.

Step Four: Determine the extent to which intermediate conclusions are proved. Not applicable.

Step Five: Determine the extent to which the final conclusion has been proved. Given the ratings, the argument rating shall be "?".

Step Six: Formulate a response. We can reply: "That he changed your tire does not definitely show he is a "good Samaritan"." He may just be chivalrous, helping young women in distress and ignoring the problems of others. Or he may have acted out of character because he was in an especially good mood and did not have to be anywhere very promptly.

EXERCISE 5 - 9

1. Step One:

A = The Prof. likes me.

B = He will give me a few breaks on the
    test.

Step Two: A U-factor that is at least as plausible as B is that the prof. makes a rule of being objective in grading, not letting personal preferences interfere. Most professors are able and willing to do this. Rate the inference "X".

Step Three: We are not in a position to provide any counter-evidence so we shall accept Alvin's word. Rate A true.

Step Four: Not applicable.

Step Five: Rate the argument "X" because of the inference.

Step Six: "That the prof. likes you doesn't prove to any great extent that she/he will give you any breaks on the test. She/he may make every effort to be objective by setting aside personal considerations when grading."

EXERCISE 5 - 10

1. Step One:

A = She doesn't like football players.

B = She won't date me.

Step Two: If A was true it would be the best explanation for Ethel's turning this fellow down. Rate the inference valid.

Step Three: Ethel's experience is a good, but not conclusive,

373

reason for saying A is true. She may be mature enough to realize that it is unfair to judge a whole group by one member of it. Rate A "?".

Step Four: Not applicable.

Step Five: Given the ratings, the argument is rated "?".

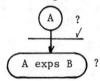

Step Six: "The explanation has not been quite proved as correct. Her experience suggests that she doesn't like football players but she may be mature enough to realize that it is unfair to judge a whole group by one member of it."

EXERCISE 5 - 11

1. Step One:

A = Capital punishment is morally prohibited in our society.

B = The Governor granted a stay of execution for Renfield, the hired killer.

C = The Governor did the right thing.

Step Two: We do not hear about any extenuating circumstances. There is some basis for saying the rule reflected by A is not defensible in terms of social justice. Some people take the view that hired killers should be executed because they deserve it. Others think this is necessary as a deterrence measure. Rate the inference "?".

Step Three: It is unclear that there is a rule prohibiting capital punishment at this time. Some people would condemn executions, others would not. Rate A "?". Rate B true.

Step Four: Not applicable.

Step Five: Rate the argument "X". (See next page.)

Step Six: "It is not clear that capital punishment is prohibited in our society, but even if it was, it would not quite prove the Governor did the right thing. The prohibition is questionable because it may prevent justice from being done."

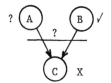

EXERCISE 5 - 12

1. Step One:

A = The psychologist has an obligation to use reasonable care to protect intended victims from harm at the hands of his client.

B = He failed to warn T. T. of the danger she was in.

C = He is morally responsible for her death.

Step Two: Evaluate the inference. The psychologist in the case had no suitable excuse that would diminish his responsibility. He would claim, however, tha he had a justification in that his communications with his client were confidential and that this confidentiality was to be respected. This was the central issue in the lawsuit the victim's parents brought against U. CA1. The court's deliberations were in a legal framework, of course, rather than a broader moral one. The court did, however, conclude that the obligation "to protect the welfare of the individual or the community" must take priority over the obligation to not disclose what was told him/her in confidence by the client. This position represents a value choice but the court also considered that by following the policy the usefulness of psychotherapy would not be seriously undermined. (The defendants argued that if it was general knowledge that the psychotherapist might disclose information given in confidence then potential patients either would not reveal such information or would not come forward for treatment in the first place.)

On the grounds that those in danger have as much right to knowledge as the psychotherapist we can rate the inference valid. The obligation to confidentiality does not override the obligation to protect potential victims.

Step Three: Evaluate the assumptions. A is a general principle that is acceptable. B is also true.

Step Four: Not applicable.

Step Five: Determine the extent to which the final

conclusion is proved. With the assumptions rated true and the inferemce rated valid the argument is rated "√".

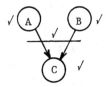

Step Six: Formulate a response to the argument. We can respond: "Although a psychotherapist has a general obligation to treat his client's disclosures as confidential, this must give way to the obligation to protect those who might be in danger. The therapist in this case is morally responsible for the victim's death."

EXERCISE 5 - 13

Step One:

A = Parents have an obligation to ensure that their children are safe coming and going to school.

B = Mr. and Mrs. X have an obligation to escort their children to and from school.

Step Two: Evaluate inferences. Two lines of criticism are open. Do these people have overriding obligations that would keep them from escorting their children? Often these days both parents work and working hours normally conflict with the periods when children are going to and coming home from school. The parents' obligation to provide for the material things of life take priority over duty to escort, although not over the safety of the children.

A second criticism is that there probably is an alternative means of fulfilling the obligation. Mr. and Mrs. S can have their children accompany older children. They can train them in pedestrian safety practices. They could even have them travel by taxi if they think it necessary.

Given these criticisms, I rate the inference "X".

Step Three: Evaluate assumptions. A should be rated true.

Step Four: Not applicable.

Step Five: Determine the extent to which the final

conclusion is proved. With the inference rated "X" and A rated true the overall rating is "X"

Step Six: Formulate a response to the argument. We can respond: "Parents do have an obligation to ensure that their children are safe coming and going to school, but it doesn't follow that they should escort them. They can have them accompany older children or teach them how to get there and back safely by themselves. They may be prevented by their jobs from providing a personal escort."

EXERCISE 5 - 14

1.   Step One:

A = You want the loan officer's job.

B = You ought to accept the Manager's invitations.

Step Two: Evaluate the inference. Of the five ways in which inferences of this kind can be criticized, this particular inference can be criticized as follows: (1) it is immoral to rely on non-job-related criteria to get promoted; (2) even if spending weekends with the Manager to get promoted was morally permissible, this approach may be less than reliable; (3) perhaps Emmaline wants to be able to believe she has been a success because of her professional efforts and getting the job by sleazy tactics would deprive her of this satisfaction; (4) she may be able to get the job by legitimate means such as upgrading her qualifications.

Step Three: Evaluate the assumption. The background information indicates that A is true.

Step Four: Not applicable.

Step Five: Given the ratings, we rate the argument "X". (See next page.)

Step Six: Formulate a response to the argument. A suitable

377

response is: "Wanting the loan officer's job cannot justify accepting the manager's invitations. This is an immoral practice, it may not be dependable, and it may rob her of the satisfaction of obtaining the promotion solely on professional efforts. Furthermore, she may be able to get the job by more legitimate means."

EXERCISE 5 - 15
1. Step One:

A = Acquiring computer skills is a good way to prepare for college.

B = Parents ought to buy their children a home computer.

Step Two: Merely buying children a home computer may not be much of a contribution toward preparing them for college because they may not learn educationally valuable skills. They might spend their time playing games. Rate the inference "?".

Step Three: It is generally conceded that computer skills are getting to be more important all the time. Rate A true.

Step Four: Not applicable.

Step Five: The argument is rated "?" because of the inference.

Step Six: "It does seem to be important to acquire computer skills for college, but this doesn't quite prove that parents should buy children a computer. They might not acquire any skills of educational value, they might play games instead."

EXERCISE 5 - 16
1.   Step One:

A = Nuclear power plants consume no natural
    resources, are fuel efficient, and give
    off no atmospheric pollutants.

B = As energy sources, nuclear power plants
    are superior to other energy sources.

Step Two: A does not guarantee B because nuclear power
plants have one deficiency other types do not--they may accidently
explode. However, they do have definite advantages. Rate the
inference "?".

Step Three: A is true if we are thinking of day-to-day
operation.

Step Four: Not applicable.

Step Five: Rate the argument "?" because of the inference.

Step Six: "Nuclear power plants do have these advantages,
but that doesn't make them clearly superior to other energy
sources because there is a slight chance they will malfunction and
explode."

EXERCISE 5 - 17
1.   Step One:

A = X has a good average with no low or high
    marks.

B = Y's average is similar but he has some
    very high marks and some failures.

C = X is a better student than Y.

Step Two: The inference is not totally satisfactory, since
being a "better student" is not entirely a matter of being a good
steady performer. Y's high grades may indicate more ability and
ability is relevant to whether one person is a better student than
another. Rate the inference "?".

Step Three: We shall have to take the assumptions as given since we have no way of checking them. Rate them true.

Step Four: Not applicable.

Step Five: Rate the argument "?" because of the inference.

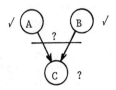

Step Six: "The data does not clearly prove X is better than Y. Y's high grades probably indicate superior ability and this is relevant here."

EXERCISE 5 - 18
1. Step One:

A = People want the unemployment insurance program to continue.

B = It is good that money was diverted from the defence budget to finance it.

Step Two: Clearly, diverting funds will satisfy the desire to maintain the program, provided that they are sufficient. On the other hand, we also desire military protection and this may be undermined by diverting funds to other things. Rate the inference "?" on the assumption that the money diverted was a substantial amount.

Step Three: A is no doubt true for people in general.

Step Four: Not applicable.

Step Five: Rate the argument "?" because of the inference.

Step Six: "It hasn't been clearly proved that it was good to divert money from defence, after all, we also want military protection and this is a matter of higher priority than

380

unemployment protection."

EXERCISE 5 - 19
1. Step One:

A = Novels are to provide entertainment.

B = A good novel must be humorous.

Step Two: Novels can be entertaining without being humorous, as detective stories, romances, and adventure novels show. Rate the inference "X" since these other kinds of novels can be good novels.

Step Three: A is somewhat dubious, as novels can be written for other purposes. For example, to make a philosophical point or to provide social consciousness-raising. Rate A "?".

Step Four: Not applicable.

Step Five: Rate the argument "X" because of the inference.

$$\begin{array}{c} \textbf{(A)} \; ? \\ \underline{\qquad} \; X \\ \downarrow \\ \textbf{(B)} \; X \end{array}$$

Step Six: "It is not necessary that a novel be intended to entertain, but even if it was it doesn't follow that it must be humorous, since entertainment can be provided without humor. Detective stories, romances, and adventure novels are examples."

EXERCISE 5-20
2. Step One:

A = Recent tests showed football quarterbacks to have above-average intelligence.

B = Football players aren't dumb like some people thought.

Step Two: The inference is not very valid because the sample (quarterbacks) is not representative. Quarterbacks are called upon to choose plays and plot strategy on the field, so that anyone who is able to play at that position is probably pretty intelligent. Other positions are significantly less demanding mentally.

4. Step One:

A = Nearly everyone at the rally is behind me.

B = It looks like I'll be elected.

Step Two: The inference is poor because the sample (those attending the rally for the candidate) is not representative of the entire voting populace. It is well known that the audience at political rallies consists primarily of people committed already to the politican's party. Those who oppose do not attend, they go to rallies for their own candidate.

EXERCISE 5 - 21
2. Step One:

A = All weapons are prohibited in the park.

B = You must not take your bow and arrow into the park.

Step Two: The quality of the inference depends upon whether "your bow and arrow" can be classified as a weapon or not. If it is a child's toy then the inference is poor.

EXERCISE 6 - 1

1. Either A or not B.   A v ∿ B.

3. It isn't true that either A or not B. ∿ (A v ∿ B).

6. A and either B or both C and D.   A · (B v (C · D)).

10. It's false that if A then not B and C. ∿ (A ⊃ (∿B · C)).

EXERCISE 6 - 2
1.   A ⊃ ∿ B / B ⊃ ∿ A // ∿ A
     T T T F   F T F T   F T
     5 6 7 8   9 10 4 3   1 2

Invalid with A true and B false.

4. A ⊃ B / A ⊃ C // B v C
    F T F   F T F   F F F
    7 6 5   8 9 4   2 1 3

    Invalid with A false, B false, and C false.

7. (A • ∿ B) ⊃ ∿ C / C // ∿ A v (A • B)
    T T   T F   F F T   T   F T F   T F F
    1213 1110 14 3 2   1   5 6 4   7 8 9

    Valid. A must be true, B false, and C true to get the second
    premise true and the conclusion false. But with these values
    the first premise cannot be true.

10. A ⊃ (B • C) / (B v C) ⊃ ∿ A // ∿ A
    T T   T T T   T T T F F T   F T
    5 6   8 7 9   101211 13 4 3   1 2

    Valid. A, B, and C must all be true to get the first premise
    true and the conclusion false. But with these values the
    second premise cannot be true.

13. A ⊃ B / C ⊃ ∿ D / D ⊃ A // ∿ B ⊃ C
    F T F   F T T F   F T F   T F F F
    8 7 5   6141312   1110 9   2 3 1 4

    Invalid with A, B, C, and D all false.

16. ((A v B) • C) ⊃ D / (C ⊃ D) ⊃ (E ⊃ F) / E // A ⊃ F
     T T   T T F F   T F F T T F F   T   T F F
     6 7   1514 1716   121113 10 2 9 8   1   4 3 5

Valid. The values needed to get the second and third premises
true and the conclusion false are such that the first premise
cannot be true. We need not obtain a value for B to discover
this because it occurs only once as part of A v B in premise one,
and, with A true, A v B is true regardless of what value B has.

EXERCISE 6 - 3
Each of the following can be done in several ways, although the
verdicts on validity cannot be different from those shown below.

1. A ⊃ B / C ⊃ D / A v C // (A • B) v (C • D)
    T T T   F T   T T F   T T T T F F
    8 910   1 2   7 6 3   111312 14 4 5

Having chosen C to be false the inference APPEARS to be valid
because the values required to get the premises all true prevent

383

the conclusion from being false. But it is possible that with C
true this won't happen so we must test the argument after making
C true.

```
A ⊃ B / C ⊃ D / A v C // (A • B) v (C • D)
  T T T     T T         T  T T T
  1 5 6     4 2         9  3 8 7
```

With C true we can have the second and third premises true but the
conclusion cannot be false. Thus, the inference actually is valid
since it cannot be shown as invalid with C either true or false.

```
4.  (A v B) v (C ⊃ D) // (A v C) ⊃ (B v D)
     T T      T          T T    F  F F F
     7 8      9          4 5    6  2 1 3
```

Inference invalid. After getting values for B and D it was possible to get the conclusion false by assigning A to be true.
With A true the premise is true because A makes A v B true and
with A v B true the whole premise is true.

EXERCISE 6 - 4

```
1.  A ⊃ B / B ⊃ (A ⊃ (C  v  D)) / C ⊃ D / ∿ (C • D) // ∿ A
    T T T   T T  T T F  T  T  T    F T     T  F F      F T
    3 5 6   7 8  4 9 11 10 12     13 14    17 15 16    1 2
```

Invalid inference, shown by making C false after deriving values
for A and B. By making this choice of value for C we get D true
at step 12 and the third premise true also. If we had chosen D to
be true the third premise would also have been true and by making
the fourth premise true, C would have been false.

```
3.  A v ∿ B / ∿ (∿ C • D) / ∿ (∿ A • ∿ D) // ∿ B ⊃ C
    T T  F    T   T F F F    T  F T F T F      T F F F
    7 6  5    10  9 8 11 12  15 17 18 16 14 13  2 3 1 4
```

Invalid inference. No value choices needed.

EXERCISE 6 - 5
1. Step One: The semi-symbolic version of the argument is:
"A. If A then B. Therefore B." The symbolic version is:
"A / A ⊃ B // B". The diagrammatic version is:

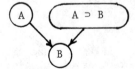

A = There is design in the world.

B = There is a cosmic designer.

Step Two: The inference is valid.

A / A ⊃ B // B
T   T F F   F
3   4 5 2   1

Step Three: Assumption A ⊃ B must be rated true since design requires a designer.

Assumption A is rated "?" because although there is a lot of regularity in the behavior of things (including animals), there is still the distinct possibility that this came about by chance. Furthermore, there is a lot of irregularity in the universe too. Lots of unexpected things happen. Stars explode, earthquakes occur, species die out through the natural selection process, and so on.

Step Four: Not applicable here.

Step Five: Given the ratings the argument should be rated "?" because of A.

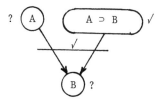

Step Six: A suitable response is this: "The conclusion is not adequately proved because it is not clear that there is design in the world. There is a fair amount of regularity in nature but this could be accidental. Furthermore, there is also a fair amount of chaos, including notable events such as stars blowing up, earthquakes occurring, and the dying out of species such as the various dinosaurs. It is clear that the universe is not in a state of perfect equilibrium."

EXERCISE 6 - 6

1. ∿ B • ∿ F
2. C v F

EXERCISE 6 - 7

1. A v D / ∿ D • ∿ G // C v D
   T T F   T F T T F   F F F
   8 7 4   6 5 91011   2 1 3

385

Invalid inference. The premises do not guarantee that C and D
are not both empty. They can be, so it is not guaranteed that
there is a Z that is not a Y, given the truth of the premises.

6.　　∿ E . ∿ G / ∿ C . ∿ D // C v F
　　　T F T T F 　 T F T T F 　 F F F
　　　1011 91213 　 5 4 6 7 8 　 2 1 3

Invalid inference. Given the premises true, cells C and F can be
empty, which is to say that there may be no Z's that are not X's.
All the Z's may be X's.

7.　　A v D / ∿ A . ∿ E // C v D
　　　T T F 　 F T F 　 F F F
　　　6 5 4 　 8 7 9 　 2 1 3

Valid inference. To have the conclusion false there must be
nothing in cell D. With nothing in cell D there must be something
in cell A. That is, there must be X's that are not Z's. This
prevents the second premise from being true, since it asserts
that every X is Z.

EXERCISE 6 - 8

1.　Step One:　The semi-symbolic version of the argument is:
"No X's are Y's.　No Z's are Y's.　Therefore, some X's are Z's."
The diagrammatic version is:

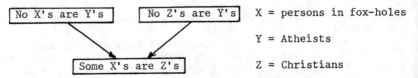

X = persons in fox-holes

Y = Atheists

Z = Christians

　　Step Two. Testing the Venn-equivalent version we find the
inference is invalid.

　　∿ E . ∿ G / ∿ F . ∿ G // D v G
　　T F T T F 　 T F T T F 　 F F F
　　12131110 9 　 7 8 6 5 4 　 2 1 3

　　Step Three:　Is it true that no persons in fox-holes are
atheists? This claim was formulated to make the point that fear
brings out the religiousness in us. Considering the claim itself,
however, we can rate it "X" because there has probably been at
least one convinced atheist who has not changed his view as a
result of war experiences. Indeed, some men have probably become
atheists as a result of their war experience. The second
assumption is obviously true.

Step Four: Not applicable here.

Step Five: Given an invalid inference and a false assumption, the argument should be rated "X".

Step Six: We can respond to the argument this way: "The conclusion does not follow from the assumptions. It is like arguing that because no cats are dogs and no pigs are dogs, some cats are pigs. Furthermore, it is probably incorrect to say that there are no atheists in fox-holes. Some people have probably kept their convictions and may even have found them strengthened by war experience."

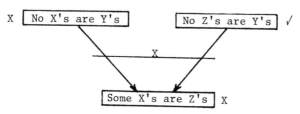

2. Step One: The semi-symbolic version of the argument is: "Some X's are Y's, but no Z's are Y's. Therefore, some X's are not Z's." The diagrammatic version is:

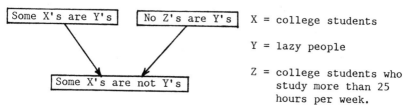

X = college students

Y = lazy people

Z = college students who study more than 25 hours per week.

Step Two: Testing the Venn-equivalent version we find the inference to be valid.

```
E v G / ∿ F • ∿ G // A v E
F T T     F F T     F F F
4 5 6     9 8 6     2 1 3
```

Step Three: Regrettably, it seems to be true that some college students are lazy. It is true also that no college student who studies more than 25 hours per week is lazy. We are assuming that this time does not include time spent in classes.

Step Four: Not applicable here.

Step Five. Given a valid inference and true assumptions we rate the argument as having proved its conclusion.

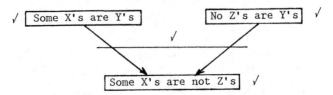

Step Six. A suitable response would be: "The conclusion has been proved."

EXERCISE 7 - 1

1. Plausible U-factor: fears about future quality of life leads to the suspension of some people's plans to have children.

Assumption: C = "English-speaking Quebeckers do not anticipate any deterioration of their quality of life with a Parti Quebecois government."

EXERCISE 7-2

1. Plausible U-factors: (1) the Stones continue to enjoy performing, (2) they want the money they can make by continuing.

Assumptions needed:
C = "They don't enjoy performing anymore."
D = "They don't care about the money they could earn."

EXERCISE 7 - 3

1. Plausible U-factor: the cramming has beneficial psychological consequences, i.e. it generates a feeling of preparedness that gives confidence.

Assumption needed: C = "There are no beneficial psychological consequences from the cramming."

EXERCISE 7 - 4

1. Plausible U-factor: on average women have less seniority (years on job) than men.

Assumption: C = "On average, women have the same seniority as men."

388

EXERCISE 7 - 5

1. Plausible U-factor: support increases complaints but not rape
   incidence--victims now come forward who would not before.

   Assumption: D ="Rape incidence is proportional to the number
   of rape complaints."

EXERCISE 7 - 6

1. Plausible U-factor: reduced physical activity allows calories
   to be stored as fat.

   Assumption needed: D = "I am as physically active as I was
   before."

EXERCISE 7 - 7

1. Plausible U-factor: people ask about others' health to be
   polite.

   Assumption needed: C = "People are not merely trying to be
   polite."

EXERCISE 7 - 8

1. Plausible U-factor: women may find Reagan's other policies
   attractive enough to offset his poor performance on sex
   discrimination.

   Assumption needed: C = "Women are influenced primarily by
   women's rights policies."

EXERCISE 7 - 9

1. Plausible U-factor: the authors are trying to make money by
   writing books.

   Assumption needed: C = "The authors do not write the books
   to make money."

EXERCISE 7 - 10

1. Plausible U-factor: marijuana use in moderation is not
   seriously harmful.

   Assumption needed: D = "Marijuana use, even in moderation is
   seriously harmful."

EXERCISE 7 - 11

1. Plausible U-factors: (1) people are entitled to put self-interest before the suffering of their children, (2) there are no feasible birth-control methods available.

   Assumptions needed: D = "Self-interest cannot override child suffering", E = "Effective birth control methods are available to them."

EXERCISE 7 - 12

1. Plausible U-factors: (1) the woman may not wish to marry him , (2) he may have some moral or religious principle that over-rides the obligation to marry.

   Assumptions needed: C = "The woman is willing to marry him", D = "He has no overriding obligation."

EXERCISE 7 - 13

1. Plausible U-factors: (1) the U.S. wishes to maintain the American way of life (which would not be possible if the U.S.S.R. was to take military advantage of the resulting weakness), (2) it is preferable to negotiate a mutual disarmament agreement.

   Assumptions needed: C = "The American way of life could be maintained if offensive weapons were eliminated", D = "Negotiations for mutual disarmament will not succeed."

EXERCISE 7 - 14

1. Plausible U-factors: (1) selling cocaine is legally, and perhaps morally, prohibited; (2) he might end up in jail (and not be able to complete his degree).

   Assumptions needed: C = "Selling cocaine is legally and morally permissible", D = "He won't get arrested."

   EXERCISE 7 - 15

1. Plausible U-factors: (1) Not an excellent boxer (true), (2) lacked punching power (false).

   Assumptions needed: D = "He was a very good boxer," E = "He had very good punching power."

   Note: experts do not require that a great heavyweight is

tops in both boxing skills and punching power. Punching power may be more important for heavyweights, though.

EXERCISE 7 - 16

1. Plausible U-factor: advertising influences preferences more than product quality.

   Assumption needed: C = "Peoples' preferences are determined solely by product quality."

EXERCISE 7 - 17

1. Plausible U-factors: (1) marriage mobility produces bad emotional side-effects (the trauma of divorce, for example), (2) the impact on children generates family problems.

   Assumptions needed: C = "There is no serious emotional suffering for those who divorce and remarry," D = "The effects on children do not result in serious family problems."

EXERCISE 7 - 18

1. Plausible U-factor: schools are state institutions and as such must respect freedom of choice in religion.

   Assumption: D = "Teaching religion is not incompatible with respecting students' freedom of religion."

EXERCISE 7 - 20

1. Plausible U-factor: most designers are not good programmers.

   Assumption: C = "Most computer designers are good programmers."

EXERCISE 7 - 21

2. $A \supset B$ / $\sim A$ // $\sim B$
     T T   T F   F T
     4 3   5 6   1 2

Invalidating Conjunction: $\sim$ A • B
Negation of it: $\sim$ ($\sim$ A • B) = $\sim$ A ⊃ $\sim$ B

4.   A ⊃ B / B ⊃ C // C
     F T F   F T F   F
     7 6 5   4 3 2   1

Invalidating Conjunction: $\sim$ A • $\sim$ B • $\sim$ C
Negation of it: $\sim$($\sim$ A • $\sim$ B • $\sim$ C) = A v B v C = $\sim$ (A v B) ⊃ C

EXERCISE 7 - 22

2.   STEP ONE. The semi-symbolic version is:
     "A only if B. But not-A so not-B."
     The symbolic version is: "A ⊃ B / $\sim$ A // $\sim$ B."
     The diagrammatic version is:

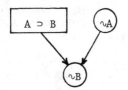

A = There will be a nuclear war.

B = The Russians attack us.

Step Two (a):   A ⊃ B / $\sim$ A // $\sim$ B
                 T T   T F   F T
                 4 3   5 6   1 2

The inference is invalid.
Step Two (b): conjunction of invalidating set is '$\sim$ A • B'.

Step Two (c): negation of conjunction: '$\sim$ ($\sim$ A • B)'.

Step Two (d): the simplest version of the missing assumption is
"B ⊃ A" ("If the Russians attack us then there will be a nuclear
war").

Step Two (e)

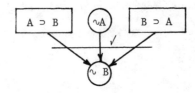

392

Step Three: taking 'A ⊃ B' as meaning the falsity of B guarantees the falsity of A, we can accept it as true, since we have no other serious opponent. Assumption ' ∿A' is dubious. No one can say for sure that there won't be a war at sometime in the future. Assumption 'B ⊃ A' can be regarded as true, although it depends on assuming they would attack with nuclear weapons.

Step Four: not applicable.

Step Five: since one essential assumption (∿ A) is dubious the argument is rated "?"

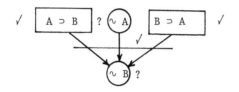

Step Six: the response is "The conclusion only follows logically if you assume that if the Russians attack us then there will be a nuclear war. This assumption is acceptable but to the extent that it is dubious that there won't be a nuclear war, the conclusion has not been proved."

EXERCISE 7 - 23

1. "Every X is Y // Some X is not Z." Since 'X' is common to both assertions we need one mentioning 'Y' and 'Z', and this would be found in TABLE ONE. A test of the inference is this:

```
∿ A • ∿ D // A v E
T F T T F    F F F
5 4 6 7 8    2 1 3
```

The assertion we need must be false with A, D, and E false so it could only be 'A v D' or 'D v E', but neither one is contained in the list. So there is no assumption that could be added to yield a valid inference.

3. "Some X is Y // No X is Z". Since X is common we need an assertion from TABLE ONE. The Venn-equivalent version of the argument is:

E v G // ∿ D • ∿ G

There turn out to be five different sets of values that show this pattern to be invalid so the only efficient way to find whether there is a validity-making assumption in the table is to insert each in the argument and test. This procedure shows that no assertion can be added to give a valid inference.

EXERCISE 7 - 24

2. "Not all men accept the double standard of sexual fidelity, so some men are enlightened."

Step One. Construct an accurate diagrammatic version:

Not all X's are Y's   X = Men

                             Y = People who accept the double
                                 standard of sexual fidelity.
      Some X's are Z's
                             Z = People who are enlightened.

Step Two (a). A fully symbolic version is:

$$(\sim A \cdot \sim D) \mathbin{/\!/} D \vee G$$

This can be rewritten as: $A \vee D \mathbin{/\!/} D \vee G$.

The missing assumption must come from TABLE ONE, and it must be false when A is true and D and G are both false. There is no assertion in the table that meets this requirement.

Step Two (b). A counter-example is: "Not all cats are Siamese, so some cats are dogs."

Step Three. The assumption is undoubtedly true, especially since it is logically equivalent to "Some men accept the double standard of sexual fidelity."

Step Four. Not applicable.

Step Five. With an invalid inference the argument proof rating is "X".

Step Six. A good response is: "Your conclusion does not follow from your assumption. It is like arguing "Not all cats are Siamese so some cats are dogs"."

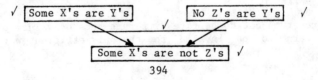

394

EXERCISE 8 - 1

2. A while B if C.

   A • (C ⊃ B)

4. If A then B when either C or D.

   A ⊃ ((C v D) ⊃ B)

6. Not A on condition that not B.

   ∿ A ⊃ ∿ B (= B ⊃ A)

8. A, otherwise B.

   (A v B) • ∿ (A • B)

EXERCISE 8 - 2

1. A[The postal clerks must be underpaid] <u>since</u> B[they strike frequently].

   A since B.

4. A[Garbage collectors should be paid more]. B[Physicians are well paid], <u>and</u> C[both groups provide essential health services].

   A. B, and C.

8. <u>Since</u> A[happiness consists in peace of mind], <u>and since</u> B[durable peace of mind depends on the confidence we have in the future], <u>and since</u> C[that confidence is based on the knowledge we should have of God and the soul], <u>it follows that</u> D[knowledge is necessary for true happiness].

   Since A, and since B, and since C, it follows that D.

11. <u>If</u> A[Cain married his sister], B[their marriage was incestuous]. <u>If not</u> A[he didn't marry his sister, <u>then not</u> C[Adam and Eve were not the progenitors of the entire human race]. <u>It follows that</u> C[Adam and Eve were the progenitors of the whole human race] <u>only if</u> B[Cain's marriage was incentuous].

   If A, B. If not A, then not C. It follows that C only if B.

EXERCISE 8 - 3

1.

4.

8.

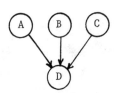

11.

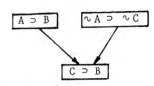

EXERCISE 8 - 4

2.

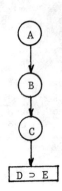

A = We have not observed everything.

B = We do not know how everything behaves.

C = We do not know all things.

D = Logic is the science of all things.

E = The certainty of logical truths
cannot be explained.

The first sentence in the passage sets out the claim the arguer wishes to argue against in the latter part of the passage.

3.

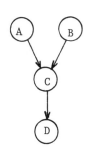

A = A closed season does not help increase the herd.

B = Legal hunters were not responsible for the failure of the herd to increase.

C = Other factors such as illegal hunting are preventing the population from building up.

D = A legal opportunity for resident hunters seems the most logical and best use of our moose resources.

EXERCISE 8 - 5

2. Step One:

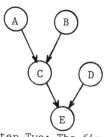

A = Some textbooks are useful.

B = All useful things are valuable.

C = Some textbooks are valuable.

D = Some valuable things are expensive.

E = Some textbooks are expensive.

Step Two: The first inference, from A and B to C is a syllogism. First we write a semi-symbolic version:
"Some X's are Y's. All Y's are Z's. Therefore, some X's are Z's."
The Venn-equivalent version is: E v G / ∿ B • ∿ E // D v G
The inference tests out to be valid:

```
E v G / ∿ B • ∿ E // D v G
T T F      F F T      F F F
6 5 4      9 8 7      2 1 3
```

The second inference, from C and D to E is also a syllogism. The semi-symbolic version is:
"Some X's are Y's. Some Y's are Z's. Therefore some X's are Z's."
The Venn-equivalent version is: E v G / F v G // D v G
The inference tests out to be invalid:

```
E v G / F v G // D v G
T T F   T T F    F F F
9 8 7   6 5 4    2 1 3
```

Step Three: There are three assumptions: A, B, and D. A is no doubt true. Knowledge is often useful and sometimes it is best acquired by reading a textbook. D is also true. Diamonds are an example of something valuable and expensive.

Is B true? Are ALL useful things valuable? Not necessarily. Air is useful but is not really valuable in dollar terms. Hired killers are useful if one wants some one murdered, but we do not as a society consider them to have a positive value. Rate B "X".

Step Four: To what extent is C proved? With A true and B false C is not proved even though the inference is valid.

Step Five. To what extent has E been proved? Given the proof rating of C and the truth of D, and the invalid inference to E, the argument warrants a "X" rating.

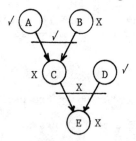

Step Six: We can respond to the argument thusly: "E may be true but it has not been proved by this argument. Given that some text books are valuable and some valuable things are expensive, it does not follow that some text books are expensive. This is like arguing "Some even numbers are greater than two. Some numbers greater than two are odd numbers. Therefore some even numbers are odd numbers." Furthermore, evem if the conclusion did logically follow it can't be proved because it has not been proved that some text books are valuable. This conclusion depends on the false assumption that all useful things are valuable. This is false because air is useful but not particularly valuable in terms of dollars. Furthermore hired killers are useful for certain purposes but we think they have negative value."

EXERCISE 8 - 6

2. Step One. A semi-symbolic version is: "A and therefore B. And because C, D."
The diagrammatic version is given on the next page.

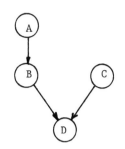

A = Matter is activity.

B = A (material) body is where it acts.

C = Every particle of matter acts all over the universe.

D = Every (material) body is everywhere.

Step Two. There are two inferences in the argument. If A were true would it make B true? If we take A to mean 'matter and activity are one and the same', as the arguer seems to do, we should rate the inference valid.

What about the inference from B and C to D? This also seems to be valid. If B and C were true this would make D true.

Step Three. There are two assumptions: A and C. According to Newtonian theory, every particle of matter does exert a gravitational pull all over the universe. In this sense C is true. A, on the other hand, is clearly false. Matter, that which has mass, is not itself activity, although it can be active. Indeed, there must be matter for there to be activity. Matter, it could be said, is distinct from and prior to the activity of material objects.

Step Four. To what extent is B proved? The inference from A to B is judged valid but A is false, so B is not proved to any extent.

Step Five. With C true and the inference from B and C to D being valid the argument rating reflects the degree to proof of B, which is "X".

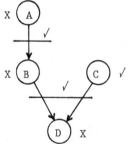

Step Six. A response to the argument could be: "Although the inferences are satisfactory the conclusion is not proved because it is simply false that matter is activity. There must be matter for there to be activity but matter need not always be active, so matter and activity cannot be identical."

399

4. Step One. The semi-symbolic version is simply "A. B. C." The diagrammatic version is:

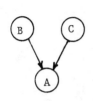

A = The current attempt by the government to pass a law requiring use of seat belts is another attempt to restrict our freedom of choice.

B = It is the right of each of us to decide whether we wish to take the risk of not wearing a seat belt.

C = This law would remove our freedom of choice.

Step Two. Given B and C, would A be true? Not really. We have here a case of an intended good effect (better protection in accidents) having an undesirable "side effect." It is incorrect to say that the legislators are attempting to restrict freedom of choice. They are attempting to increase automobile safety. An undesirable consequence is that there will be less freedom of choice. This is like the dentist giving Novocaine. He/she does not intend to hurt you, only to spare you discomfort later. Unfortunately, the injection is unavoidably painful. The legislators, like the dentist, would rather not produce the side effect, but it is unavoidable. Given that they do not intend the reduction in freedom of choice, it is false to say they are attempting to do so. The inference is rated "X".

Step Three. Assumption C is clearly true. The law contemplated would remove freedom of choice in the use of seat belts for people who feel obliged to obey the laws.

What about B? Is it "the right of each of us to decide whether we wish to take the risk of not wearing a seat belt"? The arguer is against paternalism, the position that, given adequate evidence of the value of a restriction for the individuals who would be restricted, those in a position to impose it are entitled to do so. The opponent of paternalism, the libertarian, sees personal autonomy as an important value. However, the libertarian does not advocate the exercise of freedom when it harms others. Not fastening one's seat belt can, if an accident occurs, lead to serious injury or death that might have been avoided. This can lead to harm to those who are dependent on the individual for financial support, i.e., a drastic lowering of their standard of living. Also, when an individual is relying on health insurance to pay medical expenses, others must contribute to covering these expenses through premiums or taxes. So the issue is whether

400

people would be entitled to neglect their own safety and expect others to suffer financially and emotionally as a result, if an accident occurs. The "right to decide" in this matter extends only to those whose choice will not harm others, so we should rate B "?".

Step Four. Not applicable here.

Step Five. Given an invalid inference and a dubious assumption we can rate the argument "X".

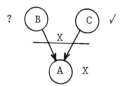

Step Six. We can respond to the argument as follows: "The conclusion does not logically follow. The legislation would, it is true, restrict our freedom of choice in this matter. But that is only a by-product or side effect of an attempt to promote safety. Furthermore, the right to decide here only extends to those who cannot harm anyone else if their choice turns out badly. Most of us have dependents or are involved in health insurance schemes, so that other people will be affected if we incur greater medical costs than necessary."

EXERCISE 8 - 7

1. Step One. The First sentence expresses a conditional. The second one can be interpreted as 'if an argument is invalid then it does not have a true conclusion'. This, in turn, is equivalent to: 'if an argument is invalid then its conclusion is false.' Thus, we can write this as a semi-symbolic version: "A when B and C. If A then C." The fully symbolic version is:

$(B \cdot C) \supset A \;// A \supset C$

The diagrammatic version is:

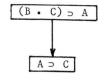

A = An argument is invalid.

B = The argument's premises are true.

C = The argument's conclusion is false.

401

Step Two. A short truth table test shows the inference to be invalid.

$(B \cdot C) \supset A \; // \; A \supset C$
         T T   T F F
         5 4   2 1 3

Step Three. Are true premises and a false conclusion enough to guarantee an invalid inference? Certainly. The assumption is true.

Step Four. Not applicable here.

Step Five. Since the inference is invalid the conclusion is not proved to any extent.

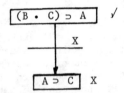

Step Six. We can respond as follows: "Even though the assumption is correct it does not prove the conclusion. This argument has an invalid inference but a true conclusion: 'Boston is more than 5 miles from New York. Therefore, Boston is more than 10 miles from New York.'"

3. Step One. The assumption is contained in the second sentence. The conclusion is "It is mostly European and non-white men who abuse their wives and girl friends." The diagrammatic version of the argument is:

A = It is false that mostly European and non-white men abuse their wives and girlfriends.

B = Wife battering occurs in all cultures and in all social classes.

Step Two. Could B be true and A false? Yes, because the incidence of wife battering may be low for groups other than European and non-whites. We can rate the inference "?". The arguer should have claimed that wife battering occurs FREQUENTLY

402

in other cultures and classes too.

Step Three. Is B true? Given the uniformity of human nature the world over we can suppose it is, without doing research to confirm this view. What is dubious is whether it is equally common in all cultures.

Step Four. Not applicable.

Step Five. With a true assumption and a dubious inference we rate the argument "?".

Step Six. We can respond as follows: "It is undoubtedly true that wife-battering occurs in all cultures and social classes but this does not quite prove that it is false that mostly European and non-white men who do it. Wife-battering may occur but not be common in other cultural groups."

EXERCISE 8 - 8

2. Step One. There is an ambiguity arising from the term 'argue'. In the first occurence it seems to mean 'present good reasons for what one wants to persuade others to believe.' The second occurrence has it being used as a synonym for 'quarrel'. Let us change these uses of 'argue' and construct the diagrammatic version of the argument. The semi-symbolic version is "A, but B. Therefore, C."

A = Studying logic teaches one how to present good reasons for what one wants to persuade others to believe.

B = People quarrel too much already.

C = I'm not going to study logic.

Step Two. Neither A nor B is a good reason for C so the inference can be rated "X".

Step Three. A can be accepted as true. B can also be accepted

403

since quarreling is generally thought to be undesirable and any amount of anything that is undesirable is too much.

Step Four. Not applicable.

Step Five. With inference invalid the conclusion is unproved.

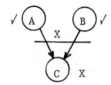

Step Six. "There is an ambiguity in the word 'argue'. In the first use it means 'presenting reasons for conclusions'. In the second it means 'quarrel'. With these different meanings the assumptions are true but neither of them is a good reason for not studying logic. So the conclusion doesn't follow at all."

4. Step One. The word 'law' is ambiguous. It has a prescriptive sense in which it is synonymous with 'enacted rule', as exemplified by laws passed by legislatures and other such bodies. It also has a sense in which it is synonymous with 'regular pattern', as exemplified by Newton's Law of Gravity. In this argument the conclusion requires taking 'law' in the 'enacted rule' sense. The semi-symbolic version is: "A . B because C." The diagrammatic version is:

A = Heterosexuality is an enacted rule in nature.

B = Homosexuals should be punished.

C = Homosexuals violate this enacted rule of nature.

Step Two. Is the inference valid? Is there any factor that might keep B from being true if A and C were true? There are various reasons why people ought not be punished when they break a law. They may have acted involantarily, or they may be able to benefit from rehabilitation measures. Since the arguer is talking about homosexuals in general, the involuntariness factor does not seem plausible. The rehabilitation consideration, on the other hand, does seem to be an alternative to punishment. We can rate the inference "?".

Step Three. Assumption A is false (in the author's opinion)

404

because there are no enacted rules in nature. Nature does not obey laws, it only exhibits regularities. (Anyone who subscribes to the Old Testament view that regularities in nature are the result of things conforming to proclamations of God would probably want to say A is true.)

Assumption C must also be considered false if one does not think there are any enacted rules in nature. If there are none they cannot be violated.

Step Four. Not applicable.

Step Five. Given the ratings we judge the argument not to have proved its conclusion.

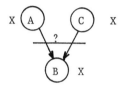

Step Six. We can respond to the argument as follows: "There is an ambiguity in the word 'law'. To have any chance of proving that homosexuals should be punished for their sexual behavior you must regard 'law' as a synonym for 'enacted rule.' But there are no such rules in nature, there are only regular patterns of behavior that are built into things. Things do not behave regularly because they are complying to proclamations. Thus, both of the assumptions are false so the conclusion is not proved to any significant extent."

EXERCISE 8 - 9

1. "Our tomatoes are at least two days fresher!"

3. "Soak the rich!" The word 'soak' here means 'tax heavily'. The vagueness arises from the term 'rich.' Who counts as rich, anyway? In most people's minds a person definitely counts as rich if they have assets of a million dollars or more. For most of us, then, the Maoist slogan means "People who have more than a million dollars in assets should be taxed heavily."

EXERCISE 8 - 10

1. 'Bald': vague.

2. 'Gold': not vague, to be gold is simply to be material

consisting of a certain element.

7. 'Recession': vague, because there is no clear point at which an economic downturn becomes a recession.

8. 'Argument': ambiguous, rather than vague. Each of the two senses ('assertion with reasons given for its acceptance' vs 'quarrel') are fairly precise.

EXERCISE 8 - 11

1. 'wetback' = 'illegal immigrant from Mexico'.

3. 'coddling' = 'providing better living conditions than necessary.'

EXERCISE 8 - 12

1. 'wasted' = 'killed'

3. 'inoperative' = 'untrustworthy'.

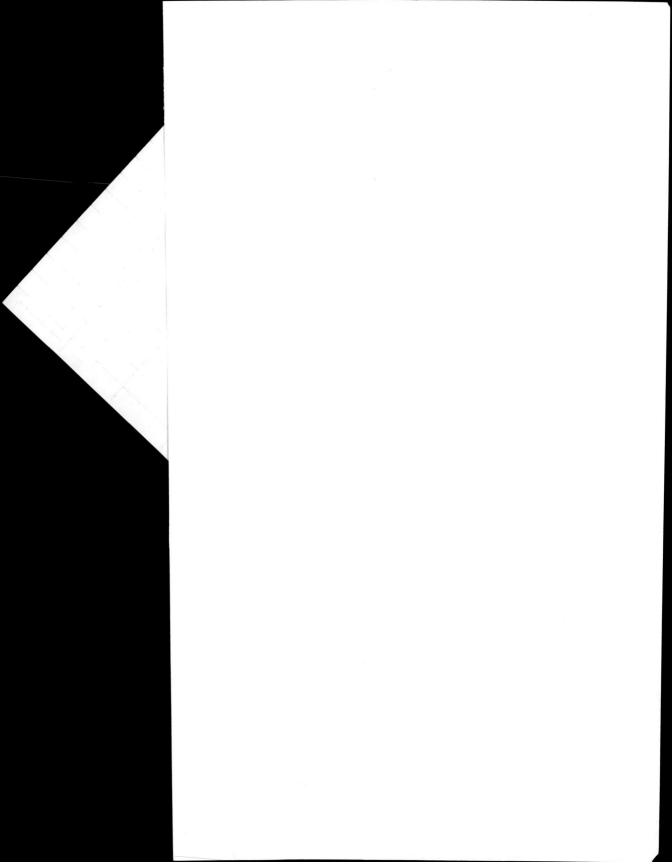

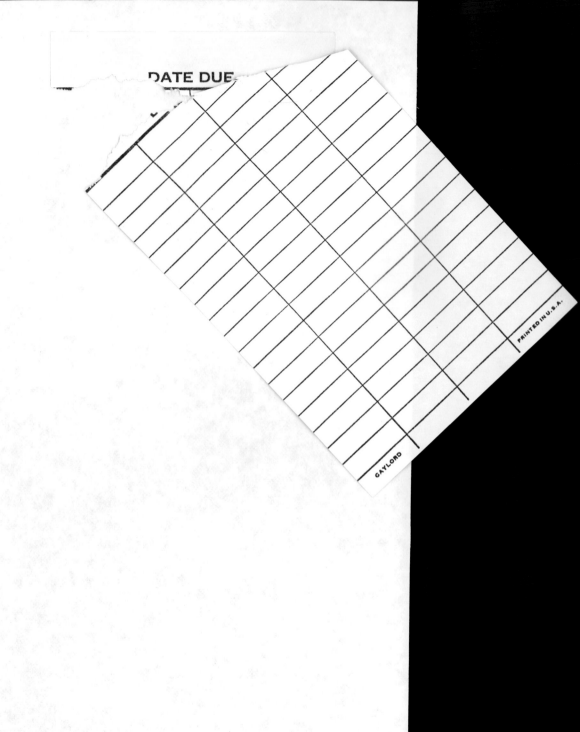

DATE DUE